SWINFORD SPALPEENS

SWINFORD SPALPEENS

Aspects of Migration and Emigration from the East Mayo Area 1815–1970

1815–1940: The Spalpeens
1940–1970: Migrants' Stories

JACK FOLEY

Galley Head Press

Published in 2017 by Galley Head Press, Ardfield, County Cork

ISBN 978-0-9542159-9-6

© Jack Foley

All rights reserved.
Every effort has been made to ensure the accuracy
of the information contained in this book.

Project manager: Claire Foley
Copy-editor: Eileen O'Carroll, Cullinagh, Kilmeaden, County Waterford
Typesetter & indexer: Dominic Carroll, Ardfield, County Cork
Printer: KPS Colour Print, Knock, County Mayo

Contents

List of Abbreviations	vii
List of Maps, Figures & Tables	viii
Foreword	xiii
Acknowledgements	xv
Note on the Text	xvii

Part I: 1815–1940: The Spalpeens

	Introduction	1
1	Socio-economic Conditions in the West of Ireland, Pre-Famine	6
2	Famine and its Effects in East Mayo	24
3	The Mini-famine of 1879–80	37
4	Emigration from the West, Post-1880	46
5	The Congested Districts Board	54
6	Emigration and the Gender Balance	64
7	Reports on Migratory Agricultural Labourers, 1880–1915	67
8	Work on English Farms in the 1930s and 1940s	101
9	Migration to the Rich Lands of Leinster	107
10	The Hungry Twenties and Thirties	110
11	Low Expectations and Stunted Ambitions in the 1940s, '50s and '60s	116
12	The Change to Britain: 'Crossing the Pond'	121
	Conclusion	129

Part II: 1940–1970: Migrants' Stories

A Window to the Past	137
Jackie Devine	141
Johnny Conlon	146
John Mulroy	151
Philip Conway	154
Stephen Farrell	158
Mary (Waters) Gannon	164
Mary (Foley) Devlin	167
John Walsh	172
Mick Foley	176
Paddy Peyton	180

continued over

Tom Morley	184
Jimmy McIntyre	187
May (Henry) Clancy	192
Joe Morrisroe	196
Martin MccCormack	200
Ellen (Foley) Reeves	205
Teddy Gallagher	211
Paddy Duffy	214
Tom Meehan	218
Kitty (Breheny) Walsh	221
Michael Goldrick	226
Tom Goldrick	228
Martin McDonagh	231
Tommy Campbell	234
Paddy Foley	236
Henry Peyton	245
Margaret (Mulligan) McIntyre	248
Brendan Swords	250
Jimmy Brennan	252
Tommy McGowan	255
Kevin Walsh	257
Paddy Molloy	262
Martin Neary	266
Eileen (O'Rourke) Killilea	269
Frank Gallagher	272
Theresa Connor	280
John Brennan	282
Conclusion	284
List of Interviewees	286
Appendices	290
Notes & References	296
Bibliography	312
Index	322

Abbreviations

AEMI	Association of European Migration Institutions
A R P	acres, roods, perches
c.	circa
CDB	Congested Districts Board
CBDHS	Charlestown/Bellaghy & Districts Heritage Society
Ch.	Chapter
ed.	editor
eds	editors
FCA	Fórsa Cosanta Áitiúil
Fig.	Figure
GAA	Gaelic Athletic Association
HSE	Health Service Executive
ibid.	in the same place
ILC	Irish Land Commission
IUP	Irish University Press
J.P.	Justice of the Peace
kg	kilogram(s)
MD	medical doctor
MGWR	Midland Great Western Railway
MHC	Mansion House Committee
MS	manuscript
NLI	National Library of Ireland
OECD	Organisation for Economic Co-operation and Development
p	pence (sterling)
PLU	Poor Law Union
PP	Parliamentary Paper
P.P.	Parish Priest
QUB	Queen's University, Belfast
s	shilling(s) (sterling)
Tech.	technical school (also vocational school)
UCC	University College, Cork
UCD	University College, Dublin
UK	United Kingdom
UL	University of Limerick
UN	United Nations
US	United States
VO	Valuation Office
Vol.	volume

List of Maps, Figures & Tables

Map 1	Poor Law Unions of County Mayo	x
Map 2:	Civil parishes of County Mayo	xi

Part I: 1815–1940: The Spalpeens

Fig. 1.1	Average number of working days available to able-bodied labourers in Ireland, 1835	9
Fig. 1.2	Common sort of Mayo mud cabin	12
Fig. 1.3	Classes of houses in Killasser, 1841, 1851	13
Fig. 2.1	Demographic changes in Doonty (Killasser parish), 1841, 1851	25
Fig. 2.2	Demographic changes in Knockfadda (Killasser parish), 1841, 1851	25
Fig. 2.3	Emigration from Mayo, 1861–1901	34
Fig. 3.1	Foxford	40
Fig. 3.2	Bellaghy, Charlestown, early twentieth century	44
Fig. 4.1	Emigration advertisement, 1881	47
Fig. 5.1	Demographic changes in selected areas, 1841–81	55
Table 1	Composition of holdings held by tenants in Cartron townland, c. 1875	57
Fig. 5.2	The Square, Charlestown, late nineteenth century	58
Fig. 5.3	Land annuity payment record	61
Fig. 6.1	Market day, Charlestown, c. 1898	65
Fig. 6.2	Male and female emigration from Mayo, 1881–1911	66
Fig. 7.1	Migratory agricultural labourers, 1841, 1880	69
Fig. 7.2	Migratory agricultural labourers, 1880	70
Fig. 7.3	Destinations of migrants from Ireland, Mayo, Swinford PLU, 1900	79
Fig. 7.4	Migrants per 1,000 population, 1894	81
Fig. 7.5	Hugh Durkan and his son Jimmy Durkan in a work gang in England, early 1950s	82
Fig. 7.6	Categories of migrant labourers leaving Mayo, 1908	86
Fig. 7.7	Density of migrant workers, 1893	90
Fig. 7.8	MGW rail fares, 1899	90
Fig. 7.9	'Sons' and 'daughters' as a subset of total migrants from County Mayo, 1905–14	91
Fig. 7.10	Bridgie (Foley) Greenwood, Ballintadder, Carracastle, c. 1950	96
Fig. 7.11	Molly and Lucy Dunne ploughing in east Mayo, mid-1970s	97
Fig. 8.1	Threshing in an English haggard	104
Fig. 8.2	Harvesting in east Mayo, early 1950s	105
Fig. 10.1	Holdings valued at £10 and under, Mayo and Swinford PLU, 1881	111
Fig. 11.1	Corthoon National School pupils, c. 1925	117
Fig. 11.2	Examination results, Miss Cahill's Secondary School, Charlestown	118
Fig. 11.3	Mary (Foley) Garvey of Ballintadder, Carracastle graduating as a State Registered Nurse from Edgware General Hospital, 1955	119
Fig. 12.1	Average family size, 1911, 1946, 1981	122
Fig. 12.2	Average annual rate per 1,000 population (1951) of persons receiving new travel permits, identity cards and passports to go to employment, 1940–51	124
Fig. 12.3	Ploughing in Ballintadder, Carracastle, c. 1950	125
Fig. 13.1	Clooncous townland as recorded in the Griffith Valuation, 1856	132

Part II: 1940–1970: Migrants' Stories

	Sculpture (Swinford) sponsored by Mr Bill Durkan and dedicated to the memory of the women who remained at home while their men sought work abroad during the mass migration of the 1950s	136
	Sculpture (Kiltimagh) sponsored by Mr Bill Durkan and dedicated to the young men and women who migrated from Kiltimagh, Bohola and the surrounding areas during the 1950s	136
Fig. 1	1950s cardboard suitcase	138
Fig. 2	Chapel Street, Swinford, *c.* 1930	142
Fig. 3	British ration book	149
Fig. 4	Martin Duffy with workmen and families on their annual outing in the mid-1950s (including Tommy Doherty (Charlestown), his wife and daughter Angela)	152
Fig. 5	Corthoon bog	159
Fig. 6	Charlestown railway station	160
Fig. 7	Visa-exit permit to Britain during the Second World War	161
Fig. 8	Nursery nurses' diploma	168
Fig. 9	Workmen at Gravesend, Thames Estuary, 1952 (Joe — (Bohola), Mick Foley (Mayo), Hughie — (Donegal); Dick — (Cork), Pat Clarke (Monaghan), Barry — (Offaly), Seán Henry (Sligo)	178
Fig. 10	Work permit of Peter Peyton, 1942	181
Fig. 11	Travel identity card, 1951	192
Fig. 12	Charlestown river (a River Moy tributary), late nineteenth century	203
Fig. 13	*Sleán* (turf spade)	205
Fig. 14	Turf made up into *gróigíns*	206
Fig. 15	Bringing home the turf from Corthoon bog, 1980s	209
Fig. 16	Channel Tunnel workmen, 1992	213
Fig. 17	Jack Duffy demonstrating the art of tying a sheaf of oats to his son, Paddy, late 1940s	215
Fig. 18	Jack Duffy sharpening a scythe	217
Fig. 19	Breheny family: Jim, Bill, Seán, Kitty, Maureen, Pádraig, Collette, Patty, Vera, Teresa, Ambrose, Madeleine, Dolores	224
Fig. 20	Bringing home the hay in the 1940s: Paddy Foley with his father, Tom	239
Fig. 21	Postcard of farming scene in Corthoon, Charlestown, 1970s	244
Fig. 22	Union card	260
Fig. 23	Market day, Swinford, 1963	263
Fig. 24	Killaturley potato pickers in Lincolnshire, 1963: Frank Gallagher, Michael Gallagher (senior), Michael Gallagher (junior), Martin Groarke, Eugene Madden, Ballaghaderreen	274
Fig. 25	Collecting potatoes, 1963: Frank Gallagher, Michael Gallagher (junior), Martin Groarke, Eugene Madden	276

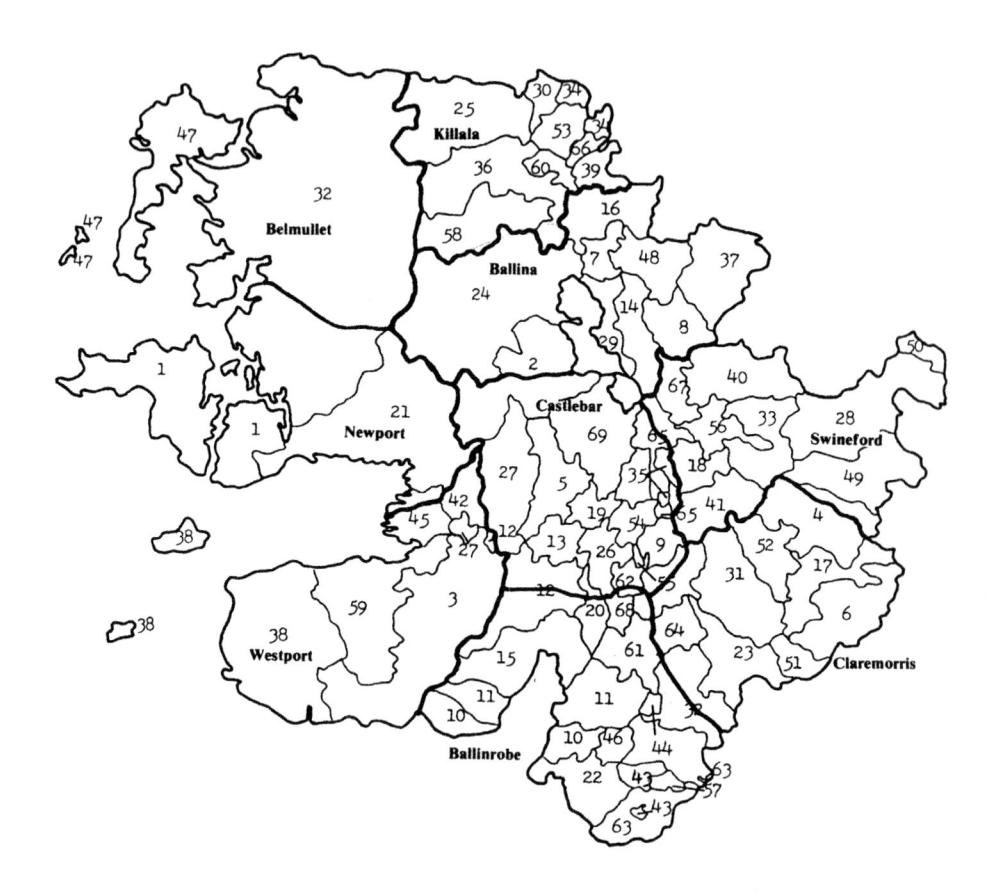

Map 1: Poor Law Unions of County Mayo. (Source: Brian Mitchell, *A New Genealogical Atlas of Ireland* (Baltimore, Maryland, 2002), p. 124)

Map 2: Civil parishes of County Mayo. (Source: Brian Mitchell, *A New Genealogical Atlas of Ireland* (Baltimore, Maryland, 2002), p. 122)

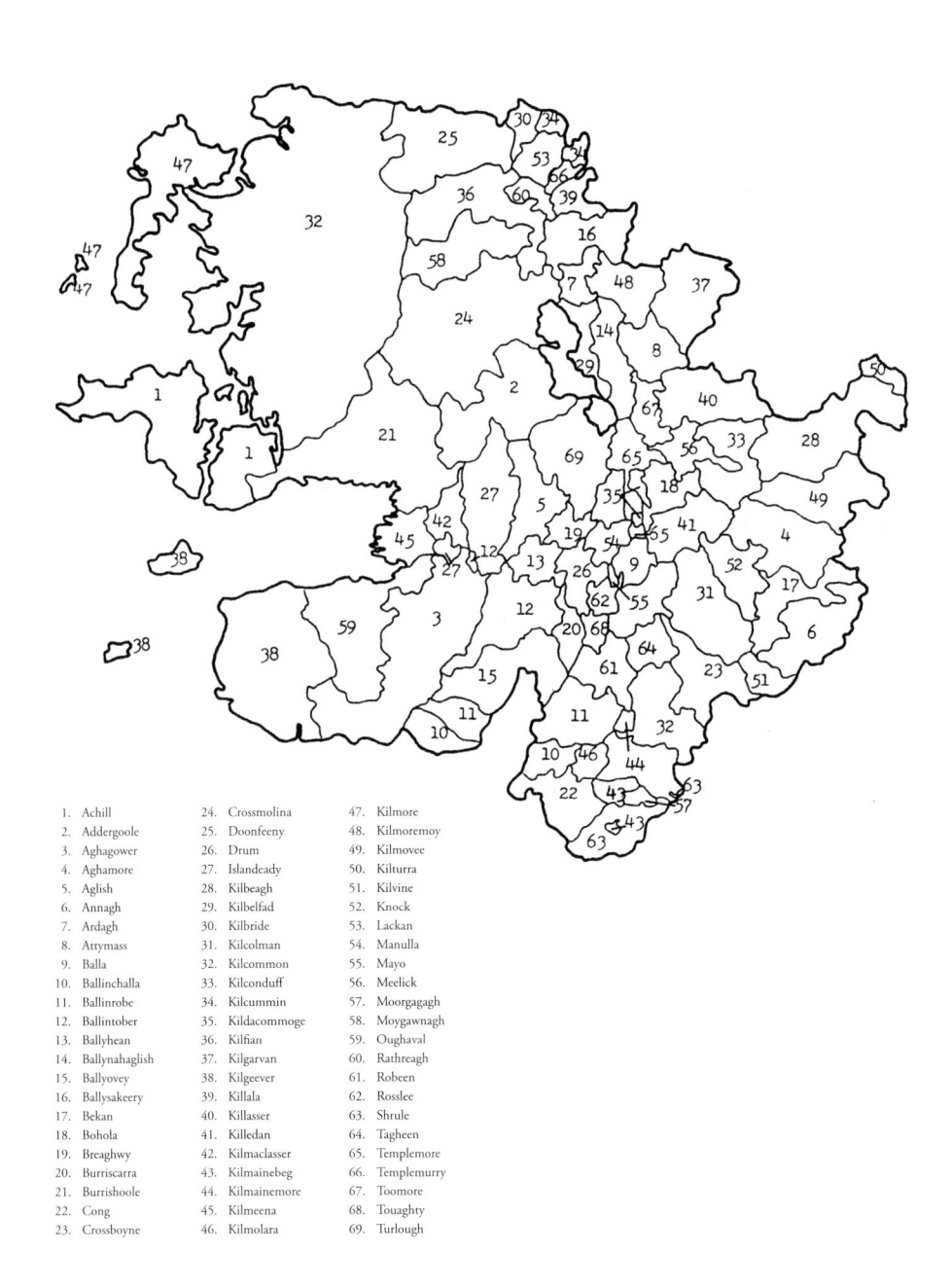

1. Achill
2. Addergoole
3. Aghagower
4. Aghamore
5. Aglish
6. Annagh
7. Ardagh
8. Attymass
9. Balla
10. Ballinchalla
11. Ballinrobe
12. Ballintober
13. Ballyhean
14. Ballynahaglish
15. Ballyovey
16. Ballysakeery
17. Bekan
18. Bohola
19. Breaghwy
20. Burriscarra
21. Burrishoole
22. Cong
23. Crossboyne
24. Crossmolina
25. Doonfeeny
26. Drum
27. Islandeady
28. Kilbeagh
29. Kilbelfad
30. Kilbride
31. Kilcolman
32. Kilcommon
33. Kilconduff
34. Kilcummin
35. Kildacommoge
36. Kilfian
37. Kilgarvan
38. Kilgeever
39. Killala
40. Killasser
41. Killedan
42. Kilmaclasser
43. Kilmainebeg
44. Kilmainemore
45. Kilmeena
46. Kilmolara
47. Kilmore
48. Kilmoremoy
49. Kilmovee
50. Kilturra
51. Kilvine
52. Knock
53. Lackan
54. Manulla
55. Mayo
56. Meelick
57. Moorgagagh
58. Moygawnagh
59. Oughaval
60. Rathreagh
61. Robeen
62. Rosslee
63. Shrule
64. Tagheen
65. Templemore
66. Templemurry
67. Toomore
68. Touaghty
69. Turlough

East Mayo landscape.

Foreword

The e/migration of ordinary people from small farming and labouring backgrounds formed the intimate backdrop to Jack Foley's life. By the early 1950s, seven siblings out of a family of nine had emigrated – Jack and a younger sister witnessed each and every departure. As a young teacher, Jack spent his summers working on building sites in England alongside Irish workers and sharing in their emigrant lives.

I met Jack Foley in 2001 when I worked at the Irish Centre for Migration Studies at University College, Cork (UCC). At the time, I was compiling an archive of individual experiences of staying during the mass emigration of the 1950s (*Breaking the Silence: Staying at Home in an Emigrant Society*). Jack, who was completing an MSSc in Irish migration studies at the Mellon Centre for Migration Studies in Omagh, agreed to contribute to the project. Of the seventy-eight life stories archived at the Boole Library in UCC, Jack Foley's narrative has a resounding quality to it. When I flinched at his depictions of those who had to go, even those 'homebirds' who tried everything to escape the inevitable, I recall Jack's refrain: 'But you don't understand Breda, there was no option.'

Jack brings the qualities of a reliable and respectful witness to *Swinford Spalpeens*, which is a unique and important contribution to Irish migration studies, local and oral history. In Part I, Jack provides a socio-economic overview of migratory conditions between 1815 and 1940. These conditions laid down the patterns that shaped mid-twentieth-century e/migration. The stories of individuals who e/migrated between the 1940s and the 1970s are presented in the Part II. Although the book addresses a variety of migratory routes and experiences, the book title pays tribute to the significance of the spalpeen, or migrant farm labourer, in the east Mayo area. Some of the stories include poignant accounts of this annual leaving and return as these workers struggled to maintain connections with family and community in their home area. While some of the women's stories of nurse training suggest greater social mobility than for the men, Jack reminds us that most Irish women went to work in domestic service and factory work. Return was a strong theme for both women and men, prompted mainly by a wish to support aging or ill parents.

Jack's familiarity with east Mayo, as well as the life trajectories of his narrators and their families, gives the reader a sense of being invited into a collective community story. At the same time, each story in its uniqueness pierces through what Liam Harte calls 'the undifferentiated mass of Irish emigrants'. I was particularly struck by the term 'lonesome' used by many of the narrators. Although articulated here by emigrants, I remember my father using the word to describe the sense of a place, house and locality with so many having left. Just as emigration gave rise to 'lonesome' feelings, so, too, did living with the absence of siblings, friends and neighbours. It is perhaps this living with absence that prompted Jack to take on the timely and important task of rescuing these extraordinary stories of survival, struggle and success from oblivion.

Breda Gray
University of Limerick
November 2016

Acknowledgements

It would not have been possible to write this book without the support, goodwill and cooperation of many individuals. Foremost among those people are the forty-four originators of the migration narratives featured in Part II of this work. They welcomed me into their homes, gave generously of their time, and provided me with memories of their own personal experiences and the effect migration had on them and their extended families. The devastation of their local communities was an aspect of emigration that emerged as the stories unfolded. This publication would not have been feasible without their assistance. and I'm very grateful for their willing collaboration.

The interviewees are drawn mainly from the Charlestown and Swinford areas of east Mayo, and consist largely of family members, relatives and neighbours. I was fortunate to be put in touch with others in the wider locality who were willing to relate their emigration experiences to me. I am very grateful to a number of people who, through their local knowledge, sourced these interviewees. My thanks, in that regard, go to Attracta Feeley, Nano (RIP) and Henry Peyton, Teddy Gallagher, Norrie Neary and Kathleen Henry.

Not all interviewees' stories have found their way into this book because of health and time constraints on the writer. This does not take from the importance of their narratives, and they are valued equally with those published.

From the Mellon Centre for Migration Studies, Omagh, I would like to acknowledge the advice and guidance generously given by Dr Patrick Fitgerald, Dr John Lynch, Dr Brian Lambkin and Dr Johanne Devlin Trew. My work in the library there was greatly facilitated by the cooperation received from other members of staff, including Chris McIvor, Christine Johnston, Joe Mullan and Deirdre Nugent, and I am thankful to them for their support.

I would like to express my thanks to the staff of the National Library of Ireland; the National Archives of Ireland; the National Archives, Kew, London; Dublin City Archives; Valuation Office; and the Department of Irish Folklore, UCD. I am conscious of, and grateful for, the support I received from the personnel of Cavan County Library, Mayo County Library and Charlestown and Swinford libraries.

I wish to record my deepest appreciation to all those who allowed me to use photos and documents from their personal collections. This material helped to enrich the narratives in this book. Among those individuals are Máirín (Peyton) Noone, Kathleen (Doyle) Foley, May (Henry) Clancy, Tom Eddie Durkin, Bernie Garvey, Mary (Foley) Devlin, Stephen Farrell,* Seamus Bermingham, Denis Walsh, Kitty (Breheny) Walsh, Gerry Brady, Paddy Duffy, Val Hyland, Frank Killilea, Frank Gallagher, Jim Foley (RIP) and Patricia (Duffy) Hannon.

A number of people very kindly agreed to proofread the manuscript, and I'm very grateful to Micheál and Maureen Murphy, Mary Rita Henry, Tom and Mary Sullivan and Norrie Neary for giving of their time and for their valuable advice and constructive suggestions. And to Brendan Nevin a very special thanks for his comprehensive feedback and objective perspective on the subject matter.

I am deeply indebted to Dr Breda Gray, University of Limerick, who responded generously and wholeheartedly when I approached her to look at a draft of the book. Her erudition and in-depth knowledge of migration studies gave me new insights into the subject. For her helpful suggestions, good counsel, and encouragement when I needed it most, I am most grateful. I am also beholden to her for her guidance and information on publishing and publishers. In that regard, I am much obliged to Dr Donal Ó Drisceoil, University College, Cork, for initiating contact, on my behalf, with Dominic Carroll and other book publishers.

I would like to express thanks to my own siblings for their patience and forbearance over the years as I pestered them for information on their own emigration experiences and their recall of the emigration experiences of previous generations. I thank them also for providing me with gentle reviews of drafts as they appeared.

Lastly, I would not have been able to complete this exercise without the practical and intellectual support of my wife, Claire, who inputted all the material and acted as referee, guide, mentor and assistant in this project over the past number of years.

---

* Pseudonym

Note on the Text

When quoting from official documents, I have endeavoured to retain the original spelling of place names and personal names. This means that several different spellings of place names and personal names appear in the book, and many of these are different from the modern spellings.

Part I

1815–1940: The Spalpeens

Introduction

Far away from the land of the shamrock and heather,
In search of a living as exiles we roam;
But whenever we chance to assemble together,
We think of the land where we once had a home.[1]

The well-known ballad about emigration from County Mayo evokes a nostalgic reaction from people who left the county and spent the rest of their lives abroad. While the tradition of emigration/migration from the county was extensive and predates the Famine, it is not intended in this book to look at e/migration from the county as a whole, but to concentrate on one area only – east Mayo – because the migrant tradition tended to be more intense and longer-lasting here than in other parts of the county. This area was also culturally homogenous, being mainly Irish-speaking through much of the nineteenth century and having an almost universally Roman Catholic population. The census records show that four parishes in east Mayo – Bohola, Attymass, Meelick and Kilmovee – were 100 per cent Roman Catholic in 1911.[2]

The narrative is separated into two parts. Part I deals with historic e/migration from east Mayo from about 1815 to 1940. Part II consists of personal stories of e/migrants who worked outside Ireland between the 1940s and the 1970s. The socio-economic conditions prevailing in Ireland, and in east Mayo in particular, which led to huge numbers leaving the country permanently towards the end of the nineteenth century and again post-Second World War, will also be explored. The book examines e/migration from the perspective of ordinary people with a rural background, particularly small farmers and labourers. Important people have many chroniclers – poor people seldom have their stories heard!

In economic terms, east Mayo has always been a deprived area with no large town to provide employment and with the majority of smallholders living on marginal holdings. The following account of one of the parishes in this area features in *The Parliamentary Gazetteer of Ireland* in 1846. It describes Kilbeagh as

> a parish in the barony of Costello, 8 miles west by north of Ballaghadireen, co. Mayo, Connaught … Most of the surface is a dismal expanse of bleak and desolate bog and moor, partially relieved by isolated hills … In 1834, the parishioners, according to the ecclesiastical returns, were all Roman Catholics, and 2 hedge-schools had on their books 164 boys and 46 girls.[3]

The world of the e/migrants of the early 1800s would not have been even vaguely familiar to the people who left east Mayo in the mid-twentieth century. At the start of the nineteenth century the majority of people in Ireland lived in clachans. These were clusters of houses inhabited, in the main, by communities of related families. Land was rented on the rundale system, a form of collective farming practised by extended family members who held the land on a joint tenancy. The population at the time was in the region of five million and many people paid their rent with money earned in the linen industry. However, as the mechanisation of the linen trade gained momentum in the 1820s, increasing numbers of unemployed workers began travelling to Leinster and Britain to work as migratory harvest labourers. The rapid rise in population – from about five million in 1800 to over eight million in 1847 – increased the pressure on available land with a consequent rise in rents. This encouraged those who could afford to, to seek a living in colonies such as Canada, Australia and South Africa, or the even more attractive destination of the United States.

The post-Napoleonic era was a period of depression in Ireland, with a number of food crises and mini-famines occurring in the 1820s and 1830s. This brought about an increase in the numbers emigrating, most trying to escape the economic malaise and take advantage of the opportunities now existing abroad. However, the rural poor – smallholders and labourers – often did not have the resources to travel abroad and, in increasing numbers, they resorted to migratory work in Britain and Ireland. By 1841 over 10,000 were leaving County Mayo alone on an annual basis to labour at the harvest in Britain.

The Poor Inquiry of 1835 looked at the condition of the poorer classes in Ireland and provided informed estimates of the numbers migrating from different parts of the country on a parish-by-parish basis. It is clear from the evidence of witnesses that there was a greater rate of migration from the parishes in the eastern part of Mayo than from anywhere else in Ireland. The Devon Commission, in 1845, also provides evidence of the large numbers travelling from this area to pursue migratory work in England. Indeed, as early as the 1820s, Lord Dillon's tenants (most of whom were located in east Mayo) were sending money home from England to help sustain their families.

Prior to the Famine much of the country had seen some consolidation of small farms and the abandonment of the clachan and rundale systems. However, the west of Ireland continued the customs of early marriages and subdivision, which led to a further expansion in population along with an increasing level of destitution among smallholders. The continuing increase in population, albeit at a slower rate, and the chronic underemployment, encouraged many migrants to seek work and a permanent domicile in Britain and it is estimated that about half a million Irish people settled there between 1815 and 1845.

The tragedy of the Great Famine has been well documented elsewhere over the past half-century and is therefore not entered into in any great detail here. However, one puzzling feature of this calamity is the relatively small decrease in population in some parishes in east Mayo between 1841 and 1851 in contrast with other parts of the country. One characteristic of the east Mayo area was the annual flow of migratory agricultural labourers to Britain to work at the harvest. This movement of workers continued during the Famine period and scaled new heights immediately after. Those migrant workers helped, through their earnings in Britain, to sustain their families on marginal holdings in the west of Ireland through the Famine years and into the twentieth century. There is some evidence to suggest that the number of migrant workers travelling from Ireland to Britain increased to about 100,000 in the decades after the Famine and declined thereafter. A contributory factor to the anomalous increase in the population of some parishes in east Mayo after the Famine was the low rate of permanent migration from the area, which was less than the national average until the late 1800s.

The food crisis of 1879–80 created special problems for the immiserated west of Ireland. While migratory earnings had enabled smallholders to survive from year to year in their home localities in a precarious way, the combination of mini-disasters which took place in a short period of time around 1880 must have made the near-destitute people of east Mayo feel as though they were cursed. From 1880 on, the numbers leaving County Mayo for abroad increased rapidly and by 1900 Mayo had the highest emigration rate of any county in Ireland. Towards the end of the nineteenth century a proliferation of shipping lines and agents, facilitated by improved communications and networks in the United States, combined with reduced fares, made it safer and easier to travel to America or other destinations for work.

Life in the west of Ireland continued to be very bleak for those who did not migrate. Housing for many was substandard and living conditions in the late 1800s varied from poor to wretched. Though the Congested Districts Board helped to educate small farmers in good husbandry and house improvements, the majority of marginalised tenants, particularly those who were domiciled in the east Mayo area, still had to undertake the annual trek to Britain.

The families left behind in Ireland after the migrants departed had to assume responsibility for managing their landholdings, undertaking essential farm tasks, such as setting and digging potatoes, mowing and saving hay, cutting and saving the turf, along with the daily chores of milking cows, feeding livestock, mending fences, and so on. Alongside the field work were the varied household jobs that had to be carried out, as well as caring for the children. With little help available apart from that provided by elderly parents and young children, a huge responsibility was placed on the spouses left at home. This led to inevitable mishaps: a cow in a drain, the death of an ass, the loss of fowl. Tragically, children were especially at risk in these difficult times. My own family history reveals just such a calamity in 1888. While my grandfather was working in England as a migratory labourer, a tragedy occurred on the home farm. My aunt Mary, at just two years old, drowned in a drain while under the care of her eldest brother, who was only six years of age at the time.

Smallholders in east Mayo were still engaged in land reclamation and the subdivision of holdings in the late 1800s in an effort to encourage family members to live close at hand and thereby replace emigration by migration. The huge numbers leaving Ireland to work at the harvest in Britain eventually came to the notice of the government and the annual reports on migratory agricultural labourers provide much information on socio-economic conditions in the west of Ireland in the late nineteenth and early twentieth centuries.

These reports, which issued between 1880 and 1915, give an insight into the life of the migratory worker, from his existence as a smallholder or labourer in Ireland, to where and when he went to Britain, what work he did there, and the amount of money he brought back to Ireland after a few months away at the harvest.

The advent of the First World War caused a hiatus in Irish emigration to America until about 1920, and while the quota system put in place by the US government placed some constraints on the numbers going from Ireland, the most important factor affecting emigration was the Great Depression of 1929 and afterwards. The number of emigrants opting to go to the US in the 1930s fell to a trickle, curtailed by the lack of employment there. Workers from east Mayo, who had built up networks of contacts in Britain over generations, started going there in increasing numbers right up to the Second World War. The war created new opportunities for Irish workers, both male and female, in the building of munitions factories and aerodromes, in the health and services industries and in farming. Emigration from all over the Twenty-six Counties, and County Mayo in particular, increased incrementally as unemployed young men and women sought to fill the many vacancies occurring in the British labour force.

A recurring theme in almost all of the interviews featured in this book is the lack of paid work in the local (east Mayo) area. There was also the recognition that local employment, when available, was likely to be sporadic and/or poorly paid. As each successive family member left home during the 1950s and 1960s to seek work abroad, those still at home were discouraged from staying as they saw siblings and friends 'take the boat' to an anticipated better life in England. Because there was work for only one adult person on a 10–15-acre farm, family members of seventeen or eighteen years of age felt they had to leave home so as not to be a drain on family resources. When they left they couldn't come back, as 'there was nothing for us there'.

CHAPTER 1

Socio-economic Conditions in the West of Ireland, Pre-Famine

'They are under a compliment for life to every man, and under the lash of the world.'[1]

Migration abroad, either temporary or permanent, was not a pervasive feature of Irish life for most of the eighteenth century. Many subtenants were able to pay the rent with money earned from cottage industries derived from flax growing. James McParlan, writing in 1802 about the barony of Costello in County Mayo, notes that 'The flax and yarn trades are here in very brisk plight; large quantities of both are sold raw and in linens.' He goes on to say 'that the migration too of the Northern weavers, during the late troubles, into this county has very much promoted the linen manufacture'.[2] The 'troubles' alluded to here refer to an engagement that took place near Loughgall in County Armagh on 1 September 1795 between feuding Catholics and Protestants, which led to the flight of a colony of Roman Catholic small farmers and weavers, in total about 4,000 persons, to County Mayo.[3] They settled mainly around Westport on Lord Altamont's estate, but some came to live around Ballina, Foxford and Swinford, adding the surnames Tunney, Devany, Daly, Conway, Diamond, McNeela and Campbell, among others, to the locality.[4]

In fact, the linen industry was fairly well established in both Mayo and Sligo before the advent of the Northern weavers. Female labour had begun to take on increasing importance in the linen trade, with women capable of earning 3*d* or 4*d*. a day, providing some or all of the rent money from their endeavours. The influx of the Northern weavers into Mayo in the late 1790s probably helped to consolidate the linen industry in the county and there were thriving markets at the end of the eighteenth century in Westport, Ballina and Sligo.[5]

Nonetheless, for the most impoverished of the tenantry, migratory labour was becoming more a feature of life as the eighteenth century came to a close. Increasing numbers were travelling from the west or north to Leinster for harvest work, and the more adventurous of those were crossing the channel to earn their rent money in England; by the late eighteenth century, seasonal migration had become a key part of both Irish and British rural life.

Post-war depression and poverty in the west

The last decades of the eighteenth century and up to the end of the Napoleonic wars in 1815 saw some economic progress in Ireland; the country had benefitted significantly from wartime demand and the expansion of British markets. In parallel with this was a burgeoning population, partially the result of early marriages and the reckless subdivision of farms. While there was a thriving cottage industry in the linen trade in the northern part of the country the smallholders of the western counties supplemented family incomes with migratory labour. However, conditions deteriorated dramatically after 1815. A severe depression led to a fall in demand for goods and reduced prices for products led to increased unemployment and widespread poverty.

Conditions were particularly bad in the west of Ireland in the early decades of the nineteenth century. James Neligan, vicar of Kilmactige parish in County Sligo, describes conditions after the war:

> The present state of the peasantry and farmers is truly distressing. Stock of all kinds have fallen one-third at least in their price, and pigs one half: potatoes and oats have lost about the same proportion of their value, as well as oatmeal; on which articles depended the payment of their rents, and the support of their families.[6]

Neligan relates that during the war prices were high and demand great. 'Unfortunately this golden age has ceased with the war; and peace … is now considered by the people of this kingdom the greatest evil that could befall them, and makes them wish for another fierce and protracted contest.'[7]

Subdivision

While consolidation of farm holdings was taking place in the more prosperous parts of the country – especially in the east of Ireland in the years before the Famine – in the west the presence of wasteland and the propensity to subdivide allowed early marriages on tiny plots of land.[8] As the population was increasing, farm size was diminishing; by 1841 almost half of all farms were between one and five acres in size. In County Mayo, where there was extensive subdivision before the Famine, three-quarters of all holdings were in this category. Consequently, Mayo had a very dense rural population prior to the Famine, second only to Armagh.[9]

Unlike the more prosperous regions of Ireland, subdivision of holdings in the west of Ireland continued for several decades after the Famine. In Swinford Poor Law Union (PLU) in east Mayo, as late as 1879 three out of five holdings were less than fifteen acres in size.[10]

Early marriages and demographic changes, pre-Famine

Contemporary official records and other written sources outline the thinking behind early marriages. John Carr, writing in 1805, suggests that:

> Insufficiency of provisions, which operates so powerfully against marriage in England, is not known or cared about in Ireland; there, the want of an establishment never affects the brain of the enamoured rustic. Love lingers only till he can find out a dry bank, pick a few sticks, collect some furze and fern, knead a little mud with straw, and raise a hut about six feet high, with a door to let in the light and let out the smoke …[11]

James Neligan relates that in the early 1800s in his own parish of Kilmactige in south County Sligo, early marriages between girls of fifteen to twenty years of age and boys from over twenty 'fill their houses with children'.[12]

Witnesses to the Poor Inquiry of 1835 agreed that 'among the labourers, poverty forms no prevention to marriage, which is contracted with the most reckless indifference to the means of providing for a family'.[13] In his evidence at Kilmore-Erris, Rev. John Patrick Lyons, parish priest, presented a philosophical view of early marriages: 'Those who are more comfortable and somewhat educated, wait longer; but persons unacquainted with comfort do not feel the want of what they never knew.'[14]

However, customs and traditions were gradually changing, even in Mayo, during the last decades of the nineteenth century. In 1864 Swinford PLU had a marriage rate of 6.3 per 1,000 people, but this had fallen to 4.5 by 1901, bringing it closer to the county average.[15] Furthermore, at the start of the twentieth century permanent male celibacy in Ireland had jumped to one in four of the population, double what it had been at the time of the Famine. In contrast to this, permanent male celibacy in England and Wales was less than half that.[16]

Employment prospects

Cormac Ó Gráda informs us that: 'On the eve of the Famine the poverty of Irish smallholding and labouring families … was legendary. The poor were wretchedly housed … and poorly clothed, and often hungry for two or three months of every year.'[17] The Devon Commission of 1845, which collected evidence from some 1,100 witnesses in various parts of Ireland, was in little doubt about the impoverished state of Irish agricultural labourers:

> A reference to the evidence of most of the witnesses will show that the agricultural labourer of Ireland continues to suffer the greatest privations and hardships – that he continues to depend upon casual and precarious employment for subsistence – that he is still badly housed, badly fed, badly clothed and badly paid for his labour.[18]

The chances of receiving remunerative employment in the 1830s depended very much on the domicile of the labourer. For example, if he lived in the parish of Kilgever [sic] in County Mayo, he would work on average only thirty days in the year. Likewise, if he lived in the village of Ballymoat [sic] County Sligo, he might get only twenty-four days, but if he lived in the Barony of Dundalk he could look forward to 210 days, or in the Barony of Fews (Armagh), 175 days per year.[19]

The period 1815–45 was one of almost unrelenting misery and poverty for the

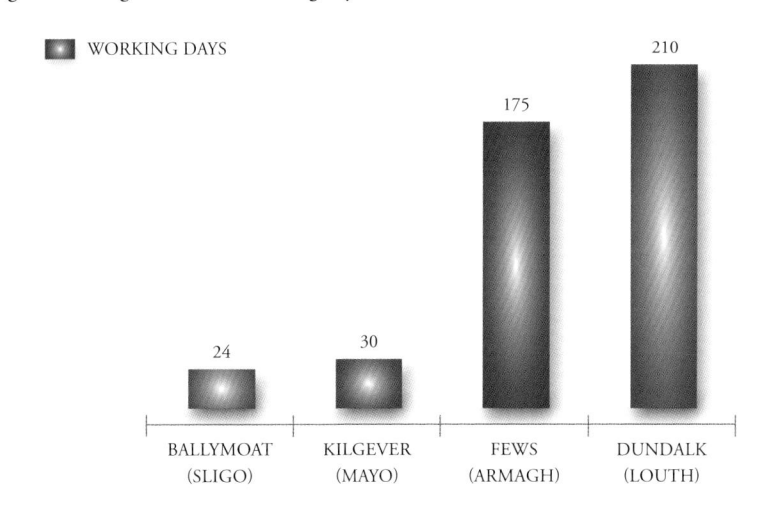

Fig. 1.1: Average number of working days available to able-bodied labourers in Ireland, 1835.

Location	Working Days
BALLYMOAT (SLIGO)	24
KILGEVER (MAYO)	30
FEWS (ARMAGH)	175
DUNDALK (LOUTH)	210

Source: PP 1835 (369) Poor Inquiry (Ireland), Appendix (H.) Part I (London, 1836), p. 12.

smallholding and labouring classes in Ireland, among whom were 310,000 smallholders, 100,000 joint tenancies and 900,000 landless labourers in 1841.[20]

Emigration and migration increase, pre-Famine

The decline of the woollen and cotton industries after the Napoleonic wars, allied to the economic depression in the post-1815 era and the mechanisation of the linen trade after 1828, led to a drastic reduction in home employment and a surge in emigration and migration. It is estimated that one million Irish crossed the Atlantic between 1815 and 1845, with about half that again going to Britain.[21] Protestants dominated emigration from Ireland until about 1830, but Catholics formed the majority after this time. The rate of departure accelerated from 1815 on, with about half of the total leaving in the last decade before the Famine.[22] The numbers leaving in 1830 are almost treble those of 1825.[23]

David Fitzpatrick links the fluctuations in the level of emigration in the decades pre-Famine to the effect poor seasons and bad harvests had on the distressed population. He points out that peaks of emigration occurred in 1830–32, 1834, 1836–37 and 1841–42, while partial failures of the potato crop occurred in 1829–30, 1832–34, 1836, 1839 and 1841–42. Thus a failure of the staple crop was usually closely followed by a sharp rise in emigration.[24]

The pattern of crisis followed by an increase in emigration manifests itself again in the 1860s and 1880s. The food crises of the early 1860s and 1879–81 are followed by a surge in people leaving the country in 1863–65 and again in 1880–83.[25] Kerby Miller, however, points out that bounties offered during the American Civil War (1861–65) may have been an enticement to young men to emigrate at that particular time.[26] Emigration from County Mayo reflects the national trend for the years shown above, with the numbers leaving in 1863 and 1864 more than treble that of the previous year; the exodus of 1880 exceeded that of the previous five years combined.[27]

The rate of emigration to the Americas, however, was still relatively low in the west of Ireland pre-Famine. Alex Glendining, giving evidence to a Select Committee in 1833, describes the relationship tenants in County Mayo had with their land: 'The habits of the poorer tenantry rivet them to their present holdings, which they will make almost incredible sacrifices to retain, and which they will not for such an object I think be induced to relinquish …'.[28] Regardless of this attachment to the land, the *Telegraph or Connaught Ranger* recorded in August 1831, that 'Among the vessels laden with Irish emigrants that arrived at Quebec to July 19, we find the following: – Medway from Westport; Manly from Sligo …'.[29] Rev. Robert Creighton, Presbyterian minister of Oughavale parish, County Mayo, recorded the number of emigrants from the quay of Westport in the early 1830s as follows: 'In 1831, 577; in 1832, 1033; in 1833, none, owing to the breaking out of cholera in America, and bad accounts from those who had emigrated.'[30]

Conditions among smallholders and labourers had deteriorated to such an extent in the 1830s that Thomas Lindsay, a land proprietor in east Mayo, declared: 'I know that my rental has sunk I should think full forty per cent. below what it was in 1814', and in relation to his tenants he remarked: 'I do not think they have ever been as well off as they were during the war.'[31] Lindsay agreed that 'great numbers' of small farmers and labourers went to England in harvest time but for those who had some capital ... 'there is no gentleman of landed property that has not lost one, two, three or four or ten decent comfortable tenants ... I lost myself five of the very best I had.'[32] People in authority in different parts of Mayo expressed their regret at losing better quality tenants at this time. A witness to the Poor Inquiry from the parish of Kilmaclash (now Kilmaclasser) described his feelings in this regard: 'There were several of the most affluent and respectable families left the parish for the Canadas, during the last three years; say, in all, 100 souls: their places, I regret to say, have been rapidly filled up by an inferior description of people.'[33] Rev. John McNulty of Killasser parish felt that it was only a lack of means that prevented greater numbers going: 'Two years since, one wealthy farmer and his family have emigrated, taking with them out of the country at least £1,000 ... Many others, both male and female, would emigrate if they had the means.'[34]

Housing in the 1830s

For those unable to raise the fare to cross the Atlantic there was always the choice of the shorter and cheaper journey to Britain. However, for those left behind in Ireland, conditions were dire in the pre-Famine decades. To make matters even worse, strewn through those decades (1815–45) were a series of food crises comprising four major potato crop failures and eleven partial potato crop failures during this period. County Mayo was particularly affected by the potato crop failures in 1816, 1822, 1831 and 1835.[35] Travellers to Ireland at this time were shocked by the appalling poverty they witnessed. John Barrow, travelling between Ballaghaderreen and Swinford in 1835, was met with the following vista:

> The country we now passed through was wretched in the extreme, and the land bore a very stony and barren appearance, except where we came upon an enormous extent of black bog, whereon was not a blade of grass or any living thing, animal or vegetable, for the eye to rest upon. This bog was infinitely the largest I had hitherto seen. The cabins, which

were wretched-looking hovels, were generally built of stone loosely heaped together, without mortar or even clay ... Altogether this part of the country presented a more general appearance of poverty than I had hitherto met with ...[36]

Rev. B. Duncan [sic] P.P. gave evidence regarding housing in the parishes of Castlemore and Kilcoleman, in east Mayo, in 1835, remarking that human habitations were 'generally wretched hovels, built of stones, without mortar, and thinly covered with straw; a pot and a few seats, called stools. Generally one set of bedsteads; bedding straw, with very indifferent covering.'[37] The parish priest in Kilmovee described the local cabins as: 'Miserable beyond description; no furniture, with the exception of a little pot, in which generally they carry in the water and boil their scanty food.'[38] Killasser parish offered no relief from the general immiseration: 'Cabins are generally built along the verges of bogs, sometimes dug into a turf bank, and covered with heath or rushes, sometimes built with sods. No bedsteads in many instances; no bed to lie on, but a wad of straw or heath, with very little bed-clothes.'[39] James Johnson, M.D., while touring Ireland in 1844, portrays the human abodes as follows: 'A hole dug in the earth, walled with sods excavated, roofed with bog-sticks, and covered with potato haulm: day-clothes scanty – bed-clothes almost none – children seeking warmth by contact with the pig!'[40]

Many witnesses to the Poor Inquiry of 1835 gave evidence about the poverty

Fig. 1.2: Common sort of Mayo mud cabin. Source: John Barrow, *A Tour Round Ireland* (London, 1836), p. 159.

and destitution in Ireland in the decades before the Famine. More accurate information regarding the standard of housing was provided by the 1841 census and there is much variation shown in different regions of the country. For example, County Mayo had the lowest proportion of first-class houses of any county in Ireland in 1841 and had the second highest proportion of fourth-class houses in that year (almost two-thirds of the total).[41] The parish of Killasser had no first-class house in 1841 and the percentage of fourth-class houses was 61.4 per cent, roughly the county average. The inhabitants of the neighbouring parish of Kilbeagh endured even worse housing, with four-fifths of all inhabited houses being in the lowest category.[42] By 1851 the number of fourth-class houses in Killasser had gone down from over sixty per cent to less than twenty per cent and the number of third-class houses had increased to almost eighty per cent of the total.[43] The increase in the percentage of third-class houses can, in part, be attributed to the dramatic fall in the number of fourth-class houses and consequently the overall number of houses.

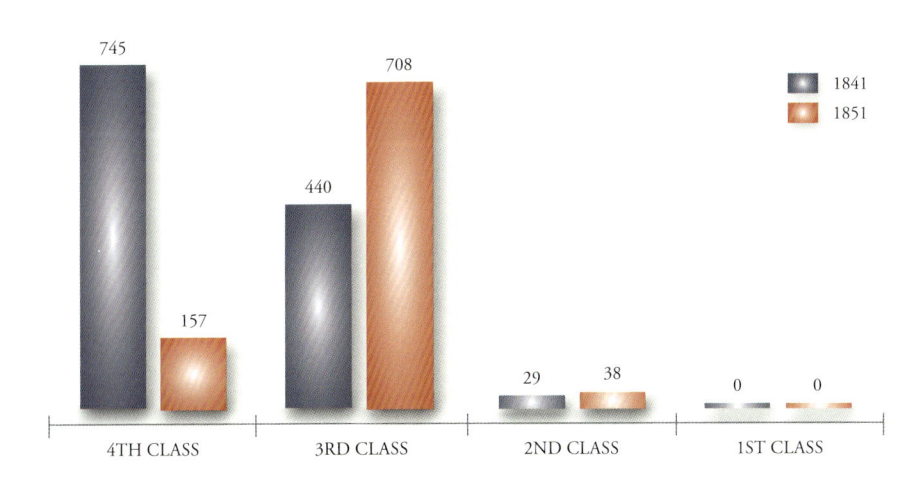

Fig. 1.3: Classes of houses in Killasser, 1841, 1851.

Class	1841	1851
4TH CLASS	745	157
3RD CLASS	440	708
2ND CLASS	29	38
1ST CLASS	0	0

Source: Bernard O'Hara, *The Archaeological Heritage of Killasser, Co Mayo* (Galway, 1991), p. 199.

Subdivision and short leases

In the pre-Famine decades most Irish farmers held tenure on short leases or at will. Many still held land in common, especially those living in the west. In County Mayo the rundale system persisted long after it had disappeared in most other counties;

as late as the 1840s almost three-fifths of the land in the county was still held in common or as joint tenancy.[44] A still rising population, pressure on land availability, subdivision encouraged by early marriages and extravagant rents, coupled with crop failures and the collapse of the linen industry, kept the population of the west of Ireland and County Mayo, in particular, teetering on the verge of starvation most years pre-Famine. Rev. John Coleman of Swinford parish commented on conditions in his area in 1845:

> A man that had ten or twelve acres was not compelled to go to England. About forty years ago land was set at half the price that it is now, and they had double means to pay it to what they have at present: they got £6 for a hundredweight [50.8 kg] of butter, and they will not get £4 now. They have no yarn to employ them, and their sole trade is rearing a pig and going to England.[45]

Lack of tenure was a cause of much complaint in many areas before the Famine. Michael Millet, a farmer and bailiff from Swinford, deposed to the Devon Commission in 1845:

> If they gave a tenant a long tenure, so that he would be encouraged to improve, that would be the most important point. When a poor tenant has improved seven or eight acres of land, the landlord raises the rent, or gives it to another tenant. That is the greatest grievance.[46]

Another witness from the Swinford area, Edward Dean, a strong farmer from Carragown, explained the tenants' attitudes to holding land at will: 'They are not encouraged to improve their lands without a lease … I see them in the wintertime idle, when they might be improving their land. They say: "We will only make the most we can of the crop this year; we may be turned out next year."'[47]

Lack of employment was a major cause of distress. Dominick Waldron, a labourer and witness at the Poor Inquiry in Ballina, spoke of the conditions endured by workmen in his area:

> The poor are willing to work, but there is no one to employ them; men are of no value at all here, and there is no regard for them; many of them have so much hunger in their faces, that no one would give them their food for all the work they could do. They are under a compliment for life to every man, and under the lash of the world.[48]

W. Sherrard, esquire, agent, referred to a major cause of distress and hardship in the Swinford region in 1845:

> I allude to the subdividing of the land, and establishing of families upon four-acre farms, which, in a country where there is no trade, where the system of agriculture is bad, and where, for want of skill and capital, the land is not made to produce one half what it is capable of, must only lead to the rapid increase of a pauper and starving population, and, consequently, to a decreased value of the property.[49]

Another contributor to the Devon Commission was Luke Collereen [sic], land surveyor and farmer from Currey [sic] in south Sligo. Collereen, in his evidence, acknowledged that three-quarters of the land in that area was mountain and bog; that the farm size in his home parish was from four to five acres in general and that for every acre of good land there were four acres of bottom land. When asked if subletting or subdividing was still practised he replied: 'Subdividing is, but we have no subletting. Subdividing is among families, and the farms are reduced to skeletons. There is nothing but three or four acres, or two acres; a father gives it to his daughters.'[50] He went on to say: 'We have no people holding in the county who are only small farmers: they are all a class of labourers …'.[51]

Mini-famines

Small farmers and labourers, such as the aforementioned, underwent much privation and hardship in the pre-Famine years. In 1822 the *Morning Chronicle* of London, reporting on distress in County Mayo, informed its readers that 'an unparalleled degree of distress exists in seven parishes that nearly compose this Barony [Gallen] amounting at least to a fourth, and in many instances a third of a population of 27,000 souls'.[52] The food crisis of 1830–32 was especially severe in County Mayo, with an excess mortality for the whole country of about 50,000 people, most of whom died of cholera.[53] A Mayo newspaper in 1831 disclosed that it was 'utterly impossible to describe the abject misery that prevails throughout this County. Last week there was on the poor list 216,643, this week it has increased to 221,843.'[54] The paper went on to report the evidence of Rev. John Coleman (P.P. Swinford), who testified that the distress in the parishes of Meeleck [sic] and Kilicunduff [sic] was very great and he asked the Committee to increase the list from 1,300 to 6,000, and issue relief for that number.[55]

Migrant harvestmen (the Spalpeen tradition)

The Irish fled the cycle of poverty in the country by emigrating across the Atlantic if they could afford to, or by making the shorter and cheaper journey to Britain if they couldn't. While upwards of half a million Irish people settled in Britain in the period 1815–45, there was a parallel movement of more transient workers – the migratory labourers – who went to the harvest in England or Scotland year after year to earn the rent money for their holdings.[56] Various observations were made from the early eighteenth century about harvestmen or spalpeens working at the harvest in Britain, with the eminent historian, W.H. Lecky, noting that at the close of that century:

> It was still true that, at the beginning of every autumn the roads were crowded with barefooted and half-naked mountaineers, who were travelling on foot 150 or 200 miles to work for the harvest in England, where they commonly fell into the hands of contractors known as 'spalpeen brokers' who distributed them among the farmers, intercepted a substantial part of their scanty wages, and imposed on them an amount of labour which few West Indian planters would have exacted from their negroes.[57]

While reference is made from time to time of Irish migrant labourers travelling to Britain during the eighteenth century, no accurate measurement was made of the numbers involved until 1841. In that year police enumerators were detailed to count the harvestmen embarking at ports around the coast during the summer and they arrived at a figure in excess of 57,000 for the whole country, with over 10,000 of those coming from County Mayo.[58]

The tradition of travelling to Britain for the harvest from the west of Ireland was a long one. Arthur Redford, writing about migratory labour in the early 1800s, claimed that most Irish migrants came from poor areas of Connaught and made the journey to Britain in great hordes, many of them settling there afterwards.[59] It is difficult to measure the settlement of Irish people in Britain pre-Famine, but reports like that on Mendicity in 1816 add to the general picture. The report alludes to 'the natives of Ireland, in which part of the United Kingdom there are no laws for the support and maintenance of the poor. Some of these come to England … in search of work, at a particular season of the year, and frequently do not return.'[60]

Most of the migratory labourers who left Ireland for Britain, however, returned to their smallholdings and it is estimated that probably 40,000 out of the 57,000 who originally left in 1841 returned to Ireland after the harvest.[61] An official report, of an earlier date, on disease in Ireland allows us an insight into the travails of the migratory labourers at that time:

In some of these villages no increase of disease was observed, until the labourers from Connaught and from some parts of Ulster, came up in 1817, in quest of harvest work. In 1817 they came up in the beginning of July, or even earlier, driven from home by famine. Thus at Kilcock (in which there are sometimes 3,000 labourers at one time from Roscommon and Mayo) no increase of fever was observed among the inhabitants till the latter end of August ....[62]

Improved transport

The advent of steam packets in 1818 facilitated the movement of migrants from Ireland to Britain and the journey was further eased by reduced fares as competition increased. By the 1820s the cost of a passage was as low as threepence a head for deck passage.[63] The improvement in transport facilitated the increased numbers who sought work in Britain in the mid-1820s and as the linen trade declined and poverty deepened it became increasingly imperative that many smallholders in the west of Ireland seek to supplement their incomes through harvest work in Britain. Writing about harvestmen in the early nineteenth century, James E. Handley contends that:

In the Twenties of the nineteenth century there was an annual influx of six or eight thousand harvesters. Throughout the Thirties the number steadily increased and by the middle Forties the Clyde steamboats were coping with as many as six or eight thousand a week during the height of the immigration and an influx of 25,000 reapers over the season.[64]

Handley felt that some of the thousands of migrant labourers going to Scotland would elect to stay there if suitable employment was available. It is difficult if not impossible to get an accurate figure for harvestmen travelling between Ireland and Britain before 1841 and while the Railway Inquiry of 1835 assesses the number as above 10,000 men annually, this figure is almost certainly an underestimation.[65]

Evidence from the Poor Inquiry

Unfortunately, there is no accurate means of tracing backwards the extent of migration from Ireland or Mayo as no official counts were taken prior to 1880, except for the census of 1841, which shows that County Mayo sent more migrant labourers to Britain than any other county – almost one in five of the total. There are, however, two major reports on socio-economic conditions in pre-Famine Ireland – the Poor Inquiry of 1835 and the Devon Commission of 1845 – and they provide countrywide information

18 *Swinford Spalpeens*

on the extent of migratory labour in specific regions of all of the counties of Ireland.

The Poor Inquiry framed the following question to elicit information regarding migration to Britain (and other parts of Ireland) from a selection of parishes throughout the country: 'What number of labourers are in the habit of leaving their dwellings periodically, to obtain employment, and what proportion of them go to Britain?'[66] The responses from witnesses were as follows:

> Castlemore parish (east Mayo), population 3,094, witness Rev. B. Duncan [*sic*], P.P.: 'About 600. All to England. Probably one half are married.'[67]
> Kilcoleman parish (east Mayo), population 5,427, witness Henry Browne, esq. J.P.: 'I have no opportunity of ascertaining the number. All go to England. Many [are married].'[68]
> Toomore parish (east Mayo), population 3,576, witness Rev. J. Henry: 'About 300 go to England, 66 to other places. A proportion of them [married] are; their wives remain in their cabins, living on potatoes, and more of them begging.'[69]
> Ballinrobe parish (south Mayo), population 8,933, witness Rev. Thomas J. Burgh, Rector: 'Not many leave this part of the county of Mayo for the purpose of employment. It is a cheap place.'[70]
> Killala parish (north Mayo), population 3,875, witness Bishop of Killala: 'Few go from this parish.'[71]
> Ferns parish, County Wexford, population 4,039, witness Thomas Derenzy, J.P.: 'About 200; none of them are in the habit of going to England, as is the case in other parts of Ireland.'[72]
> Bailieborough parish, County Cavan, population 10,480, witness Rev. John Gumley: 'Very few from this parish leave their dwellings periodically to procure employment elsewhere. None go to England for that purpose; some to Meath or Dublin.'[73]
> Magherfelt parish, County Londonderry, population 7,218, witness Andrew Spotswood, J.P.: 'Few leave their dwellings; any that do, go to England.'[74]

While the foregoing figures are taken at random from different parishes a pattern of movement from the east Mayo area to England would seem to have been well established prior to the Famine. There is less migration from other parts of Mayo where smallholders seemed to find some employment nearer home or, at any rate, within Ireland.

Martin Heveran, a labourer from Burrishoole, County Mayo, portrays the helplessness felt by people with little or no means in the 1830s:

> Some years ago I was in the habit of going to England for the harvest; I had no land then. I used to sell my pig to make up the means, and let the wife and children shift about the world for themselves, until I came home to them … When I was in the habit of going there, I used generally have 4l or 5l [l = £] home with me, having spent 18 or 20 weeks there … Latterly I have not gone to England; I could not scrape enough together to take me there.[75]

Henry D. Inglis, travelling in Ireland in 1834, found that many harvestmen were reluctant migrants:

> I accosted many individuals, travelling from Mayo and elsewhere, to find harvest work … These men had no constant employment at home … and I was invariably told, that if they could find constant work in their own country, at ten-pence, they would rather remain at home, than travel to England, even to receive the still higher wages to be earned there.[76]

Nevertheless, an Irish witness to the Poor Inquiry, commenting on his countrymen in England, felt in a position to say that: 'The Irish … have a notion that any part of the world is better than Ireland, and consequently are fond of a change. I will say unhesitatingly that nine-tenths of the Irish settled in England did not come over from necessity, but in a wild spirit of adventure.'[77]

Connaught migrants did not go exclusively to Britain. In 1835 it was noted at Naul, County Dublin, that 'the harvest of this parish and of the surrounding country could not be made up without the assistance of the spalpeens or Connacht men'. In Ratoath, County Meath, it was stated: 'In harvest and seed time we have an overflow of Connacht men to get on the work, the population being very thin.'[78]

Jerrard Edward Strickland was agent to Lord Dillon of Loughlynn in the 1820s. Dillon's vast estate of more than 80,000 acres, ran through a number of east Mayo parishes. Strickland was a witness to a Select Committee investigating vagrancy in 1828 and his post as agent put him in a pivotal position to make observations regarding the movements of smallholders within the Dillon estate, and these were recorded as follows:

> … the Committee might perhaps like to know this fact, that, in the course of the last nine years, the number of persons coming to England to obtain work has annually increased immensely; and there is hardly a cottage upon an estate in the district with which I am acquainted, which does not send at least one individual, and many, I believe send more.[79]

High rent plus low employment equals poverty

Irish migratory workers were noted for their ability to seek out work, and the frugality of their lifestyle when abroad is illustrated in a report in 1828 on Irish and Scottish Vagrants. John Allen Powell of London, a witness, had business connections with Lord Dillon's agent in east Mayo and participated in a scheme whereby Dillon's tenants in London could transmit their earnings, through him, to their families in Ireland. He described the transactions as follows:

> It was a system began [*sic*] by the late Lord Dillon, I think nearly 20 years ago, who used to receive small sums of money belonging to his tenants in London, and giving orders upon his agent in Ireland, for the payment of it in Roscommon and Mayo. After Lord Dillon's death, I pursued the same system; I think his death occurred in 1813; I have continued it since that time … I have an account here from April 1815 down to the present time; in the first year the sum paid was about 160*l* only, and that was, I believe, entirely confined to the tenantry of the estates of Lord Dillon, and there were very few of them at first. In 1816, it increased to 190 *l*; in 1817 to 230 *l*; in 1818, 230 *l*; in 1819, 290*l*; in 1820, 470 *l*; in 1821, 540 *l*; in 1822, 940 *l*; in 1823, 1120*l*; in 1824, it was about 1000 *l*; in 1825, it was 1,316 *l*; in 1826, 1,088 *l*; last year it decreased, and was only 866*l* … [*l* = £][80]

Jerrard Strickland, the agent to whom Powell refers, explains the reason for the increased migration from the east Mayo area and the need for greater remittances, to a committee on emigration in 1827:

> The small tenantry in Ireland pay more rent than any regular farmer would pay; and they pay it, not out of the produce of the land, but out of the produce of their labour in England. There is an unnatural rent paid to the landlords in the part of the country I am in, which is not derived from the produce of the land … those common tenantry will pay to middlemen twenty shillings, thirty shillings, and even forty shillings per acre for the privilege of building a cabin upon the skirts of a bog, and cultivating the bog, themselves earning the rent by their labour in England.[81]

Ten years later, Rev. B. Durcan of Killeaden parish in east Mayo, was reporting to the Devon Commission his belief that there were two main causes of the annual trek to England:

> The poverty and miserable condition of the people appear to me to be owing chiefly to two causes. First, the exorbitantly high rents and other burdens on land; and the second, the want of employment, or a remunerative price for labour … It is the want of demand for labour that causes so many to go annually to England for the harvest … In some districts of this parish, at an average, I believe nine-tenths of the male adult population go there every year. There is scarcely a house which there are not some gone from it, the younger men particularly.[82]

The evidence would seem to suggest a strong tradition of migration from the west of Ireland decades before the Famine. The decline of the linen industry and increased rents, allied to a quicker and safer passage to Britain from the 1820s on, acted as a spur to an exhausted and desperate tenantry.

Settlement of migrants

This period (1815–45) of high migration to Britain was contemporaneous with a more permanent movement there. It is generally accepted that about half a million Irish people settled in Britain during that period. Many of those who settled there may have gone on a temporary basis, found more permanent work there and eventually settled down in the vicinity. This turning of temporary sojourns cross-channel into permanent settlement is noted in official documents during those decades. John Dyas, a witness from near Kells, County Meath, when asked in 1830 if harvesters returned from England after the harvest replied: 'In some cases they do, in other cases they continue here [England], that is, if they can get employment.'[83]

George Forwood, an assistant overseer of the parish of Liverpool, told the Poor Inquiry in 1835:

> The Irish come over from 500 to 700 in a steam-packet, principally in the harvest-time … They have been brought over in numbers for 1s a head, and they never pay more than 5s for the passage to England … All these are agricultural labourers when they are in England; many of these will stay if they get any kind of employment, as hod-men, porters about the docks, &c., and become domiciled.[84]

Conditions pre-Famine

Most Irish emigrants went to North America in the pre-Famine period if they could afford the fare (about £4 up to the 1850s), while the peasantry could aspire only to a deck passage on a cross-channel steamer.[85] The cross-channel emigrants were fleeing from conditions described in unadorned language by the Commissioners to the Poor Inquiry in their third report in 1836:

> The evidence annexed to our former Reports proves to painful certainty that there is in all parts of Ireland much and deep-seated distress … A great portion of them are insufficiently provided at any time with the common necessaries of life. Their habitations are wretched hovels, several of the family sleep together upon straw or upon the bare ground … their food commonly consists of dry potatoes, and with these they are at times so scantily supplied as to be obliged to stunt themselves to one spare meal in the day.[86]

Before the Famine, consolidation of farms, increased age at marriage and primogeniture were practised in the more prosperous areas of the country, while land was still being subdivided in the west. The land available for reclamation and subdivision was greater in Mayo than in any other county in Ireland in 1841: 'This county contains a greater extent of unimproved waste lands than any other in Ireland, yet a large portion of it presents unusual facilities for reclamation and cultivation.' The Devon Commission then suggested that 170,000 acres in the county might be reclaimed for cultivation, with a further 300,000 acres available to be drained for pasture.[87] Early marriages, subdivision and a hunger for land encouraged the reclamation of this wasteland and between 1841 and 1851 over one-tenth had been reclaimed, allowing for rapid repopulation after the Famine in east Mayo, where much of this waste land was situated.[88]

Poverty was pervasive in Ireland before the Famine but was particularly acute in the west of Ireland where tenants subsisted on tiny portions of land, many relying on earnings from migratory labour for survival. While poverty was common in Europe in the mid-1800s, contemporary travellers were shocked by the scale of the privation they saw in Ireland. At this time Ireland's per capita income was somewhat less than half that of Great Britain's.[89]

Housing was of a particularly squalid nature throughout Ireland in the 1840s. For example, there were only 414 first-class houses in all of County Mayo in 1841.[90] James Johnson MD did a tour of Ireland in 1844, and on witnessing the peasantry emerging from their hovels called them 'Troglodytae Hibernica':

> The Ancient Troglodytes domiciliated in caves and caverns … But the Irish Troglodytes take rank only with moles, badgers, rats, rabbits, and other burrowers in Mother Earth! They merely dig a hole in the ground

– generally the bog – and covering it with sods and brush-wood, leave an aperture at one end for their own entrance, and a smaller one at the other, for the exit of the smoke. These wretched habitations are to be seen in all the southern and western portions of Ireland – especially in the bogs.[91]

Regardless of the poor housing, high unemployment, subsistence farms, and high emigration, the population of Ireland continued to rise before the Famine albeit at a reduced rate. By 1841 the population had passed the eight million mark and that of County Mayo was over 388,000.[92]

CHAPTER 2

Famine and its Effects in East Mayo

'... the people appear to be paralysed from starvation; they tell me they must use their little seed for food, and when that is used, they say, "We must lie down and die."'

Demographic changes

By 1851 the face of Ireland had changed irreversibly. The country had lost almost one-fifth of its population and the inhabitants of County Mayo had declined by twenty-nine per cent.[1]

The fall in population in Mayo was not uniform throughout the county. One anomalous area was east Mayo, where some parishes had steep reductions in population while contiguous parishes fared much better. For example, while Meelick, Bohola and Killasser parishes saw their populations decline by almost one-third between 1841 and 1851, Killedan parish lost less than one-fifth of its people and Kilconduff parish lost only three per cent.[2] The parish of Kilmovee actually increased its population by thirty-eight persons during that decade.[3]

A study of townlands in east Mayo shows the same puzzling features. In the townland of Ballyhine in Aghamore parish the number of inhabited houses fell from twenty-three in 1841 to just four in 1851, with a parallel fall in the population from 119 to twenty people.[4] In the townland of Knockfadda in Killasser parish, the number of inhabited houses rose from two to nineteen between 1841 and 1851, with a concomitant increase in population from thirteen persons to 112.[5]

The reason that some townlands show an anomalous increase or decrease in population between 1841 and 1851 may be as mundane as a simple mistake on the part of the census enumerators. According to local historian, Micheál Murphy, the population changes in the townlands of Knockfadda and Doonty in Killasser parish in that decade were not caused by evictions, migration or deaths, but by a simple error in determining the position of the boundary between the contiguous townlands, incorporating, more or less, the total population of the two townlands into one area in successive censuses – Doonty in 1841 and Knockfadda in 1851.

However, the combined population of these two townlands in 1851 was thirty per cent less than their combined population in 1841, in line with the trend for the whole parish.

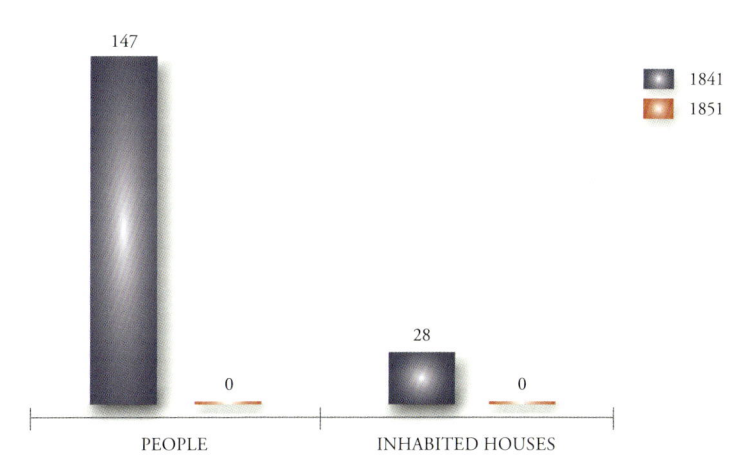

Fig. 2.1: Demographic changes in Doonty (Killasser parish), 1841, 1851.

Source: PP 1852–53 [1542] Census of Ireland for the Year 1851, part I, County of Mayo (Dublin, 1852), p. 136.

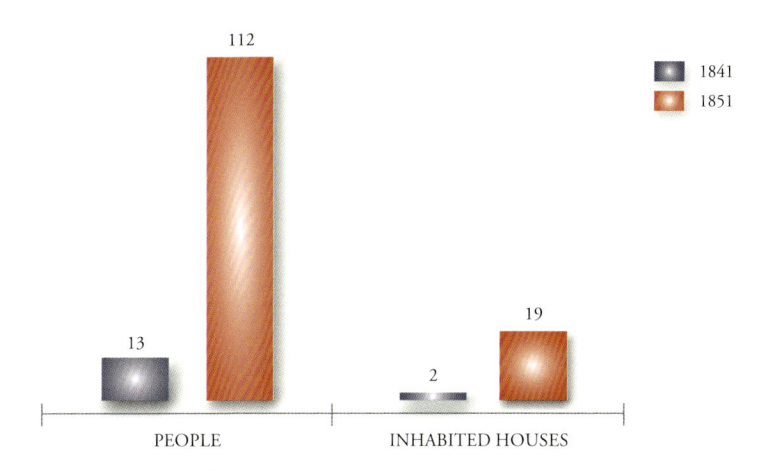

Fig. 2.2: Demographic changes in Knockfadda (Killasser parish), 1841, 1851.

Source: PP 1852–53 [1542] Census of Ireland for the Year 1851, part I, County of Mayo (Dublin, 1852), p. 136.

The influence of a good or bad landlord was an important factor in how townlands and estates survived the worst effects of the Famine, but here again anomalies arise. The 14th Viscount Dillon, Charles Henry, had a reputation as a good landlord in east Mayo, yet when the returns of population for Glenmullynaha East townland, where he was landlord, are examined, they show that there was a decline of fifteen per cent between 1841 and 1851.[6] In Glenmullynaha West, where Richard O'Grady was landlord, there was an increase in population of almost fifteen per cent in the same period.[7] To further complicate matters, in the townlands of Ballyglass East and Ballyglass West, where Dillon was landlord to both, one shows a rise in population of 111 per cent, while the other shows a fall of sixty-one per cent.[8] Did people move across townland boundaries to friends or relatives slightly better off than themselves?

Notwithstanding big losses from individual townlands and parishes in east Mayo, the Dillon estate, with a population of almost 33,000 in 1841 had lost, overall, only six or seven hundred inhabitants by 1851. Charles Strickland, agent to Viscount Dillon, worked tirelessly, it is said, to ease the suffering of the tenants. Rent abatements were allowed, soup kitchens were set up to feed the poor and, where possible, food was sold at cost price.

The *Tyrawley Herald* of 4 February 1847 was effusive in its praise of the efforts of Charles Strickland on behalf of the Dillon tenants:

> Upon the vast estate of Lord Dillon, and also upon that of Mr Costello, Edmondstown, the sleepless and unrivalled exertions of Messrs. Strickland and Holmes [local landlord and magistrate] have certainly been the means of good beyond estimation. Hundreds of lives must have been preserved by them while the condition of thousand [*sic*] had been preserved from the fearful pinching of starvation.[9]

Some areas of Swinford Poor Law Union (PLU), incorporating the Dillon estate among others, seem to have fared somewhat better than others. While Swinford Union as a whole lost less than one-fifth of its people between 1841 and 1851, some of its parishes – such as Kilmactigue and Toomore – lost over one-third of their populace during that decade.[10]

Reports from Swinford Poor Law Unions

The fact that some inhabitants of the Union fared better than others doesn't take from the destitution and hopelessness felt in general by the people. A letter from Swinford to the Inspector-General in January 1847 gives some indication of the distress felt:

> I beg to call your most special attention to the sad state of destitution existing in this district … You would be horrified, could you only see the multitude of starving men, women and children, who daily and hourly swarm the town, soliciting with prayers and tears one meal of food … I must respectfully entreat that you will use your high influence from your public position, to have food sent immediately to the very peaceable orderly people of this district, who though famishing from want of food, up to this period have observed the rights of property (food) with the strictest honesty and forbearance … the people appear to be paralysed from starvation; they tell me they must use their little seed for food, and when that is used, they say, 'We must lie down and die.'[11]

Yet later on that year, another inspector reported from Swinford to the Poor Law Commissioners that:

> The objects applying for relief were wretched in appearance, but I am bound to say, at the market held yesterday, whereat about 2,000 persons were collected from all round the neighbourhood, their appearance was highly respectable; indeed the women were rather overdressed, and no indication of want was to be observed amongst them.[12]

The same inspector turned his attention to the problem of nepotism in the local workhouse in a letter he wrote some weeks later to the Swinford Union Poor Law Commissioners acquainting them with

> the state of the officials in this workhouse on my arrival. The master, who has just been got rid of, is brother to the matron; the medical officer is brother-in-law to both; the whole either cousins or connected with three or four of the Guardians. Now, without wishing the least in the world to find any fault with the individuals, the tendency of these connexionships [*sic*] is adverse to the proper working of the system.[13]

Rather sadly this inspector reported to the Commissioners on the appointment of a new master and matron to the workhouse: 'The appointment of master and matron took place this day, the selection fell on a Mr and Mrs O'Donnell; seven applications were put in, amongst others an old police serjeant of 18 years' standing with excellent characters, but not one voted for him.'[14]

Official migrant count, 1841

Seasonal earnings were an essential component in the survival of subsistence farmers on their holdings from year to year. Captain Hanley, inspector to Swinford PLU, outlined the conditions prevailing in his area in 1847–48:

> Destitution in this union is caused by the failure of the potato crop for successive years. No union in Ireland more depended on the success of that root. Last season the unhappy people staked their all to cultivate it, which, combined with the total want of employment – not a shilling to be earned – no resident gentleman or farmer to give work, even in a small way – has tended to reduce a portion of the population to mere ragged phantoms …[15]

Regardless of the desperate conditions prevailing in east Mayo during the Famine, the population held up much better than in more prosperous parts of the county. The facility of cheap travel to Britain to earn money at the harvest may have enabled more to survive than would be expected. In papers relating to the relief of distress in 1847–48 it was noted that: 'In the Swinford Union, for the last twenty years all the male adult population have gone to England for the harvest. They go yearly to their old employers, and bring back money.'[16]

Crossing to Britain for work was becoming a familiar experience for many Irish – to build docks, railways and canals, some to work in factories and mills and more to labour at harvest work on a yearly basis –encouraged by cheap fares and the speed and relative safety of steam. No official record was made of the numbers travelling as seasonal labourers from Ireland to Britain each year, until the 1841 census. In that year the census commissioners appointed officers at each packet office to record the home county of each ticket purchaser. Efforts to count those returning from Britain, later in the year, were abandoned, because of the haste with which the migrants landed. Nevertheless, some valuable information can be gleaned from the records obtained, which were for the period 13 May 1841 to 31 August 1841.

A total of 57,651 harvest labourers were recorded at the nine ports engaged in the survey. This number is probably an underestimation of the number travelling as smaller ports were not included. Furthermore, the report itself acknowledges a possible undercounting as 'no inconsiderable number of harvest labourers embark on board steam vessels which occasionally lie to on the coast for the convenience of passengers in the summer season'.[17]

Of the total persons recorded, County Mayo supplied the greatest number (10,430) and also the highest proportion in relation to its population. The Connaught counties of Roscommon, Leitrim and Sligo came next to Mayo as major suppliers of seasonal agricultural workers. Surprisingly, County Dublin contributed over 5,000 harvestmen to the overall figure.[18] However, by the time the next official count was made in 1880, Dublin's contribution was a mere nineteen harvest labourers, with Mayo recording over 10,000 persons and still heading the list of harvestmen in the country.[19] The 1841 census also recorded almost 8,000 female labourers as having travelled to Britain.

Travel or stay put

While Henry D. Inglis was travelling between Westport and Castlebar in the 1830s, he noted numerous locked cabins and on enquiring locally was told that the owners had gone to the harvest in England.[20] However, this custom of locking doors and leaving homes for the harvest months was not universal in Mayo. Rev. Bernard Durcan, parish priest of Killeaden parish in Swinford PLU, was a witness to the Devon Commission in 1845.

> Q.71. Does a large proportion of the labouring classes go to England?
> Ans. Yes.
> Q.72. Can you state what they usually bring home?
> Ans. Some that can go early in the season for the hay harvest, and can remain there the whole season, in a good year might bring £4 or £5 home; a person going to the harvest alone, from £2 to £3.
> Q.73 What becomes of their wives and families in their absence?
> Ans. They remain in the houses attending to their little crop.[21]

The practice of leaving the family home to go begging diminished post-Famine and, from the middle of the nineteenth century on, women were more inclined to look after the crops rather than wander around the countryside seeking alms.

George Nicholls noted in 1838 regarding migrant harvesters: 'There has long been a great influx of Irish labourers into Scotland and England, at certain seasons; and it appears to be every year increasing. Many of the individuals who so migrate do not return, but remain dispersed through the great towns in England and Scotland …'. Nicholls also observed in regard to harvesters: 'They mostly resort year after year to the same districts, where they become known; and the English farmer not unfrequently [sic] engages, during the current harvest, the labourers who are to come from Connaught to assist him in getting in his crops in the next.' He commended harvestmen for being 'generally sober, well-conducted, and inoffensive, living hard and labouring hard'.[22]

From migrant to emigrant

It is suggested in the 1841 census that upwards of one in three of the harvestmen who migrated in that year stayed on in Britain on a permanent basis. While there is no information provided to support this assumption, Thomas A. Larcom, as a witness to a select Committee in 1847, gave his view regarding the movements of Irish migratory labourers: 'I do not think they all come back from England. We took great pains in the Census to count them in coming back; we set Policemen in plain Clothes at the Ports, and we have Reason to believe that a great many of them remained in England.'[23]

David Fitzpatrick contends that there was a sustained demand in Britain for Irish migrant labourers from before the Famine to the 1870s and that many who went for harvest work settled in local towns with which they had a connection of some sort.[24] Furthermore, in areas of high seasonal labour, like Yorkshire, there was a disproportionate number of Mayo and Sligo emigrants in the towns of Leeds, Bradford and York in the period 1851–71. Indeed, in York, half of Irish settlers were from either Mayo or Sligo.[25]

Peter Kilbride from Gowel, outside Charlestown, might have been one such emigrant. Peter was born about 1820 in Gowel and first came to England as a young man. He lived in the Kelsey Row area of Batley (a small town near Leeds). He returned to Ireland after a few years and married Bridget Davey while there. His son, Thomas, was born in Ireland in 1865. However, Peter returned to England and was present at his daughter's wedding there in 1886. Thomas, his son, was at this time working as a coal miner in local pits.[26]

There is anecdotal evidence of a surge of emigrants to the Batley area near Leeds in the early 1830s. This may coincide with strikes of a 'formidable character', which took place in the years 1819 and 1832, affecting the Shoddy trade in Batley. 'The latter named strike was instrumental in bringing a considerable number of Irish people into the town, to replace the refractory hands: they formed quite a colony at first, and have increased numerically since.'[27]

Many of the descendents of those Irish strike breakers in Batley are still proud of their Irish ancestry, as their commemorative parish booklet, *St. Mary of the Angels, Batley 1853–2003*, indicates:

> The ancestors of the great majority of St. Mary's parishioners came from County Mayo, and the names of the towns and villages there are as familiar to many as are the names of districts around Batley itself. Mention Charlestown or Swinford, Hagfield or Foxford, Ballyhaunis or Balla, and you will find many a one who … has a cousin there or a second cousin, or a father's cousin's uncle's son.[28]

Desperation forced many Irish workers into strike-breaking. They were willing to work harder and live harder to undercut any opposition. James Taylor, owner of a silk mill in Manchester in 1836, describes his modus operandi for dealing with recalcitrant workers:

> The moment I have a turn-out and am fast for hands I send to Ireland for ten, fifteen or twenty families, as the case may be. I usually send to Connaught ... The whole family comes, father, mother, and children. I provide them with no money. I suppose they sell up what they have, walk to Dublin, pay their own passage to Liverpool and come to Manchester by the railway or walk it ... I should think that more than 400 have come over to me after they had learnt their trade.[29]

Emigration increases

While thousands of people (mainly males) left Mayo each year to work as migrant labourers in Britain in the middle of the nineteenth century there was a parallel and more permanent movement to Britain and abroad, principally to the United States. There had been increased emigration leading up to the Famine but the Famine exodus dwarfed anything that had gone before, with about 2.1 million people leaving the country in the period 1845–55 alone.[30]

Furthermore, in the years 1856–1921, Ireland lost between 4.0 and 4.5 million people – the numbers going each year varying according to 'push-pull' factors. For example, in 1863–64 a new food crisis occurred in Ireland, which coincided with a demand in the United States for soldiers to fight in the Civil War there (1861–65). These circumstances led to a dramatic increase in emigration from Ireland to the United States during that period.[31] Even in a backward county like Mayo, which, like other western counties, had a low rate of emigration in the decades after the Famine, the number leaving the county jumped from just over a thousand in 1862 to almost 4,000 in 1863.[32]

Not everybody who wanted to emigrate could afford to do so and the *Limerick Chronicle*, cited in the *Ballina Chronicle,* adverted to this in 1851: 'we express our sad conviction that nine-tenths of the emigrants are composed of industrious, robust, and healthy farmers, with their families ... The sailings to this day from Limerick were 22 vessels for New York and Quebec, with 3,412 cabin and steerage passengers, since 1st of January.'[33] The *Chronicle* also noted emigration from nearer home, albeit on a smaller scale:

> The tide of emigration increases here with almost alarming rapidity. Two

vessels, the *Wanderer* and the *Transit,* are now about to leave for Quebec, with an average of one hundred passengers each ... but one feeling seems to pervade the minds of the people generally, and that is to get out of the country as soon as possible.[34]

Notwithstanding the poverty and lack of resources which kept many west of Ireland people from emigrating, remittances from abroad totalling about one million pounds a year between 1848 and 1900 provided a lifeline, through prepaid passages, for some of Mayo's poorest people.[35] Indeed, a local paper at the time pointed out the importance of remittances in ensuring a passage overseas from Galway port: 'Every week is adding to the numbers who are flocking away to America and Australia from this part of Ireland. The influx of money from Australia and America is enormous – every post bringing orders for large sums to the peasantry.'[36]

'Missing Friends'

As might be expected with large numbers of poorly educated and often penniless emigrants landing in American ports after the Famine, many lost their way, failed to make contact with friends or relatives and disappeared in this strange and immense new country. Advertisements were often placed in an American newspaper called the *Boston Pilot*, which ran a dedicated column called 'Missing Friends', between 1831 and 1916.[37] This column sought information regarding the whereabouts of the missing people and provided a means of reconnecting friends and family.[38]

It is both instructive and enlightening to see the human stories behind the often prosaic ads. This small selection pertains to people from the east Mayo area:

> Of PATRICK LAVIN, from parish Killinkillduff [Kilconduff], townland Castlebarnaugh co. Mayo. When last heard of was at work on the Baltimore & Ohio Railroad, and supposed to go to the State of New York since. Any information respecting him will be thankfully received by his sister, MARY, or her husband, GEORGE LAMB, Hazleton, Luzerne Co'y, Pa.[39] [13 November 1852]
>
> OF JOHN DOHERTY, from townland Lurga co. Mayo; he left Cincinnati in February last, and went to work on a Railroad near Cairo. Any information will be thankfully received by his brothers, THOMAS & MICHAEL DOHERTY, Gardner, Ms. [3 September 1853][40]
>
> OF THOMAS & MICHAEL DOHERTY, townland Livega [Lurga?], parish Killebogh co. Mayo; when last heard from were in Gardiner,

Me. Any information will be thankfully received by their brother, JOHN DOHERTY, care of PATK. MORAN, 170 Front st., Cincinnati, Ohio. [13 October 1853][41]

OF MICHAEL & JOHN DOHERTY, of Lurga, parish Kilbegha, co'y Mayo. Their sister Ellen, of South Gardner, Mass, would be glad to hear from them. [26 April 1856][42]

OF WM MCDONOUGH, of Tulleynacua [Tullinahoo?], near Swinesford, co Mayo, who left home for N York in Sept '51. Information of him will be received by Bridget Durkin, Utica, New York. [8 July 1854][43]

OF PATK LAVIN, Townland of Castle Barnaugh, parish of Swinesford, co Mayo. When last heard of was in the State of Maryland. Information will be received by his sister Mary, Hazleton, Luzerne co, Pa, or to Thomas Cassidy. [18 November 1854][44]

OF MARTIN DOUGHERTY, of Swinesford, co Mayo, who left Bradford, Vt, 5 yrs ago; supposed to be in Wiscofsin [sic]. Information received by his sister-in-law, Cath O'Brien, 18 Belmont st, Charlestown, Ms. [29 July 1854][45]

JOHN CAIN, formerly of Meelick, near Swineford, co Mayo, Ireland, and latterly of No 77 North Water street, Chicago, Ill, is hereby notified that his wife Sabina Cain and child John, have arrived in Boston per ship Jeremiah Thompson, and are on expense here, and if money is not sent to defray her expenses here, and fare to him, she intends returning to Liverpool in the Jeremiah Thompson on the 20th of May, in which ship we have offered her and her child a free passage. ENOCH TRAIN & CO., 415 Commercial street, (Head of Constitution Wharf,) BOSTON. [3 May 1856][46]

OF MARTIN NEELING, alias Jordan, of Swineford, co Mayo, by his wife Bridget Burke, to whom he was married at Pottsville by Rev Mr Fitzsimmons about 6 yrs ago, and whom he abandoned about April 20th, 1854, at Cincinnati, Ohio; was then peddling dry goods; left one child named Mary, aged 4 yrs, with her mother at Chester, Pa. Please address Bridget Burke, care of the Rev. A Haviland, Chester, Pa. [18 August 1855][47]

OF MARTIN NEELING, alirs [sic] Jordan, of Swineford, co Mayo, who was married to Bridget Burke (still alive) at Pottsville, Pa, in '49. He is a peddler of dry goods. Information to his advantage may be obtained by sending his address (postpaid) to Rev A Haviland, Chester, Del. co, Pa. [29 September 1855] [48]

Emigration from Mayo, post-Famine

While emigration was a persistent drain on the population it wasn't uniform throughout the country after the Famine and didn't take hold in Connaught as strongly as elsewhere until the last two decades of the century. If, for example, the outward movement of people from Mayo is analysed it is seen that between 1861 and 1881, 52,000 people emigrated from the county. However, in the succeeding twenty years over 83,000 people left, an increase of sixty per cent. The number of emigrants leaving annually was not a static figure and varied from year to year depending on conditions in Ireland and the receiving country. In County Mayo the number leaving yearly fell to below 1,000 persons on only two occasions between 1851 and 1911 (1876 and 1877) and peaked at over 7,000 on two occasions – in 1852 and 1883.[49]

Fig. 2.3: Emigration from Mayo, 1861–1901.

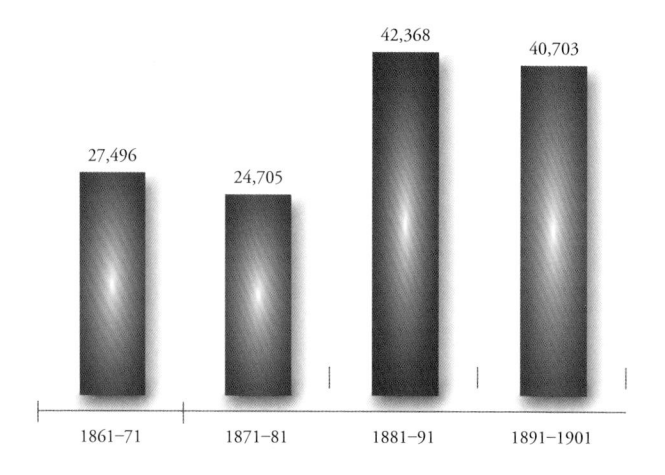

1861–71	1871–81	1881–91	1891–1901
27,496	24,705	42,368	40,703

Source: PP [Cd. 6052] Census of Ireland, 1911, County of Mayo (London, 1912), p. 173.

The county of Mayo can be divided into a more prosperous central corridor of better land, stretching from Ballina through to Ballinrobe, and two peripheral regions, west and east Mayo. The better-off central corridor followed the modernisation trend of the richer parts of the country, embracing consolidation of holdings, primogeniture, increased emigration, decreased migration, later marriages, increased celibacy and reduced population growth. It is from this more affluent area that many of the emigrants left in the immediate post-Famine period. In contrast to this, pre-Famine customs and traditions were dominant in the peripheral regions up to the 1880s.

It has already been noted that early marriage was a feature of life in the west of Ireland before the Famine and was especially so in the poorer areas of County Mayo. After the Famine the trend toward later marriage continued in most of the country but failed to take hold in much of Connaught until the 1880s. For example, the percentage of single people in Connaught at age 45–54 was as low as eight per cent for both women and men in 1851 and was still down around ten per cent in 1881. In Ireland as a whole the rate was about twelve per cent in 1851 and seventeen per cent in 1881. However, by 1911 the rate for women in both Connaught and Ireland had evened out at twenty-five per cent for both regions.[50]

Migration post-Famine

One of the strong traditions in the east and west of the county was the migration of thousands of harvestmen each year to Britain and while there are no official figures for the numbers travelling from Ireland to Britain for seasonal work between the years 1841 and 1880, Cormac Ó Gráda suggests that the numbers probably peaked in the 1860s at about 100,000 for the whole country.[51]

Nevertheless, various accounts do give some indication of the numbers travelling in the post-Famine decades. A report from a Poor Law Inspector in 1870 noted that 'the labourers and smallholders of land resort in great numbers to England, principally for harvest-work; the great bulk go in June and July and return in September'.[52] He went on to indicate that in his district alone – the counties of Roscommon, Leitrim and Galway – almost 13,000 rail tickets were issued to harvestmen in 1869. Not all intended to return: 'Some go with the expectation of procuring permanent employment, and if successful remain there. Those who go to England for manufacturing employment, generally purpose domiciling there.'[53]

John Denvir, writing in 1892, describes the spectacle presented by the mass of harvestmen as they tramped the long journey to the eastern ports on their annual trip to Britain: 'It was a sight to remember – the vast armies of harvestmen, clad in frieze coats and knee breeches, with their clean white shirts with high collars and tough blackthorns, who might be seen, some forty or fifty years ago, marching, literally in their thousands … to reap John Bull's harvest.'[54] Denvir went on to say, quoting the *Stamford Mercury*: 'That in just three or four days in August 1850 more than 12,000 harvestmen passed through Liverpool from Ireland on their way to the fens of Lincolnshire.'[55]

The *Irish Times* comments on the much improved appearance of Irish harvestmen in the 1860s: 'Lincoln was thronged on Sunday last with Irish harvesters, the major part of them being fine stout young fellows, well clothed and well fed. Indeed, the old shaggy type of Irishmen with sparrow-tailed coat and ragged breeches, seem almost to have disappeared.'[56]

Improved transport systems

The opening of rail lines to Sligo, Claremorris, Castlebar and Westport in the 1860s provided a quicker passage to Britain for those harvestmen who could afford the fare. To encourage them to avail of the train service to the ports, a special fourth-class 'harvestman' ticket was introduced and this proved very popular, as Peter Roe, former manager of the Midland Great Western Railway (MGWR) acknowledged in 1866:

> I have always been in favour of cheap fares … The first year [1849] I succeeded in getting 4,000 of them [harvestmen] to travel; the next year I got 10,000 to travel, and when I left the Midland I think the number had increased to 25,000; and now I see by the chairman's statement they carry 78,000.[57]

The movement of huge numbers of seasonal workers at particular times of the year presented problems for the railway companies and other transport agencies. In July 1877 Captain Keebles of the Sligo Steamship Company was fined £10 for over-carrying passengers – mainly harvestmen – on his steamer going to Liverpool from Sligo. The defence argued that he was unable or afraid to prevent the harvestmen boarding, as they were armed with scythes and it would be dangerous to try to do so.[58]

Considering the numbers of harvestmen travelling from the west of Ireland to Britain each year, it is not surprising that some fatal accidents involving trains occurred. One such incident happened in Ballyhaunis in 1878 when the Cannon brothers lost their lives in a tragic mishap while on their way to the harvest in England. The cause of the accident was the unusual number of men entering the carriages after the train had started, causing the brothers to fall under the train, leading to almost instant death.[59]

On the whole, the priority of harvestmen was to go to Britain, earn as much money as possible and send or take it back to their families in Ireland. They were generally well behaved, but violence could break out occasionally, especially among fellow workers, sometimes with fatal consequences. The *Freeman's Journal* of 1865 reports the death of Hugh McDonagh: aged twenty-six and from Mayo, he was killed by a blow of a sickle to the head by his sisters-in-law and others. The names of the defendants in the case were given as Martin and Bartholomew Hunt. It was accepted that drink was a major factor in the row, which took place in a pub at Constitution Hill, Dublin.[60]

CHAPTER 3

The Mini-famine of 1879–80

'I cannot recollect seeing a smile on a child's face throughout my three weeks' tour in the county.'

Mechanisation and its consequences

The early years of the 1870s saw relative prosperity in Ireland; good crops allied to seasonal work in Britain allowed for a modicum of comfort, even among subsistence farmers. However, disaster, never far above the horizon in the 1800s, attacked subsistence smallholders on several fronts in the late 1870s. Over the previous twenty years or so, the mechanisation of crops had progressed considerably in Britain after the Great Exhibition of 1851. However, machinery was expensive, prone to breakdown and could not be used on lodged crops and these factors helped keep the Irish harvestmen in work through the 1860s and 1870s. Nevertheless, as early as 1859 the *Irish Times* was recommending that with 'mowing and reaping machines, horse rakes, hay-making machines, and the like – let them all be brought into general use – farmers may discard the services of Irish reapers … on whose aid they have hitherto been too dependent.'[1]

The encroachment of machinery into the work (and lives) of the harvestmen was becoming more evident as the nineteenth century progressed. *The Times* reported that unemployed harvestmen were plentiful up around Malton in Yorkshire in 1867 and while some work was available because of lodged crops, in most instances the work was done by machinery, leaving many mowers out of work.[2] The advent of the new reaping machines heralded a slow decline in harvest work for Irish migratory labour – *The Times* in 1862 lauded this wonderful new invention, which was 'able to reap no less than between 20 and 30 acres in a day, performing the work of 20 or 30 harvestmen'.[3] However, there was still reluctance on the part of some farmers to invest in the new machinery, one man saying that as long as he could get Irishmen at one-and-sixpence a day, he would never get another machine after disappointing results with his first purchase.[4]

A looming crisis

A confluence of events led to the food crisis and distress of the period 1879–80 in Ireland. The potato yield fell from 5.1 tons per acre in 1876 to 1.8 tons per acre in 1877, to 1.4 tons per acre in 1879 because of a succession of cold and wet summers. The dearth of potatoes in 1879 reduced pig and poultry numbers, causing severe financial losses in the west of Ireland. The oat crop was also down, but to a much lesser extent.

The reduced demand for migrant labour in Britain was especially damaging to smallholders in the west and Mayo in particular, where harvest earnings formed an important component of annual income. This diminished demand for farm workers in Britain was caused by not only the increased use of farm machinery but also by the introduction of cheap American grain to the country, which led to a reduction in the area under tillage. Mayo was a prolific supplier of harvestmen to Britain during this period, with Swinford Poor Law Union (PLU) sending almost half of Mayo's total, so that the loss of migrants' earnings was felt more acutely here than elsewhere.

As conditions worsened at home in 1879, impoverished smallholders placed their hopes on potential earnings in the English harvest fields. The *Irish Times* reported that: 'The North Wall … was literally packed with great crowds of Connaught labourers seeking passage to England for agricultural work generally and the coming harvest particularly … Close on 4,000 of these Western harvesters went across Channel last night …'.[5]

Overall, though, the number of harvestmen carried by the Midland Great Western Railway fell quite dramatically in 1879. The Chairman reported that after years of progress and prosperity for the railway, the number of market and harvestmen tickets sold in 1879 fell by almost 50,000, caused, he surmised, by the great depression which overlay the country.[6] Migrants' earnings were slashed to such an extent that some had to borrow money to pay their fares home.

As a consequence of the reduced income from England it is estimated that harvestmen's earnings in 1879 fell by £250,000 nationally, with County Mayo being particularly hard hit, falling short in its normal harvestman remittances by £100,000.[7] In east Mayo, for example, the reduction in migrants' earnings was particularly severe: the postal money-orders received at Ballyhaunis post office in 1879 were down by two-thirds on those received the previous year.[8]

The crisis deepens

Eggs played an important role in the economy of smallholders in Mayo and the effect of the reduced potato crop on egg production in 1879 was exacerbated by a poultry cholera epidemic in the county in 1880, which reduced the numbers of poultry by almost one-fifth, as against the three-per-cent nationwide average.[9] The loss of poultry was even more severe in east Mayo, where upwards of two-fifths of birds succumbed to the disease, increasing the impoverishment of the local peasantry.[10]

To add to the woes of the population, credit from shopkeepers was becoming increasingly difficult to procure because of huge deficits built up over the previous few years. It was estimated that by 1879 debts of over £200,000 had been incurred by smallholders in Mayo to local merchants and shopkeepers.[11]

A series of poor potato crops, culminating in the disastrous crop of 1879, meant that the supply of home-grown food was barely sufficient for two or three months' sustenance after the crop was harvested. These factors, allied to the increasing reluctance of shopkeepers to provide credit, left much of the population in the west battling to survive. The stories that follow illustrate the effects the crippling food crisis had on the east Mayo area in 1879–80.

Relief schemes

Even before the end of 1879, food shortages were becoming increasingly apparent in some east Mayo localities. The Duchess of Marlborough initiated a fundraising campaign, appealing in *The Times* on 18 December 1879 for donations to relieve distress in Ireland. In less than a year over £135,000 was collected and dispensed by the relief committee, curtailing some of the worst effects of this minor famine.

A second major fundraising body, the Mansion House Relief Committee, was put in place in January 1880 by the lord mayor of Dublin; within a year this committee had raised and spent over £181,000 in the relief of distress.

A member of the committee (J.A. Fox) and a specially formed Medical Commission were authorised by the Mansion House Committee (MHC) to investigate, 'upon the spot', the prevalence of disease and the condition of the people in certain districts of Mayo and Galway in 1880. The gravity of the situation was exemplified by conditions in Swineford PLU, where the potato crop barely lasted two months in some localities. Because of the shortage of potatoes, widespread starvation was reported in both Charlestown and Kilmovee. As early as January 1880 over 142,000 people in Mayo were in need of relief; this had risen to over 171,000 by June 1880.[12]

Both J.A. Fox and the Medical Commission documented individual cases of hardship encountered by them in their journey through east Mayo:

> I have taken the precaution to see with my own eyes many of the recipients of relief in their miserable hovels ... I do not believe that tongue or

Fig. 3.1: Foxford. (Source: Photographic Archives; courtesy Tom Kennedy)

pen, however eloquent, could truly depict the awful destitution of some of these hovels. I asked a gaunt, starved looking man, whom I found literally endeavouring to sleep away the hunger, where his little children slept, when he pointed to a corner in the moist room, in which I could see no sign of bedding.

When asked how the children kept warm at night, the father replied 'There is a deal of warmth in children', signifying that they obtained warmth by huddling together like little animals. This occurred at Carrycastle, where Fox was accompanied by the local priest.[13]

Fox felt that while there had been destitution and privation in the neighbourhood of Ballyhaunis, Knock and Claremorris, as elsewhere, the squalor and misery were not as widespread as in the Swinford district. He tellingly remarks: 'I cannot recollect seeing a smile on a child's face throughout my three weeks' tour in the county.' Fox also visited Foxford where he found

> more than thirty hovels of the poor, principally in the townlands of Culmore and Cashel, in which I beheld scenes of wretchedness and misery wholly indescribable … In one hovel in the townland of Cashel, we found

a little child, three years old, one of a family of six apparently very ill, with no person more competent to watch it than an idiot sister of eighteen: while the mother was absent begging committee relief, the father being in England.[14]

Fox draws our attention to the honesty of the people in the face of the most severe privation:

> Notwithstanding this desperate condition of things, the police informed me that there was no crime, small or great, in the district referred to, and a retired sub-inspector of the force pointed out a large house in Bellaghy, filled from floor to ceiling with the pawned goods of the poor, which, he added, was not even protected by the presence of anyone on the premises at night.[15]

The medical commissioners also furnished reports of their findings to the MHC. 'In addition to the distressed population's privations' they intimated, there were now added 'fever epidemics of alarming extent and intensity'. It is salutary to read the account of the medical commissioners in regard to individual cases of destitution and disease in the parish of Kilbeagh:

> The house of McD——, for instance, at Kilgariff, dark as a cavern and foul as a byre, with a manure pit half full of stagnant water at the door, was devoid of all fever, though it was the worst habitation we saw in this district.[16]

> Other cases have their own peculiarly painful features. In one, that of O'H——, at Carne, the young husband is a victim; in another, that of ——, the wife lies sick, with scarce a rag of bed-clothes. At Ballintadder, in a musty, dark room, two children were tossing in fever on some straw on the floor, and another ailing on the poor bed … In the midst of their affliction the father gives a refuge to an infirm and aged sister. It may be mentioned, as adding to the sombre character of the scene, that these people are under notice of ejectment.[17]

Another case dealt with by the team of Dr Sigerson and Dr Kenny was that of D —— from Upper Lurga who lived in a lonely cabin on a bleak moor:

> There was no window – nothing but a shutter. When this was thrown

back we found the earthen floor covered with the victims of the destitution fever. At the entrance, their feet near the doorway, lay side by side two grown young women, aged respectively 21 and 19; beyond, with her head almost touching theirs, was a younger girl, aged 14, recovering but unable to move. On the left hand side, on the floor, lay the mother of the family in her day-clothes … The only person to nurse or attend on all was the worn and wretched parent, aged 50, trembling with weakness from want and watching as he stood, and expecting every hour to be stricken down, when all would be left to die 'within the walls'.[18]

Local relief committees

Local relief committees kept the MHC informed as to the depth of distress in their particular areas and kept pressure on those dispensing relief to the poor and destitute to continue the release of funds for the benefit of their own area. Canon Peter O'Donoghue of Curry parish, County Sligo, wrote to the lord mayor of Dublin on 28 January 1880 seeking funds:

> Mine is a rural parish. It has a population of ten hundred and twenty families – in all over 5,000 souls – of the ten hundred, three hundred and fifty families are at this moment, to my personal and certain knowledge, without a cow, without a stack of corn, and without a bad potato!![19]

The local relief committee in Carracastle – a small parish adjoining Curry, estimated that upwards of 4,000 people in the parish were in need of relief and that this number was likely to increase. The committee stated the following in a letter dated 2 February 1880:

> We beg to submit that we have for the week ended the 31st January distributed relief to 581 families, who are in a very poor state and a great number were obliged to go away, from the Committee Rooms hungry and exhausted, after remaining the whole day waiting for relief which unfortunately we could not give, owing to the insufficiency of funds at our disposal.

The letter was signed by P. Durcan P.P. and Thomas Davey, secretary.[20]

The members of the Charlestown Relief Committee were prolific letter writers on behalf of parishioners, keeping the MHC informed of the desperate conditions pertaining in the area and requesting funds to alleviate the hunger and hardship. On 22 January 1880 the relief committee informed the MHC that 5,000 people were in need of relief and that this number was likely to increase. A letter the following week pointed out that 'the poor people failed to earn anything in England last season'.

A day later the committee wrote again to the MHC, through its secretaries John and Michael J. Doherty, outlining the circumstances of one family in need:

> As a specimen of what we have to deal with we beg to give you the case of T. Carrol of Carn who is certainly not worse off than hundreds of our fellow parishioners: He has nine in family the eldest only 12 years. No cattle, no provisions, two beds in house; pawned one of the blankets for 3/-, and a quilt for 6/. His own suit pledged for 12/-, which cost £2 two years ago, since a week before Patrick's Day & has not attended Mass since that time. Have seen the pawn-office tickets for the above, & can afford to give him only 2 stones of meal per week. He is trying to support all for the last week by digging out potatoes where four lines of each ridge will give only three safe potatoes. We give his case here as he happened to come in while writing. We beg and trust your committee will deal generously with us, and enable us to meet the pressure of wants of our people. As an instance we can only give Carrol above mentioned two stones of Ind. Meal weekly for himself & family.[21]

Just one week later the relief committee warned that 'unless funds are forthcoming more generously from some source the committee must leave the people to their fate, and the result will be a repetition of 1847'.

Towards the end of February, the committee confirmed that 655 families (3,750 people) had been relieved in the parish of Kilbeagh. Funds of £50 from the Mansion House Fund and £25 from the Irish National Land League were acknowledged. The quantity of food supplied to the poor was 1 pound of Indian meal per head, per day: 'Should the funds run out any coming week it is a certainty that deaths from starvation will occur.'[22] In April of that year the committee recorded the worsening situation. 'It was heart-rending to hear the cries of the 263 families who were refused relief on Saturday as the majority had not the means to provide one meal and knew not how to procure it.'[23] Despite what would seem to have been outstanding efforts by the Charlestown Relief Committee on behalf of the starving people of the locality, not everybody was enthused by their endeavours. James Leo Leonard in a letter to the MHC (14 June 1880) stated that the following people from Corthoon (among other townlands) were not satisfied with the working of the Charlestown Relief Committee: Edward Morley, Patt Nedd Durkan, Widow Brett, Thomas Morley, Patt Thomas Morley, Patrick Duffy, John Foley, Andy Foley and Edward Brett.[24]

Fig. 3.2: Bellaghy, Charlestown, early twentieth century. (Source: 'Mulligans', Charlestown; postcard printed in Saxony, Germany)

The *Irish Times* quotes A.S. Deane's report on Sligo and Mayo to the Mansion House Relief Committee in March 1880:

> Swinford, in the County Mayo, was the poorest union he had visited. With a population of 53,000 and a vast extent of bad land, the people suffered very much during the past winter, and but for the relief distributed they would have been reduced to a state of starvation. The children were much in need of clothes.[25]

This paper's correspondent noted in July 1880 that between Charlestown and Swinford,

> many holdings where the crops are flourishing are filled with weeds … Doubtless this seeming want of industry is in a great measure due to the absence in England of many of the male inhabitants, but in many cases it clearly and solely arises from sheer laziness and ignorance of the proper principles of tillage.

However, the correspondent admits that

> the distress in this district and the surrounding neighbourhood has been

much worse than in other places, and were the assistance now being afforded discontinued, the greatest suffering would undoubtedly result … I visited several of the poorer houses and found there inhabitants living in a wretched condition. The beds consist of heaps of old straw or rushes thrown in a corner, while the only covering is dirty-looking rags.[26]

There was an increasing prevalence of disease during 1880 as a consequence of the lack of food and the unhygienic conditions in which most people lived. A correspondent for the *Freeman's Journal and Daily Commercial Advertiser* reported that

In this neighbourhood [Tubbercurry], in the county of Mayo, and in Swineford Union fever is raging. I heard that twenty persons were removed to Swineford Workhouse from Charleston [*sic*] suffering from what is called famine fever. It is also raging in Bellaghy … The districts of Culmore and Swinford have also been visited by the same form of fever, and the schools there have had to be closed. Fr Loftus, the parish priest of Charlestown, was about to close the schools there, but he did not, for fear of losing the bread which the *New York Herald* Fund distributes to them.[27] [A prerequisite for obtaining bread from the fund was attendance at school.]

The Dillon estate

Finlay Dun was asked in the winter of 1880 by *The Times* to inquire into land tenure and estate management in Ireland and the conditions of tenants and labourers there. His subsequent letters to that paper make interesting reading.

Dun writes of the Dillon estate in east Mayo and elicits some important facts about the estate's 4,000 tenants: 'about 3,000 or three-fourths of the total, pay an annual rent of 6*l*. and under'. He informs us that

Three-fourths of the householders annually migrate to England. Before they go they generally sow the oats, plant the potatoes, and cut the turf, leaving the women and children to hoe and work the crops, manage the cow, calf and pigs, and dry and bring home the turf. Most of the men are gone by the end of April, return towards the close of October, and bring with them from 9*l*. to 12*l*. Once a month, or oftener, many of the men now take advantage of the Post Office facilities and remit money to their families. Through the office at Swineford I am told that in one week last autumn the amounts thus forwarded reached 500*l*.[28]

CHAPTER 4

Emigration from the West, Post-1880

'… he never sent an empty letter home …'

Emigration increases dramatically

Between 1851 and 1876, over 71,000 emigrants left Mayo (twenty-eight per cent of the county's population in 1861). Nationwide, over forty-one per cent of the population emigrated in the same period. Some counties, like Cork, had an emigration rate one-third above the national average in that twenty-five-year period unlike, for example, Mayo, which had a relatively low rate of emigration up to the 1880s.[1] The emigration rate from the west of Ireland was to change dramatically after the food crisis of 1879–80. Over the next few decades the rate increased dramatically, from one of the lowest in Ireland to one of the highest. While the numbers emigrating nationally doubled between 1879 and 1880, in County Mayo the numbers more than trebled, the overwhelming majority going to the United States.[2] This upward trend in emigration from County Mayo continued up to the end of the century and between 1881 and 1901 the numbers leaving increased by almost two-thirds.[3]

For emigrants travelling abroad, transport was becoming faster and safer, as steamships took over from sailing ships and strong competition kept fares within the compass of prospective passengers. The transition from sail to steam occurred in the 1860s, and by 1865 the Liverpool, New York and Philadelphia Steamship Company was offering, through its agent P.J. Mellet of Swinford, sailings from Queenstown (Cobh) to New York on every Tuesday and alternate Mondays and Saturdays.[4] So fierce was the competition between steamship companies in the 1880s that some took out advertisements in local papers threatening 'brokers, agents, lodging-house keepers and runners' with disqualification from acting on their behalf, if they booked passengers through 'the Warren and other Inferior English Lines'.[5]

This competition between lines kept the fares low and in 1889 the Allan Line was still able to offer steerage passage to Boston for £3 16s and to Philadelphia for £4.[6]

Remittances

Remittances were a feature of emigrant life from before the Famine and for the very poor, money sent from America, often in the form of prepaid passages, offered an escape route that otherwise would not have been available. These remittances were often used to tide families over times of crisis but were also used for more prosaic purposes, such as paying off debts, replacing an animal that had died, buying farm implements, or paying rent.

The tradition of seasonal workers sending money home to their families in Ireland was also well established. A witness to a Select Committee in 1828 acknowledged collecting and sending money back to Ireland on behalf of tenants of the Dillon estate in east Mayo: 'we have connections with Lord Dillon's agent … who receives the rent when he gets this order; it is in fact a payment of rent earned in London, to be transmitted to Ireland by that means; I find we now receive upon an average about £1,100 a year.' Money was also transmitted for the migrant tenants 'through the post office orders; I believe a great deal is sent in that way; but they come to me in preference to going to the post office … the postage is rather expensive; the postage of a letter to Mayo is 17d or 18d.'[7]

John Armstrong a landed proprietor of Tubbercurry, County Sligo had an estate contiguous with the Dillon estate in east Mayo and in his

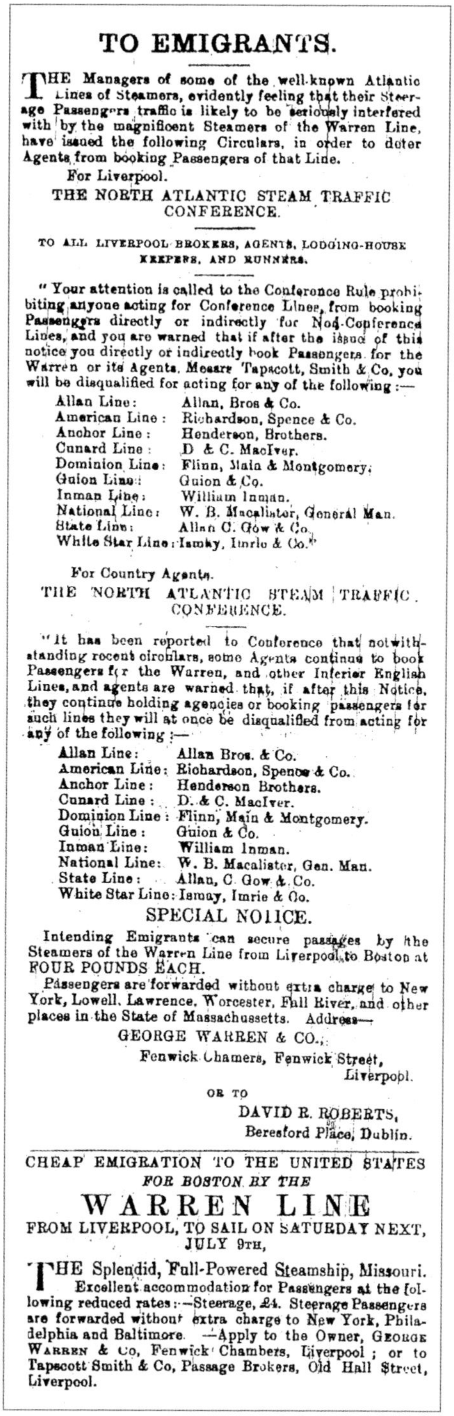

TO EMIGRANTS.

THE Managers of some of the well-known Atlantic Lines of Steamers, evidently feeling that their Steerage Passengers traffic is likely to be seriously interfered with by the magnificent Steamers of the Warren Line, have issued the following Circulars, in order to deter Agents from booking Passengers of that Line.

For Liverpool.

THE NORTH ATLANTIC STEAM TRAFFIC CONFERENCE.

TO ALL LIVERPOOL BROKERS, AGENTS, LODGING-HOUSE KEEPERS, AND RUNNERS.

"Your attention is called to the Conference Rule prohibiting anyone acting for Conference Lines, from booking Passengers directly or indirectly for Non-Conference Lines, and you are warned that if after the issue of this notice you directly or indirectly book Passengers for the Warren or its Agents, Messrs Tapscott, Smith & Co. you will be disqualified for acting for any of the following :—

Allan Line:	Allan, Bros & Co.
American Line:	Richardson, Spence & Co.
Anchor Line:	Henderson, Brothers.
Cunard Line:	D & C. MacIver.
Dominion Line:	Flinn, Main & Montgomery.
Guion Line:	Guion & Co.
Inman Line:	William Inman.
National Line:	W. B. Macalister, General Man.
State Line:	Allan C. Gow & Co.
White Star Line:	Ismay, Imrie & Co."

For Country Agents.

THE NORTH ATLANTIC STEAM TRAFFIC CONFERENCE.

"It has been reported to Conference that notwithstanding recent circulars, some Agents continue to book Passengers for the Warren, and other Inferior English Lines, and agents are warned that, if after this Notice, they continue holding agencies or booking passengers for such lines they will at once be disqualified from acting for any of the following :—

Allan Line:	Allan Bros. & Co.
American Line:	Richardson, Spence & Co.
Anchor Line:	Henderson Brothers.
Cunard Line:	D. & C. MacIver.
Dominion Line:	Flinn, Main & Montgomery.
Guion Line:	Guion & Co.
Inman Line:	William Inman.
National Line:	W. B. Macalister, Gen. Man.
State Line:	Allan, C. Gow & Co.
White Star Line:	Ismay, Imrie & Co.

SPECIAL NOTICE.

Intending Emigrants can secure passages by the Steamers of the Warren Line from Liverpool to Boston at FOUR POUNDS EACH.

Passengers are forwarded without extra charge to New York, Lowell, Lawrence, Worcester, Fall River, and other places in the State of Massachussetts. Address—

GEORGE WARREN & CO.,
Fenwick Chamers, Fenwick Street,
Liverpool.

OR TO

DAVID R. ROBERTS,
Beresford Place, Dublin.

CHEAP EMIGRATION TO THE UNITED STATES
FOR BOSTON BY THE
WARREN LINE
FROM LIVERPOOL, TO SAIL ON SATURDAY NEXT, JULY 9TH,

THE Splendid, Full-Powered Steamship, Missouri. Excellent accommodation for Passengers at the following reduced rates:—Steerage, £4. Steerage Passengers are forwarded without extra charge to New York, Philadelphia and Baltimore. —Apply to the Owner, GEORGE WARREN & Co, Fenwick Chambers, Liverpool; or to Tapscott Smith & Co, Passage Brokers, Old Hall Street, Liverpool.

Fig. 4.1: Emigration advertisement, 1881.
(Source: *Connaught Telegraph*, 2 July 1881)

evidence to the Devon Commission he intimated that his tenants earned about £3 to £5 working at the harvest in England:

> We have no persons going to Scotland … the emigration to Scotland of labourers is confined to the county of Mayo. With us they invariably go to the fen countries in England. Last year I asked a great many, and they told me the average was about £3. Some may bring home a good deal more; but those persons attend both the hay harvest and corn harvest … Some few who go and remain for years in England, come back with a great deal of money.[8]

During the Famine period both emigrants abroad and migrants to Britain made significant contributions to the alleviation of distress in Ireland. James Hack Tuke, the Quaker philanthropist, recorded the efforts of migrant labourers to help their distressed families back in Ireland:

> Through the liberality of the post-master I have been able to ascertain correctly the sums transmitted to Ireland by these poor Irish labourers, who are chiefly from Connaught, during the ten months of the present year (1847). These sums varying from 2s 6d to £5, amount in the whole to no less a sum than one thousand and forty-two pounds, ten shillings and two pence, and have been obtained in eight hundred and sixty-six orders.[9]

Tuke estimated that £20,000 was transmitted to County Mayo alone, from England, by those who fled the Famine.[10] He also wrote of the generosity of Irish emigrants during that period:

> During the pressure of the year 1846 the remittances amounted to no less a sum than one million of dollars, or £200,000; and I understand that during the first half of the present year [1847] the remittances have been on a vastly increased scale, amounting to one million six hundred thousand dollars.[11]

There would seem to have been a two-pronged approach to the alleviation of poverty in the west of Ireland: remittances from relatives abroad and the more consistent flow of harvest money from migratory agricultural labourers. John Forbes, in 1852, described the effect remittances had on some inmates of Westport Union Workhouse: 'No fewer than 300 children have gone out of the house, in consequence of money received from their fathers in England and Scotland; and 21 have gone to America, through funds sent home to them by their relations.'[12]

It is important to acknowledge that the custom of sending money to less well-off relations was common among European emigrants. In Norway the 'American money' started to come as early as the 1850s and by the early 1900s it had reached a figure of $5 million annually.[13] Remittances were an important feature of emigrant life in southern European countries also. In Italy alone it is estimated that between 1897 and 1902, returning emigrants brought home with them almost $100 million dollars, much of which went to benefit the local economy.[14]

Philanthropists

After the subsistence crisis of 1879–80 in Ireland, conditions began to improve again and an inspector's report of 1883 regarding Mayo and Galway gave room for optimism:

> The earnings in England were better last autumn, than they were in the autumn of 1879 … the remittances from America are now far beyond what they were then, or what, it is believed, they ever were before. The actual extent of these it would be difficult, of course, to ascertain, but that the money is coming in largely from America to these poor districts is a notorious and incontestable fact, and one which is easily accounted for by the large number of emigrants who left Ireland during the past two years.[15]

The large number of emigrants alluded to were fleeing the country after the distress of 1879–80, and these numbers were further amplified by the assisted emigrant schemes initiated by the philanthropists Vere Foster and James Tuke. Foster expended about £30,000 of his own money to assist over 20,000 unmarried girls from the west of Ireland to go to the United States in the period 1880–84.[16] He noted in 1882 that: 'The girls I have assisted have very frequently brought out their whole families after them.'[17]

Rev. Denis O'Hara, administrator in Ballaghaderreen, County Roscommon, writing about Vere Foster emigrants, reported that in

> almost every case I was told they [the parents] had received a good letter on such a day, meaning that the good affectionate daughter sent them some money to keep them at home from starving. Many a family in this parish would be in some distress this year but for the faithful daughter on the other side of the Atlantic.[18] The local euphemism for a letter with

money inside was alive and well over seventy years later. Sean McNicholas from Ballyvary, County Mayo left home at seventeen years of age for a job in Longford in the 1950s. Sean's main means of communication with his family was through the post and even though his wages were small his elder brother, Willie, proudly affirms that 'he never sent an empty letter home'.[19]

James Hack Tuke, a Quaker from York, was also involved in assisting prospective emigrants from impoverished areas of Mayo and Galway to travel abroad during the years 1882–84. A total of 9,482 people got assistance from Tuke to emigrate, over half of whom came from the Poor Law Unions of Swinford, Belmullet and Newport.[20] Surprisingly, there was a poor uptake by candidates in the Swinford Union; out of a population of 53,000 only 572 persons applied to travel and, of those 312, were accepted. The reason for the poor uptake may have been the strong opposition of both the Church and local shopkeepers, who saw whole families being encouraged to emigrate, leaving unpaid debts behind them as they cut their ties with the country.[21] Tuke was later to report that the beneficiaries of his scheme had sent home almost £2,000 in 1885 and that those remittances had risen to £10,000 by 1890, six years after his scheme ended.[22]

As the number of Irish-born emigrants abroad increased and communications got better, there was an improved response from overseas to crises in Ireland. The *Western People* documents one such response to the subsistence crisis of 1890–91 at the Mayo Men's Association Ball in New York: 'The affair seems to have been particularly gay and brilliant ... the substantial sum of 400 dollars was realized to meet distress at home.'[23]

Returned Yanks

Regardless of crises (of which there were three in the 1890s alone), returnees, especially women, were a familiar feature of village life in the west of Ireland in the early twentieth century. Evidence to the Dudley Commission in 1907 showed that numerous female emigrants had returned from America to the Knock area of County Mayo, carrying with them 'fortunes' to make their quest for a suitable husband that much easier.[24]

Tom Holleran, of Dromada-Duke townland in Killasser parish in Mayo, describes the situation in his own village:

> In 1900 there were seven women who spent a term in America married in our village ... They had a few dollars saved and they preferred to make

a home in their native land than toiling in a foreign land … The other six women who were married in the village never left the ashes.[25]

Cartron (Corthoon) townland in Kilbeagh parish in Mayo, whose total land valuation in 1856 was less than £40, still sustained nineteen households up to the 1950s. Eight of those households contained returned Yanks, seven of whom were women. Schrier is probably right in asserting that among Irish returnees from America, women were in the majority, frequently coming home with a dowry and the intention of marrying locally.[26]

Returnees from the US to the west of Ireland had to make a difficult choice between an independent life in America, a steady wage, a higher standard of living and a larger marriage market, as against the familiarity of people and places, the strength of custom and tradition, the warmth of family and neighbours, but also the fairly certain knowledge that life would be arduous with drudgery and hard, physical labour a concomitant of settling down in a smallholding. Quite a number must have made the choice to return permanently. According to a Swinford resident in 1905:

> All the girls in this place are going out to America when they are about seventeen years old. Then they work there for six years or more, till they do grow weary of that fixed kind of life with the early rising and the working late, and then they do come home with a little stocking of fortune with them, and they do be tempting the boys with their chains and their rings, till they get a husband and settle down in this place. Such a lot them is coming now there is hardly a marriage made in the place that the woman hasn't been in America.[27]

Many returned emigrants were willing to pay excessive prices to get their hands on farms in their home areas, as Mark Henry of Charlestown noted: 'A great many emigrants had returned that year [1908] some to settle; returned emigrants usually bought a holding of perhaps five or ten acres at an exorbitant price, or else raised the status of a poor family by marrying into it.'[28]

Emigrants returning from the US provided stern competition for local smallholders when holdings came up for sale. But the dream of successfully transplanting back among friends and neighbours sometimes turned to dust, as the grinding poverty of early-1900s Ireland soaked up hard-earned dollars, as Bernard Fox relates:

> I have been reared here in the country, and I have seen these returned policemen and Americans paying excessive prices for lands … People with capital from other countries returning home, simply from their desire and

attachment to their old country, have paid undue prices for the farms … One holding … within a few miles of this town … passed in succession through five returned Americans, and each went to work at it, but after a few years found it a complete failure.[29]

'Never go back'

Regardless of the desire of some emigrants to return to Ireland and start a new life there, the harsh reality of conditions in the country in the early part of the twentieth century must have curbed their ambitions to a great extent; the records show that Ireland's emigrants had one of the lowest rates of return of any European country. Of those European emigrants who went to the United States it is estimated that about one-third returned to their home countries. This figure is higher for some countries, such as Italy, which had a return rate of almost fifty per cent between 1880 and 1920.[30] By contrast, Ireland had one of the lowest rates of return at about ten per cent though more recent scholarship has revised this figure upwards.

The Irish seemed to have an ambivalent attitude to returning. Memories of good times, friendships and the relaxed way of life competed with memories of poverty and hardship. A Mayo emigrant in America illustrates this nicely: 'I was dreaming of home last night and I woke up dreaming of it, about buying a place in the next parish over from us, the most beautiful parish you ever saw, Lacken … But I wouldn't go back there now. I wouldn't go back if you gave me the whole county of Mayo. We were just too poor.'[31]

For those who did not return permanently to Ireland, purchasing travel tickets to bring loved ones closer was the next best option. Out of a total of 22,966 steerage passengers sailing to America from Ireland in 1905, 8,884 had their passages prepaid in the United States and between 1904 and 1910, the number of prepaid steerage tickets from Ireland never fell below thirty-two per cent of the total.[32] Irish people were not unique in wanting to have their friends, relatives and neighbours living close to them when far away from home. The Dillingham Commission estimated that about one-third of all those entering the United States in the period 1908–14 travelled on prepaid tickets.[33]

'Sending home'

While money was being sent home from America by various methods to help pay rent, buy livestock, purchase clothing, redeem debts, and so on, a major contribution to those ends was also being made by the earnings of migratory agricultural labourers (harvestmen), especially in County Mayo and particularly in the east of the county. Efforts were made in the early years of the twentieth century by government officials to calculate the annual earnings of those workers and for 1906 alone, a figure of £275,000 was estimated to have entered the local economy from this source.[34] After the 1920s, remittances sent home to Ireland came mainly from Irish emigrants in Britain, where the vast majority of Irish citizens now went. This money added greatly to the Irish economy in the 1940s, '50s and '60s, and it is estimated that over £13 million from this source was sent back to relatives in Ireland in 1961 alone.[35]

Moving forward to the twenty-first century, it can be seen that remittances are still important in Ireland, but they are now moving *out* of the country for the first time in centuries. Foreign nationals working in Ireland repatriated some €737 million to their home countries in 2008, while a mere €8 million was returned as remittances by Irish people working abroad.[36]

CHAPTER 5

The Congested Districts Board

'I do not think there are more honest people in the world having regard to their resources.'

Anomalous population increases

In the more prosperous parts of Ireland modernisation of farming life was underway before the Famine and advanced at a faster pace afterwards. However, old customs and traditions held sway right up until the end of the nineteenth century in the poorer and more backward areas of the country. This was especially true in certain localities in County Mayo. While the population fell in most regions of the country between 1851 and 1881, it actually increased in some parts of Mayo. In the county as a whole the number of inhabitants reduced by a little over seven per cent in the decade 1851–61, as against a drop of almost twelve per cent across the country.[1] In the following decade (1861–71) Mayo's population fell only by a little over three per cent, in contrast to most other counties.[2]

In the decade 1871–81 the population of Mayo remained almost static, but in the succeeding decade it declined by almost eleven per cent, with a further reduction in population of over nine per cent between 1891–1901.[3]

A number of the areas in County Mayo showing an increased population after the Famine were in the east of the county. Among those areas was Swinford Poor Law Union (PLU), one of the poorest Unions in Ireland with a dense demographic of subsistence landholders, yet it showed a slight increase in population in the decade 1871–81.

Kilbeagh, a constituent parish of Swinford PLU, revealed an even more anomalous demographic after the Famine, increasing its inhabitants from 9,733 persons in 1851 to 11,148 persons in 1881 – an increase of over fourteen per cent.[4] The bar chart below illustrates the significant increase in population in the east Mayo parishes of Kilbeagh and Kilconduff between 1841 and 1881 in contrast to the substantial decline in the number of people in County Mayo and nationally during that period. Kilbeagh parish was not unique in its demographics. The following parishes in east Mayo also increased their populations between 1851 and 1881: Annagh, Attymass, Bohola, Kilconduff, Killasser, Killedan, Kilmovee and Meelick. However, without exception, they all showed a decline in numbers in the decade after 1881.[5]

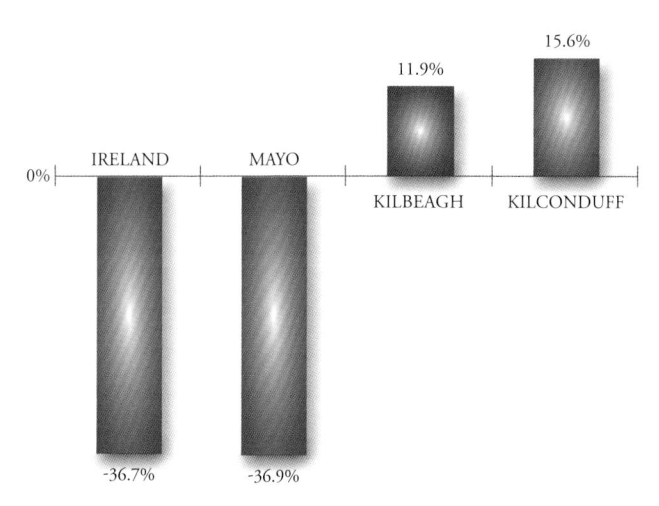

Fig. 5.1: Demographic changes in selected areas, 1841–81.

Ireland	-36.7%
Mayo	-36.9%
Kilbeagh	11.9%
Kilconduff	15.6%

Source: Bernard O'Hara, 'County Mayo', in Bernard O'Hara (ed.), *Mayo: Aspects of its Heritage* (Galway, 1982), pp. 7–8; D.H. Akenson, *The Irish Diaspora* (Belfast, 1996), p. 21; Commission on Emigration and Other Population Problems, 1948–54, *Reports* (Dublin, 1954), pp. 3, 282.

Keeping the family around you

To achieve population growth after the Famine in an area with finite land resources and little industrial employment meant that holdings had to be getting smaller. This indeed was the case. In Swinford PLU alone, the number of holdings over an acre in size increased by over 500 in the period 1851–70.[6] County Mayo, which had a large area of marginal land suitable for reclamation, was the most subdivided county in Ireland at the time of the Famine. The habit of smallholders of dividing their land into unsustainable fragments for their offspring continued unabated to the end of the century in the most poverty-stricken areas of the county.

A witness to a Commission on Congestion gave an explanation for the propensity to subdivide:

> When the young people are willing to remain in these small places, what more natural thing in the world than that a father who has a strong

affection for his son would like to keep him by his side instead of allowing him to emigrate. It is the most natural thing in the world. Many of us would do it if circumstanced in the same way.[7]

Cartron (Corthoon) townland in Swinford PLU exemplifies the willingness of smallholders to eke out a precarious existence in conditions completely unacceptable in more prosperous parts of the county and nationally. In 1856, Cartron had seventeen tenant farmers subsisting on 460 acres of mainly marginal land.[8] By 1875 three new tenants had insinuated themselves into the townland, relying solely on reclaimed land for survival. It can be seen from Table 1 that the new tenants were Andrew McEntire, Thomas McDonagh and John Morrely.

The townland of Cartron in Kilbeagh parish offers us an example of subdivision from three tenant farmers: Andrew Foly, James McEntire and James Morrely. Andrew Foly. *c.* 1897, divided his holding, valued at £4, between his sons Andrew (junior) and Thomas. James McEntire left half his holding, valued at £3 5*s* to his son Thomas and half to his daughter, Catherine. James Morrely, whose holding was valued at £2, left it between his two sons John and Thomas.[9]

Marriage rate

While the poorer areas of Ireland had followed traditional methods of farming and espoused archaic customs and practices up to the 1880s, the food crisis of 1879–80 became a watershed moment in the practices of subdivision and early marriage, both of which started to weaken and eventually went into reverse. Nationally, the number of people who were unmarried at age 45–54 was about seventeen per cent for both men and women in 1881, but by 1911 this had increased to over twenty-seven per cent for men and almost twenty five per cent for women.[10] The comparable figures for Connaught men and women in 1881 were eleven per cent and ten per cent respectively, little changed from the 1840s. By 1911, however, the figure for men had more than doubled to over twenty-five per cent and increased to almost eighteen per cent for women.[11]

Conditions in the west at the turn of the century

Despite the modernisation of society in the west gradually coming into line with the rest of the country in the late 1800s and increased emigration resulting in increased remittances from America, County Mayo – and east Mayo in particular – remained impoverished and teetering on the verge of starvation when the potato crop was reduced or the earnings of migratory labourers fell short in any particular year.

Table 1: Composition of holdings held by tenants in Cartron townland, *c.* 1875.

Abbreviations: A: acres; R: roods; P: perches.

No. on map	Name	Arable A R P	Bottom A R P	Reclaimed A R P	Reclaimable A R P	Bog A R P
1	Mary Brett	4 2 25	0 0 13	3 2 18	0 3 0	3 3 29
2	Michael Brett	5 3 33	1 3 06	0 1 30		5 2 24
3	Pat Corley	3 0 11	4 0 14	0 3 29		12 2 24
4	Andrew McEntire			3 1 1		7 0 0
5	Thomas McDonagh			1 1 5		5 1 33
6	Andrew Boyle	6 2 24				3 3 29
7	John Foly	6 2 00		0 1 26		3 3 36
8	Pat Duffy	7 3 19				4 0 15
9	Andrew Foly	6 3 32	2 2 26	4 2 19	1 2 24	1 2 13
10	John McEntire	6 1 38		6 1 36	2 3 03	
11	Thomas Durkin (Ned)	3 1 13		2 1 02	1 0 12	
12	James McEntire	1 2 16		3 1 29	1 2 01	
13	Pat Durkin (Pat)	3 0 06		0 3 0	3 3 29	
14	Pat Durkin (Ned)	6 2 12		3 0 33	2 1 21	
15	Thomas Morrely	5 2 24		6 0 29	0 0 34	
16	James McDonnagh	1 3 13		1 2 25	5 0 01	
17	Edward Morrely	1 3 32		1 0 32	3 0 25	5 0 0
18	Martin Frehily	3 0 16		0 0 19		5 0 08
19	Mary Morrely	1 2 16		1 3 32	0 3 32	1 2 07
20	John Morrely			4 0 18	1 2 33	
21	River					
22	Road					
23	Bog Reserved					63 2 08
Totals		76 2 00	8 1 39	45 3 23	25 0 15	123 1 06

Source: National Library of Ireland, NLI, MS 16 M4, p. 25.

On three occasions in the 1890s – in 1890–91, 1894–95 and 1897–98 – minor famine conditions arose in the west, caused mainly by a reduced potato crop. While the mean potato yield for the country was 3.7 tons per acre, in 1890 it fell to 2.3 tons, in 1894 to 2.6 tons and in 1897 to 2.2 tons per acre.[12] The potato yield was even lower than this in parts of the west and a depression in agricultural produce prices aggravated the situation, leading to widespread distress in parts of Mayo and Galway.

In the Charlestown area in 1891 this was somewhat alleviated by the employment of local people in the construction of the Collooney–Claremorris railway line:

> The indignation caused by the delay of opening the railway works at Charlestown has been met in Mr Murphy's section, by his local engineer, Mr Tate, who has now employed over 400 labourers. It is hoped that 200 or 300 additional men may be employed the coming week, so that the great pressure of distress may be checked; otherwise the consequences will be serious.[13]

There was distress also in west Mayo, as the following report indicates:

Fig. 5.2: The Square, Charlestown, late nineteenth century. (Wynne Family Collection; source: Photographic Archives; courtesy Tom Kennedy)

> About a fortnight ago Government Relief Works were opened in Erris for the purpose of giving employment to the distressed and destitute. Nearly 1300 hands, including men, women, and boys, are at work in different parts of the barony. The men receive the small weekly wage of 7s, and the women 5s … The town is crowded to-day with men carrying spades on their shoulders looking for work. They proceeded to the police barrack in a body, and they insist that the authorities must give them work.[14]

The inability of local workmen to work as hard as their English counterparts was noted by a Yorkshire engineer engaged in the construction of the Collooney–Claremorris railway line: 'I consider the Mayo men a good class, but they don't come up to the average English navvy. A man fed upon eggs, bread and tea cannot do as much work as a man who has beef and beer three times a day.'[15]

The Congested Districts Board and Harry Doran

After a decade of poverty in the west between 1881 and 1891, the British government eventually decided to try to alleviate the hardship and suffering endured by the peasantry by instituting a special body to educate smallholders and entice them out of the cycle of poverty in which they were mired. The Congested Districts Board (CDB) was set up in August 1891. Its inspectors were sent to different regions under the auspices of the Board, to report on the conditions of the populace and suggest improvements that might raise the standard of living of the people. Harry Doran was the inspector sent to the Swinford area and it is insightful to read his analysis of the life of the peasantry there in the 1890s.

He reported in 1892 that the District of Swinford covered an area of 80,384 acres and had a valuation of £21,364 – slightly over five shillings per acre. This area supported a population of almost 27,000 people (5,017 families), among whom were 1,550 families living in very poor circumstances.[16]

The reports furnished by Mr Doran made clear that the survival of small farmers in the area hinged on some supplementary form of income in addition to that produced by the land. He explained how people managed to subsist there: 'Most of the able-bodied men are migratory labourers. They go to England, remaining there from three to nine months of the year. The average amount saved out of their earnings would be about £8 per head. Many bring home as much as £20 and others only a few pounds.'[17]

From August to May, potatoes were still the staple food of the people of the area, as Doran indicates below:

Breakfast   Potatoes and milk
Dinner   Potatoes and milk, sometimes with herrings, or cabbage dressed with fat American bacon.
Supper   Potatoes and milk, and occasionally bread and tea.[18]

Doran was critical of the standard of housing and the character of the local people:

> The people, generally speaking, are most unthrifty. They keep their houses and surroundings in a filthy condition, and cultivate their holdings [in] a slovenly manner. The men work hard for a few weeks in springtime to 'get down the crop', and then go to England for three or four months. After returning they remain practically idle during the winter, and very few make any systematic attempt to improve their holdings.[19]

He had come to more fully appreciate the plight of the smallholders by 1906 and was able to say in evidence to a Commission on Congestion that: 'If it were not for the fact that the great bulk of these poor people, no matter how poor they are, really struggle to pay their way, they would get no [shop] credit. I do not think there are more honest people in the world having regard to their resources.'[20] He then went on to speak of conditions around the town of Ballyhaunis and the small farmers' efforts to survive:

> Even in some of those poor parts of the country where there is dense population there is more wealth obtained from the poor soil than from some of the richest agricultural districts of Ireland … I believe I am accurate in saying that for, say, twenty square miles, with Ballyhaunis as a centre, the value got from that soil is double what is got from the same area with, say Kells as a centre.[21]

It should be noted that County Meath had the highest valuation of land per person of any county in Ireland in 1891 and County Mayo had the lowest.[22] Nevertheless, while Doran may have exaggerated somewhat in his assessment of the productivity of the soil in east Mayo, it has been estimated that tillage yields in both Donegal and Mayo were similar to those found elsewhere in Ireland in the years 1850 to 1880. This was probably helped by the micro-management of the smaller holdings involved.[23]

Improvements in housing

The quality of housing in County Mayo at the end of the nineteenth century was abysmal. In 1891 there was a greater proportion of families in third- and fourth-class housing in Mayo than in any other county in Ireland.[24] The Congested Districts Board's ninth report comments on the quality of housing in the Dillon estate in east Mayo *c.* 1900: 'Fully five-sixths of the tenants keep their cattle in the rooms occupied by themselves and their children, a custom which the Parish Committees have attacked in many parishes of Co. Mayo, and have already done so much to remedy by the erection of farm buildings.'[25]

The Parish Committees alluded to were the brainchild of Fr Denis O'Hara from Kiltimagh, a member of the Board, who initiated the scheme in 1897. It was first tried as an experiment in the Swinford Union as this was identified as the poorest and most densely populated inland district.[26] The object was to encourage, by small grants of money, the poorer occupiers of land to make improvements to their farms, houses and the general surroundings. The scheme was later expanded to include

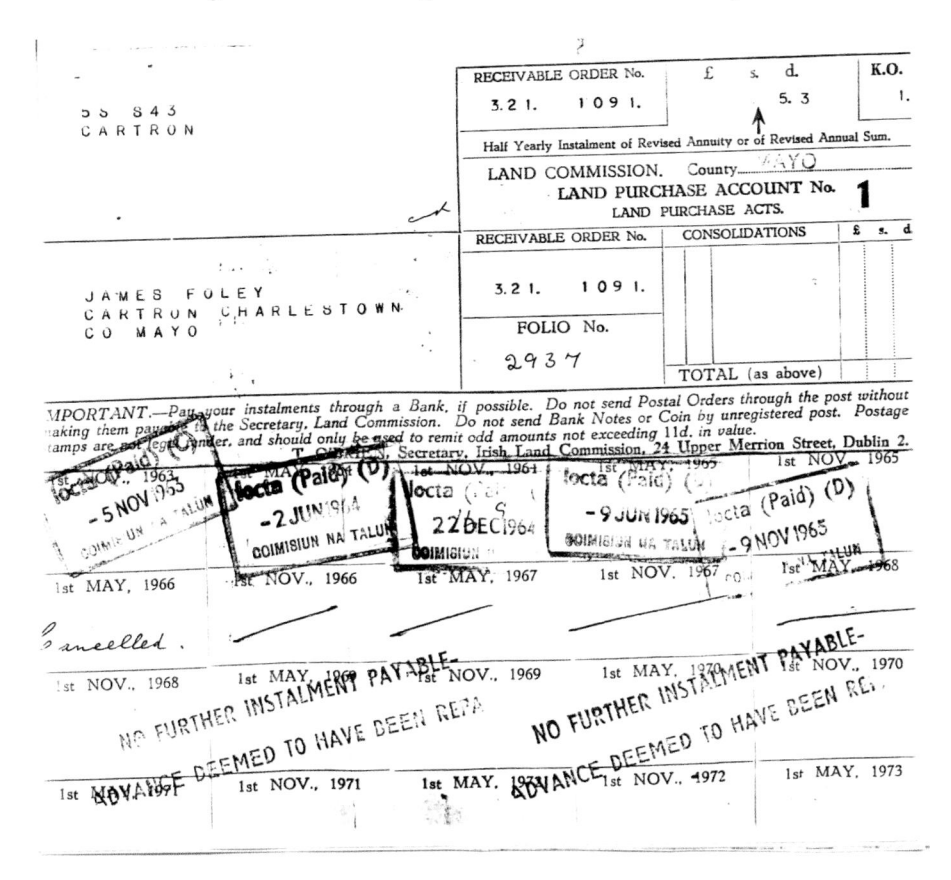

Fig. 5.3: Land annuity payment record. (Source: James Foley)

grants of up to £2 for the building of outhouses for livestock and the removal of dunghills to a minimum of twenty yards from the front door.[27] The scheme was very successful and within six years the Board was able to relate:

> Our Chief Inspector reports that the tenants on the Dillon Estate have done more for the improvement of their dwelling houses and land during the past three years than they have done in twenty years previously, and that a very considerable number of the migratory labourers on the estate, who formerly did little or no work on their holdings during the winter months, now occupy themselves during that season in affecting improvements on their holdings and houses.[28]

Sale of Dillon estate

The most likely reason that smallholders began to show more interest in their houses and land at the beginning of the twentieth century was the passing of the Wyndham Land Act in 1903. This Act provided more favourable conditions to both landlords and tenants than previous Land Acts and operated as a vehicle by which millions of acres of land ownership was transferred from landlord to tenant. By 1908, seven million acres had come under peasant proprietorship and by 1916 sixty-four per cent of rural tenants were landowners – up from three per cent in 1870.[29]

One of the largest estates bought under this Act was the Dillon estate in east Mayo. It was purchased by the Congested Districts Board in 1899 at a cost of £290,000.[30] The 4,200 tenants on the Dillon estate were not slow to show their commitment to the land and within a year of the Act being passed, 3,143 sale-agreements, amounting to £227,288, had been signed and lodged with the Land Commission, the remainder of the estate to be sold later that year.[31]

While the small farmers of east Mayo had become landowners rather than tenants at the start of the twentieth century, the level of poverty still present there meant that most smallholders still had to seek harvest work in England to enable them to survive.

The townland of Cuiltrasna, near Kiltimagh, provides an example of the backwardness of the area in the late 1800s. The striping of this townland only took place after the purchase of the Browne estate, to which it belonged, in 1899. Cuiltrasna was occupied by twelve tenants who had their land in 220 detached portions. The Congested Districts Board's report for that year stated that: 'Very little work can be done on this estate until next winter, when the tenants, who are all migratory labourers, will return from England.'[32]

Conditions improved somewhat in Mayo as the new century advanced

– emigration was down on the previous decades, the fear of famine gradually receded but chronic underemployment and a shortage of cash were still features of everyday life.

Patrick Dyar, manager of a merchant store in Tubbercurry in 1907, deposed that the tenants of Tubbercurry, Curry and Kilmacteigue parishes in County Sligo, were largely dependent on the earnings of themselves and their children in England and America. He went on to say that during December each year he cashed £700 or £800 of American cheques, which he calculated was only a small fraction of the amount sent into the district.[33]

Another witness from the same area gave evidence supporting this contention:

> In the month of December each year I have seen in the post office at Tubbercurry a fair sized table covered with invoices of American money orders. To the best of my opinion there could not be less than 500 orders on that table on some days. This money helps to pay for clothing, foodstuffs, etc., and in some cases is part payment of the passage money, outfit, etc., advanced to the emigrant or his people by the merchant years before.[34]

CHAPTER 6

Emigration and the Gender Balance

Emigration is proceeding rapidly in Mayo, especially amongst the class of single young women. From the parish of Charlestown alone more than eighty had gone, up to the middle of June, in the present year, while from Backs more than a hundred have left to this date.

The emigration trade

While living conditions had improved in the west by the early 1900s, many socio-economic problems were still unsolved. Emigration numbers had fallen but, proportionally, were still the highest in the country and unemployment was a chronic problem. Consolidation of farms was taking place, albeit at a slow rate and while the number of farms of less than fifteen acres in size in County Mayo fell by almost one-fifth between 1881 and 1917 the numbers of farms under one acre actually increased by over eight per cent.[1]

Prior to the 1880s, the rate of emigration from Connaught and County Mayo was relatively low but from the 1880s on, emigration from the west increased dramatically. By 1890, the proportion of people emigrating from Connaught was almost twice that leaving Leinster.[2] This high level of emigration was well serviced in east Mayo by a plethora of travel agents including 'M.J. Mellett, Swineford; emigration agent Thomas Leetch; the post office, Kilkelly; John Flannery, Merchant, Ballaghaderreen; Henry Neill, Foxford; M.M. Waldron, Ballyhaunis; Doherty, Charlestown.'[3]

It must be remembered that emigration was also a feature of life in many European countries from the mid-nineteenth century on and it is estimated that in excess of 50 million left their homelands in Europe between 1800 and 1914, the vast majority going to the United States.[4] Britain supplied over one-fifth of Europe's emigrants during that period with Italy providing somewhat less and Ireland, in third place, contributing over seven million people to the outflow.[5]

Fig. 6.1: **Market day, Charlestown,** *c.* **1898.** (Courtesy Tom Hennigan, Hennigan's Heritage Centre)

The gender balance

Emigration from Ireland was unusual in a European context in that the male/female ratio was fairly equally balanced. For example between 1899 and 1910, the male/female ratio for Irish emigrants was 48:52, while for Scandinavians it was 62:38. The Italians demonstrated an even greater disparity – 79 males emigrating for every 21 females.[6] Male emigrants from Ireland did outnumber female emigrants in, for instance, times of war, but over a longer period – for example, from 1871–1986 – the numbers are seen to balance out, with a net male emigration of 1,502,535 and a net female emigration of 1,511,550 in that period.[7]

Emigration was extremely high from County Mayo in the period 1880–1900, with over 80,000 leaving the county, the majority being female, It is recorded in 1898 that from a small area in east Mayo – bounded by the towns of Ballaghaderreen (recently ceded to Roscommon), Foxford, Kiltimagh and Ballyhaunis – 342 young women left for America through Queenstown in April alone.[8]

J.A. Fox draws our attention to the acceleration in emigration from east Mayo in 1880 especially among young females:

> Emigration is proceeding rapidly in Mayo, especially amongst the class of single young women. From the parish of Charlestown alone more than eighty had gone, up to the middle of June, in the present year, while from Backs more than a hundred have left to this date. Persons in America, who had not been heard of for many years, are now moved by reports of the famine to send money for their friends to enable them to emigrate.[9]

Fig. 6.2: Male and female emigration from Mayo, 1881–1911.

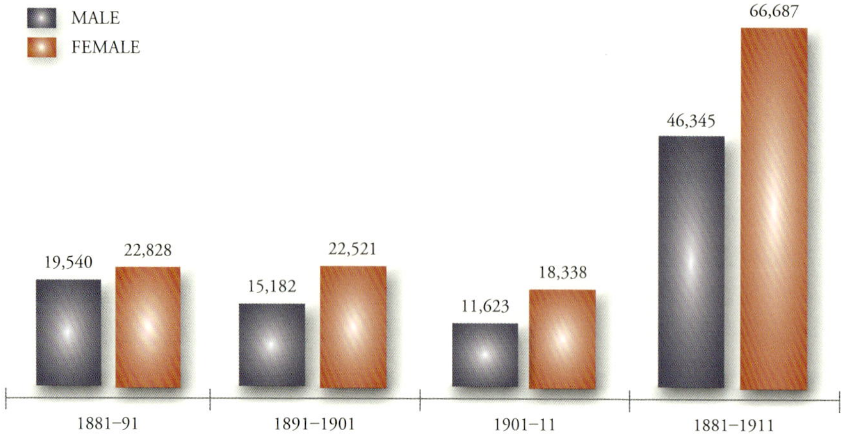

Period	Male	Female
1881–91	19,540	22,828
1891–1901	15,182	22,521
1901–11	11,623	18,338
1881–1911	46,345	66,687

Source: W.E. Vaughan and A.J. Fitzpatrick (eds), *Irish Historical Statistics: Population, 1821–1971* (Dublin, 1978), p. 338.

In the years 1881–1911, a disproportionate number of females emigrated from County Mayo. For example in 1902, 2,624 females from Mayo left the country but only 1,499 males. In 1909 the number of females who emigrated was over fifty per cent greater than the number of males. Indeed, females made up over sixty per cent of the total Mayo emigrants in the decade 1901 to 1911.[10]

Since there was chronic unemployment in Mayo in the period in question and since holdings were no longer being subdivided to the same extent as before, how did the surplus male offspring survive? The answer may lie in the large numbers migrating to Britain for harvest work each year. Most of those migrants were not householders or labourers but sons or daughters of householders who worked on the family farm when they were in Ireland. The number of sons and daughters who migrated to Britain in 1908 was estimated at 4,464 for County Mayo alone. Of this number, over nine-tenths were sons and since these were gainfully employed at the harvest in Britain each year it reduced their need to leave permanently and led to the deficit apparent in male/female emigration from Mayo.[11]

Some of those young male migrants eventually settled in Britain, while others emigrated stepwise to the US. With subdivision no longer practised in Ireland, there was room for only one son on the family farm. All other sons had to migrate or 'marry in' (marry the female heir to a farm).

CHAPTER 7

Reports on Migratory Agricultural Labourers, 1880–1915

'I never had one brought before me, as a magistrate, though there are numbers employed every year in the vicinity of my house and I have seen those men walking about the country in very great distress.'

The 'peculiar social conditions' of small farmers

There is general acceptance that the number of Irish emigrants who settled in Britain or moved stepwise abroad between 1880 and 1920 was seriously undercounted and the total leaving County Mayo for Britain in that forty-year period was underestimated to an even great extent. While official records indicate that the annual figures emigrating from Mayo to Britain rarely reached treble figures in this period, anecdotal evidence would suggest that many families from east Mayo had relatives living in different parts of Britain in the early 1900s. When entry to the United States became more restricted after the Depression of 1929, this reservoir of settled emigrants in Britain from the east Mayo area was essential in the development of networks for the new emigrants of the 1930s.

Parallel to the movement of thousands of emigrants fleeing privation and drudgery in County Mayo in the late 1800s and early 1900s was the annual trek of thousands of migratory workers to Britain to earn the rent or annuity money. This yearly movement enabled smallholders to maintain a tenuous grip on their land, which they clung to with remarkable tenacity right up to the mid-twentieth century.

Because of the social consequences of this annual journey to Britain a special inquiry was set up in 1880, as the report of the Registrar General indicates:

> In consequence of the peculiar social condition under which many of the small farmers and agricultural labourers of Ireland exist, the severe sufferings they are liable to when any failure of the harvest takes place,

and having special regard to the large amount of attention attracted to their condition in consequence of the distress which prevailed during the winter of 1879–80, it was deemed expedient to make special inquiry into the circumstances of the Irish agricultural labourers who are habitually dependent on the wages earned in England or Scotland or in other portions of Ireland as an essential part of their means of subsistence.[1]

This special inquiry provided information from three separate sources:

1. Inquiries made by the Constabulary at the homes of migratory labourers during the month of June each year regarding the number of migrants who had already left the area and the number who intended to travel at a later date. This inquiry also elicited valuable information regarding the size and condition of holdings of those migrants and the specific regions they came from.
2. Returns of migrants leaving the principal Irish ports, except Dublin, between 1 of January and 31 August each year.
3. Returns from relevant railway companies to show the number of migrants booked to Dublin or via Dublin to Britain.[2]

However, when the estimate of migratory agricultural labourers for 1880 was finalised it was seen that the constabulary figures were much lower than the combined total from ports and railways. The figure supplied by the police enumerators was 22,900 and the combined total of rail tickets and port passages was 42,272.[3] Furthermore, this discrepancy persisted over the thirty-six years the reports were published, with the authorities accepting the lower police enumerators' figures for official purposes.

The west dominates the migrant landscape

The reports, which were published between 1880 and 1915, contain much information about the lives of Irish migratory agricultural labourers, but all the figures and conclusions are based on the police enumerators' agricultural findings. To make full use of the reports it is necessary to accept the official estimates for comparative purposes.

The number of migrants recorded by the police enumerators in the census of 1841 (57,651) is in sharp contrast to the estimate for 1880 (22,900). There was no official count taken of the numbers travelling between 1841 and 1880. However, it is thought that the numbers peaked at about 100,000 in the 1860s and declined thereafter.

For the duration of the published records, 1880–1915 inclusive, Mayo held a pre-eminent position with regard to both actual numbers migrating to Great Britain and in the proportion of the population so doing and while there was a slightly smaller number in 1880 than in 1841, the proportion of the population migrating actually increased from 26.8 per 1,000 population in 1841 to 41.7 per 1,000 population in 1880.[4]

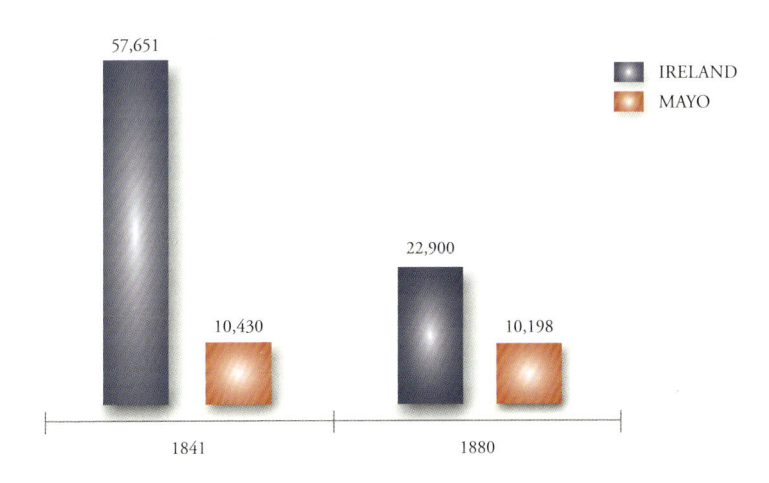

Fig. 7.1: Migratory agricultural labourers, 1841, 1880.

Source: PP 1881 [Cd. 2809] Agricultural Statistics, Ireland, 1880. Report and Tables Relating to Migratory Agricultural Labourers (Dublin, 1881), pp. 4, 7.

The number of migratory agricultural labourers going to Britain from Mayo varied from year to year over this thirty-five year period but it fell below fifty per cent of Ireland's total on only three occasions and peaked at almost sixty-four per cent in 1909. The remaining counties in Connaught also had a high migration rate, giving the province a prominent profile in the reports. For example, in 1894, Connaught's share of Ireland's migratory agricultural labourers was over eighty-six per cent and the province's contribution fell below seventy per cent of the total on only one occasion between 1880 and 1915.[5]

It is no surprise then that the Registrar General noted in 1880:

> … that as a social and commercial institution the annual migration of agricultural labourers from Leinster and Munster is of little consequence, especially as more than one-half of the labourers leaving their homes in these provinces to seek employment as agricultural labourers, merely move to other parts of Ireland. A similar practice prevails in the other divisions

of the United Kingdom where harvest labourers move about from place to place during the summer and autumn months. In Connaught and the north-west of Ulster the case is entirely different for here we find large numbers annually leaving their homes in pursuit of agricultural work in Great Britain. The social influences of such an annual movement of the population must be very great.[6]

As an indication of the disparity between the numbers leaving the different provinces, it is recorded that Munster and Leinster respectively contributed a total of 950 and 967 migratory agricultural labourers in 1880 while in the same year there were 4,862 harvestmen from Swinford Poor Law Union (PLU) alone.[7]

An important aspect of the reports on migratory agricultural labourers is that

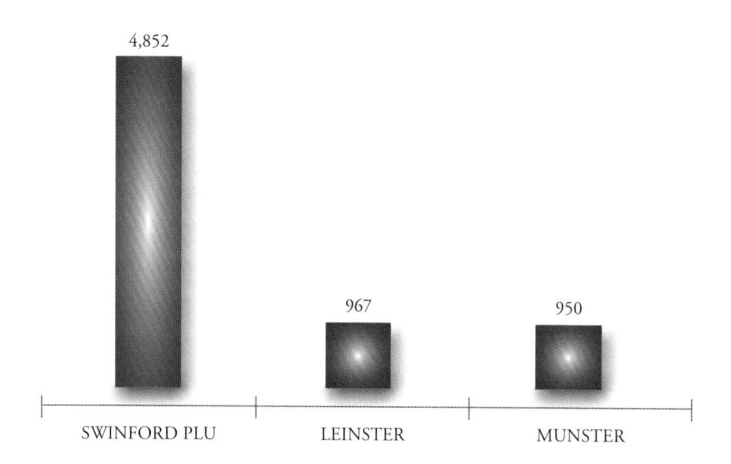

Fig. 7.2: Migratory agricultural labourers, 1880.

SWINFORD PLU	LEINSTER	MUNSTER
4,852	967	950

Source: PP 1881 [Cd. 2809] Agricultural Statistics, Ireland, 1880. Report and Tables Relating to Migratory Agricultural Labourers (Dublin, 1881), pp. 7, 9.

they provide information about the lives of migrants down to a Poor Law Union level and it becomes apparent fairly quickly that Swinford PLU supplied more seasonal migrants to Great Britain than any other Union in Ireland.

Ireland, however, was not unique in its harvest migration and around the turn of the century the movement of agricultural workers from Belgium to the north of France dwarfed the Irish flow to Britain. Furthermore, towards the end of the nineteenth century tens of thousands of Italian migrant labourers were leaving home annually seeking temporary employment in neighbouring countries such as

France, Austria and Germany. Nonetheless, the report for 1900 noted that there were features in the social economy of Connaught in particular, which were unique and that talk of 'mobility of labour' was just a euphemism for the movement of migrants designed to stave off prospective starvation.[8]

Assisted emigration

Swinford PLU had a population of 53,055 in 1871 and covered an area roughly fifteen miles square (150,000 acres) in east Mayo. Much of the land was of poor quality, farms were small and under-employment was a chronic problem. To supplement their incomes many tenant farmers and/or their sons or daughters spent several months in Britain each year at harvest work. The Congested Districts Board (CDB) calculated in the 1890s that one-quarter of family income in the Swinford and Foxford districts and almost one-third in the case of Kiltimagh were derived from migrants' earnings.[9]

The numbers of migrants from Mayo and Swinford PLU traversing the country each spring or summer for work on British farms were enormous. In 1890 over 8,000 migrants left Mayo for Britain, with almost half of those coming from the Swinford Union. However, the greatest exodus of migrants from Swinford Union was in 1881, when over 5,000 travelled to England. In contrast, by 1915 this cohort had fallen to its lowest number, with fewer than 2,000 going to the harvest that year (See also Appendix I.)

Much more significant than the actual numbers was the ratio of migrants to population and here again the Swinford Union was unmatched. The Union in 1902 had a migration rate of 101.2 per 1,000 population. Westport Union was next with 63.1 per 1,000 population, while Mayo county as a whole had a rate of 50.6 per 1,000 population in that year. [10]

It must not be thought that hardship and poverty and high migration rates ended at Swinford Union boundaries. The pattern of smallholdings with tenants (or new owners) living on the edge of destitution and relying to a greater or lesser extent on migrants' earnings was prevalent in neighbouring Unions also. For example, Tubbercurry Union in south Sligo bordered Swinford Union in Mayo and in 1906 it provided almost two-thirds of County Sligo's migrants. Castlerea Union in west Roscommon was also contiguous with the Swinford Union and it supplied ninety per cent of all the migrants sent out by that county in that year.[11]

The greatest number of migrants who left both Mayo county and Swinford Union between 1880 and 1915 went in 1881, but this number had fallen by thirty-three per cent in County Mayo and a massive forty-one per cent in Swinford Union by 1883. (See Appendix I.)

One possible reason for the dramatic fall in migrants in the early 1880s and the hugely increased emigration at that time (almost 8,000 emigrants left Mayo in 1883) was the availability of emigration-assisted schemes in Mayo, including the Swinford area during this period.[12]

A letter writer to a Mayo newspaper in 1884 commented on the exodus from the east Mayo area in the early 1880s: 'The country around is thickly populated, but when the fact is made known to you that for the past two years 3,000 State-aided emigrants left the union of Swinford, and its surroundings contributing the lions share, you will not marvel when I tell you they somewhat thinned it.'[13] This 'thinning' of the population in the Swinford area might account for the relatively low level of migrants from Swinford Union in the years between 1883 and 1895. However, the number going picked up to over 4,000 again between 1896 and 1904, before finally declining to less than half that by 1915. (See Appendix I.)

Migrant numbers start to decline

A number of reasons have been suggested for the decline in Irish migratory agricultural labourers from an estimated peak of 100,000 in the 1860s to fewer than 8,000 (enumerator's figures) in 1915. To ascertain the reasons for this decline in numbers the Local Government Board for England and the Board of Supervision for the Relief of the Poor in Scotland made inquiries in 1883 from Boards of Guardians, large farmers and land agents and so on as to the reasons for the diminution in the number of migratory labourers from Ireland. The results were as follows:

1. Of the number who answered the queries, eighty-six per cent felt that there had been a decrease in the number of Irish migratory agricultural labourers in their districts.
2. Almost equal numbers felt that the diminution was caused by either lessened demand or increased mechanisation. Three out of five felt also that the decrease in numbers was likely to be permanent.

The report of the inquiry noted that thirteen respondents recorded their approval of the Irish labourer, even though not asked on the form, and expressed regret at his disappearance from among them. However, four of the replies suggested that 'idleness', 'dishonesty' and 'misconduct' on the part of the labourers were the main causes of the decline.[14]

Conduct of Irish migrants – 'exemplary' or 'lazy, mendacious'?

Considering the tens of thousands of migratory agricultural workers who crossed the Irish Sea each year for work and the conditions they had to endure, it is remarkable that so many reports praise the harvestmen for their diligence, frugality and stoicism. As early as the mid-1800s Irish migrants were variously described as being useful, faithful and good servants to the farmer and worthy of protection and encouragement.[15]

Sir John Sebright, giving evidence to a Select Committee on Emigration in 1826, was strong in his support of Irish migratory workers:

> The advantage we receive from the Irish labourers is very great in harvest, and I am not aware that any inconvenience whatever results from them. Now I am on the subject of Irish labourers, I think it right to bear my testimony to their meritorious conduct; we have a great number of them in our country, and they sometimes arrive too soon for the harvest, and are then to be seen walking about the country almost starved, for perhaps a week or ten days, when there is no employment for them; and I can take upon myself to say, as a country gentleman, and as a magistrate, that their conduct has been invariably most exemplary; I never had one brought before me, as a magistrate, though there are numbers employed every year in the vicinity of my house and I have seen those men walking about the country in very great distress.[16]

A plasterer from Birmingham who had Irish employees was rather ambiguous in his evidence to the Poor Inquiry in 1835 regarding the character of his Irish workmen:

> I have one Irish plasterer, a very civil steady man; you would hardly think that he was an Irishman ... The Irish labourers will work any time; they generally are very industrious and very honest. I have some who worked for me ten years, and I never knew anything against their honesty; they are much trusted about houses, and there are no complaints against them.[17]

James Hack Tuke left no room for equivocation in his assessment of Irish migratory labourers in 1847:

> I know a large farmer in Holderness, who, for fifty years, has been in the habit of employing Irish labourers, chiefly from Mayo, and who has seen, at least, two generations of workmen of the same families, who declares they have never been guilty of an act of dishonesty whilst dwelling upon his premises with everything open to them.[18]

However, Tuke felt it necessary to differentiate between harvest migrants and emigrants:

> The Irish emigrants are, no doubt, as a class, inferior in moral habits and in mental and physical cultivation to most other settlers; but in a capability to acquire knowledge, and in a general readiness to labour, every one to whom I spoke upon the subject bore testimony to their full equality.[19]

Irish migratory labourers were noted for their astuteness, a quality necessary for survival when conditions were especially difficult. The census report of 1841 praises the 'singular thrift and foresight' shown by the migratory agricultural labourers in that year. When potential migrants from Connaught became aware of a small reduction in the fare from Drogheda port, they immediately set about the dissemination of this information back through the towns on the migrant route from the west, thereby channelling the traffic from Dublin to the Louth port, whose consignment that year rose to over 12,000 harvestmen.[20]

Not all contemporary accounts are paeans of praise for Irish workers. Gustave De Beaumont, writing in 1839, felt that

> The Irishman is lazy, mendacious, intemperate, prone to acts of violence. He has notoriously a sort of invincible aversion to truth. If it is necessary to make a disinterested choice between truth and falsehood, he will tell the lie. His repugnance to work is no less singular; he performs generally without pleasure, care or zeal, whatever he undertakes to execute, and for the most part he is idle.[21]

De Beaumont's analysis of Irish emigrants' behaviour may have had some truth, as official records show a tendency to drunkenness and rowdyism in Irish enclaves in Britain. Indeed, a correspondent to an inquiry on Irish migratory agricultural labourers made the point that: 'Those who remain in the large towns change for the worse in regard to civility and sobriety.'[22]

Rail travel

Trains were a major source of transport for agricultural migrants from the 1860s onwards, and tens of thousands left the west of Ireland on the Midland Great Western Railway (MGWR) on their annual trek to the harvest in Britain. A former manager of this railway gave evidence in 1866 as to the amenability to discipline of the migrants as they travelled with the Company: 'When I had a sufficient number, say, four or five hundred of them, I gave them a special train … I found them a very easy traffic to manage; they loaded themselves very rapidly, and as rapidly discharged themselves when they got to their journey's end. They were well conducted, and I have never found any difficulty in dealing with them.'[23]

Vast numbers of migratory agricultural labourers tended to travel during the month of June and this sometimes led to congestion on trains and boats. The *Irish Times*, in 1888, paid tribute to the tolerance and fortitude shown by the migratory labourers as they congregated at the North Wall while waiting patiently for passage to Liverpool or Holyhead:

> Not since the same date last year have the quays at the North Wall presented such a spectacle as they did last evening and night, when fully 8,000 Western harvestmen, as far as could be computed from the Counties of Leitrim and Mayo, were shipped for England … From an early hour in the afternoon the thoroughfares and places of refreshment in the neighbourhood of the river were literally crammed with harvestmen awaiting the opening of the entrances to the various steamers, and it is only doing justice to the enormous crowds to say that they behaved extremely well, giving the police on duty no trouble whatever. They were nearly all young and vigorous men, carrying scythes and other implements of agriculture, but among them were many aged peasants who seemed almost past their work … Notwithstanding all the efforts in placing ten steamers on the two stations for the accommodation of the harvestmen, numbers were necessarily obliged to provide for themselves as best they might about the quays during the night, awaiting the departure of boats this morning.[24]

Farmers' reports on migrants

Landowners in Britain were usually generous in their assessment of the Irish migratory labourers they employed during the late 1800s and early 1900s. While employers and workers were semi-dependent on each other the greater need was on the workers' side, where failure to get remunerative employment during the summer season could mean privation or even destitution for their families at home. One such employer from Wales gave evidence regarding his Irish workers to a Commission on Agriculture in 1881:

> Q. 7708 Have many Irish labourers come over to Wales?
> Ans. I have had for the last 20 years as many as 8 or 10 come over

	periodically every year to me. They come from the 1st of May and remain with me until December.
Q.7709	Are these the same men
Ans.	Yes.
Q.7710	How do they work?
Ans.	Very well.
Q.7711	Are they tractable
Ans.	Very tractable and grateful for anything you do for them.
Q.7712	Are they saving?
Ans.	They are very saving, and send home the money for the use of their families.
Q.7713	Do you know what part of the country they come from?
Ans.	Near Swineford, in County Mayo.[25]

The reports on migratory agriculture labourers, which were published for the years 1880–1915 inclusive, contain data from English and Scottish landowners regarding their Irish migratory workers. In 1900, a farmer of 3,000 acres from Warwickshire gave evidence that the men he employed 'usually want to borrow money as soon as they arrive, and this is always lent them, and it is a very rare thing for them to go away without repaying it. It is a rare thing for us to hear them use bad language, and we find them honest.'[26]

The report for 1901 carried an interview with a Scottish employer of Irish migrant labourers, who bore striking testimony to the excellent moral character of those who worked for him: 'The general spirit amongst them is one of extreme thrift while in Great Britain', he said, giving an example of a young lad in his employ who fainted because he had not eaten for days: 'Every penny he earned being immediately dispatched to the old people in Mayo.'[27]

The report of 1906 carried accounts from different districts of England regarding the work and wages of migratory labourers. The testimony from Corbridge-on-Tyne, south Northumberland noted that migrants worked twelve hours on a time-day and from daylight to dark on piece-work. Some men came year after year, with their sons and relatives in succession. Most of them were 'industrious, frugal, and civil.'[28] Another employer from north-west of Newcastle-on-Tyne described the Irish migrants as 'respectable, and often well educated'.[29]

Further returns in 1908 from large employers of Irish migratory labourers in England and Scotland furnished information regarding work, earnings and behaviour of their Irish employees. The report from South Ayrshire in Scotland gave the wages as from two shillings to two shillings and six pence per day, adding that: 'The workers, as a rule, work well and are sober.' Another respondent who employed about 130 labourers felt that 'mostly they are thrifty, remitting money regularly home'.

A correspondent from Lanarkshire who had employed Irish labourers for 20 years described them as follows in 1908: 'They are better clad and much better educated; they are much superior to other temporary agricultural labourers as regards hard work, skill and sobriety. We find them very obliging and trustworthy.' However, a Midlothian employer who, while feeling that the Irish migrants compared very favourably with other temporary labourers felt that 'for many years I do not think they are as satisfactory as they were previous to 10 years ago'.

A respondent from East Lothian made the point that Irish agricultural workers weren't stupid: 'If on day wages they put in as canny a day as anyone, but on piece-work they can do double and never a grumble.'

An employer from Lancashire who had experience of Irish migrants for fifty years found them at the end of this long period to be 'more thrifty, civil, obliging, and educated. Almost every farmer keeps from two to four all the year round; they are as a rule, skilful and trustworthy.'

Some correspondents, however, point to a reduction in skill and in pride of work. While the workers were better dressed and sober 'they are losing their skill on scythe work'. Another correspondent agrees, reporting that the age of migrant workers was falling and that some 'are so very anxious to make money that they are inclined to do their piece-work in a rather slovenly manner'.[30]

The good reputation enjoyed by Irish migratory labourers continued on into the 1930s, as a writer to the London *Times* attests:

> For fully forty years I have been acquainted with seasonal Irish emigrant labour and have watched, with the greatest interest, the evolution of the type, and it is only my intense admiration for the present-day men that come over here to seek honest work and wages that prompts me to try to remove a grossly unjust impression that Mr Tallack's statement might cast in the minds of many of your readers. For years I have employed 100 or more of these Irish lads – and many are mere boys – for at least four months of the year … and they have set a standard of morality, industry, sobriety, thrift and good faith which has won them admiration and a recurring welcome. Their output of work, power of endurance and cheerfulness under adverse conditions far exceed anything we look for in our young men of this country today.[31]

However, some Irish migrants were not the paragons of virtue suggested in many official reports. In his reply to an 1883 questionnaire on Irish migrant workers, a respondent from Derbyshire declared that the main reason for the decrease in numbers was a 'lessened demand for their services owing to their habitual idle ways and general dishonesty': When asked whether the decreased demand was likely to be temporary or permanent, he replied, 'Permanent, I think, and, Permanent I hope.'[32]

The final spasms of the Irish migratory labour movement took place in the 1950s and tailed-off completely in the 1960s. Seamus Dunleavy relates a conversation he had with one of the last of the migrant workers from the Charlestown area, who acknowledged that some Irish farm workers on occasion behaved in a mean and petty manner: 'We'd pay the shop every week, for the food we had, but the last week, one or two of the lads would skip off and wouldn't pay. The farmer would pick up the bill in those cases – it wouldn't be a lot.'[33]

Loyalty an essential virtue

From the foregoing accounts it could be accepted that in general Irish migratory labourers who worked in Britain had a reputation for hard work, frugal living, thriftiness and honesty, of coming when wanted and leaving when no longer required. Anne O'Dowd questions those testimonies and asks should they be accepted at face value, or was the praise because the workers were viewed as being submissive, cheap and undemanding?[34]

It is impossible to measure the probity, good character and honesty of the migrant workers but it is likely that they were submissive and loyal to their employers because for most migrants the money earned in Britain at the turn of the twentieth century was an essential component of each family's annual income. Loyalty to a particular farmer ensured work year after year and honest workers forged a bond between farmer and worker, which was often unbroken for decades.

Nevertheless, while the relationship between farmer and migratory worker was symbiotic, the balance was tilted very much on the farmer's side, as he could survive periods of reduced income much better than his employees who were therefore reduced to a more diminished role in the alliance.

Where did they go?

There had been a long tradition of migratory labourers from the east Mayo area travelling to England for harvest work extending back to the early 1800s. The data provided by the enumerators illustrate the continuation of this annual movement between 1880 and 1915 and also its extent. The enumerators' forms provided information on the home addresses of the migrants and also their destination in search of farm work. In addition the forms gave valuable data regarding the numbers going to

England, those going to Scotland or those seeking farm work 'elsewhere in Ireland'.

The reports indicate that the vast majority of Irish migratory workers went to England between 1880 and 1914. However, a significant number went to Scotland or elsewhere in Ireland during that period. Nationally, only one in ten of the migratory labourers found work in Ireland, most of those coming from the provinces of Munster and Leinster.

The lack of paid farm work in the west of Ireland is indicated by the low numbers from Mayo and Swinford PLU who gained employment in Ireland. In the case of Mayo, which provided thousands of migrant workers each year, the number of individuals finding work in Ireland never passed the fifty mark in any year and was down to single digits in almost half the years recorded.

The number of migratory agricultural workers from Swinford Union who found work in Ireland was proportionally even lower than those from the county as a whole. The records show that on fourteen occasions between 1880 and 1914 no Swinford migrant is listed as working in Ireland. (See also Appendix II.)

Fig. 7.3: Destinations of migrants from (A) Ireland, (B) Mayo, (C) Swinford PLU, 1900.

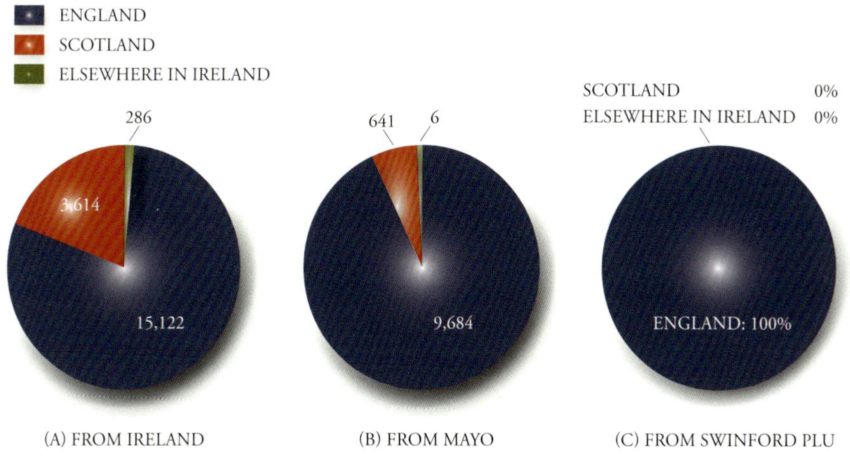

- ENGLAND
- SCOTLAND
- ELSEWHERE IN IRELAND

(A) FROM IRELAND: 15,122 England; 3,614 Scotland; 286 Elsewhere in Ireland

(B) FROM MAYO: 9,684 England; 641 Scotland; 6 Elsewhere in Ireland

(C) FROM SWINFORD PLU: ENGLAND: 100%; SCOTLAND 0%; ELSEWHERE IN IRELAND 0%

Source: PP 1900 [Cd. 341] Agricultural Statistics, Ireland, 1900. Report, Maps, Tables, and Appendices Relating to Migratory Agricultural Labourers (Dublin, 1900), p. 47.

Why did they go?

It is probable that a number of factors were at play in the migrants' decision to travel to Britain for work. In the west, the lack of suitable and constant employment would strongly influence the decision to migrate to where work was more continuous and more plentiful. The higher wages in Britain and the availability of piece-work were strong incentives for the cash-starved smallholders. For example, the weekly wages for general labourers in Lancashire, in 1907 were given as 20*s* per week, while the average weekly wage for that year in Ireland, including the value of allowances, was said to be not more than 12*s* per week.[35]

Another major factor in the choice of destination was the long tradition of migratory labour in County Mayo and east Mayo in particular, built up over generations. The movement of migrant labour from east Mayo was centred almost exclusively on England. However, in Mayo as a whole, a small but significant number of migrant workers went to Scotland, rather than England, each year. This number was in the low hundreds up to 1899 and reached its peak, 1,150, in 1902, representing over eleven per cent of the total for the county. Most of the workers who went to Scotland each year came from the west of the county, principally the Achill and Erris areas. County Donegal was the only other major supplier of migrant workers to Scotland and most of those came from the Carndonagh and Glenties Unions.

Where did they originate?

As an indication of the annual temporary denudation of rural County Mayo in the late 1800s, we need only refer to the enumerators' report for 1894. Those records show an outflow of the magnitude of 43.4 persons per 1,000 population for Mayo county, while the proportion leaving the country as a whole was a mere 3.3 persons per 1,000 population.[36]

When the figures for migrants from Poor Law Unions are analysed, Swinford Union is seen to provide more migratory agricultural labourers than any other Union in Ireland right through the years 1880–1915.

For the year in question (1894), Swinford Union provided 4,258 migrants from a population of 48,261, double the rate for County Mayo. The Union with the next highest ratio of migrants in 1894 was Claremorris Union, which recorded a figure of 45.1 per 1,000 population, slightly over half that of Swinford.[37]

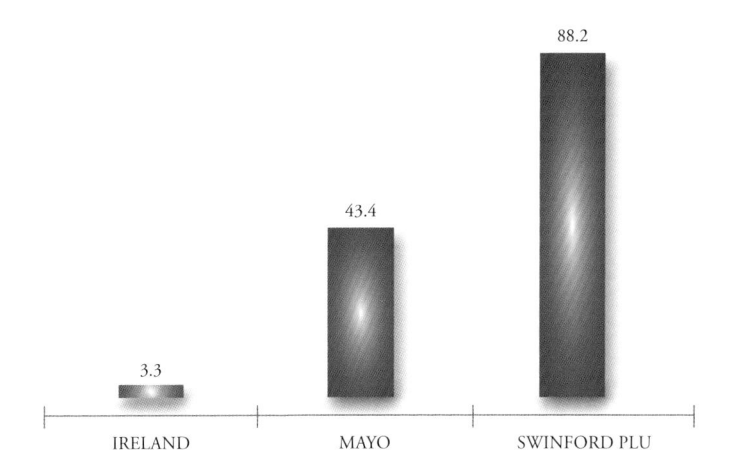

Fig. 7.4: Migrants per 1,000 population, 1894.

IRELAND	MAYO	SWINFORD PLU
3.3	43.4	88.2

Source: PP 1894 [C. 7533] Agricultural Statistics, Ireland, 1894. Report and Tables Relating to Migratory Agricultural Labourers (Dublin, 1894), pp. 4, 7.

'Adult' migrants

As well as providing information regarding the total number of migratory agricultural labourers leaving home each year to work in England, Scotland or elsewhere in Ireland, the Agricultural Statistics refined this information to quantify the adult agricultural migrants who were making this journey. 'Adult' migrants were defined as males who were twenty years of age and upwards.

County Mayo 'appears in a still more remarkable light', according to the 1891 report when the figures for the adult male migrants from the county are calculated. It is found that no less than thirteen per cent of the adult male population of the county sought employment at a distance from their homes.[38]

There is some evidence to suggest that the migrant figures for Mayo and Swinford may be even greater than those shown in the enumerators' records. It is reasonable to contend that many migrants aged under twenty travelled to Britain with parents or relatives to seek work and were uncounted by the enumerators. The report for 1905 acknowledged this and intimated that allowance be made for the fact that 'many of the harvesters who migrate to England and Scotland are not twenty years of age'.[39]

The seduction of tradition

It was a common practice for male migrant workers to bring their oldest sons to England with them as soon as they deemed them capable of holding down a position in the work gang. Those adolescents, some as young as fourteen or fifteen years of age, were helped and protected by their fathers for the first few years and in a reciprocal gesture, as the young workers matured, they in turn helped their fathers as they grew older and slower. Both fathers and sons were aware that in piecework, the gang was only as strong as its weakest link and each individual was expected to keep pace with other gang members in various types of work.

Even before the Famine the practice of family members, especially fathers and sons, travelling together to Britain was noted by contemporary writers. George Nicholls writing in 1838 regarding Irish migratory agricultural labourers noted that

> they belong, almost exclusively, to the western parts of Ireland, and the greater portion of them to the province of Connaught. They nearly all occupy small portions of land, and, as soon as their own little crop is planted, set off for the eastern ports, to

Fig. 7.5: The father-and-son team of Hugh Durkan (second from left) and his son Jimmy Durkan (second from right) in a work gang in England, early 1950s. (Courtesy Máirín (Peyton) Noone)

embark for England or Scotland, generally leaving their wives and families at home … Many young unmarried men, who do not occupy land, are found among the migrants ….[40]

Edward Dean, a strong farmer from Carragown, near Swinford said in his evidence to the Devon Commission in 1845, regarding the livelihood of younger sons in his locality: 'They go away to England for a month or two, and come back again.'[41]

Putting down roots

It was only to be expected that many sons who found themselves underemployed in the Swinford area, would eventually settle in England after a few exploratory journeys. A.J. Staunton, general merchant, farmer and Poor Law Guardian in Swinford, intimated in 1896 that of 5,000 harvestmen who had to go to England for employment from the Swinford Union in 1895, '1300 remained over here [England] … that is to say, sons that can be done without, and are not wanted to assist the parents at home.'[42] He went on to speak of the grip the annual migration to England still had on the socio-economic lives of the smallholders of Swinford Union:

> English money is coming at all times of the year into our country, because we are never without people in England. Some of our people stop there for two years without coming home, and some stop five years; but we are never without people there at all seasons of the year; but the principal number are there from the 1st of March to the 1st November.[43]

Migrate or emigrate!

The privation of the small farmers of the west of Ireland, and Mayo in particular, is encapsulated in the 1900 report on migratory agricultural labourers:

> Were it not for the annual migration to England and Scotland … these poor people, low as their standard of comfort is, could certainly not make ends meet. It is, then, not a vagabond strain in their nature but the urgency of economic circumstances that take them – men, women, boys, and girls – from their homes, for from three to eight months of every year.[44]

The 'urgency of economic circumstances' was still dictating the movements of

Swinford migrants in 1908, when some 3,000 harvestmen left the Union seeking employment in England. The population of the Union had by this time fallen to 44,000 people according to Mark C. Henry of Charlestown, a witness to the Royal Commission on Congestion in Ireland in 1908. He estimated that there were in the Swinford Union 7,700 families out of whom 7,095 had holdings of land that could not support them – roughly 35,000 people. Those smallholders, he said, were only kept from starvation by the earnings of relatives in other countries.[45]

A 1905 report from the CDB relating to the east Mayo area seemed to confirm the huge numbers of male adults crossing to English farms looking for agricultural work around the start of the twentieth century and also the extent of the parallel and more permanent emigration to America. This report provided information on part of the Dillon estate in east Mayo involving 3,847 holdings and suggested that those might be taken as typical of holdings in Swinford PLU. The report pointed out:

> That out of a total of 3,847 holdings, 1,096 of the tenants or heads of families were migratory labourers, spending on average, 5 ½ months of the year in England, and that in addition 2,401 other members of the tenants' families were also migratory labourers, making a total of 3,497 migratory labourers from 3,847 holdings. The return also shows that 1,643 males and 2,100 females of the present tenants' families had emigrated to America.[46]

Riveted to the land

The tenacity, in the face of what would seem elsewhere as insurmountable difficulties, with which many of the smallholders in east Mayo held on to their holdings is adverted to in the above report, which noted that 'for a period of thirty years only 214 holdings were acquired by the present tenants or their immediate predecessors, by purchasing the previous tenants' interest. This shows the small proportion of tenancies of this class that are offered for sale, and accounts to a large extent for the high prices which the tenants' interests in small holdings generally realise'.[47]

The reluctance to sell land is all the more remarkable when the poverty of the area is taken into account. Coupled with the destitution at home was the hardship involved in the annual trek to England – the whole exacerbated by the periods of distress visited on the west between 1880 and 1900. Further to this it should be noted that the small number of farms sold in this thirty-year period was part of an estate of some 4,000 holdings.

It can be seen from the 1905 CDB report that almost one in three smallholders on the Dillon estate were migratory labourers. The remaining migratory labourers from the estate were made up almost exclusively of other members of the tenants' families, the vast majority of whom were male.

The ratio of one migratory labourer to each household would seem exceptionally high even for east Mayo but the large families of the time – the average 'completed' family size in Ireland in 1911 was 6.77 – and the almost complete lack of employment led to a surplus of sons and daughters for many of whom migration or emigration was the only choice.[48]

The disproportionality between the numbers of male and female emigrants from the Dillon estate travelling to America (1,643 males and 2,100 females) might be explained by the numbers of sons who spent much of their early adult life as migratory labourers under the supervision or tutelage of parents or neighbours. Very few, if any, females from the east Mayo area worked as agricultural employees during the period in question, unlike their counterparts in west Mayo where females were an important part of the migratory labour force. This left a gender imbalance in the emigration statistics, as already adverted to, with many more females than males leaving the area permanently. However, some of those young male adults began to stay for longer periods in England, eventually marrying and settling down there. Others saved up and were, in time, able to pay their own passage to the States, where they were reunited with sisters and other family members who were already there.

The significance of 'sons and daughters'

It is evident from the reports that the majority of migrants were landless labourers, most of them male, with the greatest number coming from the west. However, it wasn't until 1905 that a breakdown of the composition of landless labourers was initiated and it immediately became apparent that the majority of this category was made up of family members of smallholders who, when not working on their family farm at home, were in England or Scotland seeking paid employment at farming or other work.

On analysis of the figures for 'sons and daughters', it becomes clear that this category forms the majority of all migrants from Ireland and especially so from the west. The importance of having 'one less mouth to feed' is apparent in the records for Mayo where the number of 'sons and daughters' who left the county between 1905 and 1914 never fell below half of the total migrants and reached a peak of sixty-seven per cent in 1911.[49] (See also Appendix III.)

The figures for the whole of Ireland give some idea of the staggering number of young people, many adolescent, who migrated each year from the country; close to 9,000 sons or daughters out of a total of just over 15,000 migrants left for agricultural work in Britain in 1906 alone.[50] As in other aspects of migration, Connaught and Mayo were foremost in contributing to the number who migrated. For example,

86 *Swinford Spalpeens*

while this category made up fifty-eight per cent of Ireland's total migrants in 1908, it supplied sixty-two per cent of Connaught's migrants and sixty-four per cent of Mayo's migrants.[51] 'Daughters' make only a small contribution to this category, and the number of females in this grouping who migrated from Mayo between 1905 and 1914 lay in the range of 1.5 and 5.5 per cent of the total migrants from the county. In contrast to this, the 'sons' who migrated from Mayo in, say, 1914 made up almost two-thirds of all migrants from the county. To put this into perspective, 2,756 sons migrated in 1914 but only sixty daughters left.[52] (See also Appendix III.)

Fig. 7.6: Categories of migrant labourers leaving Mayo, 1908.

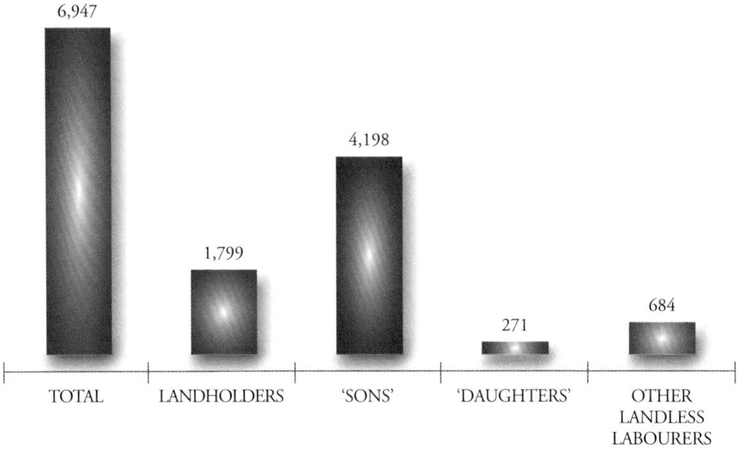

TOTAL	LANDHOLDERS	'SONS'	'DAUGHTERS'	OTHER LANDLESS LABOURERS
6,947	1,799	4,198	271	684

Source: PP 1909 [Cd. 4919] Agricultural Statistics, Ireland, 1908–9. Report and Tables Relating to Irish Agricultural Labourers (Dublin, 1909), pp. 22, 29.

Different traditions

No records were taken of the number of sons and daughters who left Poor Law Unions in Ireland, but it can be accepted that the vast majority of female migrants in Mayo came from the western regions of the county, especially the Achill and Erris areas, where there was a long tradition of female migration to Scotland. Women in east Mayo had no tradition of migratory labour, the majority going abroad instead, as emigrants to the United States. Male family members were initiated by their fathers, relatives or neighbours into the migrant traffic to England and they in turn brought over younger brothers to join them, creating a migrant stream each spring.

Poverty still endemic

All of the conditions conducive to subsistence living were still present among the smallholders of east Mayo in the early twentieth century. The soil in general was of poor quality; consolidation of holdings was very slow with the majority of holdings less than twenty acres in size and there was chronic underemployment.

Evidence gathered by the Royal Commission on Congestion in Ireland provides information on conditions in Swinford Union in 1908: 'Swinford Union was exceptionally poor, and always on the verge of famine; if the whole Union were divided into £10 holdings, more than half of the present landholders would be left without any land at all.'[53] This would seem to be true of the contiguous Foxford area also where, we are told, 'the average valuation of about 400 families within two miles of Foxford was £2'.[54]

Synge visits Swinford

Between 1880 and 1914 the enumerators provided useful information regarding the number of landholders migrating each year and the size of holdings occupied by them. The 1906 report recorded that 1,045 landholders migrated from Swinford PLU in that year and more than nine out of ten of those migrant tenants had farms of less than twenty acres.[55]

J.M. Synge, the noted playwright, stopped over in Swinford on his tour of the west in 1905 and in conversation with an old man from the locality about harvestmen leaving the area each year, he elicited the following response: 'Well, you'd never reckon them, but I've heard people to say that there are six thousand or near it. Trains full of them do be running every week to the city of Dublin for the Liverpool boat, and I'm telling you it's many are hard set to get a seat in them at all.' He then went on to point out the thin line between a successful season and a failed one: 'Then if the weather is too good beyond and the hay is near saved of itself, there is some that get little to do; but if the Lord God sends showers and rain there is work and plenty, and a power of money to be made.'[56]

Travel in fourth-class comfort or use 'Shank's mare'

The passage of migratory agricultural labourers from Ireland to Britain was made safer and quicker with the advent of steamers in 1818. However, up to the 1860s, the journey to the ports had to be made on foot by most migrants.

The first rail-line in Ireland opened in 1834, between Dublin and Kingstown (Dún Laoghaire). By 1861, the rail network had spread to Mayo with the first train station opening there on 9 September 1861 in Ballyhaunis. Claremorris and

Castlebar stations opened in 1862, while Foxford opened six years later in 1868. The rail-line passing through the most extensive migrant nursery in Ireland didn't open until 1895. This was the Collooney–Claremorris line, which served the Mayo towns of Charlestown, Swinford, Kiltimagh and Claremorris.

By the end of the nineteenth century most towns in Mayo had a rail connection. The dominant railway company in Mayo was the Midland Great Western Railway company (MGWR). A third-class rail ticket to England from Mayo cost between eleven and thirteen shillings at the beginning of the twentieth century and the records for Mayo stations would suggest that the vast majority of migratory agricultural labourers from the county used this form of transport on their journey to Britain.

Nonetheless, some migrants were very poor and so lacking in resources that they were compelled to follow in the steps of previous generations and walk long distances to the port. A parish priest in Mayo in 1893 spoke about migrants having to pawn their coats, bed clothes and everything that could be dispensed with, to secure the fare to Britain: 'Some, who could not succeed, even in this extreme way, in obtaining the necessary amount, walked scores of miles in order to save the few shillings required to take them across the strip of sea.'[57]

Micheál MacGowan talks quite casually about walking from his home in Donegal, carrying a suitcase, to Derry to board a ship to America:

> Walking was the only way of travelling then [1885] and those going to America had to foot-slog it as far as Derry. It's about thirty miles from our place to Letterkenny through Muckish Gap and twenty miles further to Derry. We had to cover those fifty miles by evening in order to make the boat … We had no anxiety about making Derry in time. We were well used to walking and we had hardly any baggage.[58]

This writer's grandfather, who was born c.1851, was a migratory agricultural labourer in the late nineteenth century, and he often spoke of 'walking to England'.[59]

Most harvestmen's tickets were bought in Mayo

Pockets of poverty were still present in Mayo in the 1920s, as John Neary describes in his memoir. John was a spalpeen from near Swinford and while he was fortunate enough to have the fare to England, some of his neighbours weren't so lucky. 'Some of the Spalpeens could not afford the fare so had to walk to Dublin. They were hard men who, to hide their plight, left their homes undetected at night. These men were known as "long-distance kiddies".[60]

There is little doubt, however, that the vast majority of migrant workers availed of rail transport to the ports on their journeys to Scotland and England in the late nineteenth and early twentieth centuries. The reports provided on migratory agricultural labourers at that time would suggest that most of the harvestmen's tickets bought in Ireland were sold in Mayo stations. For example, in 1880, out of a total of 27,659 harvestmen's tickets sold in the whole of Ireland, over 20,000 came from Mayo stations and of these almost half came from the east Mayo stations of Ballaghaderreen and Ballyhaunis.[61] By 1902, three out of four migratory agricultural labourers purchasing harvestmen's tickets were buying them in Mayo train stations, starkly reflecting the huge numbers leaving the county each year for harvest work.[62]

Categorisation of migrant workers

Irish migrants going to Britain in the late nineteenth and early twentieth centuries followed well-trodden paths to their destinations in England and Scotland. The report on migratory agricultural labourers for 1905 suggested that the workers from different parts of Ireland could be divided into three main groups:[63]

1. Achill workers: who were composed mainly of female workers accompanied by some older men and boys. This group contained workers from Achill Island, the Erris area and included a significant number from County Donegal. Between 1,000 and 2,000 of those workers went each year to the potato harvest in Scotland and were employed there for a period of about five months.
2. Donegal men: the second group were known as Donegal men and their destinations were Scotland and Northumberland, where they engaged in harvesting and other emergency work.
3. Connaught [Connacht] men: the third and most extensive group were the Connaught men. This group was exclusively male and, almost without exception, travelled to England. Their main destinations in England were Lancashire, Durham, Yorkshire, Lincolnshire, Cambridgeshire. The bulk of Connaught men came from County Mayo and, in particular, east Mayo. The report for 1893 gives some indication of the density of migrant workers in the east Mayo area. The recorded migrants leaving Swinford PLU in 1893 was 3,909 compared to the combined total of 3,933 for the counties of Leitrim, Roscommon, Galway and Sligo.[64] Connaught men were employed in all aspects of farm work and went to England as early as possible in spring and stayed as long as work was available.

Fig. 7.7: Density of migrant workers, 1893.

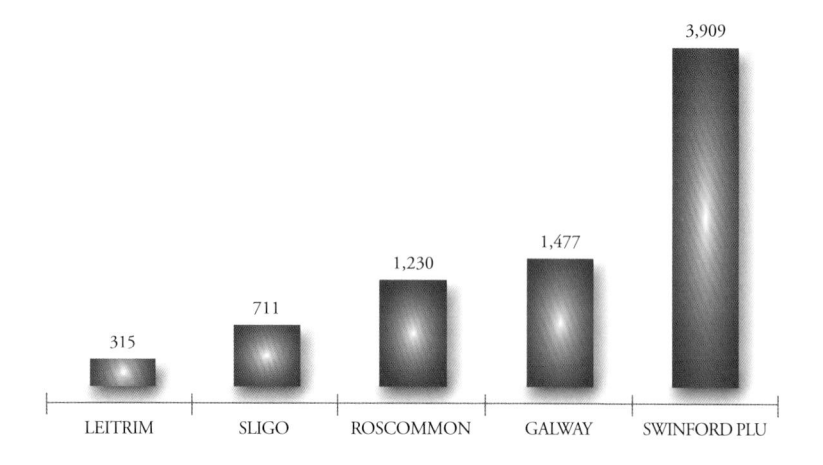

LEITRIM	SLIGO	ROSCOMMON	GALWAY	SWINFORD PLU
315	711	1,230	1,477	3,909

Source: PP 1893 [Cd. 7188] Agricultural Statistics, Ireland, 1893. Report and Tables Relating to Migratory Agricultural Labourers (Dublin, 1893), p. 5.

Coming early and staying late

Harvestmen's tickets were made available by the MGWR system from an early date each year for those willing and able to go earlier to work in Britain. 'On the larger farms the labourers begin to come as early as the middle of February, many not returning until a week or two before Christmas.'[65]

Those migrants leaving earlier and spending more time in Britain were probably farmers' sons who were underemployed in their home areas. They would be able to secure casual farm work early in the year grading and setting potatoes, cleaning out byres and spreading manure, sowing, weeding and hoeing various root crops, fencing and cleaning drains, spreading fertiliser among other tasks.

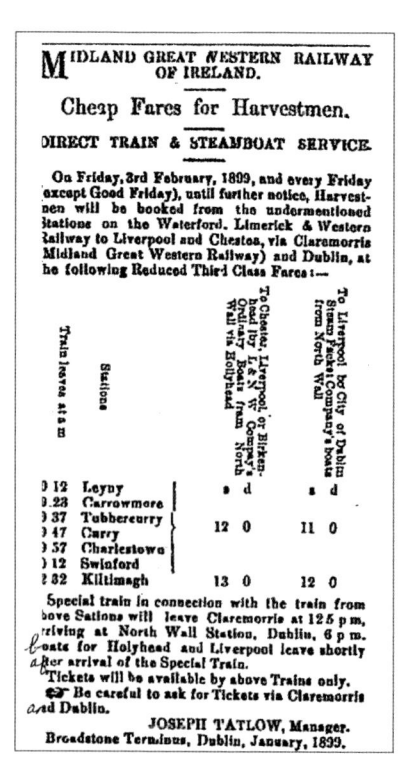

Fig. 7.8: MGW rail fares, 1899.
(Source: *Ballina Chronicle and Mayo Advertiser*, 1 May 1899)

Those left behind

For the majority, however, the stay in Britain was somewhat shorter encompassing the hay, harvest and potato crops. Work on those crops could be contracted out as piecework and earnings could be maximised in the shortest possible time. Heads of families who were also migrating agricultural workers had to synchronise the completion of essential work on their home farms with the need to be in Britain when the rush of work started or as a report neatly summarises: 'Some are employed on the same farms from June to December; others go from farm to farm in the hope of falling in with busy times and higher wages.'[66]

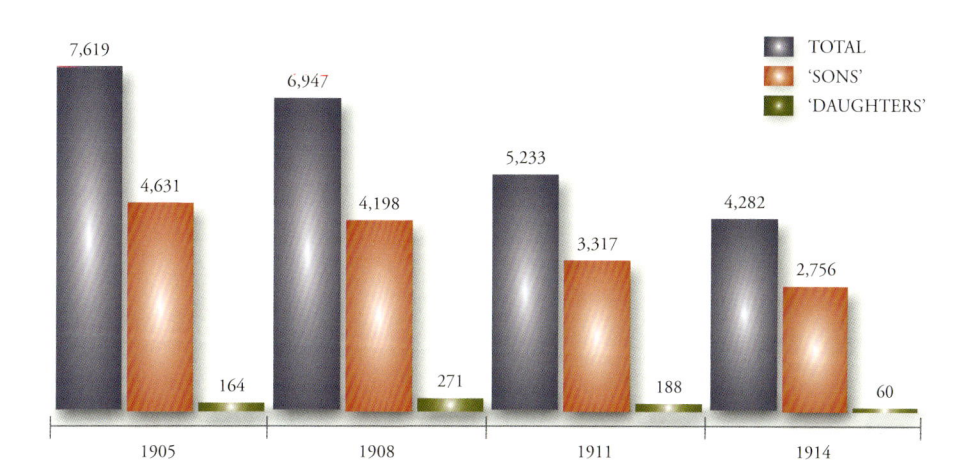

Fig. 7.9: 'Sons' and 'daughters' as a subset of total migrants from County Mayo, 1905–14.

Year	TOTAL	'SONS'	'DAUGHTERS'
1905	7,619	4,631	164
1908	6,947	4,198	271
1911	5,233	3,317	188
1914	4,282	2,756	60

Source: data derived from Agricultural Statistics, Ireland, 1905, p. 29; 1908, p. 29; 1911, p. 21; 1914, p. 19.

To minimise the amount of laborious farm work left behind for the wife and young family in Ireland, it was important that heavy work like turf-cutting, ploughing for potatoes and oats and the spreading of manure be completed before the smallholder left.

From the month of June onward, the rural districts of east Mayo were divested of many of their young people, with more than half the male adults working on farms in England during the summer season. As early as 1879 note was made of the scarcity of male adults during the summer in the east Mayo/south Sligo region: 'The tillage has to be carried on during a great portion of the year by feeble old men, women, boys and girls owing to the absence of most of the young men in England and Scotland, where they go to such employment.'[67]

Early 'time and motion' assessments

The approach to this annual trek to England from east Mayo varied according to individual circumstances. Younger, unmarried migrants could take a chance and go early on spec. Others went later and moved around from farm to farm or region to region to maximise their earnings. Most workers sought piecework and accepted a day's wages as a means of getting from one emergency period to the next. Other migrants went to the same farmer, year after year and this loyalty had reciprocal benefits:

1. Being notified in advance that work was available. English farmers often wrote to their Irish workers when their services were needed.
2. Migrants became familiar with local conditions and customs and built up relationships with local people.
3. The bond of trust built up between employer and employee increased the likelihood of the migrant getting an advance on his fare if this was found necessary.

The migrant's ambition of achieving the highest possible return from his labour in Britain was often stymied by lulls between the emergency work of hay, harvest and potato picking and work paid at day's wages. These breaks could be minimised by strategic movement between regions as crops matured. The 1905 report suggests that: 'The best paying route is commonly said to be Lancashire for haying, Lincolnshire and Cambridgeshire for corn harvest, and Warwickshire or Staffordshire for potato lifting and if a man has luck and saves he may take away over £20 for the five months.'[68]

'When on piece-work they do not mind how hard or how long they work'

From time to time employers in Britain were asked to furnish reports regarding the work and earnings of the migratory agricultural labourers they employed. One such employer from the Durham area in England, who employed Connaught men (most of them from the east Mayo region in Ireland) relayed that he had employed Irish labourers for over forty years and they were 'better fed, more intelligent, stick steadily to agricultural work and are not as quarrelsome as they used to be'.[69] He also intimated that while a small percentage stayed all the year round, most preferred to go home for Christmas and stay there until March, April or May.[70] In regard to wages he paid nineteen shillings a week for ordinary work and twenty-four shillings for the hay harvest. Lodgings were free and workers provided their own food. Employees worked a fifty-four-hour week on day's wages and some 'long days' in hay-time and harvest.[71]

A farmer from Yorkshire translates those 'long days' into seventy-to-eighty-hour weeks and describes his Irish labourers' attitude to work: 'When on piece-work they do not mind how hard or how long they work'.[72] Another correspondent from the Fen district, who had employed Irish migrant workers for fifty years noted a great improvement in their appearance and added that Irish labourers 'come to save money, but do not care to work by the day at the ordinary rate of pay for day labourers'.[73]

Even if sufficient agricultural employment were available in the west of Ireland, the much lower wage (in the region of twelve shillings per week in the early 1900s in Ireland) was a disincentive when compared to the average British wage of over eighteen shillings per week at the time. Furthermore, there was much greater access to piecework in Britain and a thrifty labourer there could save between thirty and forty pounds in a good year. As a consequence of the hard work and frugal habits of the migrants, it was estimated that up to £275,000 was carried or transmitted home to Ireland in 1907 by migratory labourers, making a significant contribution to the local economy.[74]

It is little wonder then that John Denvir, in 1892, attested that Mayo migrants spoke about the Fen country and the towns of Lincolnshire with the same familiarity as they spoke about their native localities.[75] Indeed, in 1881, the Royal Commission on Agriculture felt compelled to express alarm at the length of time migrant workers were spending away from their homes and families each year, describing their farms and houses in Ireland as merely 'roosts for the winter and spring'.[76]

Migratory agricultural and other labourers

Mixed up among some 20,000 migratory agricultural labourers who sought work in Britain in 1901 were some 3,000 unskilled labourers who followed other occupations, such as mining (819), factory work (313) and public works (270), with 115 going into domestic service.[77]

Migratory agricultural labourers who pursued occupations in Britain outside agriculture comprised almost one-fifth of the national total, many of them eventually settling down in the localities in which they worked.[78] However, among Mayo's agricultural labourers, the amount engaged in occupations outside agricultural work was just six per cent, with mining the most popular choice.[79] Just one person from Mayo is recorded as entering domestic service in Britain in 1901 from among the county's migratory agricultural labourers. This presents a stark contrast with the situation in America, where thousands of Mayo females were employed in service in the early twentieth century.[80]

Shortage of work

Life was harsh and difficult for many Irish migrant workers in Britain who had to undergo separation from their families and friends for a number of months each year. In addition to the hard work and long hours associated with piecework, migrants also had to contend with the vagaries of the English climate and the resultant effect on employment opportunities.

The significance of reduced crop yields on the earning potential of migrants from the Swinford area was noted in a local paper in 1884:

> For six months of the year a great number of the small farmers go to England, and on the most reliable authority, I can here state, that the amount of money orders to the post-office do not come to more than half at corresponding date last year – for the simple reason, that in England the turnips and mangolds failed, and consequently they spent half their time knocking around looking for work and the little they earned was scarce enough for maintenance.[81]

The year 1893 was another bad year for migrants and the effect low crop yields had on the availability of employment for Irish migratory agricultural labourers is described by A.W. Fox:

> It is worthy of note that, by the 6th of September 1893, 3,346 harvestmen had returned to Ireland, whereas only 545 had returned by that date in 1892. This it is stated, is due to the lack of employment in England this year, owing to the lightness of the crop and the increased use of the self-binder …[82]

Again, in 1905, it was noted that employment for Irish migrant workers in Britain was diminished for a number of reasons: 'The turnip crop especially suffered from drought, which lessened employment, while there was also a supply of local labour available owing to general unemployment.'[83]

'… there is a good deal of loafing and smoking …'

However, despite the vagaries of the climate and the work conditions of migrants, one observer saw the annual trek to Britain as a pleasurable and indulgent way of spending a few months:

> The man who went to England annually left a wife and four or five children, who were to work the farm and live as best they could; and

the women they had met during their inspection bore the appearance of starvation and misery, presenting a striking contrast to their husbands, who spent five or six months of the year in England, earning good wage there, and living on bread and bacon, and drinking good strong beer, were stout and hearty. They could well understand why the men wanted to go to England and why they remained there so long; but it was not fair to leave wives and children starving at home while the men sought 'green fields and pastures new in England'.[84]

There is some grain of truth in the rather jaundiced view expressed above. It was a practice on some farms to pay part of the wages in kind. For example, in 1913 the usual wage of migrant workers in England was stated to be 'about 25s a week, with free lodgings and an allowance of potatoes and milk or beer'.[85] Indeed, some migratory workers seem to have developed a taste for English beer while working there, as a Swinford native acknowledges in 1905: 'This is the only place in Ireland, where you'll see people drinking ale, for it is from this place that the greatest multitudes go harvesting to England – it's the only way they can live and they bring the taste for ale back along with them. You'll see a power of them that come home at Michaelmas or Martinmas itself that will never do a hand's turn the rest of the year; but they will be sitting around in each other's houses playing cards through the night, and a barrel of ale set up among them.'[86]

Nevertheless, it is generally accepted that migrants were on the whole extremely frugal, stoical in their attitude to harsh conditions, with a reputation for sustained hard work while in England. However, as Finlay Dun noted: 'The hard work of the absent breadwinners during summer is counterbalanced by the winter leisure; there is a good deal of loafing and smoking; reclamation and tidying up of the farm do not proceed so rapidly as they might do.'[87]

There is little doubt that the burden of work visited on the wife and family while the smallholder was in Britain was almost overwhelming. As well as household chores and care of family, the wife had to save the turf and hay and care for the corn and potato crops. This was in addition to looking after cattle, pigs and poultry where present. The possibility of accident or disease to animals or humans was ever-present and it is doubtful if it would be possible to manage without the help and support of the extended family.

Micheál MacGowan came from an area of high migration in Donegal and he praises the versatility and survival instincts of the females of his locality:

> Most of the work at home – of the heavy work anyhow – would have been done by them [men] before leaving. Many crops would be saved and the

Fig. 7.10: Bridgie (Foley) Greenwood, Ballintadder, Carracastle, *c.* 1950. (Courtesy Bernie Garvey)

turf cut. The women and children would have to look after the rest while the men were away. But there were women in our parish that would work as well as any man and there was nothing that some of them couldn't do – even to thatching a house.[88]

Underestimation of migrant numbers

As mentioned already there was a disparity between the figures produced by the constabulary enumerators and those recorded from the port and rail authorities. The Registrar General tried to provide an explanation for this in his 1880 report, which over time seemed less and less persuasive. It was probably found necessary to justify the lower figures provided by the police enumerators, since the Registrar General based all his reports on this set of data.

One important factor in the undercounting of migrants by police enumerators was the failure to recognise the migration of females prior to 1900. That year's report acknowledges this:

> For some reason no record has been published since these statistics were first compiled of the number of females who can be classed as 'migratory labourers,' though it is common knowledge that the number of women and girls who go annually to Great Britain – and chiefly Scotland – in search of work is not inconsiderable.[89]

Fig. 7.11: Molly and Lucy Dunne ploughing in east Mayo, mid-1970s. (Courtesy Frank Killilea)

Another contributory factor to the undercounting of migrants by police enumerators was the fraught relationship between the rural populace and the constabulary in the late 1800s. Furthermore, the enumerators took records only in the month of June each year, before many migrants had decided whether or not to travel.

The major cause of over-counting in the figures provided by the port and rail authorities was their inability to record repeat visits by migrants. The estimates made by the rail authorities that 'about 2,000 go twice each year' without any evidence of authentication is a little unconvincing, especially as this phrase is used without clarification for the next twenty years (until 1899). However, between 1901 and 1904 the MGWR company acknowledges finally that they 'have no means of knowing the numbers who have travelled twice in a year'.[90]

A much more likely explanation for the excess numbers provided by the rail and port authorities is the inclusion of people who travelled under the designation of migratory agricultural labourers, but were in fact rural or town labourers seeking work in Britain's cities. The reports seem to accept, from about 1900 on, that intermingled with agricultural workers were navvies, drovers, miners, among other workers who were being wrongly counted as migratory agricultural labourers.

The 1915 report was able to conclude that: 'The returns compiled in June of persons who had actually migrated or intended to migrate, which are made by the police enumerators of agricultural statistics, include only about sixty per cent of the persons who actually migrate.'[91] Further to the 1915 report, a second list was compiled which was felt to more accurately represent the true number of migratory agricultural labourers leaving home each year. This new list, which was published for the first time in 1914, went back twenty years and increased the police enumerators' numbers by about two-thirds.[92]

If the new criteria are used to estimate the number of migratory agricultural labourers who left County Mayo and Swinford PLU in 1880, it means that approximately 17,000 left the county and about 8,000 left the Union. This would indicate that upwards of one person in seven of the population of Swinford Union (53,714 in 1881) travelled from their homes to Britain to work there for a number of months each year. While the number of migrants was much reduced by 1915, some 7,000 (adjusted figures) still undertook the annual trek from Mayo county, with 3,000 of those from Swinford Union. The police enumerators continued taking records of migrants' movements up to 1918 but no reports were published for the last three years and the next official figures available regarding migratory agricultural labourers are supplied by a report of 1937, which calculated that 9,783 persons migrated for agricultural work in that year.[93]

A hostile environment

However, some snippets of information regarding migratory agricultural labourers who were in Britain during the First World War are provided by newspaper accounts of that period. It would seem that migratory labourers were still going to Britain in relatively large numbers in 1916:

> Last Friday there arrived by special train direct to the port of Dublin an immense number of Western Irish harvestmen, whose accommodation aboard the ordinary night express steamer to Holyhead was out of the question. The London and North-Western Company provided a special extra steamer for the accommodation of the harvestmen, who numbered about 900 … and embarked the harvesters, who were bound for various parts of Great Britain.[94]

Those harvestmen arriving in England found a hostile and threatening environment surrounding them, as *The Times* reported:

> In the Lincolnshire Fens, where it has been customary to employ Irish harvestmen, a difficulty has arisen this season which threatens serious trouble. At Deeping St Nicholas, near Spalding, where Irish men have always been extensively used in harvesting the corn and potato crops, the local labourers refuse to work with them and farmers are declining to employ them. The grievance of the English labourers is that while our young men are in Ireland receiving 1s. per day as Government pay, the Irish labourers – excluded from the Military Service Act – take their places in England at 5s. 6d. and 7s. per day … In view of the dearth of labour the farmers would be glad to employ the Irishmen, but are afraid of a rupture with the English workers.[95]

It was noted also that an aggravating factor in the strained relations between English and Irish workers was the 1916 Rebellion because no difficulty had been experienced in 1915, despite the war. These bad relations were having a deleterious effect on harvestmen's efforts to find work and the paper noted that: 'in Deeping Fen only three Irishmen have secured work, and it was reported yesterday that these three were leaving. A considerable number of Irishmen have come into the district expecting to find work, but they were yesterday walking about the streets of the town unemployed.'[96]

In the *Irish Times* later that year it was reported that: 'Mayo harvestmen in England are being hounded from pillar to post.' This, it was alleged, was because of their discreditable behaviour in taking up the place of conscripted Englishmen earning five or six shillings a day at agricultural work in England.[97]

The inevitable consequence of the antagonism between English workers and Irish migratory labourers manifested itself in the return to Ireland, however reluctantly, of many migrants:

> On Saturday, Sunday, and again yesterday morning straggling parties of Irish harvestmen, or agricultural labourers, again landed from steamers at the North and South Walls. These men stated they would not be allowed to work at the English harvest operations in spite of a shortage of field labour this year. A number of them returned to their homes in the Sligo and North-West …[98]

CHAPTER 8

Work on English Farms in the 1930s and 1940s

'The next day we got long, old bags and filled them with the straw and left them on these beds – just a wire mesh between the timbers – no springs or mattresses. You put in your bag of straw into the bed on the wire mesh.'

Hard times

The global Depression originating in the Wall Street Crash of 1929 led to widespread unemployment in both the United States and Great Britain. While no restrictions were placed on Irish workers travelling to Britain during the 1930s, the conditions imposed by the US for the entry of immigrants were too limiting for most Irish people. People who would have gone to the US to seek employment under normal conditions were compelled to look more closely at Britain as a source of work. This led to an increased number of people competing for all types of occupations in Britain, including agricultural work, with a consequent oversupply of labour for the vacancies on offer. Migrant workers in the 1920s and 1930s often spoke of 'tramping the roads' from farm to farm, seeking engagement of any type and surviving as best they could – often by begging – aware that conditions were even worse in Ireland.

The harsh times described above were a reality for a number of the older interviewees who participated in this study. Some related their own personal experiences while others recalled the hardships encountered by their own fathers during the 1930s. What comes through, time and again, in the personal stories of the interviewees, is the importance of contacts and networks in getting and retaining employment, especially in times of adversity.

While Martin McDonagh himself was too young to have any experience of employment in England in the 1920s and 1930s, his father had worked as a handyman there during that time:

> He went back to England when he got married. He came home once, he told me, and he spent ... all his savings were gone ... he built a house, did a few things. Then the Economic War started ... and he went back to England again to earn another bit of money and he went back and forth for several years to earn money ... into the Forties. The Twenties after the First World War, they say, was very bad in England ... and the Thirties were terrible.[1] [See also Ch. 9, pp. 108–9, and Martin's personal narrative in Part II.]

John Mulroy of Lisbrogan, Swinford had three brothers and two sisters in America when their father died in 1925. John was only fourteen at the time and, as the oldest family member living at home, he had to accept responsibility for the household. He went to England for the first time in 1930, at nineteen years of age. John had vivid memories of conditions in England during the Depression"

> Oh, sure, 'twas shocking. I knew men that couldn't get a job round London and they started off from Kings Cross station in the city and ... they left on Monday and 'twas Saturday before they landed in Peterborough. They walked and thumbed lorries and begged grub and all that on their way to the farmers to pull beet at the back end. Oh, I'll tell you there was two hundred there at the farmers when we came in the springtime.[2] [See also John's personal story in Part II.]

At the outbreak of the Second World War, in 1939, many Irishmen working in Britain for a number of years felt threatened by the possibility of conscription under the National Services Act and returned home to Ireland rather than serve in the British forces. By 1940, however, it was realised that more workers would be required for the war effort than were available in Britain and schemes were instigated to recruit Irish workers for farm work, for the building of munitions factories, in the construction of aerodromes and other work of national importance. Workers who were unemployed in Ireland were soon making their way to Britain under conditions controlled jointly by the Irish and British authorities.

It became apparent in 1940 that Irish migratory agricultural workers were an essential element of farm labour in Britain and as a consequence a special six-month visa was made available to Irish seasonal workers, allowing them to work in agriculture only, for a six-month period in that year. This period was later extended by a further three months, subject to police reports.[3]

Employment opportunities for unskilled workers increased in Britain after the war as a new motorway network was developed. Thousands of new houses were constructed to replace those damaged in the war, so that the market for Irish labour expanded in the late Forties and into the Fifties. Regardless of the many avenues of employment that materialised in the post-war period, a small number of Irishmen were still choosing farm work over construction work when they went to England. The vast majority of those men came from the east Mayo area and they no longer chose country life over city life in any focussed way and were inclined to drop in and out of farm work and construction work as the mood or inclination took them.

Accommodation

Migrant accommodation in Britain was often of a poor standard, usually consisting of empty barns, byres, old caravans, car garages, granaries, sheds and such like. The presence of proper beds in the living quarters was uncommon. On the other hand, the accommodation was free and migrants had a choice whether to avail of it or not. While older men had the experience of 'sleeping in the sack', younger migrants were somewhat taken aback by the experience, as John Walsh relates:

> The first night at the farmers we went out to this building. It was like a barn with a fireplace in the corner. The first night we went into it, there was nothing there whatsoever – just the bare walls. And one of the lads said, go down to this shed and bring up a heap of this green straw down there. And that's what we laid on the first night – seven of us. And the farmer came along then and gave us one black blanket each. There were three beds over one another against the wall [bunk beds] but we weren't organised for that. The next day we got long, old bags and filled them with the straw and left them on these beds – just a wire mesh between the timbers – no springs or mattress. You put in your bag of straw into the bed on the mesh wire.[4]

John Mulroy was reasonably well satisfied with the living quarters provided by the farmers he worked for. He found the accommodation

> was great in some places but then some of the farmers had little house huts built and there was always three or four Irishmen working together you know, pulling beet or picking potatoes or harvesting and they'd put planks down and put mattresses on top of it and there'd be a blanket. 'Twas fairly good now.[5]

The tradition of harvestmen getting free accommodation from their employers

Fig. 8.1: Threshing in an English haggard. (Source: Paddy Duffy)

went back to the nineteenth century at least. A relieving officer of Welton, Lincolnshire reported in 1867 regarding Irish labourers that 'there seems to be an objection to give them cottages, so they put them into barns and outhouses. They sleep in sacks. They are made pretty comfortable, and don't seem to dislike it. They seldom bring their wives. One man brought his wife this year to Holton Beckering to work, and he, she, and other men slept in stables, granaries, and where they could.'[6]

Some of the Irish farm labourers overwintered on English farms, braving the harsh winter conditions in the same living quarters, in which they had spent the summer. A witness in the 1860s reported that some of the Irish 'stay all the winter, and sleep in the granaries in sacks. You'll see twelve or fourteen of them lying close together.'[7]

A.J. Staunton, general merchant, farmer and Poor Law Guardian in Swinford, County Mayo gave evidence in 1896 to a Select Committee on Distress from Want of Employment. His disclosures suggest that he had a broad, general knowledge of the area and its people. In relation to migratory labourers, he saw the need for frugality during their term in England:

> I know when they go to England they are anxious to earn all they can, and I believe most of the English farmers are kind enough to them. The farmers know that these poor fellows cannot afford to go and pay for lodgings, and they give them the waste barns in the farmhouses to make

sleeping places for these men, so that they can economise and send more of their earnings home.[8]

While Irish migratory agricultural labourers accepted the accommodation provided by the farmer in most cases, it does not mean that they were always satisfied with the standard available to them. A.W. Fox, in his evidence to the Royal Commission on Labour, reported in 1893–94 that:

> Some of the men complained of the sleeping accommodation provided for them by farmers in England, and a good many said that owing to sleeping sometimes in wet clothes, having no change with them, they got bad chills and rheumatism, which sometimes injured their health. Of course it is obvious that farmers can only provide barns and outhouses for them, as they have no other accommodation. In cases where they can take lodgings they nearly always prefer sleeping in a barn free of charge.[9]

Few examples of living accommodation were as extreme as those found in Stirlingshire in Scotland in 1897, when an outbreak of enteric fever among potato

Fig. 8.2: Harvesting in east Mayo, early 1950s. (Courtesy Mary (Foley) Devlin)

diggers resulted in an investigation into migrant housing in the area. During their investigation, the medical officers came across a case where 'a byre provided for the housing of seventeen men, five women and six calves, with a heap of manure at one end and a pile of chaff at the other'.[10]

A further investigation into the conditions of migratory workers was initiated, this time by the Irish government following a bothy fire in Kirkintillock, Scotland in 1937 that resulted in the deaths of ten Achill migrants. It was concluded by the inter-departmental committee set up to investigate the tragedy that the choice of accommodation was the prerogative of the migrant and it was his choice to accept or reject it.

For the next twenty or thirty years, as the demand for migratory work waned and eventually fizzled out, the migrants' accommodation remained more or less at the same low standard as it had been for most of a century. Migrants from east Mayo were still 'sleeping in the sack' or 'making the bed with the fork' right up to the 1950s and 1960s. However, such migrants were not confined to east Mayo. Edward O'Malley, from Owenwee, Westport, was shocked when he saw the accommodation provided for him by a farmer in Habsall, Lancashire. 'Sleeping conditions were appalling … There were rough bed frames but no bed clothes of any type. Potato sacks were the only substitute. I slept in a loft over the horses with sacks and straw to act as bedding.'[11]

CHAPTER 9

Migration to the Rich Lands of Leinster

'Before us, in the 1940s, they might have to fight their way out of the town in the end of the night …'

Internal migration

Parallel with the waning migration of agricultural workers to England in the 1930s, '40s and '50s, was a form of internal migration, whereby whole families and townland groups were encouraged to move to farms in Kildare, Meath and other Leinster counties. This programme of voluntary migration was initiated by the Irish Land Commission (ILC) in the 1930s and involved the movement of young farming families from the western counties of Mayo, Clare, Galway and Kerry to what were rated as viable units of agricultural land in the more prosperous east of the country.[1]

The selection of candidates for migration was done in a painstaking and thorough fashion and prospective migrants were assessed as to their suitability by the ILC inspectors. One of the first groups to leave the Swinford area under this scheme was a collection of thirteen families from the Midfield area, who were allotted land in Kilcock, County Kildare in 1941.[2] There was a total of sixty migrants in the group, between young and old and they set off at 6.00 a.m. from Swinford station on a special train timetabled to arrive at their destination twelve hours later. Even at that early hour the station was packed with well-wishers, friends, neighbours and relations who had come to see them off.[3]

Another group of migrants, some sixteen families, left the parish of Killasser in the late Fifties and early Sixties for new homes in Meath. Around this time also five families from the townland of Woods in Midfield made the decision to move to new homes near Kilcullen in County Kildare. It was a matter of consternation to the latter group when they discovered that their new three-bedroomed cottages had neither running water nor electricity when they moved there in 1956, while they had electricity in their old homes in Mayo for several years before. The blow-ins from Midfield were made welcome, however, by their neighbours in Kilcullen, who had prepared fires in the houses for their arrival and called the next day to wish them well.[4] Between 1933 and 1973 about 2,600 families moved from the west to the east of the country, causing significant sociological and demographic changes in the two communities.[5]

Relations between migrants and local farmers were not always cordial and there was a distinctly hostile tone at a Fianna Fáil cumann meeting in Moylough, County Meath as early as 1937, where a resolution was passed condemning the introduction of migrants to the area. It was felt that there were sufficient small farmers in the area to take up any land that might become available!derived[6]

Those who migrated from the Swinford region to County Kildare in the early 1960s hadn't any real trouble with the locals. Martin McDonagh, a migrant from Swinford, describes how he avoided trouble:

> There was a lot of hassle [from local people] before my time. But I didn't have any hassle because I would avoid it. I wouldn't go into a pub if I thought that you'd be meeting guys … Before us, in the 1940s, they [migrants] might have to fight their way out of the town in the end of the night … it'd be that serious: 'You won't be there very long. You'll be gone back again to where you came from'. Some guys would say that to you. You'd get hints even yet. But now it's all mixed up … The families are … mixed up in marriage.[7]

Sport was also a great unifying force and after Martin migrated in 1961 he got involved with the local GAA club in Maynooth. This helped in his integration into the community and he was proud to be a member of the team that won the County Kildare intermediate championship in 1965.

While there was bad feeling over the influx of migrants from the west to the midlands, particularly in the early years of the scheme, it flared up also in the heart of the migrants' home territory. When the Land Commission attempted to introduce migrants to the Ballyhaunis area in 1938 it fomented a pitched battle between gardaí and smallholders who opposed the scheme.[8] However, lessons were learned over the years, and by the late 1950s it had become policy to satisfy local demand before introducing newcomers to an area.

Martin McDonagh, whose father worked in England for most of his life, was still in England himself when his father came up with the idea that the family should migrate. Martin's uncle had moved to Leinster in 1954 and his father began to favour the idea of joining him after a visit to his brother's farm in Meath. 'He got the idea from that. So he was asked in 1961 or '62 would he go. His name was put on the list and it came up and he was asked would he be interested and he said that he would and that's how that worked out. If I wasn't around he wouldn't have got the place. Like they asked him did he have sons. And he said that he did … that he had a son in England – that was me – that would be prepared to come home. Otherwise he wouldn't have got the farm … It was strange enough in the beginning [in Kildare]. The only thing was, we got to know an awful lot of west of Ireland people. My father – he knew – met men … that he went to school with. Oh yes, from Midfield – quite a few men from Midfield. Woods, yes, quite a few from that area. In fact the Irish rugby player Horgan – Shane Horgan – his grandfather was Campbell from Midfield'.[9]

Martin's father adapted quite well to the new environment but his mother, who had never before left her home area, found it hard to adjust. Integration with the local population was difficult for her even though people from home came to visit and the family had relatives in both Meath and Kildare. 'We didn't mix with the natives. Down this road there was only three farms – three of us. So there was no native really near us that we would be mixing with. The man up there [a neighbour] is from Killasser, you know, and the other man is from Westport or Newport. If I had family in the west of Ireland, I'd be down there!'[10]

Most migrants eventually integrated into the local community, built up relationships, inter-married and took advantage of the greater employment opportunities available in the vicinity of the capital city. Their experience of hardship in the west, their commitment to the education of succeeding generations and their ability to overcome difficulties became a manifest feature of migrant communities.[11]

CHAPTER 10

The Hungry Twenties and Thirties

'I was fortunate to get a job – shovelling coal at three pence a ton.'

From migrant to emigrant

As already noted there was a flow of Irish agricultural migrants to Great Britain throughout most of the nineteenth century and into the twentieth century. The numbers of those migrant workers reduced from their peak in the middle of the nineteenth century to a small fraction of that in the first decades of the succeeding century. Parallel with and complementary to this movement of temporary workers was the more permanent flow of emigrants from the country, especially to the US and Britain. However, in relation to the west of Ireland this stream of emigrants was quite slow to get started and in County Mayo in 1876 the rate of emigration per 1,000 population was only 3.4, while the rate for the whole of Ireland was over double that.[1] However, the reluctance or incapacity to leave a subsistence existence in the west seemed to have been well and truly conquered in the decades after the food crisis of 1879–80 (for more information on this crisis see Chapter 3). The aversion to leaving was reversed to such an extent that by 1900 the proportion of emigrants leaving County Mayo had risen to 22.9 per 1,000 population, over double the national rate and by now the highest of any county in Ireland.[2] The numbers leaving Ireland at the start of the twentieth century declined from their peak in the previous century, but they continued unabated from Mayo and in each of the years 1905, 1910, 1915 and 1920 the county had the highest emigration rate of any county in Ireland.

There are probably many reasons why people in the west of Ireland were reluctant to take the emigrant ship immediately post-Famine. Poverty was so endemic in many regions of the west that the ability to raise the fare was beyond many smallholders. Indeed, even the much smaller fare to Britain was often obtained on credit or borrowed at high interest rates by migrants crossing to the harvest. Networks of relations and friends abroad were not accessible to many people immediately after the Famine so that assistance in the form of prepaid tickets only became available later in the century.

An emigrant nursery

While the Congested Districts Board had helped raise the standard of living in the west of Ireland and the Wyndham Land Act had made proprietors of many small tenant farmers, all the conditions that had led to a subsistence existence were still present in the west in the early 1900s. The Commission on Emigration, in its report in 1954, outlined the conditions leading to high emigration and migration. County Mayo and Swinford Poor Law Union (PLU) had those in abundance.

1. High density of rural population: Mayo had the second highest density of rural population in Ireland in 1841 and had the third highest density in 1951.
2. Low valuation of agricultural land per head of population. Swinford PLU in east Mayo had a population of 44,162 in 1901. The total valuation of the Union was £41,783 or 18s 11d per head of population.
3. High percentage of agricultural land in smallholdings.[3]

Official records on holding size indicate that over fifty-five per cent of Mayo farms had a valuation of £4 or less in 1881, and in the case of Swinford PLU this proportion rose to just under two-thirds of the total.[4]

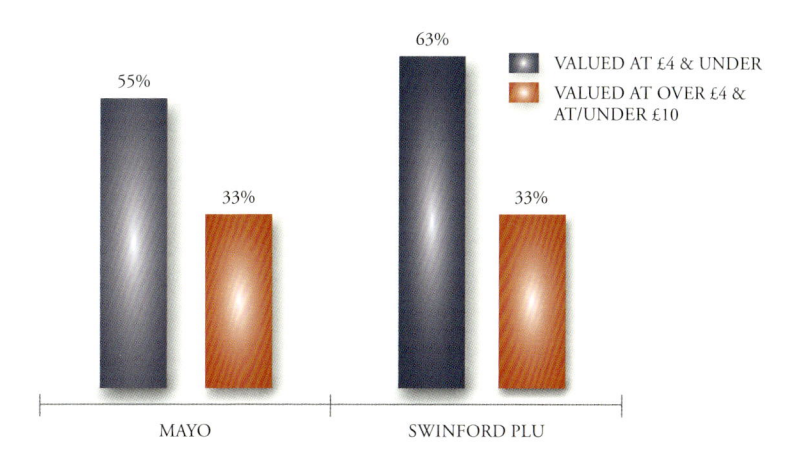

Fig. 10.1: Holdings valued at £10 and under, Mayo and Swinford PLU, 1881.

Mayo: 55% valued at £4 & under; 33% valued at over £4 & at/under £10.
Swinford PLU: 63% valued at £4 & under; 33% valued at over £4 & at/under £10.

Source: PP 1852–53 [1542] Census of Ireland for the Year 1851, part I, County of Mayo (Dublin, 1852), p. 136.

Little consolidation had taken place in Swinford PLU, it would seem if we accept the evidence of Mark C. Henry to the Royal Commission on Congestion in 1908, when he estimated that out of a total of 7,700 holdings in the Swinford Union, 4,768 were valued at £4 or less. He further stated that while Mayo had an exceptionally high rate of emigration, losing 176,817 persons between 1851 and 1908, Swinford Union had an even higher rate of attrition, making up a quarter of Mayo's total in that period.[5]

'Shovelling coal at three pence a ton'

The vast majority of young emigrants leaving Ireland in the early twentieth century went to the United States. A significant minority, between ten and twenty per cent, went to Great Britain and most of the remainder went to either Canada or Australia. In 1900 most of the male emigrants from Ireland described themselves as labourers and the majority of females went as domestic servants. Among European nations, only Sweden sent a greater percentage of its female emigrants to the United States as domestic servants. In contrast to this, just over one in five of English and Welsh females chose service as their occupation in America.[6] Indeed, there were so many women leaving the county at the turn of the century that a farm steward in Westport complained about the lack of female labour: 'You cannot get a woman to work at any price. They all go to the American mills. It kills them quickly, but there is always a demand for more.'[7]

Other counties in the west also suffered badly from emigration, especially those areas contiguous with east Mayo. A witness gave evidence in 1908 about the Tubbercurry region of County Sligo:

> Taking each estate in the parish of Tubbercurry, the rents are earned either in England by the farmer and his sons, or sent from America by the sons and daughters of landholders. The merchants and traders of Tubbercurry supply the outfit, and often advance the money to enable those boys and girls to go to America, and have often to wait for their money from one to three years before they are fully paid.[8]

Michael Neary, who had a smallholding near the town of Swinford in County Mayo, was an unusual emigrant in the early 1900s. Unlike most of the men from his village, Michael didn't go as a migrant to England after he got married; rather, he went as an emigrant to the west coast of America, where he had a sister working. He got employment there and spent a number of years in the US before returning home to his wife. Conditions in Ireland were no better than when he left and on failing to get employment at home, he set off again, this time as a migrant to England. He succeeded in getting employment with a farmer for six months each year and spent the next thirty years going back and forth to England on an annual basis.

Michael's son, John, followed in his father's footsteps and migrated to England before his seventeenth birthday in 1927. John describes how his first term in England got off to a disastrous start when he and his two companions had their first month's wages stolen from them by a confidence trickster:

> We three continued to work clearing beet for about a month, living mainly on corned beef and sleeping on our straw beds. At the end of this contract it was time to take to the road in search of more work. Eighteen miles of walking brought us to Leeds, where we worked at pulling flax for a few days at two pounds an acre. Then it was back to the road … Sleeping in haystacks and not having the means of keeping ourselves clean did little for our appearances. We were ragged when we started, imagine what a few months of hardship can do … Our little team continued its journey, a day's work here, a week's work there and lots of time in between where we found no work at all. We spent almost four months on the road that year. We often had to beg for our food, being the youngest, it fell to me to do most of the door-knocking. A lot of the people were as generous as they could be, while others chased us from their doors. Milk was the easiest to come by, we just went into a field and milked a cow! Vegetables could be acquired by digging them up. Of course when we had money we bought what we needed.

John then separated from his two companions, who had decided to return to Ireland, and sought work on his own:

> My search for work next took me to the village of Goudle [Gowdall] where I got three days work at Jackson's farm. I pulled beet, slept in a stable with the horse and came away twenty five bob [shillings] richer. Then, it was on to Snaith, where I got half a crown an acre for gathering corn. Every little helped because the weather was beginning to change. My next job consisted of three weeks on a beet farm in Clayworth, Nottinghamshire. Summer was gone, autumn was fading fast with promises of a cold winter. The roads of England were not the place to be when winter struck! Christmas that year promised little joy. I was not yet seventeen and already in the depths of despair. I had now been a whole month on the road without work, farmers don't need workers in the winter. I decided to go

back to Selby in the hope of finding work in the beet processing factory. I was fortunate to get a job – shovelling coal at threepence a ton.[9]

John was lucky enough to be befriended by the factory's chief engineer, who upgraded his status to that of apprentice steam engineer and two years later to that of boiler-house supervisor. He didn't return home to Mayo until 1932

Quota systems

While emigration from Ireland was still very high in the first decade of the twentieth century, it had fallen from the level of the previous decade and fell again between 1911 and 1920. The hazards of transatlantic traffic during the First World War reduced the numbers travelling to the United States from 340,000 in 1901–10 to 146,000 in 1911–20.[10] As might be expected, traffic was particularly low during the war years and in 1918 only five persons are recorded as having emigrated from County Mayo. Nevertheless, by 1920 the number had climbed to 1,421 and the exodus expanded and intensified up to the end of the decade.[11]

To control the large numbers of emigrants from Europe wishing to enter the United States at the end of the First World War, the US government set up an immigrant quota system for different countries in 1921. The quota set for Britain and Ireland was 77,342 persons. This was superseded in 1924 by an Act that recognised the government of the Twenty-six Counties and gave it a quota of 28,567. In 1929 this was reduced to 17,853, and a year later much more rigorous restrictions were placed on prospective Irish emigrants – they had to have substantial capital or a guarantor in the States who could ensure that they did not become a public charge.[12]

Emigration to the US from Ireland was very low during the First World War, falling to 136 persons in 1918, but it took off again after the war and by 1920 it had zoomed to almost 24,000. However, while the majority of Irish emigrants were still opting for America as their first-choice destination during the 1920s, increasing numbers were crossing the Irish Sea to Britain and settling there.[13]

The Depression of the 1930s brought a change in the destinations chosen by Irish emigrants. America had always been the destination of choice for Irish people, with Britain some distance behind, but after 1929 there was a readjustment of emigrant thinking and the majority chose Britain from the mid-Thirties on. There were several reasons for this: (i) it was difficult to get into the US because of the severe restrictions imposed on prospective immigrants; (ii) there was rampant unemployment in the United States during the 1930s; (iii) Britain recovered from the Depression earlier and more vigorously than the US; (iv) many people, especially from the west of Ireland, had contacts in Britain established through migrant labour and settlement there.

If the movement of Irish people in the 1930s is analysed it is clear that while substantial numbers went to Britain, the numbers going to the US dried up almost completely. In 1929 and 1930 it is estimated that about 8,000 Irish people went to Britain seeking employment. This had doubled to 16,000 by 1934 and had doubled again to more than 32,000 by 1936.[14] In contrast the number of emigrants going to the United States from the Twenty-six Counties fell from just over 14,000 in 1930 to 801 people in 1931 and never reached the 1,000 mark again until the Second World War had ended.[15]

The Irish Commission on Emigration, noting this change of direction, commented: 'Few things are more striking than the ease with which, after the Depression of 1929, the emigrant changed his destination from the New World to the Old, and sought work in London or Liverpool rather than in Boston or New York.'[16]

While very few Irish people entered the United States in the 1930s, life for those already there was extremely difficult, with high unemployment and low wages extending over the decade. Nevertheless, the traditional Mayo Men's Ball in Philadelphia was held as usual in 1931, with due deference being paid to existing circumstances:

> An analysis of the box office returns showed that there were fourteen hundred and forty three paid admissions at the door … Furthermore, due to the prevailing industrial depression, it was recognised that many good friends of the Mayo organisation could not afford to attend the Ball. To overcome this difficulty a sufficient number of complimentary tickets was placed at the disposal of each member of the committee to ensure that no unemployed friend of the Mayo men should be deprived of the pleasure of being present.[17]

Other nationalities living and working in the US during the Depression faced many of the difficulties experienced by the Irish. The *Belfast Weekly Telegraph* reported in 1931 on the deportation of British citizens from America because they had become a liability on the state:

> Nearly 200 men, women and children who have been sent back to Great Britain at the expense of the U.S. government because they were unemployed, landed at Plymouth last week. They comprised about fifty families who during the past ten years had left Great Britain to take up work in the US. For a time they prospered, but afterwards became victims to the general depression and lost their work. The United States Government is faced with a big unemployment problem that they must return them to their original country.[18]

CHAPTER 11

Low Expectations and Stunted Ambitions in the 1940s, '50s and '60s

'For me, access to St Nathy's College meant the difference between a University degree and a shovel job with McAlpine around London.'

Education level and achievement

Income level per head of population in the Twenty-six Counties in the late 1920s was roughly sixty per cent of that in Britain. By the mid-1930s it had fallen to half that in Britain and had fallen again to about forty per cent by 1947.[1] Thousands of Irish emigrants crossed the sea to Britain where employment was more plentiful and wages and living standards were much higher than in Ireland. Many of the workers going to Britain before the Second World War lacked specific training, the generality of men working as labourers, and most women finding employment in service or in factories.

While the majority of people in Ireland had some National-school education, the proportion of people with secondary-school education was very low. In a survey done in the east Mayo region regarding the level of education attained by adults from the pre-1930 generation, it emerged that out of 275 persons surveyed, only seven people had second-level education.[2]

It is little wonder then that the vast majority of male applicants for travel documents to Britain during the 1940s described themselves as unskilled and over half the females designated themselves as domestic servants.[3] Prior to the passing of the Vocational Education Act in 1930, post-primary education in Ireland was, in the main, provided by either convent schools (for girls) or colleges (for boys). However, there were only 416 secondary schools in Ireland in 1949–50 and most were fee-paying schools. In the west of Ireland, most parents couldn't afford boarding fees and because of the small number of schools in the country, many were too distant from home to allow pupils attend on a daily basis. In the east Mayo area,

Fig. 11.1: Corthoon National School pupils, *c.* 1925.

for example, there were convent schools in Swinford, Kiltimagh, Tubbercurry and Ballaghaderreen, but there was only one boys' secondary school in that area in the 1940s. So, while girls had the opportunity of attending day-school in the convents if their parents could afford the fees, boys from the east Mayo area were on the whole deprived of secondary education, as John Healy noted: 'If your people had money you got a secondary education: if they didn't you went without.'[4]

An effort was made in the late 1930s to bring secondary education to the Charlestown area for both boys and girls through the aegis of a private school, called St Antoine's, founded by Maura Cahill, a native of the area. Co-education was frowned upon at the time and the school closed after just a few years and was replaced by an all-girls' convent school. Miss Cahill's school was both popular and successful during its short tenure, as shown by the students' examination results, published by the *Western People* for the year 1940.[5]

Patrick Fleming, who came from Curry parish in south Sligo, appreciated the importance of secondary education: 'Ours was a distressed community in the latter part of the nineteenth century and on into the '30s and '40s of the twentieth century. For me, access to St Nathy's College meant the difference between a University degree and a shovel job with McAlpine around London. Why would I not be grateful to my parents and to my teachers? It was their help that made the difference.' Patrick Fleming graduated from university with a degree in agricultural science and ended his career as chief executive officer of County Dublin Vocational Education Committee.[6]

Regardless of the impediments imposed by lack of education, intelligence, ambition and a will to succeed often overcame adversity. Many did succeed, and the names of contracting firms like McNicholas from Bohola and Kennedy from Doocastle, among others, resonated with east Mayo workers in England during the 1940s, '50s and '60s.

Unlike their male counterparts, many female emigrants from Ireland attained professional status through the nursing profession, availing of the free tuition offered in Britain. Indeed, by 1951 more than one in five Irish-born women in Britain were in professions, many of whom were nurses or midwives.[7]

In contrast to this, the vast majority of male emigrants from Ireland found themselves in the hardest and most uninviting forms of labour in the post-war years in Britain. Their life aspirations were often unfulfilled due to their low level of education and unskilled status.

Mr James Meenan, in his minority report to the Commission on Emigration in 1954, felt that sending emigrants abroad with an inferior level of education was indefensible: 'Emigration has often been described as a disgrace. That may or may not be so; what is certainly shameful is that so many of our emigrants are so poorly educated and instructed that they must accept the most menial work abroad.'[8] Indeed, as late as 1966 one-third of Irish young people were leaving full-time education at primary-school level, and of the 16,000 students enrolled in vocational schools, almost half left without sitting the Group Certificate examination.[9]

As already indicated, there was a shortage of second-level schools for male students in the east Mayo area up to the 1960s. However, a number of co-ed schools (vocational) were built in the area in the 1950s and 1960s, which helped to correct this deficiency.

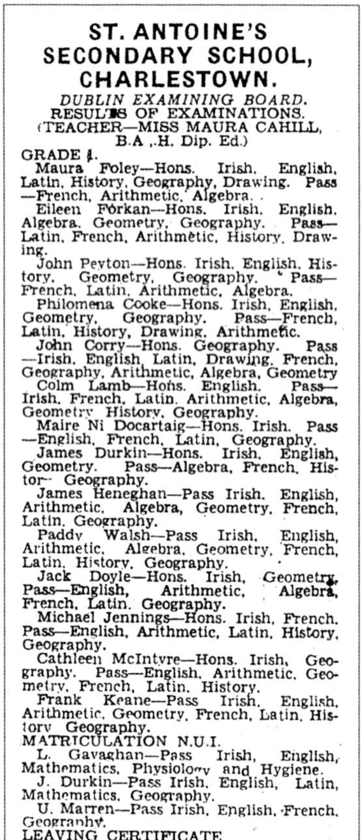

ST. ANTOINE'S SECONDARY SCHOOL, CHARLESTOWN.

DUBLIN EXAMINING BOARD.

RESULTS OF EXAMINATIONS.

(TEACHER—MISS MAURA CAHILL, B.A., H. Dip. Ed.)

GRADE I.

Maura Foley—Hons. Irish, English, Latin, History, Geography, Drawing. Pass—French, Arithmetic, Algebra.

Eileen Forkan—Hons. Irish, English, Algebra, Geometry, Geography. Pass—Latin, French, Arithmetic, History, Drawing.

John Peyton—Hons. Irish, English, History, Geometry, Geography. Pass—French, Latin, Arithmetic, Algebra.

Philomena Cooke—Hons. Irish, English, Geometry, Geography. Pass—French, Latin, History, Drawing, Arithmetic.

John Corry—Hons. Geography. Pass—Irish, English, Latin, Drawing, French, Geography, Arithmetic, Algebra, Geometry

Colm Lamb—Hons. English. Pass—Irish, French, Latin, Arithmetic, Algebra, Geometry, History, Geography.

Maire Ni Docartaig—Hons. Irish. Pass—English, French, Latin, Geography.

James Durkin—Hons. Irish, English, Geometry. Pass—Algebra, French, History, Geography.

James Heneghan—Pass Irish, English, Arithmetic, Algebra, Geometry, French, Latin, Geography.

Paddy Walsh—Pass Irish, English, Arithmetic, Algebra, Geometry, French, Latin, History, Geography.

Jack Doyle—Hons. Irish, Geometry, Pass—English, Arithmetic, Algebra, French, Latin, Geography.

Michael Jennings—Hons. Irish, French. Pass—English, Arithmetic, Latin, History, Geography.

Cathleen McIntyre—Hons. Irish, Geography. Pass—English, Arithmetic, Geometry, French, Latin, History.

Frank Keane—Pass Irish, English, Arithmetic, Geometry, French, Latin, History, Geography.

MATRICULATION N.U.I.

L. Gavaghan—Pass Irish, English, Mathematics, Physiology and Hygiene.

J. Durkin—Pass Irish, English, Latin, Mathematics, Geography.

U. Marren—Pass Irish, English, French, Geography.

LEAVING CERTIFICATE.

Agnes Kilroy—Pass Irish, English, History and Commerce.

Commercial Certificates obtained by:—Betty Walsh, Una Marren, John Durkin, Marie Sharkey, Josie Regan, Bridie O'Donnell.

Inter. Cert.—Results not yet available.

GRADE II.

Cathleen Duffy—Hons. Irish, English, French, Arithmetic, Geometry, Geography. Pass—Latin, History, Algebra.

Cathleen Doherty—Hons. English, Irish, Arithmetic, Geometry, French, Geography, Book-keeping. Pass—History, Latin, Shorthand and Typewriting.

Mary E. Foley—Hons. English, Irish, Geometry, French, Book-keeping, Shorthand. Pass—Arithmetic and Typewriting.

Margaret McCann—Hons. English, Irish, Arithmetic, Geometry, French. Pass—Latin, History, Geography, Algebra.

Maisie Mulherne—Hons. English, French. Pass—Latin, History, Geography, Irish, Arithmetic.

John Flemming—Hons. English, Irish, Geography. Pass—Latin, French, Arithmetic, History.

Eileen Doherty—Hons. English, Irish, French, Geography. Pass—Arithmetic.

Cathleen Murphy—Hons. English, French. Pass—Latin, Arithmetic, Geography.

John Murphy—Hons. English, Arithmetic, Geography, Geometry. Pass—Irish, Latin, History.

Mickie Walsh—Hons. Irish, Arithmetic, Geography. Pass—English, Geometry, French, Latin.

Fig. 11.2: Examination results, St Antoine's Secondary School, Charlestown. (Source: *Western People*, 24 August 1940)

Fig. 11.3: Mary (Foley) Garvey of Ballintadder, Carracastle graduating as a State Registered Nurse from Edgware General Hospital, 1955. (Courtesy Bernie Garvey)

A survey carried out in the area on the educational status of the post-1930 generation reflected the fact that for many males, post-primary education was either too expensive or not accessible up to the 1960s. The survey showed that almost half of this cohort had primary education only; one-quarter had some form of secondary/vocational education and one-quarter had gone on to further education such as apprenticeships, nurse-training or commercial courses.[10] Of those who went on to further education, more than half experienced it in a receiving country as emigrants.

Certainly the lack of education, as well as stunting upward social mobility, also impaired communication and other social skills among the male emigrants. This was noted by English colleagues of Irish female emigrants, as Theresa Connor remembers: 'When Bernadette [sister] went nursing to London first she said that some of the English girls used to say that you wouldn't think that the Irish girls and Irish men in those days came from the same family … For some reason the girls were educated you know and the boys weren't.'[11] (See also Theresa's personal story in Part II.)

The numbers receiving second-level education increased gradually in the quarter-century after the formation of the Free State, going from 23,031 in 1924–25 to 47,065 in 1949–50. However, it was too little too late for the vast majority of emigrants leaving Ireland in the 1940–60 period.[12] The announcement of free post-primary education by Donogh O'Malley in 1966 brought a fresh impetus, and by 1974 the number attending second-level schools had reached 239,000, a ten-fold increase on the 1924–25 figure.

CHAPTER 12

The Change to Britain: 'Crossing the Pond'

'When you'd see people coming home from England they'd be arriving up with white shirts and ties. You knew they had to go to work but it still didn't sink in that you'd have to get dirty and wet to get that suit and white shirt.'

Large families and little employment

Ireland in the first half of the twentieth century was a country with a high celibacy rate. In the age group 45–54 almost one in three males and one in four females were unmarried in 1926.[1] As a consequence of this, the marriage rate in the Twenty-six Counties was one of the lowest in the world. For example, the United States had a marriage rate almost double that of the Twenty-six Counties in the period 1930–35.[2] However, the fertility of married couples in Ireland was one of the highest in the world. The average annual birth rate per 1,000 married women in the Twenty-six Counties was 254 in 1950–52, while in England and Wales it was only 111, less than half the Irish rate.[3] Irish society consisted, therefore, of a high proportion of bachelors and spinsters, but also large families in the case of those who were married.

In the impoverished areas of the west of Ireland, uneconomic holdings, lack of resources and large families led to continued high migration and emigration. There was high migration for those living on subsistence holdings and high emigration for the excess family members who couldn't be supported locally. Because of this, emigration per head of population from County Mayo from the 1900s on was one of the highest in the country.

Family size in the east Mayo region was roughly in line with national parameters in 1911, but unlike the national trend, which was towards smaller families, the east Mayo region continued the pattern of large families right through into the 1950s.

122 *Swinford Spalpeens*

Fig. 12.1: Average family size, 1911, 1946, 1981.

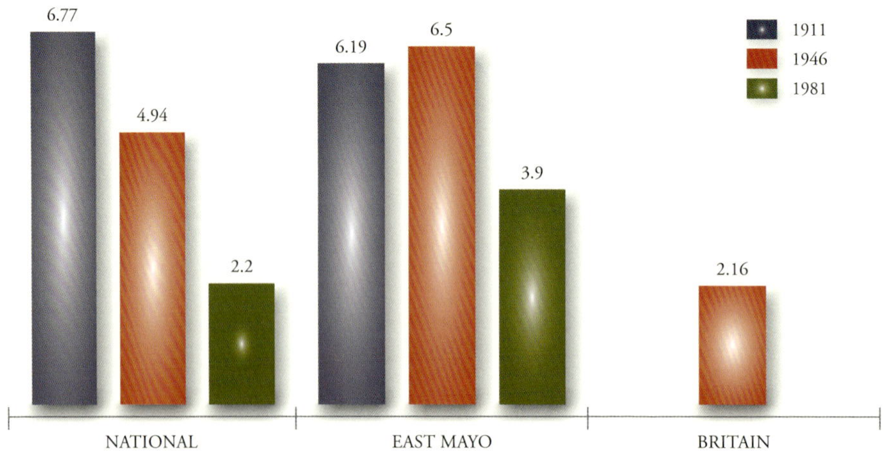

	1911	1946	1981
NATIONAL	6.77	4.94	2.2
EAST MAYO	6.19	6.5	3.9
BRITAIN		2.16	

Sources: East Mayo Migration Survey; Commission on Emigration and Other Population Problems, 1948–54, *Reports* (Dublin, 1954), pp. 94–5; Central Statistics Office, Census 2002.

Change of direction

It has been estimated that at least eight million people left Ireland between 1801 and 1921, with a further 1.5 million emigrating from the Twenty-six Counties from then to the end of the century.[4] Up to the 1930s most people leaving Ireland went to America but from then on about three-quarters of all emigrants selected Britain as their preferred destination. Nevertheless, America still attracted approximately one-eighth of all Irish emigrants, the remainder going mainly to Canada and Australia.[5] Probably the most intense period of emigration from Ireland, aside from the Famine era, was from 1940 to 1960. It is calculated that roughly 400,000 left Ireland in the 1950s, with nearly 60,000 going in 1957 alone. In contrast, less than 60,000 Irish emigrants went to work in America in the whole of that decade.

The Wall Street Crash in 1929, the ensuing international Depression, coupled with the more restrictive conditions imposed on potential immigrants to America, reduced the flow from Ireland in the 1930s. However, Britain recovered faster and more vigorously from the Depression than did the United States, so that Irish people seeking employment began to travel to Britain in increasing numbers. Britain was an attractive destination in many respects: travel was fast, cheap and regular; wages were higher than at home; employment opportunities were more expansive and varied. Furthermore, there were no restrictions on travel between the two islands and Irish citizens in Britain were treated more or less the same as British citizens.

Marrying supply and demand

However, things were to change on the advent of war and restrictions began to be imposed by Britain on Twenty-six-County immigrants in order to regulate movement between the two countries. From 1940 on, visas and travel permits were required for entry to Britain and were to be provided only to those going to work of 'national importance'.

It soon became apparent that there were labour deficits in many areas of the war industry in Britain. It was also clear that the Twenty-six Counties had a large underemployed workforce that could be recruited in the war effort. By August 1941 a set of regulations governing movement between the two countries, and agreed to by both governments, was in place.

Irish workers contracted to British firms had to be over twenty-two years of age, unemployed and go where they were needed. They had to have a work permit among other travel documents. They also had to register with the police at their destination and couldn't leave their contracted employment without permission.

The regulations weren't set in stone, however, and were simplified to a degree for seasonal agricultural workers who could apply to their local Gárda station for travel documents without going through the system set up for the general public. Wily and work-hungry east Mayo agricultural labourers found ways of circumventing the regulations, as a Charlestown migrant remembers:

> I went down to the barracks … the first guard wouldn't listen to me at all. He ran me away out of the barracks. He said 'You don't want to go to England – you're too small!' … He wouldn't give it to me at all. And the second time I went in, in about a fortnight, I got a different guard … I still had to wait about three months for the passport. In the application you had to have a farmer's letter [from England]. Jim Colleran [neighbour] who was working in England, sent me the letter. Jim was supposed to be the farmer saying he had work for me.[6]

In the period 1941–45 tens of thousands of young Irish men and women travelled to Britain to seek employment. It is estimated that 136,000 British travel permits were issued to Irish males in the period 1940–45 and 62,000 to Irish females. Since each trip required a permit it is probable that the actual number of emigrants travelling to Britain from the Twenty-six Counties was between a half and two-thirds of this.[7]

County Mayo was a centre of high emigration during the war years, with one in eight of the male population and one in twelve of the female population receiving travel permits for work in Britain during that period.[8] It has been computed that the average annual rate per 1,000 population of people receiving new travel permits, identity cards and passports to go to employment in Britain in the period 1940–51 was 11.1 for the Twenty-six Counties as a whole, 17.9 for Connacht emigrants, but 27.8 for Mayo people – the highest rate in Ireland and two-and-a-half times the national rate.[9] When the figures are broken down according to gender the results are even more compelling.

Fig. 12.2: Average annual rate per 1,000 population (1951) of persons receiving new travel permits, identity cards and passports to go to employment, 1940–51.

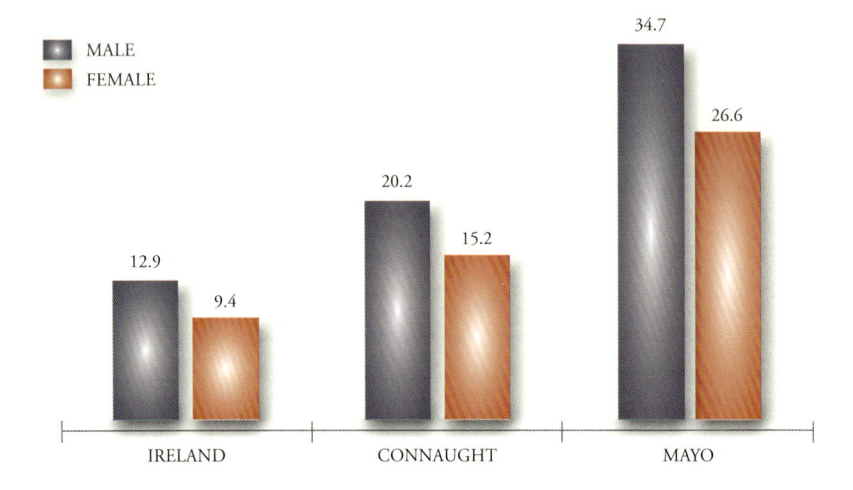

	MALE	FEMALE
IRELAND	12.9	9.4
CONNAUGHT	20.2	15.2
MAYO	34.7	26.6

Source: Commission on Emigration and Other Population Problems, 1948–54, *Reports* (Dublin, 1954), p. 327.

Fleeing poverty and deprivation

Conditions for workers in Ireland in the 1930s, '40s and '50s were very poor with a stagnant economy, low wages and a high level of unemployment concealed by the emigration statistics. Emigrants voted with their feet and between 1945 and 1948 the numbers leaving Ireland increased from 24,000 to 40,000, almost all of them going to Britain.[10] Indeed, by 1951 the number of Irish-born people living in England and Wales showed an increase of almost a quarter of a million from that indicated in the 1931 census. Of the tens of thousands of emigrants who flooded out of Ireland in the post-war period, County Mayo lost a disproportionate percentage of its population, reaching a population nadir of just 109,000 people in 1971, from a high of almost 400,000 before the Famine.

Conditions that had been present at the start of the twentieth century in County Mayo – such as the large numbers of uneconomic holdings of land, big families

Fig. 12.3: Ploughing in Ballintadder, Carracastle, *c.* 1950. (Courtesy Bernie Garvey)

and the chronic shortage of paid employment – persisted right up to the 1950s and were even amplified in areas like east Mayo. For many young people the prospect of spending their lives in the drudgery and poverty their parents were exposed to no longer held any attraction. Moreover, the tales of prosperous, well-dressed family members and neighbours, describing the attractions and good life available in Britain, just a few hours away, was irresistible: 'When you'd see people coming home from England they'd be arriving up with white shirts and ties. You knew they had to go to work but it still didn't sink in that you'd have to get dirty and wet to get that suit and white shirt.'[11]

The Irish economy performed abysmally in the years after the war and between 1949 and 1957 grew at only one-fifth the rate of other states in western Europe.[12] As a result, emigration from Ireland soared in the 1950s and between 1946 and 1961 over half a million people left the country, divided more or less evenly between the genders.[13] The building boom of the 1950s in Britain attracted tens of thousands of unskilled male workers from Ireland, who formed a transient, mobile work-force always seeking better jobs and higher wages.

While the vast majority of emigrants from east Mayo went to England rather than Dublin to find work, there were exceptions. John Cafferty's brother, who had worked in England for years, came back to Dublin to escape conscription to the British army in the early 1950s. He worked in construction in Dublin for about ten years before returning to England. John worked with his brother during his tenure in Dublin, going up for the winter and coming back each summer to work on the home farm near Charlestown. John emigrated to England after his brother left Dublin and found work in London a happy experience: 'I totally enjoyed it … the *craic* we used to have together – we never thought of home … Oh it was great fun.' John enjoyed his time in London much better than his periods in Dublin:

> Dublin wasn't as good as London for the *craic*. You wouldn't meet as many from home, you know. I mean we were all the same over there [England]. In Dublin you met Dublin people. I had no interest in drink and in my single days we [mates] used to meet in Shepherd's Bush [London] and walk the city.[14]

The aberration becomes normality

A contributor to the Commission on Emigration, illustrating the pervasive nature of emigration, points out that in the Ireland of the 1950s: 'Emigration has come to be taken as a matter of course by the public; and that is a serious feature. People have grown up into it, are hardened to it, acquiesce in it, and hardly notice it.'[15] That last contention might well be true. For instance. references to migration in the Schools' Manuscript Collection are much scarcer in the east Mayo area than might be expected – migration was not seen as something out of the ordinary.

A minority still going to the US

While it might have seemed in most townlands of east Mayo that everybody was going to England, and some 400,000 Irish men and women did emigrate from the country in the 1950s, about 60,000 of those emigrants went to the United States between 1950 and 1959. After the Wall Street Crash in 1929 revised quotas and more stringent restrictions were put in place for those travelling to America and these remained in place until 1965. The number of Irish emigrants going to America after the Second World War was only a fraction of those going in the early part of the twentieth century and in the west of Ireland some potential emigrants were still finding it difficult to finance the journey. A migrant from Roscommon describes how family solidarity managed to overcome the difficulties:

> My brother, Benny, came by boat in 1949. I came next even though I wasn't the next in line. Rory came after me and Albert came after him. When Benny came out, he sent his suit back to the next fellow, who was me, and I sent the suit back to the next brother and so on and so forth.[16]

Nevertheless, the under-educated and relatively impoverished emigrants of the 1950s made good use of the American education system to improve their socio-economic position, to such an extent that by the 1970s the emigrant Irish had the highest level of education and were the second-most affluent of all white ethnic groups.[17]

'Fifth class in school, no trade, but very strong and fit'

The ravages of emigration on those left behind in Ireland can be easily imagined. Parents worried over whether they were ever going to see their sons and daughters again. Siblings were left without the support and companionship of their brothers and sisters. This denudation of the life and energy and communality of rural districts in the west of Ireland left weakened communities behind, composed in the main of old people and children.

Ted Nealon, journalist, author and politician, was born in Coolrecuill, Aclare, in south Sligo and was one of the few who had secondary education in the 1940s. He spoke of having twenty-seven first cousins in New York and only three in Ireland and there is little doubt that his experience was replicated in many localities in the west.[18]

While about ten to fifteen per cent of Irish emigrants travelled abroad in the post-war period, the vast majority, both male and female, took the shorter and cheaper journey to Britain, where the recovering economy offered the prospect of better employment opportunities and higher wages than those attainable in Ireland. However, the ambitions of many male emigrant workers were still being stunted by lack of education and of the 43,000 young men who received travel documents between 1948–51, thirty-seven per cent gave unskilled labour as their work option, with a further thirty-one per cent going to agriculture and just one in five comprising skilled workers and clerks.[19] Among the 41,000 Irish female emigrants who received travel documents for Britain in this three-year period, over half signified their intention to go into domestic service or housekeeping, with roughly one-quarter going to factory work.[20] There was little change in the status of Irish-born male workers in Britain over the following twenty years, and it has been estimated that thirty-eight per cent were still employed as unskilled workers in the building industry as late as 1966.[21]

Nevertheless, some progress had been made in the education field in Ireland over those decades and by 1970 the number of Leaving Certificate candidates reached 19,000, a four-fold increase on the number for 1950.[22] Probably related to the rise in educational opportunities was the growth in the number of Irish-born graduates finding employment in Britain; by 1971 it was estimated that there were more Irish-born doctors and dentists working in Britain than were working in Ireland.[23]

Regardless of the increase of Irish-born professionals in Britain, the great majority of emigrants were like Seamus Dunleavy of Charlestown. He had

> always dreamed of England and the riches and the nice clothes. You would see them coming home with their gabardine coats, gloves, cigarette lighters and cigarette cases … So, in 1952, I went down Barrack Street, to the Square, and got on the Dublin bus, with my cardboard suitcase, and £6 in my pocket … I had never had a new suit in my life and never owned an overcoat. Fifth Class in school, no trade, but very strong and fit.[24]

Seamus made use of his physical attributes and mental strength to fashion a career in professional wrestling in England, appearing on the TV show *World of Sport* on a number of occasions in the 1960s.[25] In tandem with his sporting life, he developed highly successful business interests in his adopted city of Birmingham, where he lives today.

Conclusion

Ireland in the pre-Famine period was a deeply impoverished country. The post-Napoleonic era was one of economic stagnation, unemployment and misery, exacerbated by a number of factors not least of which was the decline in the linen trade and the ensuing loss of earnings. An expanding population – encouraged by early marriages and the subdivision of land – led to an increase in migratory labourers as marginalised smallholders sought to earn their rent money in Leinster or England. This growth in the number of migratory labourers in east Mayo is attested to by a witness from Killasser parish at the Poor Inquiry in 1835 who, in answer to the question 'What number of labourers are in the habit of leaving their dwellings periodically, to obtain employment, and what proportion of them go to Britain?', replied:

> Two-thirds I should suppose, or one-half, at least, of the men in this parish go to England for two or three months every season, to obtain employment. Many of them are married men. Some of the women and children mind the tillage at home, and provide fuel for winter; others are beggars through the country, and a burthen on the public.[1]

Lack of paid employment was the major reason so many smallholders and labourers sought work in Britain according to a witness from Killeaden parish [Kiltimagh] who gave evidence to the Devon Commission in 1844:

> It is the want of demand for labour that causes so many to go annually to England for the harvest, at the risk of their lives, and with certain injury to their health, and I fear to their morals. In some districts of this parish, [Killeaden] at an average, I believe nine-tenths of the male adult population go there every year. There is scarcely a house which there are not some gone from it, the younger men particularly … It is dire necessity compels them to go.[2]

The pattern of migration from Mayo, and east Mayo in particular, seems to have been well established before the Famine according to official records and contemporary sources. The most accurate early account of the movements of Irish migratory labourers is given in the census of 1841, where it is estimated that more than one-sixth of the total came from County Mayo alone. The confused perception which some migrants had of distance and familiarity is illustrated by William Cotton of Castlerea, who, when asked in 1844 if many labourers from that area had gone to work at the improvements on the Shannon, replied: 'Not immediately from here … the people that live here go generally to England. We are far from the Shannon works here.'[3]

The movement of agricultural workers to earn money in England each year may account for the anomalous increase in population in some east Mayo parishes after the Famine. The presence of much un-reclaimed land, early marriages and the practice of subdivision of smallholdings were still in vogue in east Mayo for a number of decades after the Famine and these archaic practices continued to be bolstered by migrants' earnings in England up to the late 1800s.

As well as the thousands of migratory workers going to the harvest in England each year there was also a steady stream of emigrants settling in England and even more travelling to the Americas before the Famine. Those migrants were usually people of means who could, in many cases, bring their families with them to their new homelands. However, in poor counties like Mayo, the first major movement out of Ireland didn't come until well after the Famine. The mini-famine of 1879–80 seems to have triggered off a big wave of emigration from the west of Ireland in the late nineteenth century, especially from County Mayo.

With regard to the migration of agricultural labourers, statistics and qualitative information became available through official reports published each year from 1880 to 1915. The 1880 report would lend itself to the conclusion that the number of agricultural migrants going to England from Mayo remained more or less unchanged between 1841 and 1880. Most of the conditions that encouraged migration were still present in the late 1800s: slow consolidation of farms, early marriages, sub-division of land, chronic underemployment and subsistence holdings. For example, in 1881 ninety-five per cent of farms in Swinford Poor Law Union (PLU) were valued at £10 or under and almost two-thirds of all the holdings in the Union had a valuation of £4 or less.[4]

An analysis of these reports, referred to above, shows clearly that the east Mayo area, which contains Swinford PLU, sent out more agricultural migrants per head of population than any other comparable area. In fact, in 1901, Swinford PLU, which had a population approximately one per cent of the country's inhabitants, sent out twenty-two per cent of the country's migrants.[5]

The characteristics of migration that were present in the decades pre-Famine were still present in the late nineteenth century and it could be argued that many of the same traits were still in existence up to the 1950s, when a significant number of migrants from east Mayo were still going to the 'harvest' in England. Migrants from east Mayo were overwhelmingly male and their choice destination was England, almost without exception, a tradition which was observed right up to the mid-twentieth century.

The type of work carried out by the migrants changed little between the 1860s and the 1960s, and, indeed, the accommodation offered to migrants in the 1950s hardly varied from that offered to their predecessors a hundred years earlier. Why did those small farmers and their sons persist with this toilsome way of life for so long? Different commentators have remarked on the dogged persistence with which smallholders clung on to their marginalised farms in the west and to their reluctance to leave the home place, regardless of the misery and distress visited upon them and their families for part of the year by this aberrant way of life. It has been suggested that the most likely reason that small farmers adopted this most peculiar lifestyle, spending half of each year away from their families and home, was a deep-rooted feeling for their home localities and lifestyle, which they didn't want to forsake permanently.[6]

In the book *The Great Hunger*, the attachment to home and place and the desire to be among their own kind is advanced as an Irish trait: 'The Irish have, in fact, always been a highly social people, gregarious above everything; their virtues are hospitality, good humour and wit. With an immense relish for the company of other people, they depend to an exaggerated extent on human intercourse, especially with other Irish.'[7] Micheál MacGowan from Donegal, who grew up in an impoverished part of the county, recognised the nature people had for one another in difficult times: 'There was friendship and charity among them; they helped one another in work and in trouble, in adversity and in pain and it was that neighbourliness, which, with the grace of God, was the solid stanchion of their lives.'[8]

At the beginning of the twentieth century, Horace Plunkett noted the importance of community and society in the lives of poor people:

> What the Irishman is really attached to in Ireland is not a home but a social order. The pleasant amenities, the courtesies, the leisureliness, the associations of religion, and the familiar faces of the neighbours, whose ways and minds are like his and very unlike those of any other people; these are the things to which he clings in Ireland and which he remembers in exile.[9]

VALUATION OF TENEMENTS.
PARISH OF KILBEAGH.

No., and Letters of Reference to Map		Townlands and Occupiers	Immediate Lessors	Description of Tenement	Area	Rateable Annual Valuation – Land	Rateable Annual Valuation – Buildings	Total Annual Valuation of Rateable Property
		CLOONCOUS. (Ord. S. 63.)						
1		Wm. Tarpy (Dominick)	Viscount Dillon	Land	5 0 11	1 0 0	—	} 2 5 0
2	a	Wm. Tarpy (Dominick)	Same	Land, house, and office	1 3 19	0 18 0	0 7 0	
–	b	Thos. Tarpy (Dominick) (See also 3 & 4.)	Same	House and office	—	—	0 10 0	0 10 0
–	c	Patrick Tarpy (John) (See also 5 & 6.)	Same	House and office	—	—	0 10 0	0 10 0
–	d	Thomas Tarpy (Michael)	Same	House and office	—	—	0 8 0	0 8 0
3		Thos. Tarpy (Dominick)	Same	Land	2 3 11	0 10 0	—	} 1 2 0
4		Thos. Tarpy (Dominick)	Same	Land	1 1 28	0 12 0	—	
5		Patrick Tarpy (John)	Same	Land	6 1 34	1 5 0	—	} 2 15 0
6		Patrick Tarpy (John)	Same	Land	2 3 35	1 10 0	—	
7		Thomas Tarpy (Michael)	Same	Land	7 3 31	2 3 0	—	} 3 0 0
8		Thomas Tarpy (Michael)	Same	Land	2 3 20	0 17 0	—	
9	a	John Tarpy (James)	Same	Land, house, and office	4 1 13	2 0 0	0 10 0	} 4 5 0
10		John Tarpy (James)	Same	Land	10 0 15	1 15 0	—	
11		John Tarpy (Dominick)	Same	Land	2 1 30	0 10 0	—	} 2 15 0
12	a	John Tarpy (Dominick)	Same	Land, house, and office	5 3 17	1 17 0	0 8 0	
13		Catherine Tarpy	Same	Land	3 1 26	0 8 0	—	} 2 15 0
14	a	Catherine Tarpy	Same	Land, house, and office	5 3 22	2 0 0	0 7 0	
15		Thomas Tarpy (Bartley)	Same	Land	3 1 32	0 5 0	—	} 2 15 0
16	a	Thomas Tarpy (Bartley)	Same	Land, house, and office	6 3 25	2 0 0	0 10 0	
–	b	James Tarpy (Bartley) (Also 17.)	Same	Garden, house, & office	0 0 16	0 1 0	0 9 0	0 10 0
–	c	John Tarpy (Philip)	Same	House and office	—	—	0 8 0	0 8 0
–	d	John Tarpy (James)	Same	House and office	—	—	0 8 0	0 8 0
17		James Tarpy (Bartley)	Same	Land	8 1 37	2 0 0	—	2 0 0
18	a	John Flinn	Same	Land and house	6 3 3	1 10 0	0 5 0	1 15 0
19	a	Patrick Tarpy (Philip)	Same	Land and house	10 0 19	2 18 0	0 7 0	3 5 0
20	a	John Tarpy (Philip)	Same	Land and house	8 3 8	2 5 0	0 10 0	2 15 0
21	a	Myles Grady	Same	Land and house	8 3 28	2 0 0	0 10 0	2 10 0
22	a	John O'Donnell	Same	Land, house, and office	12 3 8	3 8 0	0 12 0	4 0 0
23	a	James Tarpy	Same	Land, house, and office	17 2 7	4 15 0	0 10 0	5 5 0
24	a	Margaret O'Donnell	Same	Land and house	6 0 32	1 7 0	0 8 0	1 15 0
				Total	153 2 7	39 14 0	7 17 0	47 11 0

Fig. 13.1: **Clooncous townland as recorded in the Griffith Valuation, 1856.** (Source: Richard Griffith, *Valuation of the Several Tenements in the Union of Swineford* (Dublin, 1856), p. 42)

The communal spirit exemplified by the *meitheal* system – a support system of neighbours and friends in times of adversity – was still extant up to the middle of the twentieth century in east Mayo.

The intimate relationship small farmers had with their land and local area was not paralleled outside the west. The smallholders of east Mayo lived close to their neighbours because of the tiny farms they worked. Every foot of land was brought into production ensuring a close connection between farmer and soil. The intimate association of the landholders with the land and the environment is indicated by the naming of fields and places, streams and wildlife on their home farms and passing down this lore through the generations. Intermarriage linked communities and brought people together for weddings, baptisms and celebrations of different types. In times of family crises or family bereavements, friends and neighbours rallied round to give support and help. House visits and dances strengthened ties between neighbours and fostered interconnections – everybody seemed to be familiar with the 'seed, breed and generation' of everybody else in the locality.[10]

Clooncous townland, contiguous with the town of Charlestown, is a good example of the interwoven relationships which existed in many small communities in the west of Ireland in the late nineteenth century.

The culture that held those small farmers of east Mayo on their holdings has long since waned and from the 1950s on it became more and more difficult for parents to entice potential heirs to remain and rear a family on twenty-acre farms. Nevertheless, Garret FitzGerald would argue that Ireland still maintained 'a remarkable degree of family solidarity'. He estimated that one-and-a-half-million visits were made by emigrants to their families in Ireland in 2002 and in the same year more than one million visits were paid by Irish people to their families abroad.[11]

A steady stream of emigrants went to America each year from east Mayo in the early twentieth century, except for the duration of the First World War. However, this avenue to employment was more or less closed to them after the Wall Street Crash of 1929. The narratives in Part II illustrate the change of direction of many emigrants who were forced to seek work in Britain from the 1930s onward. The migrant networks built up over generations and reinforced year after year by agricultural and other workers from the east Mayo area swung into action and provided a fairly seamless transition for those seeking employment in Britain rather than in the United States.

The seduction of migratory work in England was still strong in east Mayo as late as the 1950s and 1960s. When the availability of farm work in England diminished in the 1960s, the beet campaigns offered an attractive alternative to smallholders or their sons, who had time on their hands during the winter months. However, even this type of work faded away as mechanisation took over. It might be said that migratory agricultural work, which employed many thousands of east Mayo men in England for at least 150 years, petered out in the 1970s.

Part II

1940–1970: Migrants' Stories

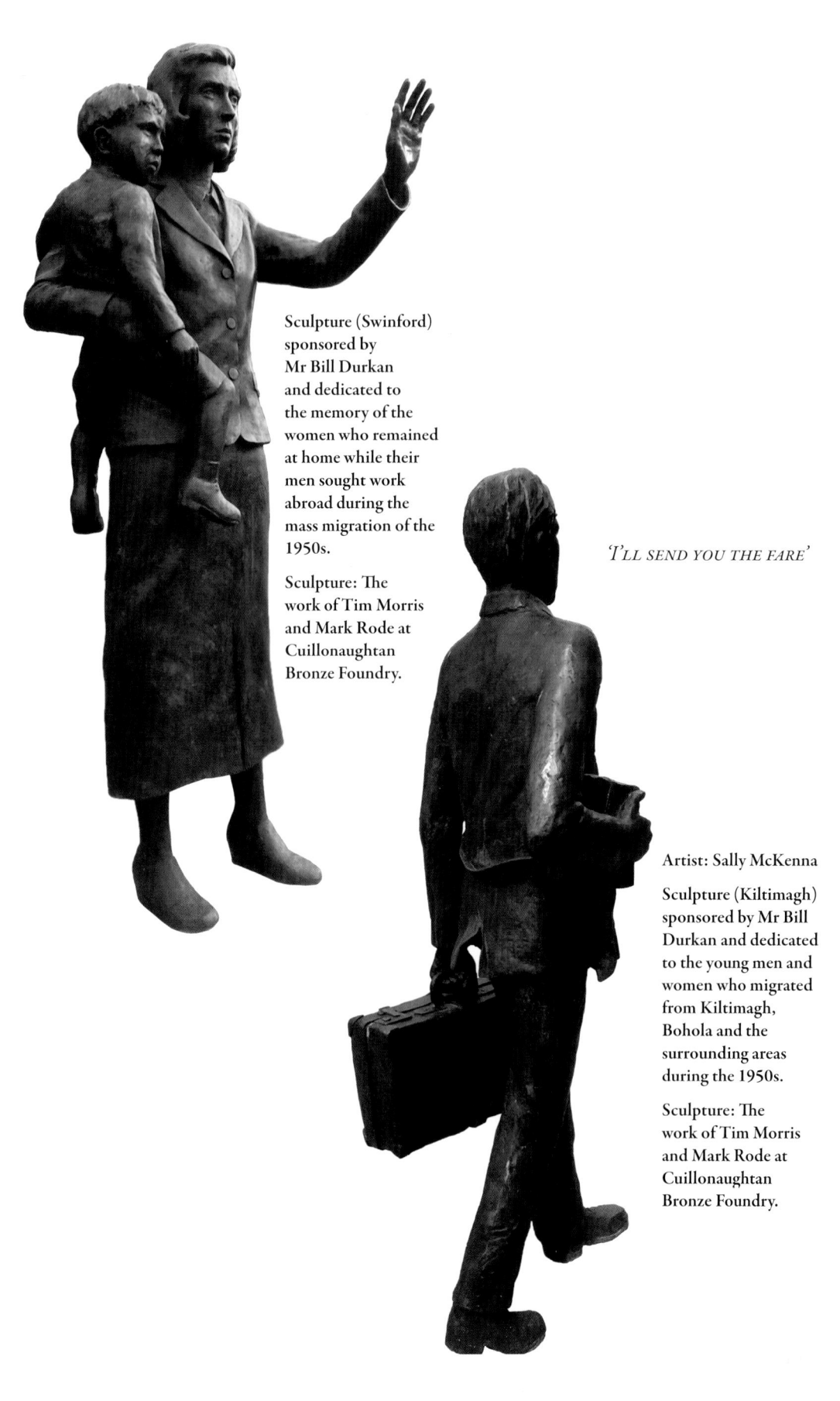

Sculpture (Swinford) sponsored by Mr Bill Durkan and dedicated to the memory of the women who remained at home while their men sought work abroad during the mass migration of the 1950s.

Sculpture: The work of Tim Morris and Mark Rode at Cuillonaughtan Bronze Foundry.

'I'll send you the fare'

Artist: Sally McKenna

Sculpture (Kiltimagh) sponsored by Mr Bill Durkan and dedicated to the young men and women who migrated from Kiltimagh, Bohola and the surrounding areas during the 1950s.

Sculpture: The work of Tim Morris and Mark Rode at Cuillonaughtan Bronze Foundry.

A Window to the Past

Single to Euston … single to Euston … single to …

There was a fairly long queue stretching to the ticket office. I was midway in the line carrying, like most others there, a cardboard suitcase and on my way to London to get work for the summer. A young lad in front of me caught my attention as we neared the office. He was talking to himself in a preoccupied manner and seemed to be repeating in a focussed way the same phrases over and over. Intrigued by his actions I watched and listened intently and suddenly the mantra made sense. He was repeating over and over to himself 'single to Euston, single to Euston, single to Euston …' so that he'd remember what to say when he got to the ticket office. The stark reality of life for emigrants from *Gaeltacht* areas hit home to me as I realised how lucky I was to have English as my first language.

I was being met by a relative who had a flat near Camden Town, and he had promised me work of some sort on my arrival. The flat was small, containing a double bed, army blankets, a stove for cooking, knife, fork and spoon each and a small sink.

The following morning in our work gear we hit the pick-up spot before seven o'clock. There was a line of men there before us, all waiting to get the nod. Murphy Cabling Company – well known among Irish construction workers – was our prospective employer. The transport lorry arrived, a ganger jumped out and walked quickly down the line – 'You', 'You', 'You' – he made his choice and those not hired walked away. About ten of us squeezed into the open-backed lorry and headed out to Luton, where a cabling job was underway. This was a spade-and-shovel job, the technical aspects of which would be very familiar to our motley crew. Some of the workmen made a cursory inspection of the storeroom when we arrived, looking for discarded clothes or boots which might be better than those they were wearing. Several sought 'subs' at 11 a.m. so that they could buy their first meal of the day. Subbing was a delicate art practised by some employers – calculating how much to give for work already done without losing the employee halfway through the day to a local pub. The shift was from 7 a.m. to 6 p.m., with a fixed wage of £3.

Fig. 1: 1950s cardboard suitcase. (Source: Jack Foley)

Our work that first day was to cut through the tarmac with picks and then dig out the heavy, yellow, sticky London clay with spades and shovels until we reached the required depth. All our group finished the shift with no one wandering off the job or being sacked. The next morning the same men appeared in the line-up in Camden Town and were rehired to continue on from the day before. Our crew was an eclectic bunch and exemplified the adage that each individual migrant has a different reason for migrating and a different story to tell. Many worked on a casual basis from week to week and day to day and some had lost touch with home over the years. One 'pincher kiddie' admitted that he had got as far as Holyhead on his journey home one year but was robbed of all his savings there and never attempted to return home again. I was foolish enough to offer him advice in relation to a job he was doing one day after developing a friendship with him. He raised the pick over his head and sank it in the ground within an inch of my foot, letting me know in no uncertain terms that he recognised one authority only on the job – the man who paid him his wages!

Many of the older workers were what was known in earlier times as 'eye servants' – they were exceptionally busy when the ganger loomed over them but were experts at taking a 'time out' when the coast was clear. One of the crew known as 'Wexford' (most workers went by their county names) entertained us and the London public each morning with operatic arias sung full-voice from the open-backed lorry on our way to work. He came from a professional family in Ireland but was forced to leave home because of psychiatric problems.

Some of Murphy's workers were employed by the day, cash-in-hand; they had no cards, no insurance, paid no tax and recognised no authority except their employer.

Most workers used Murphy's in the short term until they got on their feet and could find more consistent work and better conditions. I was fortunate in that I could leave at any time and return to Ireland to my permanent job. I had worked previously for several summers in London in factories and similar types of employment, but the hard, physical labour required by Murphy's ganger-men (among whom was the notorious 'Elephant John') added a new dimension to my understanding of working conditions in 1950s England.

It would be impossible to grow up in the east Mayo region in the 1950s without hearing all sorts of stories about life in England – not all necessarily true! I had four brothers and three sisters living in England by the early 1950s and scores of cousins, friends, neighbours who either went as migrants or had pursued a more permanent life there. Sometime in the early 2000s I began to realise that many of those early emigrants were now in their twilight years or even deceased without anyone chronicling their lives and work experiences in post-war Britain. My goal was to record the experiences of a cohort of emigrants from the east Mayo region, and this process began to take shape after I pursued a course in migration studies in the Mellon Migration Centre in Omagh. This course enabled me to put a formal shape on the process and to document in a structured way the experiences of these emigrants. Initially, I interviewed twenty-four people (as part of the migration-studies course), and I later expanded the research to a total of forty-four participants, recording all but one interview on tape.

The interviews, which took place between 2001 and 2015, were made by prior arrangement and usually took place in the interviewee's home and were between one and two hours in duration. Respondents were selected by personal contact through friends, relatives, acquaintances and so on. Finding candidates for interview was an easy task, as most people over sixty living in the area had been either migrants or emigrants at some stage in their lives. In order to record the varying life and work experiences of different categories of e/migrants, a sizeable cohort were interviewed. Many of those interviewed had been migratory agricultural labourers in the 1940s and 1950s who eventually settled back into their home farms after a number of seasons working in England. In more recent times (1960s and 1970s), sugar-beet campaigns in England offered an alternative form of migration to underemployed male workers from the east Mayo area, and many of those came home permanently after a number of peregrinations to Britain. A small number of emigrants who had settled abroad were interviewed while home on holiday in Ireland. Other interviewees had spent their whole working lives as emigrants but returned to their native area on retirement, providing another layer of diversity to the interview data. One interviewee, who for personal reasons did not wish to be identified, has been provided with a pseudonym, distinguished by an asterisk (*).

It is a source of disappointment that only twenty-five per cent of respondents are female, even though males and females emigrated from the area in roughly equal numbers. Women generally hadn't the option to return to the family farm and neither were they attracted to return and marry into a smallholding in the post-war period. The pull of home, strong though it might have been, was far outweighed by the prospects of well-paid employment, independence and a better standard of living in Britain or the US. Young girls, witnessing their mother's premature ageing as a consequence of the hardship and drudgery involved in ekeing out a living on uneconomic holdings in the 1940s and 1950s, were not inclined to follow the same path as interviewees testify. Because most female emigrants from east Mayo married abroad and remained there meant that there was a smaller number of females available for interview locally.

Oral evidence can be a valuable fount of primary information not obtainable from other sources and is a rich reservoir of tradition, culture and other aspects of folklife down to a micro level. Nevertheless, fading memories and a natural tendency to exaggerate or minimise aspects of the narrative prompt a cautious approach to such evidence The information provided by the interviewees often extended backwards from the 1940s and 1950s to earlier generations, incorporating parents and grandparents, and in this way some were able to provide insights into local migration or emigration stretching back to the early decades of the twentieth century. One way or the other, their stories illustrate how they saw emigration and their experience of it at the time they were interviewed.

The varied experiences recorded in the individual tales outlined in Part II give a flavour of what life was like in east Mayo in the mid-twentieth century and portray the life stories of some of those who left the country, either temporarily or permanently, during this period.

JACKIE DEVINE

'Anyway I got the start and the foreman asked me had I a shovel. You had to buy your own shovel that time.'

The tradition of networking built up over generations of migrants from the east Mayo area was of crucial importance in both gaining and retaining employment in Britain, especially at times of high unemployment such as the aftermath of the Wall Street Crash in 1929. Jackie Devine, who came from a small farm in Tullinahoo, near Swinford, belonged to a family in which the pattern of emigration/migration could be described as generational. Both his father, Michael, and his mother, Catherine, were emigrants/migrants. His father worked at the harvests and on the buildings in England on a seasonal basis for six months each year until he was sixty years of age. His mother spent six years in the US before returning home to marry in 1895. Furthermore, six of his seven siblings emigrated permanently to either America or England in the early decades of the twentieth century. Jackie, who was the second youngest of the family, was a migrant all his working life and managed to stay in employment in England from the time he went there in 1928, at sixteen years of age, until he retired home to Ireland in his late fifties:

> I went to England for forty-one years – all my life. My father had stopped going to England at that time. I went from Paddy Feeney's of Swinford [agent] to the sugar-beet company. Although I was only sixteen at the time, Paddy vouched for me. He knew I was a good worker. I used to meet him twice a week when I went in the four miles to Swinford with the donkey and creels to collect bread for our shop. Anyway two busloads of us set off to a place called Brigg in Lincolnshire. They were building two sugar-beet factories there at the time and they weren't quite finished so they put us working for McAlpine there until such time as the beet would be ready for pulling and when it was ready they sent us in twos and threes out to the farmers.

Jackie got his first taste of construction work in England in the building of those two factories. He was just a teenager at the time and was fortunate enough to be in a gang and with a foreman who made allowance for his youth and treated him with humanity and understanding in his first big job, as he recollects:

Fig. 2: Chapel Street, Swinford, *c.* 1930. (Source: Swinford Photography)

Maurice O'Shea and Maurice Towey were two Kerry foremen for McAlpine and one of my jobs in the morning was to make tea for the workers. They gave me two buckets and a bleddy big fire for drumming up for the two gangs. I had an hour to make that tea and an hour and a half to wash up. They [workers] used to give me a tanner [sixpence; three cent] on a Friday night when they got paid. After that hour and a half wash-up I used to have to get my shovel and work alongside the other men. I was allowed about three hours a day as a teaboy. Well now these two fellows [gangers] they were gentlemen to me and it was busy enough at the time. There were older men from round here [Swinford] working there, too, and they were very nice to me also, like. I couldn't grumble about anything the first year I went to England. I worked there for six and a half months and I came home for Christmas then.

As well as working piecework at hoeing beet and turnips, he was also involved in picking potatoes and pulling sugar beet in the short time he worked at the farmers:

It was all piecework. We were getting £12 5*s* an acre picking spuds. There were eight in the gang. We averaged two acres a man a week – about £4 5*s* each. You had to work out of your skin for that! We started at seven in the morning and in Lincoln and Cambridge the horses were pulled out at three. We got our dinner at three and then we went out spreading yard manure at five shillings an acre – a big fork in your hand. It would take two evenings anyway to spread an acre after your day's piecework [picking potatoes] was done. The farmer and his wife were very nice to us and while the accommodation was rough we had good double-beds and blankets and a big coal fire.

Did Jackie send money home to his parents?

I used to send thirty shillings a week home here that first year but I still had £25 in my pocket coming home for Christmas. After that you were making more money but if you were you were also meeting more people and spending more money.

In subsequent years in England, he was adventurous enough to follow wherever the work opportunities arose:

The second year over I went to the Peterborough area and worked there for a while and then I headed for London, you know. I was told to go to Croydon – that I'd find work there and after leaving the lodging house at 6 a.m., I was standing on the footpath looking either side of me when who came along in a lorry but one of my mates from Midfield. 'Jump into the lorry' he said, 'me and me two brothers, Pat and Dominic are working for this fellow – you might get a start in it.' I was dead lucky now to meet them fellows. Ned Campbell and the brothers Jim and Tom O'Hara were already working there. Anyway I got the start and the foreman asked me had I a shovel. You had to buy your own shovel that time. 'You'll have to get one', he said, 'and I had it got in ten minutes.'

While Jackie loved working in the construction industry and followed a very successful career there, his father enjoyed farming and spent most of his life as a migratory agricultural labourer:

My father used to go to a farmer every year and they used to send him £2 for the fare. He used to go for six months. He went twenty-five years to that farmer. Did he go after he was married? Why wouldn't he! He went up till he was sixty years, I'd say. I was the second youngest of eight and I remember seeing him coming from England myself many a time. He liked farming. There used to be a special gang from round here went tattie picking every back end. There was my father; my uncle, Tom Foley; Jack Dunleavy; Paddy and old priest Devine and Ned and Tommy Campbell. That gang went to County Durham every year to the farmers for years and years. My father used to work down there in County Durham and do a bit at the steelworks in the wintertime if he wasn't coming home.

Seeking employment in England and working there most of the year required a huge sacrifice on the part of both husband and wife. While the presence of family members dulled the pain of separation experienced by many migrants on their annual sojourn in Britain, the loss of normal family life left an emotional void, as he acknowledges:

I missed home at all times. I used to be lonesome going when the family were young. I used to come home as often as I could, you know. I used to get a voucher three times a year from Wimpey to Claremorris. I'd have a fortnight in summer-time and a week at Christmas. I'd be off early from work on Good Friday and be home [Swinford] Friday night. I'd send a wire to the wife from Dublin to meet me in town, herself and the gang. I'd be off again back to work on Easter Monday.

Networking was especially important in the 1930s when there was high unemployment in Britain. Jackie provided jobs for relatives and neighbours when he was in a position to do so in the Depression years:

There was plenty of labour in England and no work. It was very hard to get work. I was a ganger-man for Moran [contractor] when I was twenty-one and I never worked after that. I was foreman with McAlpine for a number of years but I left them and went with Wimpey. My last twenty-one years were with Wimpey. I did everything with Wimpey. I was in charge of a thousand houses in Yorkshire in 1949. They tried me out there.

On becoming a foreman Jackie had responsibility for employing men and many of those he found jobs for came from the Swinford area:

There might be an odd one here and there not Irish, but very little. The brother-in-law was a ganger up here and they were all locals with him. Butty Maye and Jim Colleran worked for me. I couldn't tell you all that worked for me – McNultys, Tom Smith the boxer, Tommy Regan the footballer (a good footballer, a good workman and a good plasterer) and Lavin, my cousin from over the road.

Jackie, himself, was a skilled Gaelic footballer and played for the Swinford club on the occasions he was at home and was selected for east Mayo on more than one occasion.

He retired home to Ireland, to his wife Mary and family, in the late 1960s. He was ninety years of age when he was interviewed in 2002. He took great satisfaction in his long retirement, which he often jokingly maintained was almost as long as his work life. Sadly he passed away in 2004.

JOHNNY CONLON

'Anyway they [the authorities] found out – they brought me to court – which was in Oakham …'

By virtue of their annual treks to England, sometimes to the same farmer, certain Irish seasonal labourers built up relationships and friendships there and if they remained single it was difficult sometimes to decide where to settle down finally. Johnny Conlon from Esker, near Swinford, who was a migratory worker for over thirty years was unequivocal about where he wanted to retire to eventually: 'Well I always thought at the end of the day, Esker was where I wanted to be.' Nevertheless, he enjoyed his annual work trips to England, both to the farmers and to construction projects.

In his work life Johnny moved around to many different areas in England but remembers St Helens in Merseyside with particular affection: 'I didn't want leaving St Helens. St Helens was more like home to me, short as I was there [two years]. I got to know an awful lot of people working there from Carracastle and other places.'

He also built up relationships with local people over the years when he worked at the farmers: 'Well when I was out the country then, out at Wakerley, near Stamford, there was hardly any Irish people out there – it was all English people. I was as well known there as … as pretty well as around Swinford.' He got on well with his English neighbours and found them 'lovely – if you were alright they were fine'.

Johnny first went to England at nineteen years of age to a construction job in St Helens. He went there because his father, Tom, was working on this job and *he* was there because his cousin, Pat McNeela, was a walking ganger on the job.

What were his expectations of life in England?

> As a matter of fact when I left Ireland I had no great expectations at all. The only thing I didn't know was the sort of work I was going to. I knew where I was going. I knew my father was working for Pat McNeela and I knew it was road making. The first job I got was shovelling concrete and that was hard work.

Johnny was familiar with the culture of emigration/migration as exemplified in his own extended family. He emigrated first in 1931 and for the next thirty-four years he spent at least six months of each year working in England, either in construction and/or at the farmers. He was an only son and the eldest of four. Two of his three sisters emigrated and eventually settled in Britain. The third sister didn't migrate and married locally. In his father's family of six offspring, two settled in England and three went to America and remained there. Tom himself, Johnny's father, who was also a seasonal worker, migrated to England each year for between thirty and forty years, before retiring to his home farm in 1949.

Tom Conlon migrated first to *his* father who was working in Yorkshire at the farmers in the early part of the twentieth century. He continued to go to England on a seasonal basis for the next forty years – going when the heavy work on his home farm was completed in April or May – and returning at Christmas when the farming season in England was drawing to a close. Johnny remembers his father coming home finally in 1949:

> My mother died in '51 and I think he didn't go back to England anymore after she died. He was going every year since I got to know him. His work was on farms except the couple of years he was in St Helens. He came back permanently a few years before my mother died because she was no longer able to do the work on her own.

Johnny's mother, Ann Durkin, didn't migrate and married relatively late, as he explains:

> She was thirty-two years before she got married because she got a job as a monitor [junior teacher] in Killasser school. She got the job because she was bright and had a good National school education. She was employed by the head teacher. She didn't want to get married because she knew if she got married the few shillings would stop.

Love, however, seems to have won out in the end and she and Tom married in 1910.

It had always been Johnny's ambition from a young age to follow his father to England:

> Well, when I was growing up [in the 1920s] – even before I left school I always thought I'd look forward to the day I'd be leaving school and going to England. There was a lot of my neighbours going to England and I thought that something great was over there, something that I'd like to see and be a part of. They [returned migrants] would have a nice white shirt and a couple of ties. If you were here you wouldn't have that.

He had contacts in America as well as in England but these were the Depression years and it bit deeper in America than in England and he found himself attracted more to England than the US:

> I had an uncle and two aunts in the United States and they used to keep in touch with my father. It was too difficult to get the money to go there unless you had friends in the States good enough to bring you out. I couldn't go to America because my father hadn't the money to send me there. I didn't care about going to the States anyway. My first preference was England.

During his time as a migrant, Johnny was employed both at the farmers and in construction work. He was a seasonal worker with the same farmer for over twenty years. He remembers following a set routine over that period. 'I used to come home and do the work in spring and as soon as I got the spring's work done – my father and the girls [sisters] – took over and carried on from where I left off.'

In his early years in England he moved between farm work and construction work as conditions determined. He would generally go to the farmers first for beet or turnip hoeing:

> If it was turnip hoeing now myself and Pat Rowley [brother-in-law] … we used to hoe eighty acres between us. The rate for hoeing turnips was a shilling [six cent] a row. A row could be one hundred and twenty or two hundred yards long. Do as many rows as you could in a day – work as many hours as you wanted in a day – all piecework. However if there was a better job on the buildings we'd go into that. We'd spot opportunities and we'd take them. A better job or more money would have us moving.

Johnny was kept more or less in constant work during the 1930s but conditions changed dramatically for Irish workers when the war started. He recalls how the pressure to join the army was quite persistent:

> The year the war broke out there was little or no work in England. If you went into a labour exchange looking for work you were told 'join the army' and who wanted to join the army? My mates and me got letters to call into the local police station in England to register. All my mates went home but I stuck it out. I was working at the farmers at the time and I got a letter from the farmer to say I was needed on his farm. I was supposed to stay working on his farm and of course being an Irishman – a chancer – I went into public works as well. The money was more sure anyhow

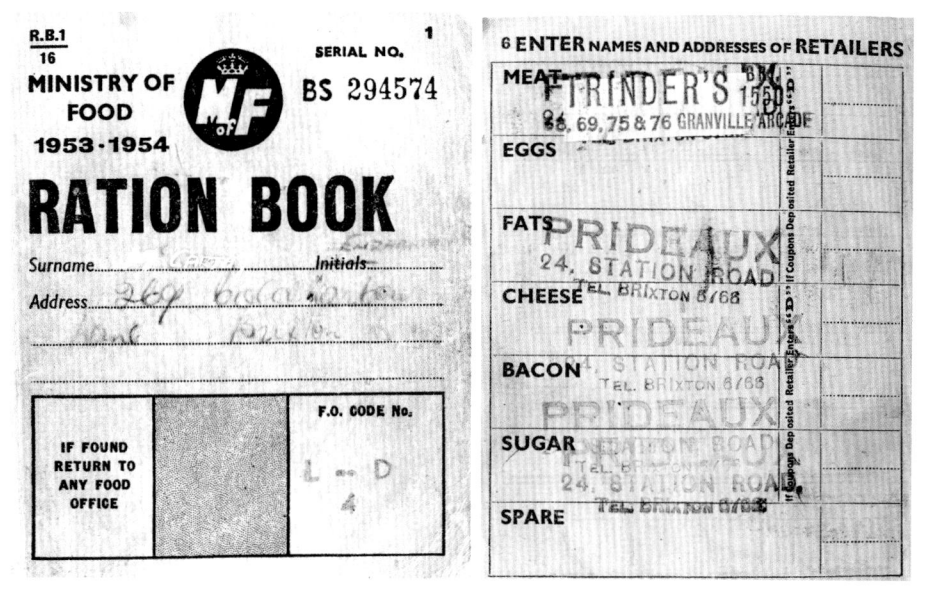

Fig. 3: British ration book.

in public works but the working conditions could be harder than at the farmers betimes. That was during the war.

While he managed to avoid conscription he soon found himself in trouble with the authorities with regard to food rationing. In that period and right into the 1950s, workers, especially those engaged in hard manual labour, found the issue of food rationing hard to deal with and Johnny thought he had solved the problem, as he relates:

> There was ration books at the time and I got a ration book when I was in public works and I got another ration book as a farm worker. Anyway they [the authorities] found out. They brought me to court – which was in Oakham. Of course I played it ignorant – awful ignorant! I got away with it – with a caution.

In the 1950s and 1960s Johnny returned to the same farmer year after year until he came home finally in 1965. There was piecework available on the farm from late spring to December between the hoeing of beet, the picking of potatoes and the pulling of beet:

> My last job in England was pulling beet. That was in Wakerley, Oakham.

> The nearest town to me was Stamford. I worked for twenty-three years for this Charley Gilman. Myself and Pat Rowley [brother-in-law] worked for the same farmer. He had two farms. One of them was 1,800 acres. Beet and spuds were the only crops he grew.

Living conditions on the farm were comfortable by the standards of the time, as he recalls:

> Accommodation, when I was working with Gilman was fairly good – even though we had only one room [bed-sit]. It was nothing like the kip houses – no – not at all. I had a good bed (I never shared a bed) and free heating. Anything that grew on the farm was free to us – milk, potato, vegetables etc., a big open fire for cooking and plenty of pots and pans.

At fifty-three years of age he decided to capitulate to his father's pleading and return finally to Ireland: 'My father wasn't getting any younger and his preference was for me to stay at home. He was on his own and he had four cows and fourteen or fifteen dry stock to look after.'

Johnny never married and returned permanently to his native locality in 1965. He took over the farm and continued farming well into his senior years. He was still in good health at ninety-two years of age when he was interviewed in 2004.

JOHN MULROY

'Irish men were the worst men you ever worked for. The English men would have some pity on you.'

John Mulroy was born in 1911 in Lisbrogan, Swinford and was another emigrant/migrant from east Mayo who worked in England during the Depression years. All of John's siblings, except his sister Kate, had emigrated to either England or America before the Depression. John stayed at home to look after the farm and saw England as his best prospect for employment and money while still keeping in touch with home. Contacts in England and networking were of huge importance in finding and keeping jobs during the 1930s. John describes how a gang of workers from his home area got employment when they first went over:

> Four of us went. There was this man, Tom Loftus, he was used to going. There was a man from back here – Carrowreagh – in the parish of Meelick. He was a contractor in England. Patsy Gallagher was his name and he got us all started. Páid Quinn – he was from back that way – a ganger-man – I was working for Páid. I was working for some of Patsy Gallagher's nephews, too. They were ganger-men.

Like many of his peers, John sent money home to his parents: '£2 every fortnight. All the time I was away. And even the family that went to America, the cheques 'd come at Easter and Christmas.'

John wasn't lonesome for home or disappointed at being away: 'Oh no, I wasn't … I wasn't fainthearted like that, do you know. Because with all the company you hadn't time to be. It was like being at home. There were lots of lads there I went to school with up at Lislackagh.'

Outside men from his own locality, he hadn't much respect for Irish contractors: 'Irishmen were the worst men you ever worked for. The Englishmen would have some pity on you. He wouldn't put you down, but some of the Irishmen, they'd want to get a name for themselves.'

While John's experience of Irish contractors in England soured his perception of his countrymen as employers, there were instances of good relationships between Irish companies and their employees. An example of the rapport which could exist between employer and employees was the firm of Martin Duffy of Charlestown. Each year during the 1950s Duffy's company provided a fully funded outing for all

Fig. 4: Martin Duffy (employer, standing, sixth from left) with workmen and families on their annual outing in the mid-1950s, paid for by the company. Sitting, right: Tommy Doherty (Charlestown) (employee), his wife and daughter Angela. (Source: Seamus Bermingham)

his workers and their families. The photo shows Martin Duffy and his employees and family members on their annual outing *c*. 1957.

John remembers the first time girls started going to England rather than to America. Even in the 1930s there were lots of Irishmen and women in London where John worked:

> There was a pub there called The Crown. You'd meet an awful lot of Irish men and girls there. That was the time the girls started going to England, too [1930s]. Even round here now there was a lot of girls from up the village there, going. What did they work at? Factories or housework – Oh yes, they'd do any job.

Before the 1930s most Irish emigrants went to America rather than to England, and this was true of John's own family:

> I had two sisters went to America. There was better money in America. I had four aunts in America at the time and I also had a step-uncle there. Yanks used to send a 'package' to a lot of people that time. Like one aunt now she brought the first one [John's sister] over [to the States]. She sent a 'package' – a ticket to her and when that girl got work then she'd send

a 'package' to her next sister or brother. That's how it worked out that time. Oh they were very keen that time, looking after their own family.

Stepwise migration from England to the US seems to have been a popular method of going overseas for men. Migratory workers could save the fare to America if they so desired after a couple of seasons in England, as John explains:

All the young fellows 'd always have a year or two in England before they'd go to America. There was nothing here at the time. They used to get finer jobs in America. They'd get as much in a week in America as they'd get for a month in England especially if they had any education.

Inheriting the home farm was no longer an attractive proposition for many men, even in the 1930s, when a better living standard was available just a short distance away in England. However, it is clear from the interviewees that a substantial proportion felt obligated to return to the home farm to support aged or vulnerable parents, who were no longer able to look after themselves. After nine years going back and forth to England, John eventually settled back on his holding near Swinford: 'I couldn't go [back to England]. 'Twas a case of having to stay because there was no one here but my mother then, you see. She was getting on in years. [My brother] came back several times but he wouldn't stay.'

PHILIP CONWAY

'For everyone there was work for, there was twenty people for the same job.'

Philip Conway, from Lisheenabrone, worked as an apprentice carpenter in Swinford in the 1930s before he went to England: 'I got no money until my last year [as an apprentice] when I got the very big salary of one shilling [six cent] a week and I must tell you I was still the richest of the lads round the area because nobody had a shilling that time.' He sought work locally after completing his apprenticeship and even though there was a big number of houses built in rural Ireland in the 1930s he was unsuccessful in his quest for employment, as he explains: 'For everyone there was work for, there was twenty people for the same job. Carpenters were getting £2 10s a week in the Thirties and that was big money if you had work.'

He recalls his experience of emigrating to England in 1936, at just eighteen years of age. He went to his father who was working there for Wimpey:

> I went on my own to my father. There were local lads with me to Holyhead but we separated there and I went to a place called Gateshead-on-Tyne where my father worked. I got there on Saturday and I was at work on Monday. He had a job waiting for me.

Having a job during the Depression years, when so many were unemployed, was much appreciated by Philip, as he recalls:

> There was no use complaining about anything because there were fifty men for every job and you just had to put up with the conditions no matter how bad they were – until work got a bit better or you had a few pounds in your pocket. I cannot understand young people today saying they're homesick or bored – you don't know you're born! [how lucky you are]. As soon as I put my feet in England and got my first week's pay – £3 12s, I thought 'that's great now'. I gave my father so much for my room and board and I'd go to the post-office every fortnight and send money home to my mother. I never had no problems in England.

Philip soon found his feet and was making great money – over £5 a week as a carpenter – soon after he went over. He stayed about a year there before he left to work on a job in Carlisle, even though his father, his brother and his sister all worked in Gateshead.

He was still working in England when the war broke out and recollects his involvement in massive construction projects connected to the war effort:

> When the war came there was plenty of work for everyone no matter where you went. I worked for a while in Carlisle and from there I went to South Wales and worked for a firm who were building a great big munitions factory. I stayed there for about four months and I left there and went with two other fellows – Mick and Johnny Keane. They came from Ennis, County Clare and they'd got word of a big job in Stoke-on-Trent and the three of us went there to suss it out. I never seen anything like it! It was a massive, massive size. It was fifteen miles round the site. There were thousands of men working there between labourers, carpenters, plumbers, sheet metal workers, electricians, steel fixers, steel erectors, etc. I worked there for about a year and while I was there I got friendly with a lad from Stoke-on-Trent. We were working together and he got made charge-hand and then he got made foreman and he made me charge-hand. We got on well together. Then I got called for the army. I was supposed to register at the office but I didn't register. I didn't go in the army – I went to Coventry instead. Coventry was a good place for work. There was a lot of bomb-damage work. Soon as you'd come home from work in the evening there was nothing but air-raids – air-raids! That was 1940–41.

Employment opportunities for Irish emigrants opened up in England as the war progressed and in the post-war period the demand for labour increased substantially. The Irish appeared to be drawn to particular jobs and to certain regions in England. Philip reflects on that period:

> There were very few Mayo people on the jobs I worked. They were only in certain areas or certain jobs. That big job I was on in Stoke-on-Trent, I don't think there were twenty Irishmen on that job. If you went to work in Warrington in Lancashire it was full of Irishmen from round here [Swinford]. There was another big job in Chorley in Lancashire … there wasn't a house round here that didn't have men working in that job. McAlpine or Wimpey would transfer them from one job to another so they always had work.

As a youngster growing up, Philip had always wanted to go to the States. However, he was deprived of the opportunity of going there because of the Depression in the 1930s and the war in the 1940s. Going to England was not a daunting experience for him as he had plenty of knowledge of what life was like in England from his father on his visits home and from migrant neighbours:

> I never remember my father when he wasn't going to England. As long as I remember he was in England, you know. When I was a kid, your father would be coming home for Christmas. Even though he worked on the buildings he'd wait at home and do all the spring work. A fellow would write to him and bring him over later in the year and he used to work up around County Durham. He was a plasterer's labourer – carrying the hod but he was elevated to ganger on other jobs. He had travelled round most of the north of England, from one place to another. When times were bad you'd go from one place to another to see could you find a job. He went to County Durham and Gateshead 'cause that's where he went when he was going to *his* father. A lot of the old-timers used to go to Middlesbrough to the steel mills and those that didn't work in the steel mills worked in the coal mines. Very few went to the farmers. There wasn't much farming in County Durham. An awful lot of them went to the coal mines especially from up around Midfield [Swinford]. There wasn't that much building earlier on and if you got a job in the coal mines you went to the coal mines – one [person] brought the other. Midfield men went to the coal mines and down around here, Lisheenabrone [Swinford] they went to the farmers. You'd go wherever there was work – you had no option.

The custom of sons travelling with their fathers before making the journey on their own was well established in migrant families. Philip describes the tradition of migration in his own family:

> None of us ever went to the farmers. My father never went to the farmers because *his* father never went to the farmers. They'd work around the coal mines – my grandfather and my father worked around the coal mines. My father was only sixteen when he went to the coal mines to my grandfather.

Looking at the movement of his uncles, aunts and siblings gives a good insight into the migration history of Philip Conway's extended family. His father, who was a seasonal worker in England most of his working life, had five siblings, three of whom emigrated to America – one emigrated to England and one married locally. On his mother's side he had six uncles. Three of those married into local farms and were seasonal migrants to England for between forty and fifty years. One uncle emigrated permanently to County Durham in England and settled there. Another uncle spent two terms in America before returning home to buy a farm and retire. His sixth uncle farmed his home place and while he worked as a seasonal worker as a young man he didn't migrate after marriage. Of Philip's own siblings, all seven emigrated to England and spent all their working lives there.

The pattern of seasonal migration was well established in Philip's own townland of Lisheenabrone in the early-to-mid-1900s, as he describes:

> The fathers would be going to the farmers every year – going in May or June and coming back after the beet was pulled in November and December. Would they be doing this after they were married? Oh God yes! – the only way you could live. In some houses here in the winter-time there'd be five or six in the family. In summer there'd be no one. And then eventually in the Thirties when they started working on the buildings and staying there [England] they didn't come home at all. And these would be more or less the farm labourers because the miners didn't have to come home – they could work all the year round.

Philip was in no doubt as to the reasons his own family (including his mother) emigrated during the 1930s and 1940s. Was the main reason economic? 'Migration for economic reasons? We never heard them kind of words. Starvation, more likely – hunger, no money, no work. Everybody went – boys and girls.' As well as the poverty there was also the influence exerted by returning migrants. 'Most of the people of our generation you'd hear them coming off the bus talking about Camden Town or Manchester or Birmingham and you always wanted to go. But I always wanted to go to the States. I had an awful lot of cousins and uncles in the States.'

As a skilled tradesman, Philip worked in construction all his life, while many of his neighbours went to the farmers. Consequently he was familiar with the harvesters' joke about 'the landlady making the bed with the fork'. So what was his assessment of the standard of accommodation offered in England to workers in the cities and towns in the 1930s?

> We were better off than the people who worked on the farms. When the Irish labourers went over, the cattle went out of the barns and that's where you slept. The accommodation in England didn't bother us. The water might be running down the walls but it never bothered you. You were brought up to it – sorta rough and tough. From living at home we were well used to the conditions. You had no bathroom and no electricity [at home]. People were brought up that way.

It was very common at that time to be sleeping two to a bed and sometimes three, as he acknowledges:

> The Keane brothers from Ennis and myself had been walking the town looking for a place to stay and this landlady told us she had only one bed left and we said 'Fine' and the three of us shared the bed for a week until I got another digs across the road and I stayed with her for a year.

Philip worked in England between 1936 and 1947. However, after the war ended he fulfilled his ambition of going to the States leaving his father and most of his siblings behind him in England. He had cousins and uncles in America and moved first to Canada for two years before entering the States in 1949. He worked there for over thirty years before he retired. He then completed the circle by returning to Ireland with his wife Peggy to spend his final years in his home town of Swinford.

STEPHEN FARRELL*

'You felt very embarrassed … the first time away from home, with strangers and everything and to be there in a line naked along with all these guys.'

Stephen Farrell, from the Charlestown area, went to England for the first time in January 1944 at age nineteen. He had worked for several summers previous to this, saving turf in a local bog. There was big demand for turf in Ireland, as a substitute for coal, during the war years and much-needed employment was provided on many bogs throughout the country to cater for this market. Stephen was one of many workers in the Charlestown region who appreciated the employment provided, as he acknowledges:

Fig. 5: Corthoon bog. (Source: Jack Foley)

* Pseudonym

Fig. 6: Charlestown railway station.

> What was I doing before I left home? I was emptying turf lorries below at the [train] station. It was wanted at the Phoenix Park to give to the people of Dublin … It was coming from Corthoon bog, and coming in from Cloonmore and up Kilgarriff and all the different places. We used to get four shillings, Jack, for emptying the lorry of turf. Now that was between four of us … that was the going rate. We were kinda on piecework. So the more you emptied the more money you got. I suppose, Jack, you could put down an average of ten shillings a day [wages]. That's ten lorry loads in the day. The fellows now abroad in the bog, they were filling the lorries and they got five shillings to fill it and we got four shillings to empty it. I'll tell you, Jack, I was getting more money when I was at home than I was when I went to England. The rate in England when we signed on was 1s–2½d an hour.

The big drawback to this type of work was that it was only seasonal – at most six months in the year – so Stephen set his sights on England. Local agents for English firms were offering year-round employment at good wages with plenty of overtime, so he decided to give them a try:

> We signed on, signed the contract with Paddy Feeney. Paddy was the agent

that time. When you signed the contract with Feeney your name was sent away and a voucher came back and a badge with the firm's name on it and a number. The firm I went with was G. Walker and Slater. In Holyhead when we landed, there would be a shout – 'G. Walker and Slater men this way.' Another gang would follow John Laing. 'Wimpey this way' and another gang would follow Wimpey. You had to go where they sent you. You had no choice. I was sent to help build an aerodrome and runway in Norfolk in a place called Diss. It was an advantage to be away from London and the south coast where there would be more bombing.

However, before he got to Diss he had to undergo a fumigation process in London, which he remembers vividly:

We landed at Holyhead and we were transported by train up to London. Liverpool Street station [London] was the venue for bringing you to Diss. The day we landed we were brought to a big hostel. 'Twas a hotel turned into a workman's hostel and we got a bit to eat there. Next thing they told us we had to strip off and we stripped off and there was a big line of men maybe fifty or sixty in a line and two men came with hoses, one in the front and one in the back and dosed us with this fumigation stuff they put in the water. You felt very embarrassed ... the first time away

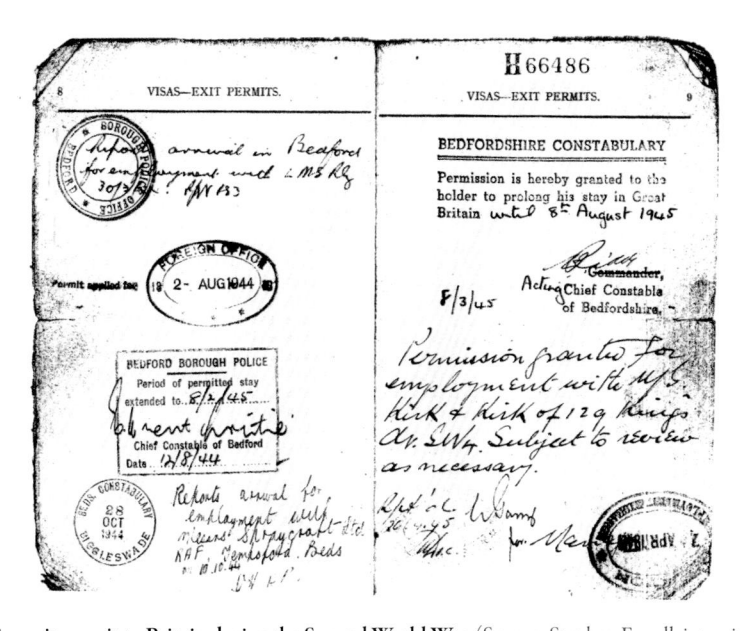

Fig. 7: Visa-exit permit to Britain during the Second World War. (Source: Stephen Farrell, interviewee)

from home, with strangers and everything and to be there in a line naked along with all these guys.

The fumigation process that Stephen Farrell underwent in London was a consequence of an outbreak of typhus in the west of Ireland in 1943. To reduce the spread of the disease a delousing programme was initiated, which allowed the process to be performed on the migrants either in Ireland or Britain.

Mr James Deeny, chief medical adviser to the Department of Local Government and Public Health, witnessed the procedure at Dublin's Iveagh Baths, where he described hundreds of naked men milling about as they were hosed down and bathed with disinfectant in an atmosphere that reeked of abasement. He noted that 'the atmosphere of shame, fear and outrage was easy to feel'.[1]

Stephen Farrell remembers clearly the atmosphere in east Mayo during the war years when thousands of young men and women were 'taking the boat'. He describes the procedure used for recruiting workers and organising the transfer to England :

> That time everyone was going to England nearly. Feeney [agent] was sending away sixty or seventy men every day of the week except Saturday. You'd go up to Nan Moffitt's … up there in Chapel Street [Charlestown]. You'd look in the window there to see and there'd be a list of men – about fifty men – Monday, Tuesday. And she'd put more fresh ones in Wednesday, Thursday and Friday, telling you which day you were going and which train you were catching.

Living conditions for him and his co-workers when they reached their destination were disappointing. The accommodation consisted of Nissen huts, with twelve people sharing each hut. The bed clothes were damp when the workers arrived and the heating was completely inadequate – one small stove was supplied to heat each hut. Stephen paints a dismal picture of the general living conditions in the huts:

> To wash ourselves we had to go to a separate building – a wash-house – that'd be maybe a hundred yards from your hut. You brought your towel with you, washed yourself and came back again. That'd be about half-six in the morning. As well as that the grub was very bad. You got auld horsemeat and sure you didn't know what it was. When you were hungry you ate it. For your tea break in the morning you got a slice of bread and jam at a penny a time.

In the circumstances, a food parcel from home was much appreciated: 'I used to get the *Western* [local newspaper] every week. My mother used to send it and she'd put in a bit of ham, you know, in it and wrap it up.'

Stephen knew the type of work he was going to and wasn't fazed at the thought of hard work:

> When you went to this firm you knew they were building an aerodrome – they were building a runway … levelling concrete and digging trenches. Them times there were no JCBs or anything like that, you know. They were all hand-dug – the trenches.

Nevertheless, he was disappointed with his weekly earnings in his first few months in England which more or less mirrored his wages in Ireland: 'You'd have to work a long week to earn £3. You'd have to do overtime or Sunday work.'

After the war there was big money to be made working on bomb-damaged buildings and he describes how some workers used the system to enhance their earnings:

> There were chancers who went into London as carpenters and roofers and slaters and painters making big money. Every six weeks on the bomb damage you'd get a travel voucher, you see, to go back to where you came from. Some firms gave you the ticket. Other firms gave you the money. By getting the money you were getting maybe fifteen or sixteen pounds. You'd say you were coming from the furthest ends of Scotland – from Inverness or somewhere like that. That was good while it lasted.

He was employed on different types of jobs after the war when you could choose where and for whom you worked: 'You went to where the money was. I got work on the railways as a plate-layer. You were always sure of Sunday work on the railway. You got an extra few pounds on the Sunday shift.'

One way of meeting people from home was after Mass on a Sunday, as he relates: 'It depended whether you were on Sunday work or not. If you were on Sunday work you'd meet nobody. I used to go to church in Camden Town on Arlington road and you'd be looking around for this one or that one to see what news they'd have.'

Stephen enjoyed both his work and his social life in England but after about seventeen years as a migrant he decided to come home finally because of his mother's illness: 'My mother got sick or I never would have gone home.' It was a deciding factor for him but once he had made the move home he had no regrets and lived contentedly as a single man in his home environment until his death in 2009.

MARY (WATERS) GANNON

'My father and mother were always longing for her to come, do you know. They were absolutely longing for that letter to come to say "I'm going home."'

While the vast majority of people interviewed for this book were e/migrants, Mary Gannon from Montiagh in south Sligo was neither and spent her whole life within a radius of a couple of miles of her birthplace. Mary was born in 1923 and experienced at first hand the hard times and straitened circumstances experienced by the majority of the population during the 1930s and 1940s. Unemployment was high, wages were low, opportunities were few and big families were still the norm in rural areas. These dispiriting conditions prevailed and were exacerbated in the 1930s and, as Mary remembers, 'making do' was an important feature of survival in the east Mayo–south Sligo region at that time.

Like most of her contemporaries, secondary education was out of her reach for diverse reasons, such as cost, transport, and so on:

> It was a very odd one got secondary education. Schools weren't local that time and people didn't have the transport to go to them. A while after that then people had bicycles and they would be able to go to Charlestown when the convent opened up or to the Tech. in Tubbercurry. But we didn't have bikes either [that time]. Odd ones had them, but then the war started and everything was tight, you know – you could only get two ounces of tea and half a pound of sugar a week [per person] and you were lucky if you got that. We thought we'd never see food plentiful again. If the tyres got worn on your bike – sometimes the tyre came off the wire and we used to sew it on and it would go for another couple of weeks. That's the gospel truth, Jack. You'd sew it with a darning needle and thread. You know the thread that'd be in a flour bag. The women used to rip the flour bags and bleach them – take the brand [name] out of them. 'Cause the brand that time was written on the cloth, you know. They'd wash them and they'd boil them in washing soda and put them out on the hedge so that the sun and the bleach would get at every corner of them and they'd come out as white as snow.

Mary spoke of the different uses flour bags were put to:

> Oh, make sheets [from them] or underwear for the women or pillowcases or little things for the kids. Or they used to maybe make aprons out of them. They'd dye them, you know – dye them black or blue or whatever. The bags for Indian meal were used to make bag aprons. Bag aprons were used for carrying troughs, pots of spuds etc.

Although she had no paid employment as a young woman she was kept busy caring for two grandmothers, doing chores in the home and working in the fields when necessary:

> I worked at home, in the bog, moulding [earthing up] spuds [with a shovel] and doing all that kind of thing. I'll tell you what kept me at home, I'd say, apart from meeting my husband or boyfriend at that time. My sister went to live with one of my grandmothers and she was with her from once she was nine years old till she went to America at eighteen and when she went to America I went to stay with her [grandmother]. The other grandmother lived at home with us. So my mother couldn't watch the two. People weren't put in [nursing] homes that time. So I used to wait with my grandmother at night and then go back and help my mother with the other granny and work in the fields as well.

What effect had the emigration of an only sister and daughter on Mary and her parents?

> Peggy went when she was only eighteen. Yes, we were very lonely and my father and mother were very lonely and my grandmother – she was devastated altogether. She [Peggy] didn't come back for thirty years! She went on the last day of July, 1939. We went to Galway with her. She emigrated from Galway that time. They used to go out on a tender to get to the big boat. She was gone for thirty years. Of course the done thing that time was to save as much money as they could and send some home and all that. It was a different way of living to now!

Mary points out the advantages of living in one's own locality with parents and extended family close at hand:

> Well I was happily married and I had a big family and I was near my parents and they came to visit me and I was able to go and visit them and I had a happy life. My sister [Peggy] came back [on holiday] in 1971

– after all those years! My father and mother were always longing for her to come, do you know. They were just absolutely longing for that letter to come to say 'I'm going home.' She came and spent a week or a little more with them. And then she came a couple of years after that but they were dead at this stage.

Describing the farewell party the family and neighbours had for an intended emigrant to America, she recalls:

They used to have – 'A Farewell' – they used to call it, for anyone going to America. Now I hear people calling it the 'American Wake'. Down our ways they called it 'A Farewell' which I think is a nicer name for it. And they would all gather and have music and everything. There'd be dancing and drink – a drop of poteen, you know, on the quiet and a cup of good strong tea, I suppose. Home-made butter and home-made bread – that was all the go at that time. This would be all during the Twenties and Thirties and that, and I'm sure, before that.

Mary's brother, Pat, went to England as a migratory labourer before and during the Second World War. He was forced to abandon those seasonal trips due to ill-health probably caused by the substandard accommodation provided by the farmer. Mary recalls her brother's migration experience:

Pat went with some neighbouring men that used to go, you know, every year. We'll say '38, '39. He came back when the war broke out and he went again in '42 maybe '43. He didn't go after '43. He had pleurisy actually that year when he was in England. He was very sick and you know that time they used to live in old barns … the doctor sent him to hospital for a while. He got over it, Thanks be to God.

Mary married in 1947, and she and her husband Patrick had eight children. Unlike previous generations, her family found work in Ireland and consequently were able to provide comfort and support to her and Patrick as they entered their senior years. There were features of life in Ireland which Mary felt would be hard to replicate overseas – the strong familial ties in the extended family and the powerful community bonds supporting family friends and neighbours in the locality. This, in Mary's view, could not be replicated anywhere else.

MARY (FOLEY) DEVLIN

'They were so unhappy they ran away and they went down to their father who was working at the farmers and the police brought them back.'

Mary Gannon and Mary Devlin were second cousins, born within two years of each other and though they never met, the villages in which they lived were only two miles apart. Their lives diverged in their formative years, and while Mary Gannon spent her whole life in Ireland, Mary Devlin spent all of her working life in England, where she still lives. Mary emigrated from Corthoon, Charlestown in 1943 on the promise of a job as a trainee nurse from a local nun who was in contact with a hospital in England and acted as a recruiting agent for this hospital. She had just completed three years of secondary education in Miss Cahill's ill-fated private school in Charlestown.

Mary was the second eldest of nine children and it was inevitable she would emigrate, like her peers in the locality. At just seventeen years of age she left for Edmonton (London), where she had been accepted on a nurse-training course. She was accompanied by an older female neighbour who was also seeking work in London. Even at that stage of the war many Irish people were finding employment in Britain. 'Everyone was going to England. You knew that's what you were going to do 'cause everybody was going. The oldest children definitely had to go then.'

Leaving Ireland in the 1940s, 1950s and 1960s was much different from leaving Ireland today. Back then it was seen as a more permanent decision, with the possibility of returning once a year for a holiday if circumstances allowed. Communication was by letter and contact between the emigrant and home for those whose writing skills were weak could be infrequent. Emigrants' experiences in the middle of the twentieth century stand in stark contrast with those of the well-informed emigrants of today, who have cheap transport and a multitude of communication systems enabling them to stay in contact with home on a weekly or even daily basis.

Parents seeing offspring emigrate in those earlier years understood well that only a small number could aspire to return permanently, because of the chronic unemployment in the west. Mary understood this, too:

> I think mother broke her heart when the children left and I being a mother now myself understand what she must have gone through. I know when Tom [brother and eldest of the family] went she was broken-hearted. But they [parents] hid their anguish from us. For my own part

the first year was probably the hardest, 'cause you're green; you don't know anything; you have no one to talk to, you're on your own and you're very, very homesick.

She found her work as a trainee nurse was very different from what she had expected and she hated every minute of it. Her training began in a private nursing home:

They were moneyed people who were in there – but they were all more or less dying. And we had to clean them – and we had no training whatsoever. There were one or two cases of, like, venereal disease that we had to deal with. We weren't fed very well – the food was terrible. Two girls from above Swinford who came over the same time as me – they ran away. They were so unhappy they ran away and they went down to their father who was working at the farmers and the police brought them back.

The National Society of Children's Nurseries
Carnegie House, 117, Piccadilly, London, W.1

Nursery Nurses' Diploma

This is to Certify
that

Mary Foley

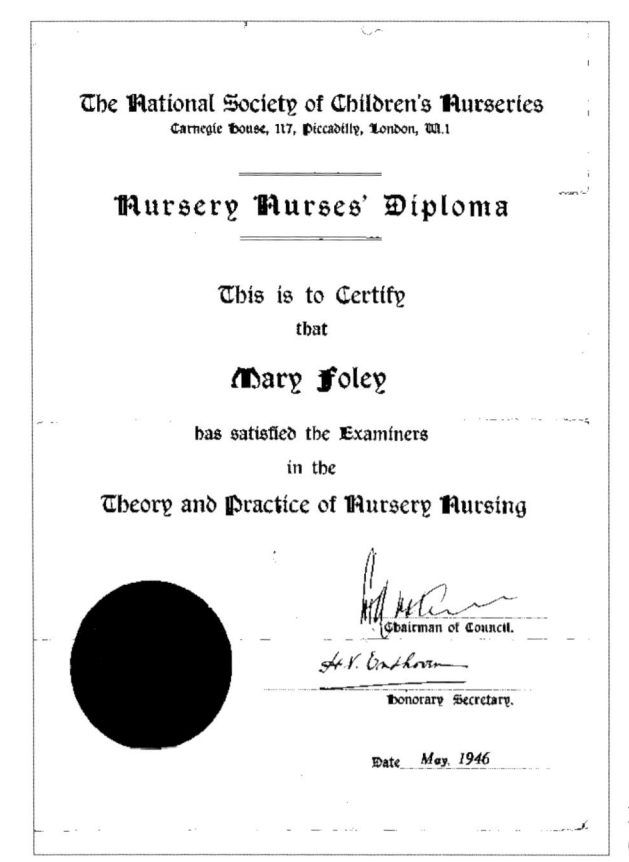

has satisfied the Examiners
in the
Theory and Practice of Nursery Nursing

Chairman of Council.

Honorary Secretary.

Date May 1946

Fig. 8: Nursery nurses' diploma.
(Source: Mary (Foley) Devlin)

As already alluded to, Mary had been sent to this hospital through the patronage of a local nun, who, on being told of her discontent got her released from her contract. Instead, through a network of contacts, she got employment as a nanny with the family of an American officer in the Irish Guards, a Captain Grant:

> I got twenty-five shillings a week and my keep and all I had to do was look after the couple's two children from morning till they went to bed at night. Actually that was a lovely job. Then my brother Tom came down from London and I got itchy feet and I went back with him. When I went up to London, I got a job in an office, no bother. I could do shorthand and typing and bookkeeping and all that. I don't think I was great at it but they'd take anyone that time [1943]. Then you had to go to the labour exchange to sign on to go to these jobs.

However, she was told in the labour exchange that she hadn't the right to pick and choose jobs and that if she didn't go back to the hospital she was originally sent to, she would have to take their choice of factory work 'or go back to Ireland!' She agreed to take the factory job, but putting caps on lipsticks was not a very challenging occupation and she went back again to the labour exchange, this time with more positive results:

> I'll never forget it – one week in the factory, Jack, sitting on a seat putting tops on lipsticks, hour after hour. I went back [to the labour exchange] and I said 'Alright, I'll do whatever you want' and they said 'There's a hospital in the east end of London – a children's hospital, and it's very nice, would you go for an interview?' That's where I spent most of the war – in this children's hospital. All the trainees stayed in a hostel and they paid me – where they didn't pay the English students – because I was from Ireland – twenty-five shillings a week. I was the only Irish girl in my group.

After two years as a trainee, Mary graduated with a nursery nurses' diploma. This diploma opened up opportunities to her and she secured employment fairly quickly:

> I went out then and took this job in the Green Man [pub] looking after these two little boys and I was there for a while but you see it was a pub so I lived upstairs with the children. You were looking after children – putting them to bed and you had no social life. I could hear all the great time down in the pub and I wanted a bit of life.

Mary threatened to leave but was persuaded to stay by being offered a job as a wine waitress in a select area of the bar: 'It was after the war and everyone was drinking. The best time of my life … And you were treated as one of the family, you know. I did that up till I got married to my boyfriend, Patsy, in 1948.'

Life in post-war England was difficult for many people. There was a housing deficit and food rationing was still in place. Mary found this period, up to the mid-Fifties, the most trying period of her life. She and Patsy lost their accommodation in 1951 after she became pregnant. Rented accommodation was almost impossible to find, especially if you were pregnant and more especially if you were Irish and pregnant:

> We walked the streets every evening after work looking for a place to live. Eventually after three months and when I was seven months pregnant we found a tiny, unfurnished room up three flights of stairs in West Kensington. We paid 32*s* and 6*d* a week for this flat, which had no running water. You had to go down to the first floor to a communal bathroom if you wanted to go to the toilet. If you wanted water to wash or clean or cook, you had to haul it by the bucket up two flights of stairs. I had to rear my first-born child, Stephen, in these conditions. We were there for twelve months before we managed to get improved accommodation with our own toilet. This was like heaven to me because I had my own kitchen and toilet and we no longer had a cantankerous landlady shouting up the stairs to 'keep that child quiet!'

This new two-roomed flat became too small after a few years, as the now increased family (Stephen, Tom and Una) grew up:

> We had to reorganise our sleeping arrangements, Patsy sleeping in one room with the two boys and Una sleeping with me in the other room. This put pressure on both Patsy and me and I went to Ealing Town Council to see could I get a bigger flat. I explained our position to an official and the first question she asked me was 'Are you Irish?' and when I said 'Yes', she said 'You have to go to the back of the queue.' I explained our situation again but all I got was a shrug. Some years later, in the mid-Fifties, while we were still in this flat, Patsy had a bad accident at work and was assessed for disability benefit. The following years were the worst of my time in England. We now had to live on family allowances and Patsy's disability income as I couldn't work because of the children. It was a very tough time and it lasted over five years until our compensation claim was finally

settled. This was one of the best days of our lives as we were able to buy our own house and get back to a normal family life.

While her husband Patsy eventually went back to work after rehabilitation following his accident, Mary felt it was important to be a stay-at-home mother during her children's schooling and she left the workforce for a long period of time: 'When I was expecting Stephen [first child], I left the job at Christmas and never went back to work again until Stephen was fifteen years old.' Mary's first job, after this lengthy period out of the workforce, was as a waitress in a dining room for managers in Wall's. She worked there part-time for over four years. Then a vacancy arose for a nursery nurse in a local primary school and she applied for the post, as she relates:

> A job was advertised in a local school and I went for interview and got the job. It was the best thing I ever did 'cause I got a pension out of it that went back to when I worked during the war. In addition to that I was delighted to get the opportunity to get back into the type of work I was trained for. I worked in this school for fifteen years – until I retired – and I loved it. Forty pre-school children came into our school each morning and forty more came in the afternoon. We had a staff of four to look after the children – two nursery nurses and two teachers. I used to start work at half eight and finish at quarter to four.

Mary retired in 1985 and she and her husband Patsy moved from London to Luton to be near their daughter, Una. Patsy sadly passed away in 2001. Mary returns to Ireland on holiday each year, where she visits her extended family, friends and neighbours, and still calls Mayo 'home'.

JOHN WALSH

'You were busy all the time and you were among people and you hadn't much time to be thinking about home.'

Many of the bogs in east Mayo and elsewhere provided summer work for adults and teenagers during the war years and while young people could also be employed on the home farm, it would almost certainly be without remuneration. John Walsh, from Coolrawer in south Sligo, worked in the bogs saving turf in 1942, when he was just fourteen years of age:

> I worked at the bogs with Bord na Móna and also did a bit at the land. I went working in the bog on my school holidays – we used to have six weeks and I had earned £12 at the end of the six weeks. The bog was here at the back of the house. They were short of coal and they used to get the turf here and send it off to Dublin and different places. They used to draw the turf with horses and carts in to Charlestown and send it off [by train] to Dublin. We used to wheel out the turf in the wheelbarrow at the time they were cutting it and then of course it had to be turned and footed and brought out then with the donkeys – out along the road and there'd be a crowd of men looking after it on the road – piling it up and all that sort of thing.

John was the second youngest of a family of seven and all his siblings had emigrated, except one, by the time he left home in 1951:

> I migrated to Lincolnshire – Scunthorpe in Lincolnshire. That was my first stop. All my pals had more or less gone and I said 'I'll see what it is like, too.' I should have waited at home, I suppose, because my father was more or less an invalid at the time. He was very bad with arthritis. I had a younger sister – she was at home, too.

It wasn't essential for him to go to England to earn a living. His father's farm was over eighty acres, enough, as he acknowledges, for a number of families to survive on before consolidation – 'there were six families reared where I am now'. However, he was tempted by a friend who was working in England: 'It was a pal that was already in England. He was home on holidays and he was going back and I travelled back with him.'

He was very disappointed with his first impressions of England:

> I thought everything would be great there. I got a bit of a shock when I landed there first, to see the place the people were living in, like. It was these huts, you know. They were like army huts. They were galvanised right to the ground. There'd be eight beds inside but it would be only one room – they weren't partitioned off at all. And there was a stove in the middle of the room where you could light a fire in the cold weather. There was no privacy whatsoever. It was bed after bed. And then there was all the black blankets as well – army blankets. This wasn't the farmers – this was Public Works!

The first job he worked at was in a steelworks plant in Scunthorpe, Lincolnshire:

> The work wasn't too bad, like, you know, when you'd get used to it. Making-over roads and digging bits of trenches for pipes and all that. Then I worked another while in a cooling tower. I liked that. But then they [firm] moved on when that job was finished. I could have gone with them, alright, but I didn't like leaving. I knew a good few around there and I didn't know anybody who was going. If there was anybody I knew at all who was going I'd have travelled with the firm but I didn't at that time.

Scunthorpe is at the centre of a large farming area in Lincolnshire, so John and a few workmates decided to engage in farm work for a few months:

> It was August the time we went down to the farmers. Usually they don't go into the farmers until about late September or early October for the late spud-picking. We went down at that time for the early spud-picking. These early ones would be put into bags right away and be sent off in lorries. But the late ones, then, these were put into pits and left there for the winter.

The back-breaking work didn't seem to worry him:

> The day wasn't too long, you know. We started soon after eight and we were finished at five o'clock. We were getting £8 an acre that time [1951] for the spud-picking at the back end. I'd say if you'd do [pick] two acres in the week it'd be as much. It depends then, like, on how heavy the crop was.

In his seven-year sojourn in Britain, he spent only one season at the farmers:

> My last job in England was what they call pile-driving. I spent most of my time at that work. We used to bore holes in the ground, on average about twenty-five to thirty-five feet. When we had the hole bored we had to put steel in and fill it up with concrete. Whenever we had a job finished we'd move on to the next job. We used to travel with the firm. We used to travel to a lot of different places. I liked that work, now, I liked that work … it was in Wales we finished up. I worked a good while in Wales – Port Talbot, Cardiff and round there.

What did John think of his accommodation? 'I found them alright [digs]. The beds were good enough in it. Sometimes you might sleep two to a bed but mostly you'd be on your own. The standard of accommodation wasn't too bad.' (See Ch. 8, p. 103 for John's view of accommodation at the farmer's.)

As well as enjoying his work-life in England, he savoured the social aspect of life there, too – going to clubs and dance halls with his workmates was the main activity: 'No I wasn't ever sad. No I was quite content, like. You were busy all the time and you were among people and you hadn't much time to be thinking about home. I was satisfied enough. I was quite content in England.'

While he was pleased with his life in Britain, John, nevertheless, returned to Ireland permanently in 1958 to take care of his widowed mother and assume control of the home farm. He married Theresa a few years later and settled down to life on the land until he retired some years ago. His retirement allowed Theresa and himself to indulge themselves more freely in their favourite pastime, dancing.

Three of John's older sisters worked in munitions factories in London, during the war years and despite the hazards they faced on a daily basis, they had an ambivalent attitude to returning home:

> 'Twas tough old going for them alright. They used to have to go out many's the time at night and go to the air-raid shelter. That was the worst part of it. Oh, it was very frightening that time. Sometimes they wouldn't go to the air-raid shelters at all. They'd take their chances. They'd go under a big table or maybe a bed or something, hoping that the stones or stuff wouldn't fall on top of them. No, they didn't [think of coming home]. There was no work [at home]. I think that was it and they were having a fair good life there and they were collecting a bit of money.

After surviving the war years in Britain, two of John's sisters left England and with their Irish-born spouses emigrated to Australia, where they settled permanently. Two more of his sisters worked in England for a number of years but returned to live and work in Ireland with their Irish husbands. Only one of John's siblings did not emigrate. She married a local man and lived all her life in Ireland. John's only brother worked in England for seven or eight years before emigrating to Australia, where he spent five years before returning to his home area in Ireland to marry a local girl and settle down.

MICK FOLEY

'You got £7 a day to knock down a section of a building. We used to knock it down in a day with sledgehammers.'

As already noted, many men from the east Mayo area got work in local bogs, cutting and saving turf during the war years and Mick Foley from Corthoon, Charlestown availed of those employment opportunities for a number of years before the work finally dried up shortly after the war ended. Seeing little prospects locally he and three neighbours – Mick Burns, Tom McIntyre and Eddy Gallagher – set off to the farmers in England in May 1946. The four separated after landing and Mick ended up in Boston in Lincolnshire on his own. He worked that year for a farmer outside Boston – hoeing beet, pulling peas, picking potatoes – before he returned to Ireland in late autumn. His accommodation with this farmer was typical of the time: an empty shed without heating or cooking facilities. Nevertheless, this didn't stop him returning the following year:

> Myself and Jim Colleran [neighbour] went back there again. The next time we went back, mind you, we were still in the shed but we had a fire in it! The farmer fixed us up with a shed and a fire (a stove) so that we could have a fire and cook on it. At that time of the year – it was winter – you couldn't have stayed in the shed without a fire.

While the money was good at the farmers, it was hard earned. He describes the long hours and the intensity of the work and gives an example of how good his workmate was at this type of job:

> A better worker over there than he was in Ireland! Oh he'd go mad stooking wheat. He'd be going round running for the sheaves. Running all day long – no time to relax. The stooks were chucked up any old way at all as long as you got them up. Morning to night. We made good money alright but we worked very hard.

Before the next batch of piecework started, Mick's companion left and got a job on the railway:

> He used to go into the pubs – I used to go to the pictures – and he got

to know blokes in the pubs. So he got a job on the railway. The farmer said he didn't want me on my own so I went with another bloke, riddling spuds for a different farmer. After that we got in with this fellow – a builder. He got us [work] cards and that's where I ended up – in the buildings in Stamford. We lived down in the field in a tent then. We got digs in the end in Stamford, myself and this lad from Swinford – Páidín Moore.

Living in digs was a new experience for him and the house rules imposed by the landlady became a problem: 'No smoking in the room and we had to be in at ten o'clock at night. One night we didn't come in until two o'clock in the morning so she ran us then.'

The work Mick did on the buildings was typical preparatory labour, taking the scraw off the site and digging trenches: 'It was piecework and Joe Moore from Swinford was the ganger on that job. There were five or six working for him. I don't know what happened but myself and this Limerick bloke went away to Nottingham on our own, sometime in the middle of the year and went working on the railway – taking up old lines and putting down new lines. That was heavy work and all, yeh!'

In 1948 Mick came home and because of ill-health, didn't return to England until 1950. On his return he found work much harder to come by than he expected, as he recounts:

Myself and Patrick Durkin [neighbour] set off the next time. When we came [to England] we went to Nottingham. We couldn't get no work. No matter how we tried we couldn't get no work. Both of us were broke and we went to Paddy [brother] in Grimsby. He was in public works building houses. So he put us up. I was working at the same job as Paddy for two months, I think and then he went away to the farmers. He wanted me to go with him and I told him I'd never go back to a farmer again and I never did. I didn't like farming work anyway. He went off and I got another job with a pile-driving crowd. They were doing a bridge in Derby. When that job was finished we left there and went to Harwich. I was getting a lodging allowance there. I stuck with this firm and kept getting the lodging allowance. It was only fifty bob [shillings] a week but it was good. I worked with them for years then. Pile-driving was their game more than anything else but then we moved to London and started pulling down buildings. I was making £7 a day there. That was great money – piecework. You got £7 a day to knock down a section of a building. We used knock it down in a day with sledgehammers. It only lasted about two months. I went from there to Southampton. We were

Fig. 9: Workmen at Gravesend, Thames Estuary, 1952: front: Joe — (Bohola), Mick Foley (Mayo), Hughie — (Donegal); back: crane driver, unknown, Dick — (Cork), Pat Clarke (Monaghan), Barry — (Offaly), Seán Henry (Sligo). (Courtesy Kathleen Foley)

only there a fortnight when we had this job in Gravesend to come to. That was another pile-driving job. When that was finished we all packed up. The whole gang walked off Millers' [firm] over a bonus that wasn't coming up. We went down the road to Fareham and started another job. Sometime later I went back to Millers again. The old ganger [in Millers] got after me – he said 'There's a job for you here if you want it.' So I went back to Millers. We went to Luton first, pile-driving for these offices. The airport was just starting up then. From that we went to Stevenage building a new bridge over the railway. After that we went back to Southampton and we worked at pile-driving there.

Digs in England in the 1950s and 1960s were of variable quality and it was not uncommon to 'shift' beds under some landladies. This entailed a person on a night shift sharing a bed with a person at work during the day. Sleeping two to a bed was more or less obligatory and this involved, on some occasions, two strangers getting into the same bed. 'It was always two to a bed. You wouldn't get a bed to yourself. I slept in between Jim Colleran and Mikey Ted Stenson [neighbours], two big blokes – in the middle of summer! You'd be that tired you'd sleep no matter where you were.

You were glad to lie down anywhere.' Many interviewees spoke about their digs or lodgings, sometimes with venom at their perceived shortcomings, or with praise where they were happy with the standard. The impact of these lodgings was so profound that quite a number of the interviewees could still recall at this remove the names and addresses of the landladies with whom they stayed. Mick Foley, without hesitation, could list fourteen addresses where he stayed during his first ten years in England:

- Boston, Nr. Peterborough, Lincolnshire
- 115 Lambeth Walk, Stamford, Lincolnshire
- Ketton, Stamford, Rutland
- 12, Dryden Street, Nottingham
- 327, Rutland St., Grimsby, Lincolnshire
- 71, Grisborne St., Derby
- 87, Bristol Rd., Gloucester
- 12, Church St., Harwich, Essex
- Greenwich, London
- Onslow Hotel, Southampton
- 6, Pier Rd., Gravesend, Kent
- Eaton Green, Luton, Bedfordshire
- Monkswood, Stevenage, Hertfordshire
- 52, Springfield Rd., Totton, Southampton

Sending money home was a tradition which was adhered to by many migrants right up to the 1960s and Mick followed this custom, albeit reluctantly:

> I used to send nearly every penny I earned, that time. I was earning good money at the farmers then. I sent money home for years. Everybody sent a few quid home. Well it was drummed into your head. You were brainwashed to send money home and that was it. You never thought to do anything else. You just kept enough to keep yourself going.

After many episodes working with farmers, in construction, on railways or pile-driving, he got a job with the city council in Chiswick, London, where he worked for about two years. He then worked in a nearby factory that manufactured television sets, and he was employed there for a further two years. His final move was to Tottenham, where he worked for almost thirty years with an engineering company called TI (Tube Investments), from which he took early retirement in the late 1980s. He lived out the remainder of his years in London with his wife Kathleen and daughter Catherine. Sadly, Mick passed away in 2008.

PADDY PEYTON

'You didn't mind hard work when you were getting the money.'

The similarity of the migration narrative between one generation and the next emerges in many of the migrants' stories told in this book. The migration experience of Peter and Paddy Peyton (father and son) from Tumgesh, Swinford, is an instance of such similitude. Peter Peyton's life story is an example of the inconstancy and uncertainty that pervaded the lives of many migratory workers. He was born in 1878 and worked as a migratory labourer at the farmers in England in the early 1900s. He continued to migrate after marriage until the untimely death of his wife at forty-nine years of age. By this time he had a family of twelve young children and eschewed further migratory work until his family was reared. He did, however, return to England to work in a munitions factory in 1942 and didn't come home finally until 1944. Paddy Peyton, like his father, worked at the farmers and in factory work as a young single man in the 1940s. However, he returned home to Ireland in the early 1950s, got married and didn't go back to work in England until his family had grown up. He returned to England in the 1970s to work in the beet industry, mirroring his father's late sojourn to work in the war effort in Britain in 1942 when he was in his early sixties.

Paddy tells of remaining at home looking after the family farm until his father finally returned to Ireland in 1944. He recalls why he first went to England:

> The agent came from England to Paddy Feeney's [Swinford] a couple of times a year. You put down your name if you wanted work. They sent me to Birmingham. I worked in a factory – an aircraft factory – where they used to make sheets for covering the plane. We made everything there, even the propellers. It was hard work – hard work surely – twelve-hour nights and twelve-hour days – six days a week. That time the wages on the night shift ran about £5 10*s* to £6 a week. You had a higher rate at night than in the day but in 1944 the tax came in and sure you paid half of it in tax.

There were plenty of other men from the locality going to England at this time but Paddy went independently:

> I went on my own. There was a crowd you know from other parts, not out

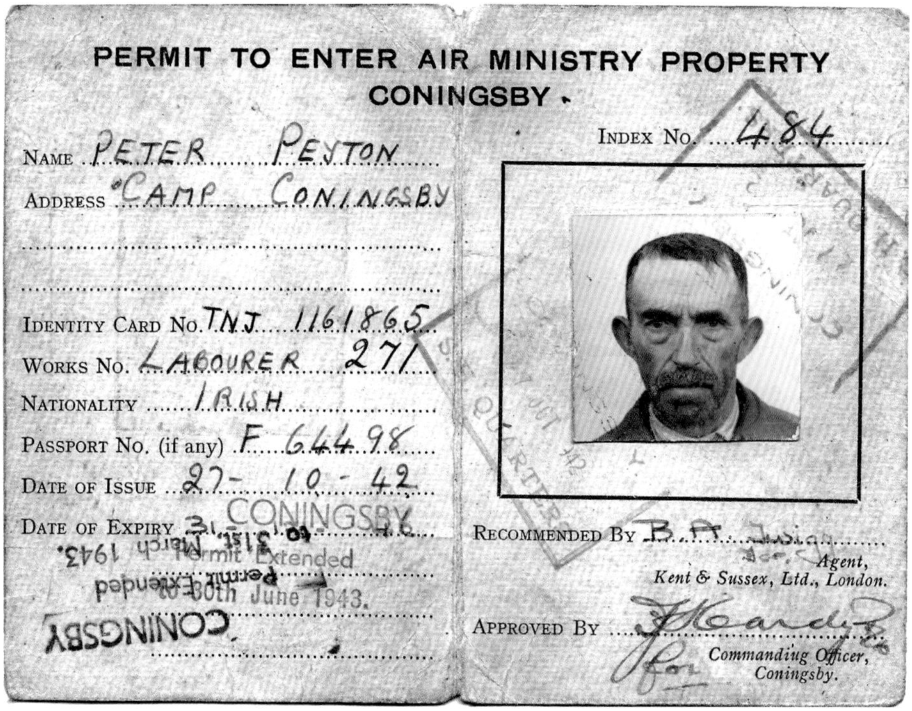
PERMIT TO ENTER AIR MINISTRY PROPERTY
CONINGSBY.

Name PETER PEYTON

Address CAMP CONINGSBY

Identity Card No. TNJ 1161865

Works No. LABOURER 271

Nationality IRISH

Passport No. (if any) F 64498

Date of Issue 27-10-42

Date of Expiry

CONINGSBY Permit Extended to 31st March 1943.

Permit Extended to 30th June 1943.

CONINGSBY

Index No. 484

Recommended By ... Agent, Kent & Sussex, Ltd., London.

Approved By ... Commanding Officer, Coningsby.

Fig. 10: Work permit of Peter Peyton, 1942. (Source: Máirín (Peyton) Noone)

> of Tumgesh but above from Carrowcanada, Kilbride, all going together – ten, fifteen, maybe twenty. Other parts of the country, too – Kerry, Clare – from every part. You went where you were sent. The firm paid the fare.

What expectations had he of life in England? 'I thought I'd make money and be rich. There was nothing in this country.' He remembers how bad conditions were in 1940s Ireland and how difficult it was to get employment and how poorly paid it was:

> I worked for 3*s* 4*d* [twenty-one cent] a day. That was the Land Commission or the Council. That's all they paid, and then along with that, they only gave you three days a week – about 15*s* 0*d* [ninety-six cent] a week. You wouldn't get fat on it. Ah, no, they were hard times. You couldn't get the work. That'd be around '39 or '40.

After a year working in the aircraft factory, Paddy returned to Ireland and the following year [1946] went back to the farmers in England with his brother-in-law.

'We paid our way and went over on our own. We went to a farmer and asked him for work. Between harvest and beet there was always work at the farmers then. They could get no one else to do it. The English wouldn't do it.'

Paddy supported the anecdotal evidence regarding the quality of accommodation at the farmers: 'You slept in the car shed. Pull out the car, put in a bed of straw and we slept in it. Straw thrown on the ground and a bag over it – that's where we slept. There were rats in it, too!'

Food was scarce during the 1940s, even at the farmers, as he recalls:

> You cooked the food yourself. You had a little electric stove. We used to bring the spuds home and boil them. You could eat as many spuds as you liked free of charge but you had to pay for milk. When the farmer went to the market at the weekend he used to bring bits of bacon and herrings and mackerel to us. You're telling me we'd be hungry – very hungry. In the middle of the day you'd be very lucky if you had a sandwich with you. That time you couldn't get bread because of rationing. You done with very little.

Regardless of the inadequacy of their diet, he and his brother-in-law worked pulling beet piecework through the winter of 1946 in Lincolnshire. It was hard, unrelenting work, as he describes:

> Twelve hours a day – as long as there was light. 'Twas piecework – £5 an acre – I remember it well. If you done an acre and a half a week you were working hard. The two of us worked together and we could do three acres in the week. £15 divided – £7 10*s* each.

Between his time in the aircraft factory and a couple of seasons at the farmers, Paddy spent about three years working in England in the mid-1940s before returning home. He settled back into his home farm and got married in 1952 and didn't return again to work in England until 1973, after his family was reared. He was fifty years of age at the time, but was lured back to England by the relative ease of finding good employment in the sugar-beet factories. He acknowledges he had good living and working conditions in the factory and the wages were commensurate with the work done:

> I spent eight years in the beet factory. Oh, I liked it there. There was money there. You were inside all the time. Oh God aye! I was old when I went there the second time. I was twenty-seven years at home here until

the family grew up and then I went back again and I done eight more years. I was happy at the beet factory. Good money and looked after. I had a couple of good campaigns. As well as working my own shift – I used to do a second shift. I often done two double-shifts. I often worked 16 hours a day and for that 16 hours you got [paid] 20 hours. I liked it there. You didn't mind hard work when you were getting the money. Getting the money and well fed.

As already noted, Paddy was one of a family of twelve children and it is instructive to see what happened to his other siblings as they reached maturity. His two oldest sisters emigrated to America in the late 1920s, while still in their teens. Because of the stringent regulations imposed on prospective emigrants to the US after the Depression of 1929, Paddy's other siblings, including five sisters and one brother, all went to England and settled there permanently. It is not too difficult to imagine the huge sense of loss visited on their father (a widower) as he watched successive members of his family leave home, some never to return. The real tragedy is that this was a common experience in many households in east Mayo in the 1930s, '40s and '50s.

Paddy and his wife Mary, both now deceased, were more fortunate than previous generations in that their children benefitted from the educational opportunities that became available in Ireland from the mid-1960s on. Their sons and daughters were able to secure employment in Ireland and in the vicinity of the homestead and this ensured that Paddy and Mary Peyton had the support and companionship of their family throughout their lives and into their senior years.

TOM MORLEY

'A fellow from the town would be no bleddy use to you. He wouldn't stick it an hour.'

Another migrant from the Swinford area was Tom Morley of Carrowcanada. He was born in 1922 and didn't go to England until he was twenty-four years old. The reason he didn't migrate before this was because his father worked in England during the war and didn't come home permanently until 1946:

> When he [father] stopped going I went that year then. He was going right up to that. He was going to England all during the war. He was home here for a long time while I was growing up … and then when the war started you see there were free passes and there was work laid on – one place was Reading, and Chorley was another place … Paddy Feeney down here was the agent.

Tom worked in England for about twenty years, going back and forth each year. Like many of his neighbours he worked in Lincolnshire, near the town of Scunthorpe. While there he worked at the farmers and recounts his experience of the different types of farm work he engaged in. The hiring fairs for the hay crop were still in existence in Yorkshire in the late 1940s, as he outlines:

> There were fellows around here [Swinford] and they used to go every year to the farmers about the first of May for the beet hoeing and they'd come home again when the potatoes were all picked. If you went over to the hoeing now you'd be on piecework – hoeing sugar beet and hoeing turnips. It'd be a shilling a hundred yards for hoeing turnips and it'd be one and three [1s 3d] for beet – beet is harder hoed … that'd be 1946 or 1947. After that then there might be early hay there at the farmer you were at and you might have a week or two there. You'd go up then to the hirings to a place called the Hawes. Oh yes and Leyburn, too. Leyburn is the first big town and then the Hawes. There used to be hirings there. There'd be a whole pile of blokes there and a whole crowd of farmers looking for men and they'd hire them – so much a month. They'd [farmers] know what you were there for. There was nobody there only fellows that were going hiring or the ones that were looking for hiring. You'd be hired then and you'd be taken out to the farm on the bus or maybe some farmers had

cars, though there weren't many had cars then and there weren't many had tractors either. It was all bleddy horses!

Working at the hay was a contract between the farmers and his hired men. There was an agreed price for saving the hay and the objective of the workers was to get it saved in the shortest possible time and then move on to other paid work:

> You'd get about £35 maybe for your month's work – you were hired for a month. If you got a real roasting summer you might be finished in two weeks. You'd be working long hours. I remember working until about half twelve or one o'clock in the morning bringing in hay. I think there must be a forecast of rain coming.

Picking potatoes was a particularly onerous job; not alone was it heavy work but the necessity of keeping the back bent for long periods caused excruciating pain in the first few days:

> It's a busy job I can tell you. The two fellows in front of the horse have to be very good pickers, you know. The ones at the side are near the cart but the ones at the front have to come back [to the cart]. A fellow from the town would be no bleddy use to you. He wouldn't stick it an hour.

As well as the Irish men working on the farms there were local English men who were more or less permanent employees and for the war years and for some time after there were land-girls employed also. The land-girls were a corps of women established in Britain for work on the land, especially during war time:

> There used to be land-army girls there – they'd be staying in hostels. Good workers they used to be and all. They'd be working with you. We'd be out stacking corn and everything together. There'd be girls that time leading the horses, you know, when you'd be pulling sugar beet. You didn't work Sundays now [at the farmers] – you worked six days. You'd go to the town, maybe on a weekend – Saturday night. There was a good bus service. You'd get on well [with the English] in the pubs. They were used to the Irish fellows going in there.

Tom was surprised at how backward rural England was at the time:

> After the war they were just the same as here. I often stopped in villages

now just out from a town … and they had no flush toilets. They were no more forward than they were here. Fellows came round at the dead hour of night … went to every house and cleaned them [dry toilets] out.

He spent the latter years of his time in England working in the steelworks in Middlesbrough as a platelayer:

We were always working seven days a week … year after year – you got a break every … I think it was every six weeks – a long weekend, from Thursday 'till about Tuesday, you know. You were paid during the breaks. You got vouchers to Ireland every five or six weeks and you got travelling expenses to the nearest town to home.

Tom, a single man, came home from England in the late 1960s and settled permanently in his home farm in Carrowcanada. Sadly, Tom passed away in 2011.

JIMMY McINTYRE

'We separated in Boston and I set off walking to Scunthorpe which would be about thirty miles, say. I had my case with me and I got a lift.'

A munitions factory in Belfast was where Mary Theresa McIntyre went when she sought employment in Ireland shortly after the start of the Second World War. She was the eldest of a family of eleven from the townland of Corthoon, Charlestown and probably felt safer in Belfast than in England, where her father engaged in farm work for most of each year. Mary Theresa's younger sister, aged seventeen, joined her in Belfast a year later to work at the same factory. However, both of them left Belfast in 1943 and found employment in England, though the war was still on. The McIntyre girls were no strangers to migration and emigration. They had three uncles and three aunts who spent all their working lives in America and their father had worked as a migratory labourer and in construction in the north of England for more than ten years before he got married.

Jimmy McIntyre, brother to Mary Theresa, came fifth in this family of eleven children and by 1948 had seen three of his sisters and one brother leave the family home for employment in England. Eventually all but two of his siblings emigrated. Jimmy had got summer employment from the county council cutting and saving turf in Corthoon bog: 'The last year in the bog it was 1*s* 7*d* an hour for cutting turf – that'd be the spring of '47 and for underage workers it would be 1*s* 3*d* to 1*s* 4*d* an hour.'

In April, 1948, just after his seventeenth birthday, Jimmy joined the outflow of young men and women from the locality going to England:

> You felt you had to go because everybody was going. You were going with the flow. The farmers used to send letters to you to come over. My father [who was in England] used to write out the letters. He was back and forth to England every year. You'd get a visa to go over and a passport and you took off.

Jimmy's father didn't work in England while his family were very young but he resumed his seasonal and other work there between 1938 and 1951. Tom, Jimmy's older brother, had been brought to the farmers by his father in 1946 and it was now Jimmy's turn to go and he left home with his father in April 1948. Because Jimmy's father had returned to the same farmer year after year, he was a trusted employee:

> You only seen the farmer once or twice a year. The foreman ran the show. The farmer used to talk to my father a lot. My father was well known to a lot of them [farmers] because he used to get men [Irish workers] for them. They'd [workers] move to a new place for a few pence extra, you know.

The working environment at the farmers was challenging and Jimmy gives some details of the pay and daily routine of the workers:

> The conditions we had here in Ireland at the time were a lot better than we found in Lincolnshire. The basic wages, with the farmers in '48 was £2 15*s* a week and that was for five days and a half, working from seven till six in the evening. That'd be for dossing about. You wouldn't want much of that work [day's wages] because we were there for piecework. That's where the money was. The first job that might come up in piecework might be sieving potatoes – grading them and bagging them. And then the hoeing of the beet would be the next job that'd come on. You'd start say at seven o'clock in the morning and you'd work till about half eleven and then you'd have an hour's break. If you had horses and carts there'd be land army girls driving them so you could get back in about five o'clock for your tea. [The horses worked shorter hours, so the hours for the workers were reduced accordingly].

One of the reasons Jimmy found conditions difficult on English farms (aside from the hard work and long hours) was the primitive accommodation provided by the farmer:

> In Lincolnshire they were called the 'Kips'. They were just the four walls – a barn! Some of them were cow-barns or horse stables containing straw mattresses and hessian sheets. Hessian sheets were sometimes called mustard sheets because they spread them under the thresher when they would be threshing mustard. You'd fill big bags up with straw and lift them off the ground with pallets and fold the huge hessian sheets over and under the straw mattresses. You'd lie on the straw mattresses. Our 'bed' was the full width of the shed with two sleeping on each side of it. I stayed in some 'kips' that might have six or eight sleeping in them. No wardrobe – you hung your clothes on a nail up on the wall.

Jimmy recollects that to rent a house in Grimsby in 1949 cost thirty shillings per week – a substantial charge on one's weekly income – while the accommodation at the farmers, such as it was, was free of charge. Not only was accommodation unsatisfactory at the farmers it could be substandard also in the cities, as he remembers: 'Accommodation was never very good – you got good ones and bad ones. I spent a couple of years moving about the south of England and you could get great digs – better than living at home. We got very good digs in Portsmouth and very bad digs in Southampton.'

It is hard to conceive, in the present day, Jimmy's description of workmen sharing beds back in the 1940s, '50s and '60s:

> I shared beds regular – complete strangers. In a new town you might have to go into a bed and breakfast the first night, you know. You could be put into a bed with a complete stranger. We never seen anything wrong with it. It would be an awful crime now, wouldn't it?

After his first year at the farmers, he returned home to Ireland for Christmas and early in the new year he set off again to Lincolnshire with a friend:

> I came back home in '48 and me and a neighbour went back to Boston [Lincolnshire] a couple of weeks after the Christmas – which was the wrong place to go in the middle of winter – in the middle of farming country! We separated in Boston and I set off walking to Scunthorpe which would be about thirty miles, say. I had my case with me and I got a lift. They brought me down to the steelworks in Scunthorpe, which was booming at the time. This would be January '49. So I got work there but digs were very hard got in Scunthorpe. So after walking round for a couple of hours I came on a Wimpey site. I popped in and of course, there was one of my cousins, your brother Paddy. So I started with Wimpey's in Scunthorpe. That was the first time now I was away from the farmers.

However, Jimmy was enticed back to farm work, principally because his older brother, his father and some neighbours were employed at a farm he had worked at the previous year: 'I left Wimpey's and went back to the same farm because I wasn't happy with the builder. That was about April or May time and I had work there for that year.'

His move to another farm on his third and final year at the farmers, gave him a different perspective on the accommodation: 'The third year we didn't stay at the same farm as the previous year. We moved – myself and Tom – in 1950. We had beds and blankets in this place – army bunk beds. Things had improved slightly.'

Like many of his compatriots, he sent money home:

> Oh yes. For the first three or four years you'd send money home every week – that's now if you were on piecework at the farmers because you could make up to £10 or £12 with the farmers, piecework. That's why the lads were all going there. That was great money at the time. When I went on the buildings in Scunthorpe [1949] it was 1*s* 9*d* an hour, I'm almost sure and we had 27*s* 0*d* lodging allowance and I think it was £1 bonus and we worked sixty hours a week – that was £7 12*s* 0*d* for a sixty-hour week. We could earn £12 a week at the farmers.

Because he was living and working alongside his father and brother as well as other young men from his home area at the farmers, the question of loneliness never entered his head: 'You'd never think about that. You'd be palling around with a crowd of local [Charlestown] lads – the Burnses, the Garveys, the Duffys – all going round together at the time. Homesick never came into it.'

Jimmy still enjoyed the social aspects of work even after he moved away from the farmers into construction in the early 1950s. It was apparent in the post-war period that machinery was taking over what was heretofore the domain of manual labourers. The interaction between workers was being lost and although Jimmy was philosophical about the changes in work practices, nevertheless he regretted the diminution in personal contact: 'In earlier days before so much machinery you'd have great *craic* on a job. Twenty or thirty Irish lads and plenty of banter. I used to love going to work but the machinery did away with that – you couldn't have a chat with a machine!'

Transience was a way of life for many workers in construction seeking better wages, improved conditions or adventure and so on, and Jimmy was no different from his workmates. While he only moved away from his base in Manchester a few times after he married, he was quite mobile in his early years in England: 'I worked in Birmingham, London, Southampton, Plymouth, Portsmouth, Gillingham, Canterbury, Deal, Carlisle, Manchester and Faversham at different jobs including motorways, oil refineries, store-keeping and concrete work.'

For the duration of the building boom in post-war Britain, employees could more or less choose jobs at will, but conditions could be quite harsh for workers when employment opportunities decreased, as Jimmy explains:

> If you worked on the buildings in England the duration of a job might be two years which was about the limit. Sometimes you were asked to go – you had no security. If you got past three o'clock on a Friday, you were okay for another week. There was no security whatsoever up to the Seventies or Eighties when they had to give you a week's notice. Men were sacked every week and fresh lads started on the Monday. On the other

hand if you got a chance of a better job, you were gone [to it]. There'd be a constant movement of workers. I couldn't count all the firms I was with. You could be in ten different jobs in a year. But if you were lucky enough and got into a good job – a government job – such as power stations, where the unions would be strong and conditions would be good, nobody would be leaving that. And they couldn't sack you either because the unions were too strong. But with the small builders – you could be moving every few weeks, like you know.

Jimmy kept in touch with home in his first few years in England through letters, visits home and by listening to Irish radio programmes. Being part of the Irish community was very important to many emigrants. It was a way of keeping in touch with Irish affairs and facilitated the exchange of news about friends and neighbours left behind in Ireland:

We always lived in a very big Irish community – Church, bars, clubs – Mayo, Sligo, Kerry associations. Every parish had a club – all Irish. We'd have no contact socially with the English. The [Irish] radio programmes were very important. In Hyde Park somebody would have a banger of a radio and everybody would gather round to listen to a match. It kept us in touch with the GAA at home. When I came back to Manchester in 1955 you'd go to the park and all the Irish couples would be walking round with radios listening to the Irish programmes.

Considering the strong attachment to all things Irish shown by Jimmy McIntyre when in England, was it not surprising that more effort wasn't made to find work in Irish cities? 'We could maybe have gone to Dublin, Cork or other cities but that was never mentioned. You either had to go to America or England – that was the policy. Nobody from the west would stop in Dublin to work. You had a very good life in England.'

When asked if he felt he had realised his potential in his work-life he indicated that lack of education was a drag on his progress: 'I suppose we were tied by the lack of education to go very high. I would have spent maybe twenty years as a foreman. Education would have been important if you wanted to go any higher because you're more involved with book work.'

At this distance Jimmy can see the importance of education when he looks with some satisfaction at the achievements of his own family of eight, who all progressed to third-level education and now enjoy very rewarding careers as a result. Jimmy and his wife Bridie retired back to his native locality in Ireland in 1993, after forty-five years living in England.

MAY (HENRY) CLANCY

'I had never used a telephone or seen a telephone in my life.'

The majority of young people in Ireland in the 1940s and 1950s completed their formal education at fourteen years of age. Advancing a child's education into second level was beyond the financial capacity of many parents but those young people who were fortunate enough to attain an Intermediate or Leaving Certificate had avenues opened up to them, both at home and abroad, that were closed off to many of their peers. Scholarship schemes attempted to address the imbalance between those who could afford the fees and those who could not. May Clancy from Barnacogue, Swinford was one of those talented students who was encouraged by her National school teacher to apply for a County Council scholarship, which would gain her free entry to her choice of secondary school:

> The teacher had put two of us in for scholarships. The exam was in Ballina and both of us were successful. I got my fees paid for five years as a day-pupil in Swinford convent school. I attended the school for three years and passed my Inter Cert. examination but I didn't want to go any more. Instead I went to Miss Duffy's commercial school to do shorthand, typewriting and bookkeeping. I completed the course which lasted eighteen months and got my exams. That was the year I went to England. My qualification was as a shorthand-typist and I had bookkeeping as well.

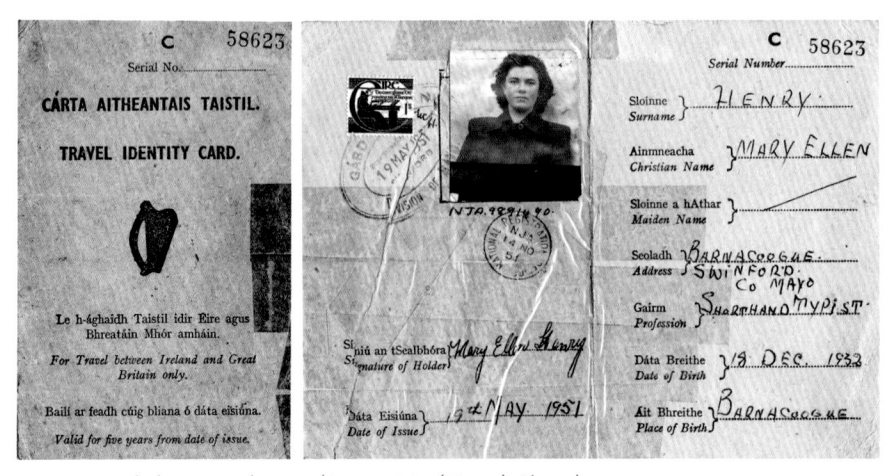

Fig. 11: Travel identity card, 1951. (Source: May (Henry) Clancy)

After two abortive attempts at getting employment locally, May reassessed the prospects of getting a worthwhile job in her home area, commensurate with the qualifications she now possessed. In one case the wages offered to her were so low she couldn't afford to pay for the accommodation in the local town where the job was and in the other case she blamed nepotism as the reason she failed in her second foray into the job market in Ireland. While there were employment opportunities in Dublin, she was loathe to go there as she had no friends or relatives in the city, whereas her older brother and several of her uncles were living in England and it was there she went shortly after her eighteenth birthday, in 1951.

May stayed with her uncle in Manchester and soon after arriving applied for a job as an office junior with the firm of Brown and Polson. She describes her experience of dealing with a 'new world' far removed from the rural environment she was familiar with and the gulf that existed between the educated teenagers of her time and communications-savvy youngsters of the present day:

> My uncle John encouraged me to go for this job because it was near where we lived – to reply to the ad. for the job. It had a telephone number to ring up. I had never used a telephone or seen a telephone in my life. I didn't ask anybody to ring up for me. I think I pretended to know what to do. I left the house and I met a policeman and I said, 'Would you show me how to use the phone, please?' 'Have you got three pence', he said. 'No', I said. He put his hand in his pocket and took out three old pennies, dialled the number from the piece of paper I had, pressed the button and handed the phone to me and walked off. That was my first experience of a telephone in England. I rang the company and arranged an interview. I attended for interview and got the job.

The job was both interesting and exciting to May. There was a big staff, large offices and a laboratory section for analysing foodstuffs, where she was sent from time to time with messages. She had no difficulty in adjusting to her work and soon began to find her feet and make new friends both in the workplace and outside and here relates how she integrated into the Irish community in Manchester:

> When I went to church at St Wilfrid's, I met a Fr Duggan. He was chaplain to the Legion of Mary and I got into that. I got to know some of the girls from Church. Then I got to know the Irish Clubs and we all used to go dancing there.

However, she found it very lonely in her first year in England, especially the first

Christmas after she went, but somehow she found a mechanism for coping with it: 'I'd be stubborn enough not to come back home much as I wanted to. Then I met a lot of people through the clubs and I loved going to the pictures and the sadness faded over time.'

May's qualifications as a shorthand-typist and bookkeeper, acquired before she left Ireland, enabled her to have a very successful and rewarding career in England. She changed jobs on just a few occasions, often because she and her Irish husband John wanted to move house. She was employed principally as a clerical officer and she worked in this capacity in both the private and public sectors. Her longest stint was with the Manchester Ship Canal Company, where she worked from 1969 to 1984. She also worked for a number of years in a labour exchange, where it was not uncommon for a job seeker to acknowledge: 'I just come out of the nick [jail] love, what do I do?'

Not all jobs offered equal pay for equal work at the time, and May was cognisant of this fact when applying for any new job: 'When I left the Labour Exchange I had to look for equal pay. It was only in the likes of the Civil Service or the Ship Canal Company that you got equal money because men got more than women for the same work that time.' Her last post was with the Co-op and she retired from that in 1990, after arranging a severance package she was happy with.

Her experience of migration through her extended family replicated that of many of her neighbours in the Swinford area and she has vivid memories of her father, Andy, returning from England at Christmas each year in the 1940s:

> My father, Andy Henry, worked in County Durham in the pits and he has two brothers buried in Durham – Tom and Michael. Tom was in the British Navy. He was awarded a medal 'for services rendered in the Royal Navy'. Dad had another brother called Pat, who didn't marry and lived in Blackburn. I only ever met him the once. My father went to England when he was very young and then he had to come back because there was nobody else to care for *his* father, you see. My father had two sisters who went to America but I never entertained going to America. They [aunts] used to send things home during the war – tea and clothes. When their daughters got married they sent parcels of clothes that they wanted to get rid of, probably. I thought I was the bee's knees in those American clothes. My father went only once to the farmers. He went from October to Christmas. He didn't like the farmers – the accommodation in huts and pulling beet. When he went again he went into Public Works.

Andy had a long career as a migrant. He was born in 1891 and his early work as a single man was in the pits in Durham in the early 1900s. After his marriage and as his young family grew up in the 1930s and 1940s he found he needed to return to England, though now in his middle years. May remembers his visits home as she was growing up:

> He'd come home every Christmas and he'd stay maybe for a few months – I'd say for ten years of my growing-up time. I used to be waiting for him at Christmas. He worked for Gleeson's in Public Works after he got married. They'd be taking down Nissen huts and building prefabs to replace bomb-damaged houses after the war.

It's May's understanding that her father was in England during the war also, as his letters home were censored:

> You'd get a letter with a big piece cut out of it. He always sent his money by telegram because it was safer than a registered letter. He'd be gone for nine months or so every year and sometimes he only had a month at Christmas. In the later years when Jim [oldest son] was stronger and bigger he [my father] used to stay shorter periods at home. Then when Jim went to England he [father] stayed home altogether.

In all, May had five uncles and two aunts, all of whom emigrated and none of whom returned to Ireland permanently. Four of her uncles settled permanently in England, one went to Canada and her two aunts spent all their lives in the United States. Both of her own siblings emigrated: Jim returned home to take over the home farm after about ten years working in England, and John settled in England permanently, where he worked on major contracts as a steel-erector:

> He worked up in the Windscale Power Station for a long time. He also worked on the oil rigs and on the construction of the Humber Bridge. He was employed by his firm at the building of the Alcan Refinery at Aughinish in Limerick – the only time he worked in Ireland.

After forty-two years working in England, May and her husband John returned to Ireland in 1993. They settled into retirement in Swinford, where she still resides. Sadly, her husband passed away in 2010.

JOE MORRISROE

'Once I came home in '56, I never went back to work in England. It was the happiest day in my life.'

While Joe Morrisroe's narrative is not too dissimilar to that of many other east Mayo migrants, it differs in that he was reared on a substantial farm of land unlike many of his contemporaries. However, conditions were so poor in Ireland in the late 1940s that Joe felt compelled to seek work in England to supplement his farm income in Ireland. He was the youngest of the family and most of his brothers and sisters were already in England, and, indeed, three of his siblings spent all their working lives there.

The tradition of going to the farmers for a few months each year was strong in the area and when his neighbour suggested they go together, Joe agreed: 'Michael Rushe was going to the farmers and he was looking for a man and I went with him.' Joe had good anecdotal knowledge of what life was like at the farmers: 'It was easy to get to the farmers and there was work there but I didn't know what the bleddy work was like.' However, he soon found out: 'We arrived there in the evening time and we were out working the next morning at seven o'clock.'

Joe was lucky in his first few weeks and recounts his work with the farm gang: 'We started the harvest and me not knowing the name of the game. There were only five of us wanted for piecework and I was number six and they said to me "you go on the fly gang". I didn't know in hell what a fly gang was but it was great.'

In reality Joe's job was to facilitate the pieceworkers in any way they needed, while they concentrated their energy on the main task. He got paid the same rate as the pieceworkers: 'I was the lucky one. I was told to do this and that – all kinds of bits of jobs. There was no [hard] work to it. It lasted for a good few weeks.'

It was 1948 when Joe ventured to England for the first time. He was twenty-one years of age. He got married the following year to Mary Frances, a girl from his home locality and except for periods when he stayed at home for the birth of his children, he returned each season to work at the same farm for the next six or seven years. Elsham Top Farm near Brigg in Lincolnshire was Joe's initial destination in England: 'It was all runways and everything. During the war they had an aerodrome there and where we were staying was the guardroom.'

He got the surprise of his life when he discovered that the farm 'beds' provided in the guardroom were not of the kind he expected: 'The first thing I had to do when I went there was to go out along with Michael Rushe and start pulling straw out of this stack and bring it in [to the guardroom] to make a bed, Jack.' It is possible that the acceptance by the migrants of a low standard of accommodation led the farmer to conclude that the housing he provided was equivalent to what the migrants had left in Ireland. Later on that year Joe got the opportunity to disabuse the farmer's wife of any such notion. He relates how he got the opening to do so:

> One day while I was working alone in the field straightening stooks that had fallen, this lady arrived one side of me … where she came from I hadn't a clue. So she started asking me questions … 'What did I do in Ireland?' And all this, that and the other – and of course I [said] I was farming but on a lot smaller scale. We kept chatting away for maybe a quarter of an hour and she said 'Are you happy, like?' 'Well', I said, 'when I had to go out and bring in the straw, that was a bit of a shock,' I said … That evening, you won't believe it, there were three double beds and a single bed arrived with mattresses and everything. That was the farmer's wife. I was told she was a teacher. Now that was the only time I ever saw the lady.

Joe was delighted with the new arrangement, 'very happy with the accommodation – nobody could grumble'. The foreman's wife did the cooking and laundry and Joe describes her as a marvellous woman: 'She did all our shopping and got everything we wanted. When we'd get up in the morning going to work just after seven o'clock she'd have all our washing out.' She also cooked dinner for them: 'We gave her about £1 a week or something like that.'

The length of the sojourn in England was generally from August to December and this period incorporated the harvesting of three major crops – corn, potatoes and sugar beet. Those journeys to England were not made lightly: 'Leaving a wife and child after you is the most difficult thing a man can do. It was hard to speak to anybody for a long time after you left the house. Very lonely, Jack. Terrible time, Jack.'

While Joe never participated in haymaking in England – it was too early in the year for him – he heard stories about the work and the method of recruiting workers:

> Lancashire for the hay! You were hired for a month. You worked [hard] there, too. I knew Tommy Fay from Tavneena. He was a great man for Lancashire – £40 for his month. That'd be in the '50s. The farmer picked you out of the crowd [at a hiring fair]. I often heard them talking about 'were you at the Hawes?' [hiring fair].

Working on a farm in England reduced the opportunities for socialising, except during weekends, because of the long hours and the five-and-a-half-day weeks. When the opportunity arose at the weekends, Joe socialised with his workmates, mainly in the local pub and cinema. However, the culture of attending Mass every Sunday was so strong among the Irish that Joe found going to Mass was a great way of getting to know people, too: 'I never missed Mass. A bus collected us and a crowd of boys from Belmullet [working on other farms] every Sunday morning and brought us in to the nearest Catholic church and just gave us enough time to have two pints after Mass and home again.'

Joe's parents had a similar experience of migration as he had, with its concomitant social and economic effects on home life. His mother never left home, but his father, Martin, spent a number of years working as a seasonal worker in England in the early 1900s and was likely to have experienced the hiring fairs that were customary at that time in Lancashire and Yorkshire. After a period in England he ventured further afield and emigrated to America before the First World War. He was conscripted into the US army in 1914 and worked as a cook for the duration of the war. He came back to Ireland in 1918 and married a local girl the following year. Martin Morrisroe returned to America to work on at least two occasions in the 1920s before finally settling permanently in his home locality in 1932.

After some time working with the farmers, Joe moved into other jobs, including civil engineering. Even when working in civil engineering in his last term in England, Joe was very impressed by his landlady and lodgings: 'The old lady in the digs was very good. She used cook and have the breakfast ready but on a Friday morning you got two boiled eggs – you got no rasher' (Catholics abstained from meat on Fridays at that time).

For his last term in England, Joe went to work on the building of a power station in Bradwell, Essex rather than to farm work. He found the sociability of local lads on this job helped to ease the disruption and sense of loss he felt at being separated from his wife and young family:

> It was nearly all Mayo at McAlpine's [in Bradwell]. There was an awful lot of people that I knew and of course we met an awful lot of Midfield [next parish] people there, too. Pake McCann from home had the shout there [was the ganger]. Anybody from Mayo that came the way, they found work there. When we walked down the field in the morning I knew so many people, I'll be honest with you; I think that's what kept a lot of people, what you might call, happy. They met their own neighbours – people from the next village and the conversation went on about what happened in our village and their village. I think I had three or four

months with McAlpine's. That was it! Once I came home in '56, I never went back to work in England. It was the happiest day in my life.

Joe speaks pragmatically about life in England in the '50s and how he found life in Ireland when he returned finally:

When you got there [England] you got work and you had a few pounds – the few pounds made all the difference. You knew the weekend was coming up and you were going to get these few pounds. You weren't used to that [in Ireland]. Then [after returning] I started working for the county council – here, there and different places off and on – and God, no matter what the ganger said to you, you couldn't open your mouth back to him. Because you wanted that pound again.

In 1956 Joe settled back permanently on his home farm in Barnacogue, Swinford with his wife Mary Frances and their young family. Both are retired and enjoy their leisure time in the company of their children, grandchildren and great grandchildren. He still remembers vividly many of his exploits at the farmers and recalls with some pride the day he and three workmates entered a forty-five acre field of cut wheat at seven in the morning and left it just before dark with the whole field 'standing' (stooked). When they got back to the farmhouse, the foreman wouldn't believe them: 'He jumped on the tractor and was down the field in seconds. He thought it was impossible for us to do.'

MARTIN McCORMACK

'And you'd hear them when you'd lie down, grinding at the straw under your head.'

Martin McCormack from Lisloughna, Swinford worked for a number of years in his local bog as an employee of Bord na Móna in the late 1940s and early 1950s. However, when this type of work dried up after the war, he, like most of his contemporaries, sought work in England:

> [I worked] down at Bord na Móna – Cloonainra bog – from about sixteen years to twenty roughly. You had turf machines there, you know. You filled them with peat with your shovel and the sods came out from the machine, two at a time. There was so much money a thousand [sods]. I seen us getting £12 a week that time – that's the truth. I didn't get it in England when I went! 'Twas piecework of course. It was twelve-hour shifts – six days a week. You were working seventy-two hours for that. Now you'd get weeks that wouldn't be as good as that.

Martin migrated to England, initially in 1953, at twenty years of age. So why did he go?

> That's a good question. Work on the bog must have been finishing out at home. If the work was in it, we wouldn't have gone, I guess. I know Bord na Móna finished at that time. Most of my pals went as well. That was a lot of it, too. There was no other work only the bog you know and as for signing on the dole you'd only get four or five shillings [a week].

After work in the bog finished, he signed on for a sugar-beet factory campaign in England:

> I went to the beet factory the first time – to Bury St Edmunds. You went on the free pass – you didn't pay at all. My uncle, Michael Groarke over here, brought me up to Swinford and there was a fellow there, like you, with a piece of paper. 'Show me your hands' he said and I'd say there were caubs [callouses] sticking out of them. He didn't look the second time. Down with your name and you were finished [the interview]. He was an agent who came to Jimmy Groarke's to recruit for the beet factory.

Successful interviewees received a voucher from the sugar-beet company and all travelled to Dublin on the same day:

> You had to stay a night in Dublin. Did you ever hear of the Iveagh Hostel? You had to stay there overnight. I don't know what in hell we stayed there for in bleddy cubicles – one to a bed. We were kept there for the night. We were on the boat the next day and there were coaches that picked us up to take us straight to the factory. You went where you were sent.

He was happy enough during his time at the beet factory. There was a hostel and accommodation provided for the employees and he had the company of several workers from the Swinford area:

> You had Paraic Meehan, Jack Groarke, Tommy Doherty [neighbours] were with me. The hostel was supplied by the beet factory. You didn't have to pay for it. There could be five or six or maybe ten of those little huts [for living in]. The heating was stoves with pipes coming out the top. There could be ten or twelve men in every one of those [huts]. Each one had his own bed.

As well as being employed at the beet factory, Martin being a versatile worker, also engaged with the building industry, opencast coal mining and the farmers. He found the work at the farmers hard and the accommodation atrocious:

> Oh I did harvesting and tattie picking. It was pretty rough. Well, at the harvest now you'd start at seven o'clock. The day would be longer if there was tractors. If it was tractors you could work away till seven or eight o'clock in the evening. But if it was horses you'd finish at three o'clock because they wouldn't let the horses work past three.

Both harvesting and tattie picking were paid at piecework rates – so much an acre – but the price varied in accordance with the density of the crop: 'The last place we were in it was only £10 an acre because it was only 10 tons to the acre. If you were the other side of Peterborough it might be £20 to the acre because there might be 20 tons to the acre.'

The lack of continuity of piecework at the farmers was a serious drawback for seasonal workers, as he outlines:

> While you'd make more money at the harvest and tattie picking, the work

would only last so long. You'd come home then [to Ireland] or you'd go back into some town and start whatever job you could and be thankful for what you got. Go down to the pub and you'd meet someone – you wouldn't be long out of work.

Martin worked for farmers around Peterborough and also in the Huntingdon area. He found the accommodation offered by the farmer in Peterborough to be abysmal:

> Don't mention it! Sort of a shack, you know. Lie on the floor on bags of straw and you'd hear the mice eating under your feet. Old grey blankets, same type over you as under you but you'd still be lying on straw. As I put my foot under the blanket one night a mouse shot out. That's the God's truth, Jack. And you'd hear them when you'd lie down grinding at the straw under your head.

In Huntingdon he worked on a farm with some neighbours from home and although they had a two-storey house there, conditions weren't much better. He shared the house with James Bernie Walsh, Tom Strick Gallagher and Paddy Bawn Gallagher (workmates) and each had his own room.

Working in the opencast mines driving a truck was another job he engaged in while in England. He lived in digs at the time and the standard of accommodation and quality of food varied from one place to another:

> Some of them were terrible. Myself and Joe Henry over here in Cloontubrid stayed in a place in Dollis Hill. £2 10*s* 0*d* a week we were paying. The dinner would be ready for you. It was so poor that the men would later go to a local cafe to satisfy their hunger.

Because these men worked so hard, their energy requirements were very high. The landladies of the day were more concerned to keep costs to a minimum rather than to provide meals with high calorie content for their clientele. Martin did, however, have one good experience of digs, in St Helens where the landlady, Mrs Grady, came originally from near Ballaghaderreen:

> That was a good digs. It was £3 a week. You'd come in in the evening and she'd have the dinner ready – eight or nine of us round the table. And you surely couldn't see across the plate with all the bacon and cabbage that'd be on it. She was the greatest feeder you could want.

The custom of sharing beds while in digs was familiar to Martin:

> Well I did [shared beds], aghrá and I'll tell you what we did do – we double-shifted beds. When I got out another man got in off the night shift. Two in a bed – no problem. This is when we were on the opencast coal mining. You done twelve hours at night. We came in off the night shift. The other six or seven men were going out. The beds never got cold.

Willing to go wherever there was work, Martin spent a couple of terms in London on the buildings, working as a lorry driver. He got married in 1961 and came home finally with his English-born wife in 1962 to his home farm. He was fortunate at the time to find work in the local bogs, cutting and saving turf, some nine years after he originally left:

> After Bord na Móna finished another fellow started then – Lee from Sligo. I worked down here [Cloonainra] and in Derrykinlough, Cloontia and a bog over near Ballaghaderreen. Then we started working on what they called the Moy drainage – cleaning the river and tributaries and building bridges. We had five or six years on that. Things were getting a bit better.

Fig. 12: Charlestown river (a River Moy tributary), late nineteenth century. (Wynne Family Collection; source: Photographic Archives; courtesy Tom Kennedy)

The wages went up to £10 a week and I said 'We're sound now.' No problem after that.

The culture of migration and emigration was deeply embedded in Martin's family, as with many other families in the locality. His father's four brothers emigrated to England a generation earlier and settled there. Three of his mother's brothers worked seasonally in England for a number of years before coming back permanently to their local area, while another brother went to the US and spent the rest of his life there.

Martin is retired now from active work on his farm and lives in his home area with his wife Kathleen, and has the comfort of having his sons, daughters and grandchildren living close by – a much changed situation from that experienced by his father's generation.

ELLEN (FOLEY) REEVES

'It was very, very hard. Let nobody think it wasn't. Because you had to learn right from scratch.'

It must be incomprehensible to many young Irish people of the twenty-first century that teenagers of sixty or seventy years ago were engaged in hard manual labour, day in, day out, on small rural farms and didn't resent it, and, indeed, as Ellen Reeves suggests, even enjoyed it. Although she was only about sixteen years of age when she first went to England, she had worked on her home farm in the townland of Corthoon for several years before that:

> Oh yes, I worked on the farm. I did lots of things – saved turf and hay … dug potatoes, picked potatoes, dug fields. I'll always remember that. I think Mick [brother] was one side and I was in the middle and I think it must have been Paddy [brother] on the other side and we were digging a field [with spades] and we were sort of having a competition between us to see who would dig the most and I think we worked really hard. It was fun in a way. I suppose I was fourteen at the time.

She and her brothers spent many days digging this field and what really upset her was what she considered unjust treatment when she went in for dinner:

> We'd all go in for dinner and the boys would disappear after dinner with a book [to read] and father would get into his book. I was expected to do the washing up and I used to resent that because I had been working in the fields as well. We were all supposed to have a rest after dinner before going back to work but I didn't get any rest.

Like many of her peers Ellen was lucky enough to get employment in a local bog during the war years, saving turf for the county council. The employees working in

Fig. 13: *Sleán* (**turf spade**). (Source: Henry family)

Fig. 14: Turf made up into *gróigíns*.

the bog consisted mainly of adult men (turf cutters) and adolescent boys and girls (spreading and footing turf). Cutting turf with a *sleán* (turf-spade) was laborious work and paid a higher rate than other work in the bog (see p. 187):

> The men would cut the turf and we were part of a gang and we would spread the turf and then there was another place where the turf was partly dried and then you would put the sods up in 'gróigíns' to dry more and then load it onto the donkeys and take it out of the bog when it was completely dry. You'd sit down and have your lunch and your cup of tea and you'd all get round the rick of turf and sit there and chat. There were quite a few in the bog. I enjoyed that. I would imagine this was during school holidays.

The wages Ellen earned were usually taken by her father, as she outlines below. Her brother, Paddy, also had his wages appropriated, as he relates in his narrative (see p. 236):

> The cheque came and father took it. I didn't expect it either. Sometimes I got a shilling [from father] and I would walk into the town and go to a matinee in the cinema. That used to be on a Sunday, I think.

When Ellen left school at fourteen she was employed for about six months in a small industry in the local town. She earned in the region of 10*s* 0*d* [sixty-three cent] for a forty-five-hour week.

> I worked in Parsons'. A little factory at the end of Charlestown and they did woollen garments there. There were three girls employed there and they were on machines and they would knit the backs and sleeves of cardigans or whatever they were doing and we would join them together. The lady there [owner] would come in and she would pull them this way and that way and heaven help you if they came undone. It was very important that you had it sewn properly.

Ellen was the middle child of a family of nine and by the age of sixteen was conscious that four of her siblings were already in England so she decided in 1946 that she would join her sister, Bridie, in London:

> I went because I wanted to be with Bridie and I thought it was going to be great fun. I went over there and it was during a real bad winter and I

was homesick and as miserable as sin. I found out what it was like to be an emigrant and I never wanted to be an emigrant any more.

Bridie (Ellen's sister) worked in a bar, but Ellen herself was too young for bar work and she got employment instead doing some housework and looking after a baby in the establishment. After a while she graduated to working as a barmaid and this brought her into contact with many English people:

> I met a lot of English people. English people are very, very kind. Both of us [sisters] were just young barmaids and they would invite you to their homes – they didn't know us from Adam – 'Come and have a cup of tea' you know and 'Come and have a meal.'

It took her quite a while to adjust to her new life. Her expectations of 'the good life' were severely restricted by the limited income she earned:

> You see when you had your day off from work, you were supposed to go out and enjoy yourself. Well you didn't have a lot of money to enjoy yourself with, you see. £3 a week and my keep, was what I got when I first of all came to England. Well then you see you were supposed to save some money and send it home. I must admit I never sent an awful lot home to Ireland. And of course you'd see clothes that you wanted to buy and you wanted your hair done. You had to watch [be thrifty with] your money! We [sisters] would have thought it was the height of luxury to go into a room where we could sit down and make ourselves a cup of tea and just chat.

Regardless of the kindness she encountered, Ellen found her new life in England a challenging experience:

> It was very, very hard. Let nobody think it wasn't. Because you had to learn right from scratch. I used to think 'Why don't they speak English?' Of course they were all Cockneys where I worked [English pub] and they had a proper English accent and I thought 'why can't they speak in a language I can understand?', and then one night I was serving somebody and he said 'I wish you'd speak English' and it suddenly struck me that they were having the same problem with me as I was having with them.

Ellen worked as a barmaid for about two years in London and then got a job in 1948 in a Lyons' Corner House, where she became a manageress responsible for

Fig. 15: Bringing home the turf from Corthoon bog, 1980s. (Courtesy Tom Eddy Durkin)

opening and closing the shop, the supervision of staff and the payment of wages – a job she thoroughly enjoyed. She got married the following year and didn't take up paid employment again until her youngest son was eight years old. However, this didn't mean she wasn't busy. During this hiatus she partook in a number of night classes:

> I went to night school for quite a few years. Yeah, Bill [husband] and I went for German lessons, probably for three years. Then I did typewriting and I could do thirty words a minute. You could apply for a job as a typist at that speed. But I never went for a typing job.

While Ellen never used any of the subjects she studied for work purposes, her expressed sentiment was 'I wasn't sorry I did them.' When her youngest son was eight years old, Ellen sought to enter the job market again:

> I went into school dinners. I went into doing dinners because the school was convenient to where I lived and I was appointed assistant cook. That was my first job after the children came. I was there for about five years.

> Then I went into a tobacconist shop because I got fed up with that [school dinners] and I worked there for about three years and then I went as an escort on an ambulance for handicapped children.

This area of work appealed to Ellen and she continued to work in different aspects of social services, including caring for the handicapped and young delinquents, until her retirement. She derived a lot of satisfaction from working in social services and recalls the daily routine this type of work entailed:

> The driver and I would pick up handicapped people and make sure they were secure in their seats and take them in to a centre and I did that for five or six years. Bill [husband] and I then decided to go in as residential social workers. You started work at three o'clock in the afternoon and you worked till three o'clock the following afternoon. We were on duty overnight and saw our charges off to their centre or whatever. First of all we looked after – I suppose they would be called delinquent boys. That was our first job with social services and we did that for three or four years. That was when we did our stint at college – taking out qualifications. Then after a while the boys' home was shut because of shortage of money and they [authorities] said 'Would you like to go and help the handicapped?' So we went in and we worked with the adult handicapped. I would say it was five years with the [delinquent] boys and seven years with the handicapped, as far as I can remember. We thoroughly enjoyed working with the handicapped. It was very satisfying.

Even though Ellen lived all her life in England from the age of sixteen to the present day, her strong attachment to Ireland never waned. She and her husband Bill were frequent visitors to Ireland, particularly in their retirement years. Sadly, Bill passed away in 2009. Nevertheless, Ellen maintains the practice of holidaying in Ireland each year and enjoys linking up with family and friends in her home locality.

TEDDY GALLAGHER

'It's harder when you're going away and leaving young kids, you know. It's tough – tough on you and tough on them – everyone is lonely.'

A survey carried out in the east Mayo region in 2002 found that most emigrants left the area for economic reasons and Teddy Gallagher from Tavnaglass, Midfield was no different from most of his contemporaries:

> My father got killed when I was fifteen and the two girls [older sisters] were in England and there was three of us at home – myself and two younger brothers, you know and there was nothing [money] coming in, like, so it was kinda like 'you'll have to go somewhere'.

Nevertheless, he managed to get some labouring work in the locality and stayed in Ireland looking after his mother and younger brothers for three more years. His wages at that time [1964] were £5 a week.

Teddy went to England at eighteen years of age and travelled to Leeds first, rather than London where his sisters worked. He went to Leeds because his cousin's father was a ganger there and had promised to provide jobs for both him and his cousin on their arrival:

> When I went to Leeds the wages for seven days, working four o'clock Saturday and four o'clock Sunday, were about £18. You'd have ordinary time up to twelve o'clock [Saturday] and time and a half between twelve and four and on Sunday then you'd get double time all day. There was three of us, like, together and it was a pound each for the room and three pounds each for food. My wages were £18 and that'd leave me with £14 and I used to send £10 a week home so I had £4 10*s* left [for myself] but £4 that time was a lot. £10 was a nice bit that time coming in [to a house]. I was getting a fiver when I was working here at home and could [now] send ten from England and while I was getting the fiver here [in Ireland] I had to be kept [fed etc.] out of it.

As might be expected of a young lad away from family and friends for the first time, he was very homesick, as he recalls:

> Very lonely – I used to cry my eyes out when I went first and especially when I'd go up to bed at night – the streets were lit up there, you see and just across the back of the house there was a field or fields. I remember that and I used to think if I was at home I'd be out in the fields doing something or walking around – cry me eyes out, cry me eyes out. I suppose me father only after getting killed and me two younger brothers at home – you'd be thinking of them.

After his first year in England, he took a trip home to Swinford but on his return in the New Year, he decided to go to London. Jobs were more plentiful and wages were better in the capital but not all jobs were of equal value:

> Well you could be in a job for a few years or six months. You might go into a job and find out it wasn't a lot of good. You might stay in it for a while until you found something better. If it was good you'd stay in it. Oh yeah! You'd get the good jobs and you'd get the bad jobs. And the good jobs – it wasn't easy to get into them. Anyone that got into them looked after them [didn't leave them].

Teddy had no difficulty meeting other Irish, or, indeed, men from his own locality in the England of the early 1960s. Social interaction for many Irish workers was with their own ethnic group, as Teddy soon found out:

> We'd all meet at the church. Then we'd go for a few pints and then go to the dance. I would socialise with local people from round here [Swinford] who were there. They were from Charlestown, down around Foxford, Bohola, up around Kiltimagh, Kilkelly – all that circle – it was full of them, full of them around London. Just from this side of Swinford, up to Cuiltybo, just up the road there, there was thirteen of us on the one job – from the Midfield area, really. We used to all pal around together.

Again, like many Irish workmen, he was employed on a variety of jobs in a range of locations:

> I worked in the tunnels different times. I worked in them – in the tunnels – on the Victoria line [tube] in 19 … would it be … '66 or '67? I was a shuttering carpenter on the buildings and steel-fixing. That kind of thing. I worked in Leeds and in London and Southampton and I was in Folkestone and Dover.

Fig. 16: Channel Tunnel workmen, 1992. (Courtesy Val Hyland)

After six years working in England, Teddy got married to Maureen Walsh, a neighbour of his from Killasser. They remained working in England for a further six years before returning to Ireland to rear their family at home. However, in 1987, eleven years later, he returned to England to work on the channel tunnel. He spent four years working on this project and came home finally in 1991. However, he regretted very much the time lost away from home while his family were growing up:

> It's harder when you're going away and leaving young kids, you know. It's tough – tough on you and tough on them – everyone is lonely. Oh, I would love to have lived at home all the time. If things were right I would have stayed at home. I was gone for four years from my family, which is four years I lost. I missed them [children] growing up for four years.

PADDY DUFFY

'I wrote him a letter and he sent me a telegram – "Come immediately!"'

Paddy Duffy from Madogue, Swinford came from a large family, all but two of whom emigrated. Five of his sisters went to America between 1949 and 1963 and he and his brother, John, went to England in the late 1950s:

> My first step in England was to go to the farmers and Peterborough was my first port of call. Mike Groarke [neighbour] and the Duffy lads in Killeen [cousins] were, like, a farmer's team over there for a few years. News came through that Mike wasn't going to go to the farmers that year. He was in England doing public works. So I immediately got on the hotline to Paddy Duffy in Killeen [team leader]. I wrote him a letter and he sent me a telegram – 'Come immediately!'

Paddy jumped at the chance: 'It could have been Timbuktu or the heart of London', as far as he was concerned. He had been brought up on stories of working life in England: 'Over the years I'd been listening to the Burns lads from Madogue and the McIntyres from Corthoon talking about the good money to be earned in England. They'd be talking about getting work with such and such a contractor and earning £15 to £20 a week.'

While at home, Paddy got work with the council occasionally, earning 13s 4d a day (two-thirds of a man's wages). He spent the rest of his time working on his father's farm for little more than pocket-money. Although he was used to laborious farm work in Ireland, he found piecework in England was at a new level:

> We had about eighteen weeks that year at the farmers [in England]. We were there until just before Christmas. The harvest was first, then we moved to potato picking, to the beet and then the farmer employed us for a few weeks, on a day rate, planting Brussels sprouts. The farmer was attractive that time to a lot of Irish people. Most farmers paid you cash-in-hand. We harvested at so much an acre – stooking wheat for example was ten shillings an acre. We spent three weeks stooking, day in – day out. Take it off the field and cart it in and thresh it was twelve and six pence an acre. Roughly three weeks carting and threshing. Twelve hours a day, five and a half days a week. We always finished twelve o'clock on a Saturday.

Fig. 17: Jack Duffy demonstrating the art of tying a sheaf of oats to his son, Paddy, late 1940s. (Source: *Corthoon National School: A Social History* (1998); courtesy Duffy family)

> Be in the field at seven, till seven in the evening. It was helter-skelter! Okay, you were earning about £20 to £22 a week and factory work was probably £10 a week at that time, you know, and the beauty of this was it was cash-in-hand.

There were several farming teams in the vicinity of where Paddy worked, the members of which were acquaintances of his from home. For example, Tom McIntyre, Paddy Duffy (Killeen) and Martin Duffy were all team leaders with their own gangs in the locality. Unfortunately a disagreement arose among the members of the team Paddy was working with, and as the last man in, he was let go:

> All the teams were made up of five or six workers. So Tom McIntyre [neighbour] had his own team. Now Tom was in public works over the summer waiting for the farmer's date. Tom, God bless him, realised I was out of work and he took me under his wing – 'There'll be no neighbour's child out of work', he said, 'while I can help it' and brought me into his team. I waited there until the potatoes and beet were done and myself and Tom waited for a further two weeks at day's wages – £2 10*s* a day. That took us to within three weeks of Christmas. That was it. Tom McIntyre

went to the same farmer year after year. Once you built up a rapport with the farmer it was probably easier. The job was waiting for you and the farmer was expecting you. They [farmers] did take advantage of you. It was cheap labour. No doubt about it and the accommodation was chronic.

Like many emigrants he was lonely at first in England, as he admits:

The first year probably you're still homesick. But you're also resigned to your fate, you know. Well there's no point going back. First of all they'd [neighbours] laugh at you. I was fortunate getting in with the Burnses and McIntyres [neighbours] in the first months – we had our own little clique.

While he found living conditions in England very good during his later career with a railway company, he was very critical of the accommodation offered by the farmers he worked for:

The farmer gave us what they call the 'kip house' – nothing better than a cow shed. Straw bed, couple of old army blankets – one to cover you and one to lie on. The mattresses consisted of hessian bags [stuffed] with straw. The beds were bunk beds filled on each level with straw mattresses.

However, the living conditions at the second farm were a little better:

It was still what was called the 'kip house', but it was a slated building – just one big room with a fire up at the end of it, like you'd have in the house at home. There were proper beds there and he [farmer] had a woman who came in and did a bit of housework and made the beds and changed them.

After a season at the farmers, Paddy joined his uncle John Halligan in Ellesmore Port, Cheshire on the promise of a job in public works. John was general foreman with a railway engineering firm and Paddy soon found work with the same company. It was at this juncture that he saw career opportunities open up and by dint of determination, hard work and courtesy of the British education system and a three-year course in North Lindsay Technical College, Scunthorpe, he gradually moved up the ladder to hold the position of UK contracts' manager with responsibility for all UK sites before he retired.

Paddy Duffy spent his whole working life in England and is retired there now but he would still have chosen to live in Ireland if he had the career options open to him there that were available in England.

Fig. 18: Jack Duffy sharpening a scythe. (Courtesy Patricia (Duffy) Hannon)

TOM MEEHAN

'You wouldn't put on too much weight – I'll tell you that – you'd get more gravy than meat.'

Another emigrant from the Charlestown area, and the last of his family to go, was Tom Meehan from Brackloonagh. He was the youngest member of a family of six, all of whom emigrated to either England or the US during the 1950s. His oldest sister, Mary, spent one year in Cornwall, England as a trainee nurse, before going to her aunts in America. She graduated as a psychologist and married a US citizen and thereafter spent the rest of her life in the US. Tom's brother, John, and his sister, Bríd, also went to the US. Bríd, however, worked in Dublin for three years before deciding to join her siblings in the US. Paddy, another brother, lived all his life in England.

Although Tom came from a farming background, his first wage-earning job, as a fourteen-year-old, was in a local bottling firm. He worked there for four years by which time his wages had increased to £3 per week. Like other young people in the area he was influenced by stories he heard from neighbours and family members home on holidays from England: 'I seen them coming on holidays and they seemed to be a lot better off than I was.'

In 1964 he left his job in Charlestown and went over to London where he had two brothers working: 'I went over with one of them. He was home on holidays and I went back with him. My brother had it all laid on – digs and work and the whole lot.'

The first job he worked on was the construction of a multistorey car park at London airport and he adjusted to the work and life quite well, considering the changed circumstances he found himself in: 'Well, building work was new to me, of course – and machinery. We didn't see much machinery around this part of the country [Charlestown] then, or buses or anything else. But we soon got used to it.'

Wages were even better than he expected: 'My first week's pay was £15 and my second week was £25 with bonuses and I left £3 here.'

Tom found his accommodation in England good and he was fortunate to have a workmate from home who shared a room with him until, eventually, both went their separate ways when each of them married:

> Myself and my mate went together to England like, and we had a room in a house and the use of a kitchen for £3. I was in digs once in

Wolverhampton and bad digs they were. You wouldn't put on too much weight – I'll tell you that – you'd get more gravy than meat [for the dinner].

Like the majority of young emigrants at that time, he sent money home: 'I did – every week. I used to send a tenner [£10] every week to my mother. My father was dead of course, that time.'

How did he feel about being away from home: was he homesick and did England live up to his expectations?

Ah, no, we had a great time. London was a great spot you know. You could be out every night of the week if you wanted to. And the money was good. I didn't drink at the time at all as I was a pioneer [teetotaller]. There was one thing I found and I'd have to say about England – it was a very fair country. I got paid for every minute I worked and paid for a lot of minutes I didn't work. And I never was a day out of work while I was there. I was eleven years without ever being late for work. I got an award for that from the firm. Being a non-drinker was a big help in time-keeping. We used to get three and a half hours extra if you were early for the five shifts. A lot of people could never make it on time you know.

Unlike many young emigrants, he was reluctant to change jobs:

Well I never changed jobs too often. I was eleven years with one firm – Taylor Woodrow. They used to transfer me from one job to another, like. I worked with the brother for a couple of years before that. Then we went our different ways and I went with Taylor Woodrow and I was transferred to Birmingham and ended up in Lancashire.

Tom kept up links with home through letters, visits home and Irish newspapers. He went home 'once a year – to do the haymaking. My mother used to rear cattle here and I'd come home to get the hay for her. That was the holiday! It was all hay that time – there was no silage.'

Though he had a very fulfilling life in England, he and his wife Ann and young children decided to come home permanently to Ireland in 1977:

I'd advise anyone to go. I enjoyed my time there. We had our own house over there. We were well settled really. We were living in a seaside town and a grand spot but my mother was not in great health and of course the kids were coming up and we decided we'd come back. And if I'd stayed there, I'd be retired now and I'd have a bloody good pension – or I might have been killed as well!

KITTY (BREHENY) WALSH

'You had to take every stitch of your clothes off in front of four doctors.'

The townland of Clooncoose, where Kitty Walsh grew up during the 1930s and 1940s, was dominated by the surname 'Tarpey' and while Kitty's own name was Breheny, her mother was a Tarpey. She recalls that at the time, 'there were nine houses in Clooncoose and they were all Tarpeys. We were the only Breheny there.' Her recollection of growing up in Clooncoose was of the closeness of neighbours and the great sense of kinship and community that pervaded the townland.

When she left National school in 1944, Kitty Walsh went to the convent secondary school in Charlestown, but left after a year to help at home because her older brothers were in England working at the farmers:

> You had to pay £8 that time to the school. It was a lot of money. The lads [brothers] were in England, you see, and my mother needed me at home to do the work. I was kinda responsible for getting the turf and everything else at home. I worked on the farm all the time [before going to America]. I worked at digging spuds or maybe haymaking. We helped at all the neighbours. I never worked away from home in a [paid] job.

Kitty was the fourth in a family of thirteen – eight girls and five boys. During the period of the 1940s, '50s and '60s she and all of her siblings emigrated to the United States. This exodus was a repeat of what had happened to the previous generation of her family. She had four uncles and two aunts in the United States and an uncle living permanently in England. She had no aunts or uncles living in Ireland. Her three older brothers worked seasonally in England and when the opportunity arose they moved stepwise to their relations in America, as Kitty recalls:

> When I went [to America] first, my two older brothers, Bill and Seán, came with me and we sailed on the *Queen Mary* from Southampton. I was lucky I had the two brothers with me. They were in England at the time and we went from there. I don't think I'd ever have gone only for that. Jimmy, my oldest brother, was already in America. He was there since 1948 and we were waiting for him to meet us at the boat only to discover he had been conscripted to the army and we didn't know it. He was stationed in Fort Dix in New Jersey. He won the 'soldier of the month' in Fort Dix and

was featured on the Ed Sullivan Show on TV. We didn't have television in Brooklyn [where we lived]. We had to go down the street to see it.

Back in the 1940s, well before the advent of Green Cards or Morrison Visas, the process for entry to America was even more rigorous than it is today, with very intrusive procedures to go through. Kitty emigrated to America in 1949 and explains the steps that had to be followed at that time:

> You had to be claimed out that time. An uncle or an aunt had to put up a bond and they had to have property in America to claim you out. My uncle claimed Jimmy first and then my aunt Mary [Breheny] claimed me. My other aunt and uncle in Brooklyn claimed Bill and uncle John claimed Seán. They were responsible for us while we were there. The relations in America sent a written affidavit to the Consul in Dublin and they assessed it and called you up for interview and examination. You had to take every stitch of your clothes off in front of four doctors. Walk up and down the floor to see if you had any deformity of your limbs, your hips or your body. Can you imagine doing that to girls of that age? The aunts and uncles in the US put up the money for us to go. They had to send the money home [for the fare] which was £60 each that time or $300. We had to work hard that first summer and pay that money back. You were lucky to get the money, I suppose, just to get to the States. My first job was down in Bowling Green with American Express. Jim Breheny, a retired cop and distant relation, got me in there for a while. Then they figured there was a better job paying maybe five dollars more and I got that job with Westinghouse [Electric Corporation] at 40, Wall Street.

However, Kitty was still not satisfied with the money she was earning and eventually decided to take up a waitressing job in an hotel in the Catskills, run by her uncle. While the hours were long the tips were good and she had saved enough money to bring her sister to the US the following year, as she recalls:

> I remember going up to the Catskills to my uncle's place and working in it. We were up at seven in the morning and we didn't go to bed until nine at night. We took Maureen, my sister, out the next year. We started saving in 1949 to bring her out in 1950 and she came in April that year.

Why did Kitty choose America over England as a work destination when most of her contemporaries were taking the shorter and more familiar journey to England?

> America was my first-choice destination because we heard so much about it from our relatives there. My mother always talked about America. And we always got parcels from America. They were always sending stuff home to us and that. We never thought about England. Isn't it funny that? My older brothers went over to Lincolnshire for a few years to the spud picking but they never went to England to live permanently. We had an uncle in Spalding and they used to go to him. They were always home for Christmas. England wasn't great that time either – in the late Forties and Fifties. I know a few that went to England and left it and went to America.

The knowledge gleaned from her relations about life in America was that it offered a better lifestyle, and, indeed, Kitty's own experience bears this out:

> America was a much more progressive country and the weather was better and you had a cleaner way of life. There was more family life in America, I think. The churches would bring the parents out for a night and all the parents would come. St Francis of Assisi Church in Brooklyn was our church and we used to see John Healy's aunt [who is featured in his book *Nineteen Acres*] at Mass there every Sunday. My aunt was great for visiting houses – we never went to a bar.

Throughout Kitty's time in America she lived with her aunt and cousins, and when her sister, Maureen, arrived, she also stayed in her aunt's house. The work practices of the time seem strange from a present-day perspective, Kitty admits:

> When we started working as waitresses we took home our work clothes. You had four uniforms and aprons and you had to take them home and iron them. That's what we spent our weekends at. And then we might go to a movie, if we had the dollar.

Like many of her contemporaries, Kitty sent money home to her family on a regular basis:

> I sent money home every week or two. Indeed, I did. We had a Christmas club and we saved two dollars a week up till October. By that time we had saved sixty-six dollars, Jack, and that went home for Christmas. And we sent money home in between, every time we'd have a few dollars to spare.

The good work practices and ethics that Kitty got from her mother when growing

Fig. 19: The thirteen brothers and sisters of the Breheny family at Collette's wedding (groom not present in photo): (left to right) Jim, Bill, Seán, Kitty, Maureen, Pádraig, Collette, Patty, Vera, Teresa, Ambrose, Madeleine, Dolores. (Courtesy Kitty (Breheny) Walsh)

up in Clooncoose were invaluable to her throughout her working life, and Kitty recalls a multitude of chores she had to fulfil as a young girl:

> We were lucky we had the upbringing we did because she [mother] had you doing something round the house all the time – sweeping the street, dibbling spuds for a neighbour or you were scouring the teapot, or ironing, or haymaking. She never left us idle which I think was a great thing because you didn't have time to sit down or get depressed or get fed up with yourself.

While life in America was good and Kitty enjoyed her time there, she admits to suffering from homesickness, particularly during her first year:

> I cried myself to sleep every night for six months when I went there first. The loneliness hit most when I went to bed. I was too busy during the day but when I went into bed all I could think of was the fields below the house and all the kids [siblings] and everything at home. But when I'd got enough money to go home – I figured I can go home now if I want to and I didn't mind so much.

Kitty maintained links with her parents and siblings through weekly letters from the US. 'It was too expensive to come on a visit. The fare was $300 or more then, Jack. That took a bit of saving and we were also sending money home.' Nevertheless, she determined to come home to Ireland after she got word her mother was seriously ill. She realised how much the visit would mean to her mother: 'Mother had to watch three of us going off at the one time when we left for America. She never saw Jimmy or Bill [sons] again. It was hard times!'

One of the consequences of belonging to a large dispersed family was brought home to Kitty when her sister, Collette, got married in 1970: 'My brother, Jim, came in from California when Collette got married in New York and he had never seen her until then. He was gone [emigrated] before she was born in 1948. I hadn't seen him in seventeen years myself.'

Although Kitty enjoyed her time in America and thought it was a great experience, she came home finally in 1953 to marry her boyfriend, Seán, and set up in business in Charlestown. Living in America had widened her horizons, sharpened her business acumen and gave her an insight into what was necessary for success in Ireland: 'We were a progressive business and we weren't afraid to try out new things and maintain high standards.'

Kitty's husband, Seán, sadly passed away in 1992. She is now retired and lives in Charlestown, but she maintains links with family in the US through frequent visits to Florida, where she spends part of each year.

MICHAEL GOLDRICK

'I hated England after I went and that lasted three or four years. I didn't adjust. I cannot explain it.'

While there was much unemployment in east Mayo during the 1940s and 1950s, there were sporadic work opportunities available through the county council or small industries in the area. Michael Goldrick from Corthoon, Charlestown, worked for the county council for two years before he went to England to his brother, Tom, in 1955. He was pleasantly surprised with his first work experience in England:

> 'Twas a bit of an eye-opener. The work was easy enough, like. It would have been easier than it was here, like, put it that way. 'Twas easier than working at the council at that time. Ah yes! It was hard work at the council. Above in McGuinn's pit [Carn] taking out stones for the crusher. Hauling out stones and putting them into carts. You'd have to break some stones [with a sledgehammer] before you could lift them to carry them to the cart. You spent the full day at that. It sure was heavy work. The council was terrible that time, Jack. You'd be lifting half a hundredweight [25 kg] at a time. No gloves and no rainwear – 8.30 to 6.00 – and a half-day Saturday. The dust was terrible, Jack – no mask that time. The field next to the crusher would be covered in white dust, never mind the person. I had two years at that and no holiday pay or nothing. The ganger-man promised me he'd get me holiday pay leading up to Christmas. I didn't get it and I packed it in at Christmas.

Michael got paid £4 a week, plus a stamp, while working with the council, and got a job with a local bottling firm for the next six months, for which he was paid £2 10*s* a week. He then decided to try England where he felt his labour might be better rewarded. He found work in England 'more easily than I expected' and was engaged in construction in Newbury, Berkshire within a week of leaving home. For the next ten years he worked in construction in various places, with his last job involving the building of a nuclear-power station in north Wales. He lived in camps most of the time and found the accommodation 'good, two to a room, clean, well run, with good food in a wet canteen'. However, social outlets in camp life were limited and activities revolved around interaction with workmates in the canteen, except for weekends, when the workers might visit the nearest big town. He changed jobs only about five times in ten years: 'I was 4½ years on one job and you'd get awful fed up on the one job – oh you would.'

Although he worked for ten years in England and kept in contact with home through letters and visits home, he always wanted to return to Ireland: 'I hated England after I went and that lasted three or four years. I didn't adjust. I cannot explain it. I don't know why but I never liked England, that's for sure.'

Michael Goldrick's father, also called Michael, was an example of an emigrant who worked abroad for a number of years and then returned to his home area, bought a farm of land and settled back to country life in Ireland. Michael senior came originally from Tourlestrane in south County Sligo. He emigrated to America in 1927, joining his four older siblings in Chicago. While his older brother and three sisters went on to live permanently in the US, Michael returned home after five years, married a local girl, Mary Deehan, and went on to buy the farm where Michael junior now lives.

How did Michael junior's emigration and that of his siblings compare to that of his father's? The records show that while emigration was a prominent feature of both families, the destinations differed substantially: the older generation chose America while the younger chose England. The rate of return migration was much higher from the younger generation: four of Michael's siblings returned to Ireland to either to work or retire, while none of Michael senior's siblings returned.

In 1965 Michael junior returned permanently to Ireland to take over the home farm where he and his wife Bridie, still live.

TOM GOLDRICK

'I mean we left it to make it good for the next lot coming up. We couldn't all have stayed here.'

Smallholdings and big families meant, in many cases, that when children left National school they had to seek work outside the home 'to pay for their keep' and to add to the family resources. Having a brother or two younger than you who could take on your duties on the farm meant that you had to get wage-earning employment away from the farm or emigrate. Jobs outside the farm were few and far between in the west of Ireland in the 1940s or 1950s and often involved teenagers in heavy, arduous labour for poor recompense.

Tom Goldrick from Charlestown, brother of the aforementioned Michael, got a job in the local bakery after he left National school in 1948: 'I was bringing in the turf and bringing in the flour. The flour was in ten-stone [60 kg] bags. I used to be out in the bread vans with the drivers, as well.'

Fortuitously, a new bakery was being built while he worked there and he was later employed as a labourer in its construction. His work involved:

> Mixing concrete and whatever had to be done. It was hard going anyway. I was probably only fourteen years of age when I went in there first. The wages were ten shillings a week in the bakery and it probably would have been £3 on the building. I was just sixteen years of age when I worked on the building.

With work drying up and another brother snapping at his heels, Tom decided to emigrate in 1952, at eighteen years of age. Through a tortuous set of interconnections involving a Welsh sub-contractor, who happened to be married to a Swinford girl, he got work in Milford Haven, Wales, joining two of his next-door neighbours who were already working there.

At the end of his first year in Britain he left Wales and headed for London and worked in or around the capital for the next couple of years:

> I was in London from 1953 to 1955. I had another period then at the building of a power station down in Essex. I lived in a camp there for eight years. The job went on for ten years altogether. It was as good or better than what was around London at that particular time, like, you

know. Accommodation was first class. All prefabricated wooden huts and there'd be two people in each living part – heated and everything to the last. There were up to 2,500 people staying in the camp.

While Tom was more or less labouring when he first joined the workforce there, he was promoted to ganger-man before the job terminated. Being in charge of men was a different experience for him. However, he had no difficulty in adapting to the new role: 'It wasn't too bad – no fighting or anything. The fighting would be with subbies' [subcontractors] men – say the likes of Murphy and them gang. As bad as things got they were a different breed altogether.'

Managing one's work-life was an important component of survival in the harsh working environment of the construction industry and Tom's astuteness ensured that he was never unemployed:

In all my time in England I never was one day out of work and I never left a job until I had one to go to. Another thing was that when you packed in [left the job] on the Friday all you had was the few shillings to come and in them times you mightn't get work for a couple of weeks, you know.

Tom never worked at the farmers in England, although he and a neighbour, Jack McIntyre, made an abortive attempt to get work on the land in Lincolnshire in 1957:

That's where I met Paddy Duffy [neighbour] and he was only after arriving in England that time. Jack [McIntyre] said 'We'll go to the farmers.' I was out in Luton working for McAlpine [at that time]. Paddy Duffy was in Peterborough and we pulled into Peterborough to meet him. We waited a week there but we didn't get any work [at the farmers] and we went back to where we came from [Luton]. We'd have been there, I suppose for the potato picking.

For the last twenty-seven years of his working life, Tom stayed with the one employer. He worked on many diverse jobs: 'Building roads, erecting a big record factory in the Seventies out in Milton Keynes, on the Underground system, building a defence wall for the River Thames, erecting a big hotel at London airport.'

While Tom was a teetotaller, he enjoyed socialising, in Irish pubs mainly, with relatives and people he'd be working with. He expounds further on the pub scene: 'When I say I'd go to the pub, I'd go one night a week anyway. Saturday night I'd go to an Irish pub in the area where there'd be Irish music. I'd go to Irish dance halls for the company.'

Tom's view of the prospects facing himself and his siblings in Ireland in the 1950s and 1960s was prescient, and by 1963 all but one of his own brothers and sisters had emigrated to England. His fatalistic view on emigration is very understandable. 'The way I looked at it afterwards – if we didn't leave, where would we be? I mean we left to make it good for the next lot coming up. We couldn't all have stayed here [Ireland]. There was only room for the odd one.'

He retired home to his local area in 1999. Would he have stayed at home if conditions were as good as in England? 'I suppose I would have. If conditions were like now [2007] I wouldn't have gone.'

MARTIN McDONAGH

'Sometimes you'd get digs and sometimes you'd get insults and all sorts of things. Ah, you would – yeah. They'd tell you to get back to your own country.'

Martin McDonagh (who features elsewhere in this book; see Ch. 8, pp. 101–2, Ch. 9, pp. 108–9) was one of the migrants who left the west of Ireland in 1962 for a Land Commission farm in Leinster. Martin had already worked for six years in England before taking up the challenge of permanent migration to Kildare. He emigrated to England from Drumshinnagh, Swinford in 1956 at age nineteen, satisfied that he could improve on his council wage of £7 per fortnight:

> I knew very well when I was going I wasn't going to get anything for nothing. You'd hear the stories about guys, you know, that would go before you and come back … with some great spoof … but other men would tell you the truth, like. My own father, like, he had been going back and forth. He knew the whole story … so he could tell me what to expect.

Scunthorpe was where he went first though he would have preferred to have gone to London where his sisters were.

> I wanted a bit more life [than in Scunthorpe]. You see Scunthorpe was a real English town. Manchester wouldn't be – there's an awful lot of Irish in Manchester. I only stayed in Scunthorpe a few months – the work was bad and the money [was bad] and I left and went down to the Isle of Grain 'cause my cousin was there and I was able to earn better money down there. It was all about money! I lived in a hostel in England in the Isle of Grain for about a year. It was sort of a … you could say it was like an army camp. It was okay. In wintertime you had central heating which was great and there was plenty of hot water. There was four of us in a cubicle or room and you had your [own] bed. You had a canteen. There was even a church – you could go to Mass on a Sunday – on the site. It was very handy … you didn't have to do any travelling. We were actually building an extension to an oil refinery. It was huge.

During his time in England he worked in a number of British cities, such as London and Manchester but he liked his time in Newport, Wales, best of all:

> I enjoyed my two years in Newport. I enjoyed it, yeah I did. 'Cause I played [Gaelic] football there as well. We had a football team and we did enjoy it. So that was a help, you know, to keep in contact with the guys from home. Oh there was a lot of lads there from down Swinford. My first cousin, Tom O'Hara – he was a foreman there and his sons worked there. Three sons had come and gone while he was there. [The plant] was the most modern steelworks in Europe. It was five miles in length.

The Newport project was extensive enough to furnish a Gaelic football team from among its Irish employees, who were sufficiently skilled to win the Gloucester league and championship in 1961. Martin was an integral part of the 'Pride of Erin' club and team at that time.

He stayed with an English landlady while working in Newport. 'I was happy enough with the digs – it was clean, comfortable. The landlady was very strict though about coming in late. She would expect you to be in shortly after the pubs would close. You wouldn't be busted with food!'

Some antipathy between locals and Irish workers was evident while he was in Newport:

> Sometimes you'd get digs [barbed comments] and sometimes you'd get insults and all sorts of things. Ah, you would – yeah. They'd tell you to get back to your own country. I got it twice in Newport! There were two guys that I lived with [in digs] and they'd hardly bid you the time of day … they weren't too sociable now.

During his time in England he became aware of some of the disadvantages associated with poor communication skills.

> I met lads in England … I must say they were from a *Gaeltacht* area … they had no English, which was very, very hard. They'd pick it up [English] as they went along but I knew one lad he was just after coming over. He was one day in a place where he got injured – a cut or something – a nurse was dressing his hand – and she was asking me could I interpret what he was saying … and I couldn't understand him. This lad was young – I would say seventeen and I thought it was bloody awful.

He returned permanently from England, after about six years working there, to take possession of a Land Commission farm and house on the outskirts of Maynooth in exchange for his own farm and dwelling on the periphery of Swinford. Now in semi-retirement, he continues to farm on his holding in County Kildare. He still has a strong attachment to the area from which he originated and visits his home town of Swinford quite frequently.

TOMMY CAMPBELL

'The buildings was hard. I mean, in them years you'd have to carry everything, bricks and the like, on your shoulders.'

The county council was one of the few sources of employment in east Mayo in the 1950s and 1960s and while the wages earned by employees were quite low, they were a valuable addition to the income derived from small landholdings. Tommy Campbell from Cloonaghboy, Swinford worked for the council on leaving school at fourteen years of age and describes his work and wages:

> I think it was £7 a fortnight. The reason I was getting that was that I was drawing water to the crusher and I was on a man's pay for having the ass and cart. I was out there at fourteen. I had a few good spells – two winters and I got nine months in one spell. They were tarring the road here right back into town. Every morning I used to be up at six to be at the hospital – that's where the council yard was – for work at eight o'clock.

Like most young men of the area he experienced serial unemployment and even when work was available the wages were low. In 1956, aged eighteen, he decided to seek work in England:

> Well, I was always on edge to get going [to England], you know. Well, it was the done thing. Everyone around was going. Once you're out of work, you're out of work. You could get nothing else. I went to Middlesbrough first. I went with a neighbour … Lord have mercy on Pat McDermott [neighbour]. It could have been anywhere. It didn't matter a bit to me, 'cause I really didn't know where I was going, you know. Pat McDermott was over there working. He used to come home here regular. The last time he came he said, 'Come, there's plenty of work.'

To get a job and earn good money was Tommy's only motive in going to England. He found his first job, working on the railway, through Pat McDermott, who was based in Middlesbrough:

> We'd be doing twelve hours [shifts] a lot of the time. Work week-ends if there was a rush job on. The money was fair. I think my first week's wages

were around twelve quid. A big change from here, you know. I was sorta used to the [hard] work – it didn't make a lot of difference to me.

As an only son he felt it his duty to come home each year to help his father with the heavy work on the farm:

I used to come back to help him every year. I'd come home to help with the hay out in June and the turf – he'd have it cut himself. I'd stay on until maybe July or August – say three months of the year at home. You'd have to go back again [to England] looking for a new job. That was the system. You'd get used to it, Jack.

Tommy talked in some detail about his life in England. Unlike many of his compatriots, he didn't do any farm work in England: 'That's one thing I escaped.' Nevertheless, he found the work on the railways and buildings arduous:

If I was to stay there [England], I'd have got away from the building trade and that, you know, into a factory – something a bit easier. The buildings was hard. I mean, in them years you'd have to carry everything, bricks and the like, on your shoulders. Oh yeah, it was all hard work. Nothing mechanical at all.

The railways provided employment for Tommy in his first years in England but he wasn't wedded to this type of work:

If work was plentiful you'd change jobs often enough. You'd be looking for a better job, you know – more money. If you thought you'd get a few bob more, you'd go. I was a long time on the buildings. I was on the Chiswick flyover – three or four years. I worked there with a neighbour and relation – Pake Foley.

Being employed in a beet factory in Ipswich was to be his last experience of work in England before he returned to Ireland to take over the home farm: 'In the beet factory you'd be back [home] again in March. I did that for four years.' Unlike building work, the beet campaigns ran over the winter period and were ideally suited to small farmers who wanted a steady source of income for the winter months.

Tommy spent over twelve years travelling back and forth between his farm in Ireland and various work locations in England. He returned finally in 1968 to settle back into farm life and to rear a young family, supported by his wife Margaret.

PADDY FOLEY

'I come home one night and there's a bleddy letter from the War Minister or someone. 'You got to report tomorrow for … the army in Korea.'

Paddy Foley was born in Corthoon, Charlestown in 1931 and worked for his neighbours and in a local bog, spreading and footing turf in the mid-1940s. He worked in the bog, among other enterprises, for about two years after leaving National school before he went to England to the farmers in the spring of 1948.

He was very clear about his reasons for wanting to emigrate even at that early age: 'Money I earned in Corthoon bog went to my father. I got none of it. All the time I worked in the bog and I worked two years in the bog – I got a shilling [six cent] on Sunday nights.'

His main expectation of England was 'getting paid for the work for a start off – not to be working for nothing'. He also had a sense of adventure which had to remain unrequited as long as he was at home: 'I always looked forward to getting away. I watched the cars going round the bend [at Durkins'] as far as you could watch them. I'll be around that bend one day, too, I thought.'

In the spring of '48 he migrated to a farm near Boston in Lincolnshire. He was accompanied by his two older cousins, who had worked for this particular farmer, Jack Risdale, the previous couple of years. The foreman, Ted Rose, had written to them informing them that work was now available on the farm: 'That's how you knew when you'd be wanted there.'

Their first job after arriving at the farm was spreading fertiliser by hand, a task he recalls vividly:

> We got there before lunch and were out in the field spreading what they called 'guano' directly after lunch. The sooner you started the sooner you got paid. There's big fields there – eighty or 100 acres. The tractor and trailer dropped off the bags of guano in rows up and down the field – every twenty yards – and we'd go along as quick as we could and spread it from buckets – with your bare hands! You wouldn't do it now! If the wind was blowing the wrong way you'd be swallowing the bleddy stuff.

While Jack Risdale came down to the farm every so often 'with his plus-fours and his Jaguar to inspect the place', he seemed oblivious or indifferent to the living conditions of his Irish workers:

> The year we were there we lived in the granary. We didn't live in a house. You paid no rent then you see. That's what some people wanted. Fill a few sacks up with straw and you got a few blankets and there was a heavy sheet made up of potato sacks all stuck together. Throw that over the top – that was it!'

Regardless of the quality of the accommodation, Paddy and his cousins, Jimmy and Mick Burns, got on well with Ted Rose, the foreman. He used to join them in the granary regularly for a game of cards. Ted's wife did the cooking for them and they were very satisfied with the quality of the food:

> They used to do the cooking for us. Jimmy used to go in and get the trays out, you know and we'd take it up to the granary and eat it. Every now and again Jimmy would go in and do the dishes and other chores in the house. He had great nature and would chat with the women. I couldn't do that. Good food, yeah, the best of food. When we went there first the flat-rate wage was £4 10*s* a week. Ted's wife used to take thirty shillings out of that for our keep.

Food was still rationed in England up to about 1950 but he explains how they found ways of tweaking the system:

> You had to have ration books. This is what used to happen on the farm. The women liked chocolates and sweets and things. We didn't want them so they'd ask us for them – the foreman's wife and his daughters. So we'd give them the sweets or whatever they fancied and they'd give us coupons maybe for clothes or shoes or butter or something, you know, in exchange.

Paddy's gang of three – he and his cousins – was supplemented by three brothers from the Erris area when the heavy harvest work started. He recalls how laborious the work was:

> There was Tony, John and Mick Gaughan. They came from Tullachan Bawn near Geesala. Tony was a big fellow and he used to do the forking – the heavy work – in the field. The weighty sheaves of wheat – you'd be pitching them up on the carts all bleddy day. I was only driving a cart but we were all getting the same wages. One couldn't do without the other. There was no good putting me out forking the wheat – I wouldn't last.

It must be remembered that this was his first year in England and he had just turned seventeen years of age.

He went home for Christmas the first year he migrated and in the New Year he joined a few lads from the village who were going to work on the buildings in Oxford. However, while his mates, who were older, found work readily enough, he encountered difficulty in getting employment: 'I was talked into this job in Oxford where they were getting £20 a week and I said that'll do me.' However, things didn't turn out as he expected. Unlike at the farmers, he had to get a set of books [work documents] before he could take up employment:

> I had to go to the labour exchange but when they saw my age – I wasn't eighteen – I couldn't get books [registered to work]. I could get work probably but not a man's wages. Anyway after a few weeks I got a job. Marty Walsh [neighbour] got the job for me with Wimpey's, down in Leicester, building an atomic power station at Harwell.

Like so many young men who had to find work in a foreign country, the experience of finding a job and integrating into the community was very daunting. Paddy found moving away from friends and neighbours an unnerving experience. His cousins had looked after him at the farmers the previous year and now he was going into the unknown: 'I was a sorry man going to Leicester, I'll tell you. I had no friend or nobody to ask there. I was on my own properly now. Before, with my cousins it was like being at home.' Nonetheless, being obliged to think for himself and form his own judgement about matters gave him confidence and after working for a while in Leicester he decided to go back to the farmers:

> I was working for Wimpey's in Leicester after coming down from bleddy Oxford and I got itchy feet – I think about this hay business. So myself and these two fellows hit off to Skipton. Hadn't a clue about the hay – never been there before and they were worse than me – they were townspeople from Ireland – from Kildare or Meath. They hadn't a clue – they didn't last long. The hay – that was a game of its own, you know. There's a hiring in Skipton and the Hawes is another one. The streets was lined with Irish men – and they'd pick you out, you know, if you were suitable. As soon as we got there we spread out straight away through the farms – ignoring the hiring fair. We weren't supposed to do that but we did it. A farmer took us on – he took two of us and the other fellow got another farm somewhere that took him on. They hired you for a fortnight [to get the hay in]. You were gone then. They got their money's worth out of you.

Fig. 20: Bringing home the hay in the 1940s: Paddy Foley with his father, Tom. (Courtesy Kathleen (Foley) Henry)

> I don't think I ever worked as hard in my life. The hours we put in. Six o'clock in the morning he'd [farmer] give you a scythe to get down there cutting around the dykes you know, and they'd bring you up a breakfast around 9 o'clock and it'd be between 8 or 9 o'clock at night when you'd finish and all you'd do is fall into bed. I got £16 for the fortnight. It wasn't much at all [1949]. It'd be a bit better than the buildings, I think.

After completing his time at the hay, he got work near Spalding with another farmer called Butty Jackson. The potato crop was maturing on the farm and Paddy elected to provide a team of pickers. His four-man team consisted of Joe Walsh, a Galway man, Ted Parsons from Carracastle, his (Paddy's) brother, Tom who was coming down from London and himself:

> Deeping St Nicholas was the name of the area around and then there was the Fen country. The Fen country was a different price from the Deepings – heavier soil and better crops. It could be ten tons to the acre in one area and fourteen tons to the acre in another area, you know.

He gives details of how the team operated:

> You'd have the horse and cart and you'd put the two best pickers in front. The rest would be on the side – they'd be the closest to the cart. All they'd have to do is pick them, stand up and empty the potato basket into the cart. The two in front had to run back to the cart, to put their potatoes in, you know. I was good at tattie picking.

Picking spuds was back-breaking work and he describes how it affected some men: 'I used see some of them and just about in tears at night time with their backs. They'd be down in the huts not able to get up to make a cup of tea for themselves, you know.'

Paddy had an adventurous or restless spirit and it didn't take a lot of persuasion for him to head off to another job, in another part of the country, when the gang had finished the potato picking:

> Me and this Joe Walsh and Parsons – we headed off. There was a job down in Southampton. They were building an oil refinery and we set off for there. We got a job straight away – the three of us – yeah, an American firm – Foster Wheeler and they were rough and tough. So we only stayed a short while there. Parsons stayed on in Southampton while me and Joe Walsh headed for London. 'Twas coming up for Christmas when we got to London – the two of us – we hadn't much money either. Stupid thing to do in the middle of winter – jacking up a job. We never thought of that. So I went to Mary's [sister] for a few days and then we went to Camden Town one day – myself and Joe. We were in the 'Dublin Castle' [pub] in Camden Town and there was a great big fellow there … a Belmullet man – big Jack Reilly. Anyway somebody said 'He's looking for men.' So we went up to him, had a talk with him. 'Ah yeh, looking for men, yeh, yeh, for Scunthorpe!' That's how I got to Scunthorpe. Back down in Lincolnshire again, you know. We signed up with him anyway. So the two of us set off and sure enough he was there in Grimsby. He put us up in lodgings there and out to work the next day for Wimpey in Scunthorpe. Housing we were doing. We were there up till nearly summer time. We left there then and went to Derby. I used to be driving the big mixer for the concrete – that was my job.

Serendipity plays a role in the lives of young mobile workers as it did when Paddy was settling into a new job in Hanley, Staffordshire some time later. He was happy in his work and things 'were going good', when out of the blue an official letter arrived at his digs:

> I come home one night and there's a bleddy letter from the War Minister or someone. 'You got to report tomorrow for … the army in Korea.' It was about three weeks before Christmas and this thing rolled up. There was three of us got word – two Galway fellows from Clifden and myself. So those two fellows went home to Ireland. But I thought to myself, I cannot go home, I have no money or what am I going to do there for the bloody winter. Maybe better off going to Korea. Anyway I went in the next morning with another fellow – a fellow from Longford, Tully was his name. I went to the agent – a Cork man and I said, 'I want my books as soon as I can.' 'Is there something wrong?', he said,' I'll make them up for you as soon as possible.' He had them by ten o'clock. So straight down on the train with myself and Tully to Gravesend in Kent. He knew a place in Gravesend – he was down there a long time [working]. So he wanted to get back there and he wanted a mate to go with him. So it just suited him and me. I wrote a letter back to them [Authorities], 'gone to Ireland'.

After a while in Gravesend and when the threat of conscription had faded, he came back to Liverpool. It was early spring and he found work was hard to come by. So he went from there to Manchester, where he met a few fellows and got started again:

> There was a job in Manchester with this 'Eagre' firm. All they done was railways – laying lines and sleepers. So I went in there looking for work. There was snow on the ground and everything … I was getting low on money and low in morale, too, and luckily I got the job. So I spent a good while with them – maybe twelve months or so. Then this Grant Lyon firm started up offering big money and lots of overtime and people were leaving Eagre and going with them. A lot of fellows that was around Manchester were switching from Eagre and making big money with Grant Lyon. They were seven days a week. 'Twas double pay on Sunday, you know and time and a half on Saturday. There were blokes from Ballyhaunis and Kiltimagh and places like that looking for work there. They used to come over after they'd sow their crops in Ireland. They'd come over for a few months to work for Grant Lyon. All they wanted was seven days a week!

Paddy worked in many different locations in Britain and showed his capacity for multitasking in the variety of jobs he was engaged in during his thirteen years there. However, after he got married in 1956 he settled in Manchester, a city he was very familiar with. Then a new opportunity arose that stimulated the interest of both Paddy and his wife Sheila, and in 1961 they and their young family decided to join the £10 Poms and emigrate to Australia, under the Assisted Passage Scheme. The establishment of this scheme after the Second World War made Australia an attractive destination for some emigrants. The subsidised fare for Britons was £10 per adult, with children going free. It was not quite so appealing to Irish people, who had to pay £30 per adult.[1] The scheme was operated from 1947 until 1971, and it is estimated that over one million British citizens participated in it.[2] However, while there was a high take-up rate, many were disappointed with life in Australia, blaming misleading and overly optimistic advertisements that promised full employment, big wages and high-quality accommodation. Not surprisingly, it is estimated that upwards of one-quarter of post-war Britons were so disillusioned with their new lives in Australia that they forsook their new homes and returned to Great Britain. In a further twist, half of those returnees went back again to Australia to try and pick up where they left off.[3]

Life was very hard for Paddy, Sheila and their young family in their first few months in Australia. Employment opportunities and wages were at a much lower level than they were led to expect and the accommodation was of an inferior quality. He recounts his experience after arriving in Australia:

> When we came first we were put in hostels. They were only Nissen huts, you know – like the army have. If you stayed in the hostel and didn't go to work it was free. So you could live there for a month or two months. It was hard to get a job when we came here [1961]. There was a recession on or something, they kept saying. But when we left home [England] they told us there was jobs everywhere … plenty of jobs, you know – but there was nothing. We were there two or three weeks looking for jobs and we couldn't get one. If you got a job you had to start paying straight away. If you didn't get a job, you could live there [in the hostel] three meals a day. But you were scared of getting a job. You might be there [at work] only a week or a day and they'd sack you. That was too bad for you. You had a job and that was it, you started paying then. You could still stay in the hostel, but you had to start paying – tariff, they used call it. After a week or two I got a job with Roche Brothers – earth moving you know. The foreman was Cookie a Northern Ireland fellow.

It wasn't long before Paddy made the acquaintance of the term 'useful', as applied to some employees in Australia at that time. This meant that you could be called in to work at any time and you could be sent home at any time. He soon discovered he was 'useful' after being sent home by Cookie at 11 a.m. on his first day at work:

> Back in England if you went out you got a day's work whether there was a day's work there or not. They paid you for the day. Cookie of course was on a salary. He got paid no matter what but he sent me home many a day at eleven o'clock or twelve o'clock and there wasn't much you could do about it.

His introduction to life and work in the new world was an eye-opener and he became very disheartened by his reduced earning power and his inability to provide for his family as he would have liked:

> The money that time was £17 12*s* 6*s* a week and I was earning about £20 in England. I wasn't too happy about that. Anyway I got talking to different people and a truck driver, an Australian, said to me. 'You want to see Paddy Meehan. He's an Irish foreman for the company.' So I went down to see Paddy and introduced myself. 'Come with me tomorrow,' he said. And I was with him the next day. He had great time for the Irish, you know. I wasn't the only one he took in [helped]. Any Irish fellow that was without a job they went to Paddy.

He worked for Paddy Meehan for a number of months, but again experienced short hours and low weekly earnings, well below what he had been achieving in England. Frustrated by this he decided to change jobs once again:

> So I got Saturday morning's paper and somebody wanted a couple of labourers for digging trenches – no experience needed! I got a bus to see these people. They were two Hungarians, father and son and they were in pipework. They had a tractor but there was a lot of places that you couldn't use the tractor. It was a bit different to what I was used to but I got a go there. I was determined to stick to this you know. The best of it was – it was piecework – like so much a yard, you know. A difficult job or something you couldn't do piecework, 'twas £5 a day which wasn't bad and you could work seven days a week. So that was a big help getting £35 instead of £17. After a while, I could dig one a day, you know, about 50 yards – 5 feet deep at one end and maybe 2 feet deep at the other end. In sand I could do one a day – no problem.

Paddy was not daunted by the hard physical work involved in digging trenches and after some time he began to realise that his knowledge and expertise were as good, if not superior, to those of the bosses for whom he worked. As this realisation sank in, he decided to get qualifications in this area of work:

> I went for my test [to use plastic pipes instead of concrete ones]. You had to do a theory test and a practical test. I done the theory test and passed that – now I had to do the practical test. I done that and passed that. So now I got my certificate. I was right then. I should have got it a long time before. I made good money after that. People used to ring me up and say 'name your own price'. I never had a day off work since, you know, flat out all the time – Saturdays, Sundays …

Having his work certified gave him the impetus to set up and operate his own business in pipe-laying services in the city of Adelaide. P&S Pipe Laying, Adelaide, South Australia was established soon after, and he and his wife Sheila operated this business very successfully until his retirement some years ago. Sadly, Paddy passed away in April 2015, seven years after being interviewed by the writer in Adelaide, Australia.

Fig. 21: Postcard of farming scene in Corthoon, Charlestown, 1970s.
(Courtesy Peter Zoeller, photographer)

HENRY PEYTON

'Work was very plentiful in London at the time. You had no worries about being unemployed for long.'

Henry Peyton from Madogue, Swinford had a job of sorts in Ireland – an unpaid apprenticeship in a local bakery – when he decided to emigrate to England a few months short of his eighteenth birthday. A sister home on holidays from England provided him with the impetus he needed: 'I suppose everybody was going to England at the time and there didn't seem to be much here. There didn't seem to be any other alternative but to go to England, you know.'

His purpose in leaving was not solely economic and had an element of escapism in it:

> I suppose it was adventure as well as economic. I suppose as a seventeen-year old it was probably adventure, too, you know. You were venturing out into the world. Everybody was going. My sister, Mary, was home on holidays at the time so I thought 'I'm going back with you.' Pauline [another sister] was over there as well – she was doing nursing and I suppose my cousins were there – it was kind of a home from home if you like – we were one big family there.

Employment opportunities in 1950s London were even better than he had imagined:

> As it happens there was lots of jobs. When I went to the labour exchange, I was asked what would I like to do or what did I want and I said. 'Well, I worked in a bakery at home' and he looked up his file listing the jobs and he said 'I have one here for you.' That was the next day after I went to London. I had got the job straight away.

Adjusting to life in London posed no problem for him and the fact that he lived with his sister and cousins helped considerably. He was shocked, however, by the huge chasm that existed between life in his home town of Swinford and life in a big city:

> I was flabbergasted at how far advanced London was compared to where

> I left, you know, even after coming out of a world war. I was very happy in London. My sister was there, the cousins were there. You were working and there were so many things to do and so many places to go. It was a different world altogether from the world I left.

Henry didn't work for long in his first job (in a bakery). Through a network of relations in the building industry he was offered an apprenticeship to the painting trade and he spent the rest of his time in England (1955–63) as a painting contractor in the construction industry.

Like many young Irish workmen living in England in the 1960s he changed jobs 'a good few times'. His explanation for this transience mirrored that of other Irishmen: 'extra money maybe. That time you could change jobs today and get another one tomorrow. Work was very plentiful in London at the time. You had no worries about being unemployed for long.'

Social life typically centred round the pubs, dance halls and cinemas. Although a non-drinker at the time, he found pubs a congenial place to meet friends: 'We always went to the pubs because, you know, the crowd would be going to the pubs. The Crown was a favourite place.'

Did he socialise with workmates?

> No, never. Once you finished work you never saw your workmates any more. They were mostly English – married men. You'd have nothing in common with them outside work. Nothing whatsoever! You'd socialise mostly with lads from around Charlestown. You'd meet them at the dance hall or in the pub – or you'd arrange to meet.

Henry maintained links with home through annual holidays and letters, but he didn't buy Irish papers or listen to Irish radio.

Chance plays a part in the lives of many emigrants and the weather played a big part in his decision to return to Ireland after eight years in London:

> I came home with Frank [brother] and it happened to be the winter of '63 and everything was frozen up in England for four or five months and it was bad here as well and there was no point in going back to England, so I didn't go back. I just happened to get a job with John Duffy, God be with him. And from there I hit out on my own. It wasn't my intention to stay, believe it or not. There wasn't much happening in Ireland, that time, around here. It just so happened a job came up.

Would he have stayed in Ireland if conditions in the mid-Fifties had been better? 'I'd have gone anyway. I wanted to see it [England] but I never wanted to really settle in it. So when the opportunity arose I stayed in Ireland.'

Work opportunities increased in Ireland from the mid-Sixties on and Henry was able to find constant employment in his home locality. His principal employers were Mayo County Council and the Western Health Board (now the HSE) and he was able to carve out a fulfilling work life, ably supported and sustained by his wife Nano (now sadly deceased) and his four sons.

MARGARET (MULLIGAN) McINTYRE

'Well maybe there were better opportunities there, 'cause there certainly weren't any here!'

While the vast majority of Irish emigrants went to Britain after the Second World War, a significant number began to go to the US in the 1950s, averaging about 6,000 annually between 1950 and 1959. Among those leaving Ireland during that decade was Margaret McIntyre from Madogue, Swinford, who went to America with her twin sister, Kathleen, in 1959. The ostensible reason for the trip was to attend their older sister's wedding but they were attracted to America and decided to stay there: 'Well I had an older sister Mary who was there. We went to her wedding and when we went we stayed there. I had aunts over there, too.'

Her recollection is that there was no clear notion in her head as to what she wanted to do at that stage:

> Well, I don't think, at eighteen we thought of it [job opportunities] in that way. Well maybe there were better opportunities there, 'cause there certainly weren't any here! So that was probably part of it, but at eighteen I don't think we were thinking, like, that far ahead, what kind of career we were going to get into. We were just going to work wherever it might have led.

Margaret had worked for two years in Ballinafad College in Belcarra, from the time she left secondary school at sixteen till she went to America at eighteen. Her food and accommodation were provided by the college and her wages were £7 10*s* per month.

From the simple life in Belcarra to the hustle and bustle of life in America was a challenge that Margaret embraced with relish and succeeded in integrating quite successfully into the workforce in the US, as she recalls:

> I had hopes anyway of getting a job and making decent money. Get a job and that was it. Found work six weeks after we got there. Got a job through a friend of my brother-in-law who was working in an insurance company and he recommended that we [twin sisters] go for the jobs. It [job] was in Philadelphia and it was with an insurance company – The Insurance Company of North America – and I worked in the personnel

department. I made $42 a week and I was there from '59 until '64. That was it then. I married Patrick Walsh from Galway in '63 and worked for six months afterwards. Then I was self-employed – my husband and I had a landscaping business in New Jersey and I worked in that up until '95.

While life in America could be a daunting experience for many girls coming from rural Ireland, Margaret was fortunate in that she had the support and guidance of an older sister who was already settled there as well as the companionship of her twin sister who had accompanied her there:

I lived with my sister, Mary, when I first went there. She and her husband had a house. I was there from '59 to '63. I don't remember being homesick. We emigrated in '59 and the first time we came home was Christmas '61. Went back again – I never had a problem with it really. We were making – not great money – but enough to live on and have some savings but I don't think I needed or wanted for anything, really. I never went through a hard time or a difficult time or anything like that. Of course there was always Kathleen [twin] and I. Even going out at night there was always the two of us.

There was just one area of life she was disappointed with: 'It wasn't a very Irish area where we lived. That was the only problem – that we didn't get out to mix with the Irish – we would have liked to, but living with Mary [sister] was like living at home.'

She was ambivalent about her feelings regarding emigration. When asked if she would like to have remained at home permanently she responded:

I don't know. I don't regret having to emigrate. I think it was an experience and I learned a lot from just moving home. At the time when I did emigrate it was interesting and it was what I wanted to do and it was exciting and all that. Looking back now it would have been nice if I had lived at home and not emigrated.

After the death of Margaret's husband, Patrick Walsh, in 1991, she returned to Ireland. She met and married Paddy and now resides in her home area. However, for part of each year Margaret returns to the United States to spend time with her now adult children and extended family there.

BRENDAN SWORDS

'It was such a big change from the restrictions at home. It was a new-found freedom and I thrived on it.'

Like many of his peers in the south Sligo area, Brendan Swords required little encouragement to migrate from his home farm in Sandyhill to England in 1963. He was nineteen years of age at the time and had already spent a couple of years working at home with little or no pay, because the small farms in the area couldn't sustain a paid worker. Brendan was the youngest of eight children and all of his siblings had emigrated before this. So he decided to leave home and join his older brother, Tom, who ran a successful business in Gloucestershire, England:

> My brother invited me over to work for him. He was in partnership with another guy in a fencing business. I worked for him for about four months and then I came home for a few months. I went back to England again and worked in London. I stayed with my sister and brother-in-law in London.

He worked in London for about six months and then went home for a short period before returning again to Gloucestershire. He worked in an army military barracks there for a while and then moved up to the north of England.

What were his expectations when he migrated to England first?

> I didn't really know what to expect but it exceeded any expectations I might have had. I was absolutely enthralled by it and by the people – the friendliness of them. The work was extremely hard but I enjoyed every minute of it. It was such a big change from the restrictions at home. It was a new-found freedom and I thrived on it. We used to go out two or three times a week to pubs or clubs. It was great!

While he was fascinated with life in England, his ultimate preference was to return and work in Ireland. He had aspirations to better himself and was not afraid to seek employment in different types of businesses with that end in mind. So after about three years in England he came home and applied for a job in Dublin: 'I got a job as a bus conductor in Dublin. I was working at that for about two and a half years and then I left the buses and worked for a few months on the buildings.' After leaving the buildings he applied for and got a job in Roches Stores in one of their warehouses, where he worked for over two years. His next job, which was to be his last in Dublin, was with Quinnsworth. He was transferred by that firm to their new branch in Galway in the 1970s to work as a warehouse manager and he spent the rest of his working life in that city:

> I was in Quinnsworth in Galway for over two years and then I joined Digital [Equipment Corporation] and started working in the stores. Later I went into production control and I was production-control planner for about eight years. We had a technical library there. I trained as a technical librarian and worked there for two years. We used to order stuff from the British Library and from different branches of Digital in the States, for our workforce.

The culture of emigration/migration was deeply embedded within Brendan's own family. He had ten uncles and three aunts on his mother's side all, of whom emigrated. Eight of his ten uncles went to America, the remaining two settled in England. His three aunts also went to America and lived there all their lives. His mother was the only one of the family who settled down locally. When he decided to emigrate he was not short of destination choices. He had plenty of contacts in both England and America, through uncles and first cousins in America and uncles and siblings in England.

While he enjoyed working in England for a few years, his desire at all times was to return to work in Ireland. His hard work and foresight in pursuing opportunities within the organisations he worked for enabled him to have a very successful and fulfilling work life. He settled in Galway and married Margaret in 1974, with whom he had three children. He retired from Digital a number of years ago to spend more time with his family. Sadly, his wife, Margaret, passed away in 2008.

JIMMY BRENNAN

'There were nine beds along one side of the room and nine beds along the other side …'

'The day I was fourteen I left off school.' Jimmy Brennan knew from an early age that he had to assume full responsibility for the work on his home farm since he was an only son and his father was a migratory worker who spent much of his time in England. As well as looking after his holding of land he also worked part-time for the council, when work was available: 'It was £9 something for a fortnight at the council and you worked forty-eight hours a week. We were up at Lynskey's pit [Culmore] quarrying stones, and at the [stone] crusher and the tar boiler.'

In 1957, when Jimmy was eighteen years old and finding himself underemployed on his home farm, he decided to go to his father in England, who at the time was working in a mine in Yorkshire. He went with a neighbour who was as naive as himself: 'The first year I went, Paddy Sweeney was with me. We were gormless enough, too, you know.'

Within a week he was working with his father in the mines in Mexborough, Yorkshire. He was a bit disappointed in the early stages:

> When I went to the pits, you know, you'd say 'Oh they'd be getting great money' but when I had to go training it dropped back a bit – to only £6 a week. Well that was for the first few weeks. But then when you went down the mine after training they put you on haulage – engine driving and there was ponies there, too. There were so many seams – Parkgate seam I was in, I think. It was about £1 4s a shift. But when I was there a while, you'd get to know someone and you'd be getting overtime and that. I done a lot of overtime and I had about £14 or something in the week and there was £4 or £5 taken in tax. I was in no hurry doing double shifts after that! Well, when you done a double shift you done your eight hours and they let you up to have your dinner for an hour, there was a canteen above, and then you went down again for another eight hours.

Jimmy's father, Michael, first went to England in 1920 while still in his early teens. Jimmy's understanding is that his father went to England when he was fifteen and went to his own father who was working at the farmers: 'He always said that the next year he went on his own. He spent a certain length at the farmers and like a lot of them [migrants] he worked his way then until he got into the pits and he spent fifteen years in Lancashire in the pits.'

Michael Brennan was a versatile worker who had a variety of occupations during his time in England, including farm work, construction and the sugar-beet campaigns. He spent most of his working life (fifty years) in England. As Jimmy recalls:

> He spent three years at home at one stage and then he went off to London or somewhere. He worked eight years for McAlpine and then fifteen years in Lancashire. He went down to Scotland then and from there he moved to Mexborough. He spent a good few years there because when I was eight he came home and I was sixteen when he came again.

Like many families in the area most of Jimmy's close relatives either migrated or emigrated. He had uncles in America and England, an aunt in Canada and a migrant aunt who bought a farm in Meath and settled there. Furthermore, both of his sisters worked in England for a number of years before returning to live in Ireland. The custom of fathers initiating sons into the tradition of migration is clear to be seen in his own family:

> My mother's father went to the same farmer for years and years. There was nine in family and he brought the sons with him and they went at about thirteen or fourteen. Then they went to some other part of Lincoln, maybe to the harvest and they went to the tattie picking but there was no sugar beet in my grandfather's time. So they all came back to Ireland again at Christmas and went off again [the following year]. They'd be going like that for a couple of years and gradually they'd work their way into the pits. That's all the work there was that time, I'd say. Irish men were mainly on the sinking pits – sinking shafts or they were coming along making roads. When I worked now at 'Menwells' [mine] there was a lot of fellows from round about [Swinford] – Heaneys and Campbells and that – but they weren't on the coal – they were more or less coming along making roads and putting up girders.

Jimmy didn't go back to the mines on his second trip to England, but went instead to work in a sugar-beet factory. Work at the factory commenced in autumn and went on to early spring. Seasonal work of this nature dovetailed very well with urgent farm work in Ireland and he settled down to a routine of spending the spring and summer working on his home farm and in the sugar-beet factory in England during the autumn and winter: 'You had to go … nothing else. On account of having the bit of land at home you'd go for a few months and come back again.'

Working conditions in the sugar-beet factories were fairly good according to Jimmy. So keen were workers to optimise their earnings, that they were prepared to double-job as well as double shift. Local farmers offered work to any factory employee willing to spend a few hours picking potatoes between their factory shifts and some workers, like Jimmy, were glad to get the opportunity to earn extra money. The factory was shift work – a fortnight on nights and a fortnight on days:

> You could go out to the farm in the evening once you'd finished your shift at the factory at three o'clock. The farmer would be waiting and he'd bring you out from half three to half six. But then if you were on the night shift you'd come off the night shift at seven o'clock and have your tea and the farmer would be there at eight o'clock and he'd bring you out to the field and you worked until one o'clock. You'd get £12 off the farmer and maybe, say £20 from the factory – all clear.

Jimmy worked about four and a half months each year at the beet factory: 'that was in the Sixties because I went in '61 and I think I finished up in '68 or '69. I'd enough money then to put towards [the cost of] a new house.'

The living accommodation attached to the factories was good in some cases and not so good in others, as he recalls:

> There were nine beds along one side of the room and nine beds along the other side – a total of eighteen in the one compartment – rough accommodation. All you got was one old wardrobe and the bed. In Newark [Nottinghamshire] they had a great set-up when I went there. They had [only] three in every room there – great accommodation – very modern.

He returned finally from the sugar-beet campaigns in England in the late 1960s and settled back on his home farm in Culmore. His interest in farm work never waned and Jimmy, now retired and living in Swinford with his wife Mary, still continues to engage in some farm activity, although of a much more relaxed nature.

TOMMY McGOWAN

'The first year I went to England I left a job here where I was getting £7 a week and my first pay packet in England was about £22.'

Wintertime was an especially slack period for small farmers in Ireland and to supplement their incomes, some joined the beet campaigns in England, which ran from about October to March during the 1960s and 1970s. Tommy McGowan from Charlestown was one of those who took advantage of the beet campaigns for a number of years in the early 1960s, although he was an only son and neither his father nor his mother migrated.

During his teenage years Tommy worked alongside his father on the home farm but also sought paid work outside the farm when it became available. Prior to migrating in 1962 he had been employed sporadically by the county council: 'Well, I know that myself and Val Moffitt [neighbour] worked for the council with the two horses and carts, carting from O'Brien's pit [Bushfield] above. I think for a six-day week the wages came to about £7.'

Describing his journey to England, he recalls:

> We travelled by train to Dublin, stayed in the Iveagh Hostel overnight – that was organised for us. I think it was about a shilling [six cent] a night at the time. I think it was, kinda, to keep all the workers together. They were easy collected then to get on the boat.'

Different groups were sent from the hostel to the various beet factories all over England. He was sent to Bardney, in Lincolnshire:

> I knew where I was going was a country area. There was no town at all. The nearest big town was Lincoln city – you never went into town. It was too far away. Instead you stayed in the hostel and played cards or watched television. There was a pub down the road and we'd go down now and again for a few pints.

The main object of the Irish workers was to make as much money as possible in the few months of the campaign. Some workers were so keen to augment their wages that as well as their seven days a week shifts in the factory, they sought work from a local farmer picking potatoes, as he relates:

> If we worked in the morning at the factory we'd go out in the afternoon to the farmer. And then when you were on the afternoon shift at the factory you'd go out in the morning to the farmer. And if you were working nights you'd also go out in the morning [after doing your shift]. There'd be seven or eight of us in a gang and we'd work at our own pace.

Although he had no great expectations of life in England, he was pleased with how things turned out:

> I was surprised, pleasantly surprised. The first year I went to England I left a job here where I was getting £7 a week and my first pay packet in England was about £22. That was in 1962. Plus we used to pick potatoes for a local farmer in our free time and we'd get another £7 or £8 a week along with that.

While there were many Irish people working in the factory, Tommy knew just one or two: 'Jimmy Brennan from Culmore was one of them.' Like many Irish migrants he sent money home: 'Every penny I could. Every fortnight or that you'd send whatever you could. My mother would bank it for me. She wouldn't spend it.'

Employment opportunities were increasing in Ireland from the late 1960s on, and after four campaigns in England, Tommy settled back permanently into his home farm, where he still resides with his wife Mary and family.

KEVIN WALSH

'He had a hold of my hand, I remember it well. He said, "Whatever you do, don't work like a horse and spend like a donkey."'

Although an only son and heir presumptive to the family farm, Kevin Walsh from Brackloonagh took a few years out to work in England as a carpenter in the late 1950s. As a teenager he had attended night-classes in the local town hall (under the auspices of Mayo Vocational Education Committee) and had developed skills that would be of good service to him in his time in England: 'We did around two years [night-classes] in there and I was only fifteen at the time and you had to be sixteen to get into it. He [teacher] never passed no remarks because I was big for my age. The training stood to me when I went to England.'

Kevin had paid employment for a year in the early '50s as the Rural Electrification Scheme passed through the local (Charlestown) region. His wage was £5 6s 8d a week on this scheme but he lost his job after one year when the project moved on to the next district. As there was little or no employment locally, he began to look to England as a source of work.

The thought of emigration didn't faze him. His own father had worked as a seasonal labourer in England – at the farmers in summer and autumn, and in the mines during the winter – for a period of about ten years. His mother, Kathleen Dwyer, was a returned Yank who had worked for almost eight years in America as a cook. Unusually for the times and for the region, she had second-level education. Fortuitously, domestic science was her favourite subject in secondary school and this gave her an edge when she sought employment as a cook in the US. 'You see her two older sisters had gone ahead of her. She'd have been over there in '27. She was there in the Depression along with Walter [brother]. She later came on a holiday, never intended to stay but met my father and married into the land here.'

Furthermore, he had two uncles who had settled in England and a total of two uncles and three aunts who had lived all their working lives in the US. 'I had aunts in America who wanted me out there but I wouldn't go. I had an uncle that was in America during the Depression and he never had anything good to say about America.' So Kevin joined the thousands of other young emigrants going from the Charlestown region to England in the 1950s. He had a job arranged for him through the aegis of a local tradesman when he first arrived in England in 1956:

Ben Garvey, I went over to. He had seen some work I had done in the vocational school on one of his visits home and he said 'You'd do very well in England.' He told me there was loads of work there and that they were looking for carpenters. We worked together in England for a short while and then, you know, you'd be split-up and put with somebody else.

His first job in England was on a massive construction project in the south of England:

To give you an idea – in the Isle of Grain, where we went first – there were 3,000 carpenters at the peak of it. The job was an oil refinery similar to the one they're talking about doing down at Bellanaboy [Belmullet]. The site would be anything up to thirty miles long – that was from where the boats anchored. We were brought in for our breakfast in the morning by bus and if you missed the bus going back you were as well to go home because you wouldn't be able to find the place you were working in, the site was that big.

What expectations did he have of life in England? 'Well I knew it was going to be better than here, you know – from talking to people and from seeing people coming home. They were always well dressed and they seemed to have a few bob [shillings] to spend and they were anxious to get back again to it.'

He remembers clearly the good advice he got from his uncle before he went to England: 'He had a hold of my hand, I remember it well. He said, "Whatever you do, don't work like a horse and spend like a donkey."'

His first job in England brought back good memories to him and he recalls an incident in one place he worked when he paid a nostalgic visit back there a few years ago:

I left here on Friday and I was working Monday morning. Ben Garvey gave me directions how to get to Gravesend. I even remember the number of the house I went into – 39 Harvell Street and I was back in it there some years ago. I went back to Gravesend to look at it. I was going down the street and I met a man the same age as myself and he was looking at me and I said, 'I wouldn't know this town,' I said. 'Why, were you here before?' he said. 'I was' I said, 'a long time ago.' He said, 'I've been here all my life.' He was a man from Kerry and he had stayed around [in Gravesend] and made his home there.

The standard of accommodation offered by landlords and landladies drew a mixed reaction from him:

> We were in digs in the beginning and then eventually we started taking rooms. Well, the English landladies and landlords, I couldn't say enough for them and the Irish I couldn't say enough about them. They were the pits. I had a Cork man and Cork woman and a Tipperary man and I never will forget them. Bad food and not enough of it.

One incident he recalls involved his Tipperary landlord and three Scotsmen who were staying there:

> This Tipperary man was deadly [focussed] on time and if you weren't in by six o'clock he wouldn't give you your dinner. Now I always beat the time and I got my dinner. However, one evening all three Scotsmen got held up [were late] and the landlord wouldn't give them their dinner. I was woken the following morning by the shouting downstairs. The evening before I had looked out and he [landlord] had ten or fifteen sheets out drying on the line. However, hearing the uproar, I went over to the window and every one of the sheets were cut into the size of bandages and the three Scotsmen gone.

Kevin was the only one to speak up when the police were called: '"Well," I said, "If you gave them three Scotsmen their dinner yesterday evening that you'd cooked for them, your sheets would still be hanging on the line. You're a disgrace to the Irish," I said. So I gathered up my stuff and went down and got another place.' However, he acknowledges that his experience of digs wasn't all bad and there were some landlords/ladies who were very solicitous:

> We were in digs where they'd have a dartboard, draughts, card playing, an old piano and they'd want to know where you were going, when you were going out [adopting a parental role] … We weren't drinking and I always went round with a crowd that weren't drinking and we were causing no bother in the house.

Like many of his compatriots, he sent money home on a regular basis: 'Oh I did surely – every week. I don't think I ever sent them an empty letter and along with that I built this house while I was still in England.'

On the whole he enjoyed his life in England and had many positive experiences during his time there: 'I was happy in England. I fell in with a great crowd of lads.

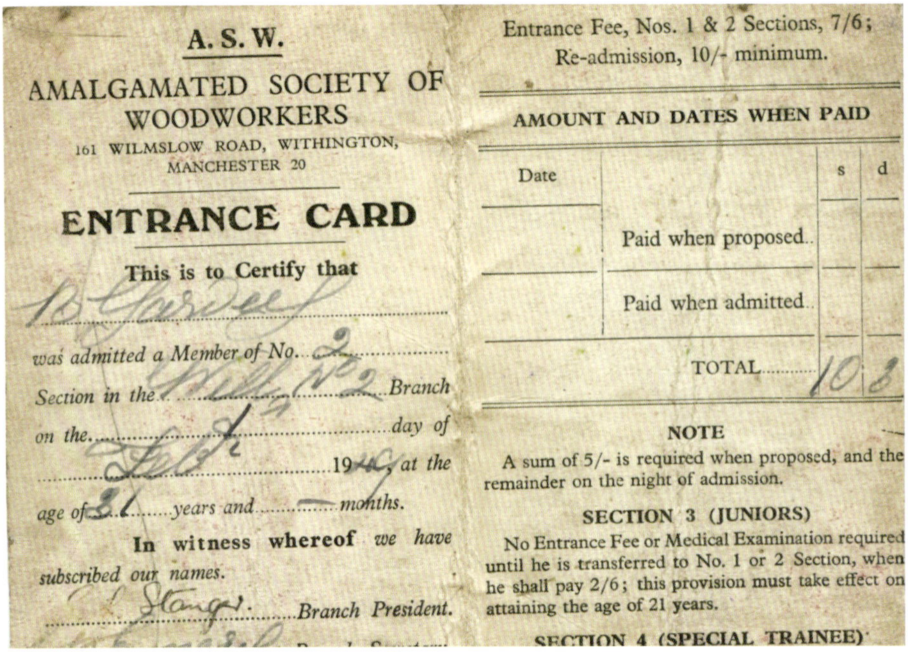

A. S. W.

AMALGAMATED SOCIETY OF WOODWORKERS

161 WILMSLOW ROAD, WITHINGTON, MANCHESTER 20

ENTRANCE CARD

This is to Certify that

B Garvey

was admitted a Member of No. 2

Section in the Well No 2 *Branch*

on the 1st *day of*

Feb 19[illegible] *at the*

age of 21 *years and* — *months.*

In witness whereof *we have subscribed our names.*

Branch President.

Entrance Fee, Nos. 1 & 2 Sections, 7/6; Re-admission, 10/- minimum.

AMOUNT AND DATES WHEN PAID

Date		s	d
	Paid when proposed		
	Paid when admitted		
	TOTAL	10	8

NOTE

A sum of 5/- is required when proposed, and the remainder on the night of admission.

SECTION 3 (JUNIORS)

No Entrance Fee or Medical Examination required until he is transferred to No. 1 or 2 Section, when he shall pay 2/6; this provision must take effect on attaining the age of 21 years.

SECTION 4 (SPECIAL TRAINEE)

Fig. 22: Union card. (Source: Bernie Garvey)

Ben Garvey was there – a kind of father figure. He wouldn't put you astray.' Kevin socialised mainly with Irish people: 'Well, every county in Ireland. Whoever was in the house with you. We all went off together. They were all Irish – very few English you'd have with you.'

During his tenure in England he worked in several different locations:

> Gravesend was my first stop – then over to Gloucester – then up to Nottingham to another power station at High Marnham. Then I was on the M1 motorway when they started that. We were on the bridges there at Northampton. Then I went with another crowd and I finished up back in London. The whole thing was to get seven days a week. It didn't matter what the work was. If there wasn't seven days a week in it, it was no good. There was a book came out there. They called it 'Paddy's Bible' – the *Labour News* – and every week there was a list of carpenters wanted. So you just rang up. We knew the rate – it was union rate and you got subsistence allowance – three guineas a week.

Kevin had learned the importance of further education from his time as a student attending woodwork night-classes in Charlestown town hall in the early 1950s and when his friend, Tom McGoldrick from Leitrim, suggested attending a course in carpentry in the local technical college in England, he was willing but apprehensive:

> He [Tom] came to me one night and he said 'Would you go down here to the Tech. with me if we get in?' 'Jeez,' I said, 'Sure we won't be let in.' 'Ah we will,' he said, 'I made a few enquiries.' So we set off one night and we went down to the Tech. We did a bit of an interview and told them we were working out on a site. I learned there about drawing and we did a bit of bench work. It was all English fellows in along with us. We were a bit of a novelty, I suppose. We were used to working with English people. I found the English working class – I could never say enough good about them. The English working class were lovely.

In 1961 he returned to Ireland to care for his widowed mother and to look after the home farm, to which he was the heir apparent. When he returned to Ireland permanently, he discovered that money was still very scarce in the building industry. He decided to try and find work in his own locality and was contracted to build a house for a client: 'I was getting £20 a week when I left England and I worked once and a half times as long [in Ireland] and I got £9.' However, over the intervening years he has developed from scratch a prosperous and substantial business linked to the construction industry, running it alongside the family farm and its specialism in pedigree animals, ably supported by his wife Maureen and their family.

PADDY MOLLOY

'The agent would look at your hands – see were you a worker.'

Paddy Molloy from Cloonlara, Swinford grew up on a small farm and like most of his peers in the area migrated to England while still a teenager. He had, however, sought work from a county council ganger-man shortly after leaving National school but found the available work sporadic and unfulfilling:

> I asked John Horkan [ganger-man] was there any chance of a bit of work. 'Ah, you're too young for work – what kind of work would you want?' I said I had a great ass and we could carry the water to the steam engine. 'I'll tell you what I'll do, I'll put you on the waiting list,' said John. Within three days I was working. I was fourteen at the time. Wages were 14*s* 8*d* a day for the ass and cart and myself. That was a man's wages at the time. I worked for four or five months at that.

He went to secondary school for a time afterwards but found it hard to settle down to study after his stint in paid employment. He got his chance to leave school when he was about sixteen years of age: 'What I done was I signed on for the beet and I got accepted for the beet [sugar-beet campaign in England]. He [an agent] used to come every year from England into the local labour exchange [to assess possible employees].'

The interviews were quite perfunctory: 'The agent would look at your hands – see were you a worker. They knew the workers – soon as they'd look at you they'd know. [If successful] you were called to the beet factory – you had no choice – you had to go to where they sent you.'

Recruits to the sugar-beet factories were brought by train to Dublin on a free pass, as he recalls: 'The first day we went [from home] you had a medical to see were you fit. When you came off the train in Dublin you were met by a factory representative and you were supposed to carry a white handkerchief' [for identification].

The prospective employees were brought to the Iveagh Hostel where they had their medical and stayed overnight. When they reached Holyhead the recruits were taken by coach to their workplace in Bury St Edmunds: 'All the factory employees were there together on the coach. We were put to work the following day.'

Working on the farm and elsewhere before he left Ireland meant that Paddy was

Fig. 23: Market day, Swinford, 1963. (Source: Swinford Photography)

used to hard, physical work, even though he was only sixteen years of age when he first migrated. The heavy work at the factory didn't faze him:

> The production line had to be kept clear. If that wasn't kept clear you might as well go. We went for hard work. I was in pulp – all piecework – loading wagons and stacking pulp. We were at the top of the elevator. We took bags as they were coming [off the elevator] – ten-stone bags [60 kg] on to wagons. The best mate I had there was a man from Kerry, Michael Moriarty. He was a great worker. To work with him you had to be something special or he wouldn't take you on. He took me as a mate and I tell you, the two of us pulled [worked well together]. A good week's wages when we started was £25 … and everything found!

The sugar-beet factory work was constant and unrelenting once the campaign started:

> It [the job] started in the middle of September and then it'd go to sometime in February. One year it lasted up to Patrick's Day. You could do eight hours and lie down if you wanted – 'twas up to yourself. The

factory paid time and a half for overtime and if you worked Sunday you got double time and if you worked Christmas day you got treble time. We started the morning shift at seven o'clock – seven to three. The following fortnight we'd do three to eleven and then the following fortnight we'd do eleven to seven. Christmas day was the same as any day. That's the way we wanted it. A seven-day week and, if possible, sixteen hours a day – if we could get it. I bought a tractor with it!

Recruits to the sugar-beet factories came mainly from the west of Ireland with a substantial number coming from the east Mayo area. Paddy met many Mayo men both on the journey over and in the factories. He recalls that 'among those going were lads from Swinford, Kiltimagh, Foxford, Ballina and also lads from Kerry and Donegal. There'd be about twenty or thirty of us from Swinford. We met up with the others on our journey over.'

He had few expectations the first year he went to the beet factory and he was pleasantly surprised at the working conditions and living accommodation: 'I didn't think it would be as good. Very happy. There was a lovely hostel attached to the factory – polished and clean. Every week the sheets were changed, the floors were mopped. There was a recreation hall as well.'

Since the beet campaigns usually ended in early spring, he took the opportunity to seek further employment in England for a month or two before returning to his home farm in Ireland: 'At the end of the season after the beet was finished I'd always go to Eddie [brother] who'd be in London or John [another brother] down in Wales and have another couple of weeks before I'd come back home. They'd fix me up with work.'

Much as he enjoyed working with his brothers on the conclusion of the beet campaign, there was one aspect of his life in England which discommoded him somewhat. He found it difficult to adjust to English digs and English landladies after the comforts of the hostel at Bury St Edmunds:

> I remember going down to Wales to my brother John who got work for me. I had a landlady who didn't want you in the house. You had to get out to the pub and next thing … such a one came in to the pub and a whole round of drinks followed and I said to myself 'This is not my life whatsoever!' You go into these pubs and you turn out to be a proper *latchiko* [layabout].

Time eventually caught up with him and much as he enjoyed his annual trips to the beet factory, the fact that his parents were ageing and no longer able to look after the farm in his absence caused him to reconsider his options and he reluctantly decided to stay at home permanently in 1969, having completed thirteen seasons at the beet factory in Bury St Edmunds:

> The last year I was going to go I had everything ready to go out the door and I thought to myself, 'what am I doing?' They [parents] won't be able to do nothing and I had a lot of cattle out the fields. I fired the case from me and told my father – 'No, I'm not going!' And he laughed with joy.

He never went to England to work after that. However, he had an entrepreneurial streak and immediately got involved in farm-contract work in his home area. He bought a threshing machine, which he had seen advertised in the *Western People*, and travelled the country during the autumn months threshing corn for local farmers. He continues to farm and still engages in different associated enterprises. He and his wife Mary, together with their family, live on the home farm on the outskirts of Swinford town.

MARTIN NEARY

'I thought the work would be awful hard, like, you know. I was shocked! It was away easier than I expected.'

Another farmer from that era was Martin Neary from the Swinford area, who worked in English sugar-beet factories during the 1960s and 1970s. Martin was an only child, who lived with his widowed mother and migrated to England for the first time at twenty-three years of age. As he points out, 'The only place I would have gone to before that was … I was in the FCA [Fórsa Cosanta Áitiúil/Local Defence Force] going to camps and that.'

As well as the economic reasons for going, there was a social aspect to it, according to Martin: 'You wanted to make a break, like, or get away for a change. You were getting bored with what you were doing and it was encouragement to move on. Moving out of here and going to England was a bit of an adventure.'

Martin liked the conditions in the factory well enough that he went to the same workplace for eight successive campaigns: 'Well, I used to go for about four months in the wintertime and that went on for eight years. '74 would have been my last year.'

Prospective employees were assigned to a particular factory and had no choice in their destination. Was he upset by this? 'I never thought about it. I didn't care where I was going. I didn't care as long as I was going.'

The interviews took place in Swinford and a group of about ten workers was recruited for a particular factory by the agent. Martin recalls some of the locals who made up the group:

> The two Groarkes from Cloontubrid, Paddy Groarke out in Meelick, that was three and myself four and there was Conway and his son from up in Kinaffe and probably Padhraic Durkin, seven. The first agent that recruited me was an ex-army officer. There used to be a big crowd in there in the recruiting office. This would be in September. The first year that I went, there were one hundred and twelve recruits. They were mostly Kerry people, Connemara, Mayo and Roscommon going to one particular factory and the last year that I went I think there were only twenty-seven.

He explains how the numbers taken on by the factories began to reduce substantially in the early 1970s, as a result of more and more mechanisation in the factories:

'It wasn't that they were taking on locals [English men] or anything like that. It's that the machinery had been modernised. Every year there'd be ten or twelve gone [let go].'

Martin recollects how recruits were overseen before they travelled on to the factory in England:

> We used to stay in the Iveagh Hostel [Dublin] for one night and you'd be processed there and you'd be getting your ticket there. People were complaining about the food in the hostel. There was nothing wrong with the food – it was as good as we were used to. The fare was paid by the company but you paid it back after a month or so working in England. A good few would go and avail of the cheap fare and maybe work a week, get their wages and then hightail it [leave without refunding the fare]!

The factory provided year-round employment for local labour but emergency work required people to take on the more arduous tasks and this work was more or less reserved for the Irish recruits: 'It was seven-day shift work and the locals wanted nine to five. They'd be worse paid than we were.'

What were his expectations on his first trip to England?

> I didn't allow myself to have much expectations. I thought the work would be awful hard, like, you know. I was shocked! It was away easier than I expected. There was no hard work at all. You wouldn't be put in a hard job if you couldn't do it. The accommodation at the factory hostel was fine. The hostel was just beside the factory and was about two miles from the village of Allscott in Shropshire. The laundry came every week and changed the sheets. There was a certain amount of heating and you could apply for extra blankets if it was cold in wintertime. Grub was okay. When I came home I was a lot fatter than when I left!

The main outlets for socialising were the pub and cinema: 'You'd socialise with your own type in the hostel and going into town. I used to work with nearly all English people but you wouldn't socialise with them.'

This area of Shropshire was, it would seem, a destination for an earlier generation of Irish migrants. Martin came across a number of people whose ancestors had come from the Swinford area: 'People from Swinford – like second generation. People who emigrated there and their sons. There was a big power station around there one time. I've a feeling that there was a power station around Ironbridge and that a lot of Irish worked there for a time and probably settled there.'

Martin enjoyed the change of environment provided by his seasonal work in England:

> I was quite happy to go – glad to go and glad to come back. I had the urge to stay over there sometimes and if I didn't have to come home – if there was nobody here – I would have stayed over there but there was that attachment to the land and my mother and you were expected to go home.

As he was preparing for his ninth season at the sugar-beet factory his mother fell ill and he had to change his plans: 'My mother was in bad health then – she was losing her sight and I had to stay at home to look after her.'

Like many young Irish migrants, he sent money home on a regular basis:

> Well that's the way I used to save it. You had to write every week so you would send it then. I would earn about £15 a week that first time I went [1966]. That was the average unless you did overtime. You might get £20 if you did some overtime. Now, I was a few years there and I did night shifts – worked twelve hours at night – and you could get up to £50 [a week].

Martin settled back finally to his home farm in 1974 and remained a single man all his life. He developed his farm over the years into a modern unit of land and has the reputation of being a progressive farmer. His holding has provided a comfortable standard of living and being in his home environment has given him much contentment in life.

A much deeper disparity is evident in the migration history of his extended family. His father, Martin senior, emigrated to the US in 1915 and served a period of time in the army there. He returned to Ireland in 1939 and married into his wife's home farm. He migrated again for a further two years before returning finally in 1941. He died in 1949 when Martin junior was just five years of age. All but one of Martin senior's siblings emigrated – four to the US and two to Britain. Two of his uncles on his mother's side also emigrated to England and settled there. Out of a total of eleven aunts and uncles, eight emigrated permanently to either America or Britain, further weakening the already attenuated community in east Mayo.

EILEEN (O'ROURKE) KILLILEA

'You'd be vetted if you wanted to go outside the door at home. Migration was freedom for me.'

Bill O'Rourke, Eileen Killilea's father, was from Cork and spent ten years working in England in the 1930s before he met and married Eileen's mother, Winnie Marren, in 1943. She was also an emigrant and had worked for thirteen years in England before she married. They both returned to Ireland in 1953 to take over her home farm in Sonnagh near the town of Charlestown. Bill, however, returned to England to work at the beet factories and in construction for a number of years afterwards.

To add to the migration narrative of Eileen's family it is necessary to go back over the movements of her aunts and uncles on her mother's side from the 1920s on. Eileen's mother had ten siblings – three sisters and seven brothers – all of whom emigrated permanently from Ireland. Four siblings had emigrated prior to 1929 and all went to Chicago. However, in the 1930s it was difficult for intending emigrants to enter the United States and she and five of her remaining siblings went to England instead, with two of them settling there permanently. The remaining three siblings worked for various lengths of time in England before going to America to join their older brother and sisters in Chicago in the 1950s. None returned permanently to Ireland except Winnie.

Notwithstanding her family's migrant history, Eileen decided to try and find work in her local area when she completed her secondary-school education in 1962. She applied for and got a job with a family in a neighbouring town, looking after children. She was just seventeen years of age when she started her new job:

> I was up in Kiltimagh … kinda looking after children. I was only there for six months. The pay was very bad – £2 a week it was. That'd be about '62, I think. These live-in jobs are not good either, 'cause you're there all the time. You had no hours to yourself at all. Oh 'twas dire! … I remember when I first got the job I went in on trial for a month … they had seven children – seven children! It was my first job.

She left her job at Christmas and remained at home, helping on the farm, until she spotted an ad in a local paper looking for trainee nurses in England:

> I saw this advert in the *Western* [*People*] in July. I answered the ad and

they wrote back to me and they sent me the date to arrive and sent me the fare and all. So I went over then to the hospital. I had to do a test, like, and passed that grand and then I had to get measured for a uniform. Then I went to the doctor and he asked me all these questions. I had TB [tuberculosis] when I was fifteen and they [hospital] wouldn't take me for another five years on that account and when you're eighteen, five years is a lifetime. I've always regretted not getting into nursing.

The memory of her first big journey from her native Charlestown to Manchester still evokes strong feelings; a mixture of excitement and alarm is how she describes it. Journeys that now seem inconsequential had much more apprehension and anxiety built into them for those travelling alone than can be imagined nowadays. Adding to the excitement and alarm she felt on the day she made the journey to England were the headlines splashed across the national newspapers on that day of 'The Great Train Robbery' in England:

I remember when I got on the bus down the road here it was the morning of the Great Train Robbery in England. I didn't know when I was getting on the bus out here I could have booked all the way to Manchester. When I got to the boat the official kept telling me I could book to Manchester but I said no! no! He got sick of me anyway and gave me a ticket to Holyhead only and the boat sailed out. It must be one o'clock in the morning when we got off. I had no ticket then to get on the train [ticket office was closed]. I was in an awful state. What was I going to do? Fortunately a porter came along anyhow and I told him. So he said 'Come on down here and I'll get a ticket for you.' And he brought me down and got me a ticket. I never will forget that!

After her disappointment in the hospital, she quickly readjusted her sights and got a job as a shop assistant in Woolworth's: 'Woolworth's were first. Then after about a year I got a job – a bleddy great paying job – in a factory fitting parts for fridges. It was piecework. Oh it was mighty.' However, the factory started laying people off and she lost her job:

So then I got a job in an office. The work was grand – it was, kinda, a catalogue place. They were all old women in it and they were the most horrible women and a few of them were Irish and all. I didn't wait long there. Then I got a job on the buses as a conductor. I loved that job. There was great money now in that – nearly £20 a week. When I got married in 1968 I left that job.

It was a coincidence that the house she and her husband Frank moved to happened to be located just opposite a hospital, and Eileen, still hankering after a career in the nursing profession, applied for a job there: 'I got a job in the hospital as a nursing auxiliary. The kids were small then you see. What I should have done that time was apply for nursing again. If I was as wise then … but the kids were small and it would have been awful hard.'

While her main reason for migrating was economic, Eileen looked forward also to the freedom that was lacking in Ireland at the time and which living away from home would give her: 'You'd be vetted if you wanted to go outside the door at home. Migration was freedom for me. You were on your own there and you made your own decisions.' However, after sixteen years in England and with a family of three young children, she and her husband Frank decided to leave Manchester and return to Ireland permanently to take over her home farm in Sonnagh in 1979:

> I enjoyed my sixteen years there but I was glad to be coming home. I was delighted, you know. You know over there you'd have to watch them [the children] the whole time. The little fellow [third child] was only five weeks old when we came back finally.

Eileen worked on her home farm and had a part-time job as a receptionist in a local business before sadly passing away in 2006.

FRANK GALLAGHER

'When I got as far as Holyhead there were that many people there I knew, 'twas like going to the bog.'

While employment for Irish agricultural workers on English farms was drying up rapidly by the 1960s, there were still pockets in east Mayo where the migrant tradition persisted. It might be asked why workers would put themselves through the hardship involved in corn harvesting, potato picking or beet pulling in England when there was plenty of work available in construction there, offering better conditions and a more convivial social life. However, despite the harsh conditions endured by the agricultural workers, there were some crucial advantages accruing to them which were not readily available to building workers. They were assured of work through prior contact with the farmer. There was a guaranteed price per acre agreed in advance of travel. Lodgings were often free with vegetables and potatoes supplied by the farmer. The wages were cash-in-hand and outgoings were kept to a minimum. The work was available when farm work was slowing down in Ireland and the work-term was short, allowing workers to return home to their families before Christmas.

Frank Gallagher from Killaturley, Swinford was a migrant worker who served a number of terms at the farmers in England during the 1960s. He still hadn't reached his sixteenth birthday when he first set off for Lincolnshire as part of a potato-picking team:

> I went on my own but I wasn't on my own for long. The *Princess Maud* [ship] was waiting for us at Dún Laoghaire but we had to wait till they put the cattle on first. So the cattle were down below lowing and the Paddies were up top crying. When I got as far as Holyhead there were that many people there I knew, 'twas like going to the bog. That was my introduction to England.

Frank was one of a team of potato pickers organised locally but liaising with a gang leader *in situ* in England:

> There would be a fellow in England who would sort out a 'take' of spuds with a farmer that might give them forty or fifty acres or a couple of hundred to pick and they'd arrange so much an acre and then they'd send for the crew – mostly local lads or lads that we knew. We'd land back

there then and if we were short one, we might get one in the pub that night. You could pick up a crew of seasoned workers in the pubs fairly handy. But sometimes you'd get a crew that wouldn't agree too well or someone of them would go on the tear at the weekend and wouldn't turn up or be half dead and he'd have to be replaced, to put it mildly, and then some of them might be leaving a lot [of potatoes] behind. Those missed potatoes still had to be picked in the 'harrowings' and so time would be lost in the second picking if too many were overlooked or 'buried' in the first picking. Oh it was tough going. You'd have to be up at five o'clock to have your trousers on at seven – you'd be that stiff! But then again we were reared and brought up on small, little holdings and the going was tough here at home also. The only mechanical device [at home] was the wooden wheelbarrow with the big wooden wheel and it was a big change to see how they lived on the other side of the fence. We learned quite a bit and we saved a few quid and came back then for the Christmas with a new suit of clothes and a pair of pointy shoes.

As the eldest of a family of six children – three boys and three girls – it was a given that Frank would migrate. In fact the three boys migrated to England for varying lengths of time, but all came back to settle permanently in their own locality. Only one of his sisters emigrated from Ireland. She and her husband worked as teachers in Japan and China and are at present working in Europe, in Prague.

Both of Frank's parents were emigrants. His mother worked as a receptionist in a doctor's surgery in England for about ten years before returning to Ireland to marry during the Second World War. His father spent all his working life in England, returning home permanently when he reached pension age. He worked in England at the farmers, in construction work, in mining and in the beet factories at various times, keeping himself employed throughout the year.

Frank spent six consecutive autumns in England before his twenty-first birthday, all of them involving picking potatoes piecework with a team of men from home, including his father, Michael: 'They'd be local [Swinford] men – my father, Michael; my brother, Michael; Martin Groarke, Tom McDonnell, Joe Gallagher and John Gallagher, brother of Joe. We were in Peterborough most of the time, sharing a house.'

Because of his long tenure picking potatoes at the farmers, he amassed a great amount of knowledge associated with the work:

> The average day would start about half seven. You could see the spuds then – it would be getting bright. You'd have your dinner about half ten under

Fig. 24: Killaturley potato pickers in Lincolnshire, 1963: (left to right) Frank Gallagher, Michael Gallagher (senior), two English farmhands on tractors, Michael Gallagher (junior), Martin Groarke, Eugene Madden, Ballaghaderreen. (Courtesy Frank Gallagher)

> the hedge. You'd finish at one or two o'clock. People would often say 'why didn't you keep going' ? But physically you couldn't. Some would but the majority couldn't. You'd be really crocked. Sundays you'd be licking your wounds [recuperating].

As well as the English farmhands who drove the tractors and the Irish team of pickers, there were also teams of local women engaged in the potato-harvesting process:

> When the gangs of women used to pick the spuds – there might be fifty women in a field picking. They wouldn't fling the baskets into the trailer at all [they'd be too heavy]. They'd take another empty basket and keep filling. There was a trailer coming down the field behind them and there was a man emptying the [women's] baskets into the trailer. There would be a woman looking after their kids and things, at the end of the field under a bush [an open-air crèche]. The female pickers were generally English girls of maybe Irish descent and my golly they could pick spuds and they didn't mind the *craic* at all. They'd be generally in the twenty [age] bracket – maybe students or young teachers trying to get a few quid together.

Arrangements were made in advance with the farmer, through a gang master, in regard to the area to be picked and the price per acre:

> We found them [farmers] to be fairly good. We never had any disagreement with them. £17 10*s* per acre was the average price in '63/'64. The average picker would pick half an acre of spuds in the day. If there was a heavier crop they would look for more money.

At this time, in the mid-1960s, supermarkets were being built in the area and it was realised by the pickers that the metal basket used in supermarkets was more suitable for collecting potatoes than the old *ciseán* (wicker basket), which collected a huge amount of soil on its base and was hard to clean.

Manual potato picking was fizzling out in the mid-1960s, as the mechanical tattie pickers were coming in, as Frank recollects:

> They were in their infancy at the time but some of the land around Peterborough, out around Eye and them places, they were reclaimed from the sea and it was cloddy land and the potato picking [machine] used to pick the clods as well as the spuds and the Paddies got the job instead. Now that was tough going because your fingers would be skinned up to here. Come home in the evening you'd rub salt into them [to prevent infection] and you'd be yelping with the pain.

However, some ingenuity was applied to the problem and a practical solution was found by the team, as Frank explains:

> You'd get a pair of tight gloves and you'd cut the fingers off and you'd pull the [glove] fingers up on your fingers and you'd bang away. When a wet day would come or a bad day you had the option of going home or riddling spuds. The farmer had a Nissen hut, a big thing on wheels and within the Nissen hut they had a mechanical screener and there was a bagging unit and weighing scales and they'd push it up against the end of the pit of potatoes and you'd fork the spuds into it. The boys [workers] would pick out hard ones, or rotten ones or leaves and they [potatoes] went out into bags. There'd be another fellow watching them there and he'd stack the bags and in the evening you'd get so much a bag as they went up the conveyor into the truck. It was piecework. It wasn't big money but it was better than sitting within looking out the window.

Fig. 25: Collecting potatoes in plastic baskets, 1963: (left to right) English farmhand, Frank Gallagher, Michael Gallagher (junior), English farmhand, Martin Groarke, Eugene Madden. (Courtesy Frank Gallagher)

Frank, who was born in 1945, left school at fourteen years of age – 'I could just write my name' – and after some time doing odd jobs at home decided to emigrate, just before his sixteenth birthday: 'I borrowed £20 and I went to England. It cost me £17 10*s* to go at the time [1961] and the change [from the borrowed £20] had to keep me going till the following Friday week if I got a job.' The abrupt end to his formal education didn't deter him from trying to better himself, both educationally and in the pursuit of expertise in a range of vocations or occupations, as he reveals:

> The rest was self education – correspondence courses and night classes. I was interested in radio above all things. I got hooked on radio (technical side) and spent twelve and a half years studying that – engaging with correspondence courses and night classes under the aegis of the National Radio School, Reading [England] taking any chance I got to work with old radios. I wouldn't be in England any full year so these [courses] would be mostly at the back end for a few months.

Opportunities to study and advance his knowledge in the radio business were available while he was in England he acknowledges:

England was a great place to get going on correspondence courses or night school. I was moving up on the radio side of things and I was at the stage where I could nearly make a living from it and then the technology changed. They went from the valves down to the micro chips and transistors and after twelve and a half years I went over to electrical full time – industrial wiring.

A course he followed with the British Institute of Engineering gave an impetus to his new career in industrial wiring. However, that, too, changed in a few years: 'It went into different hi-tech stuff.'

As well as working at the farmers picking potatoes for a number of seasons during the 1960s, he also engaged in building work after the farm work ended, before he came home for Christmas. Frank was just sixteen years of age when he was first employed as a construction worker in England:

I'll never forget my first introduction to that. Seven o'clock in the morning I was told: 'There's a lump of concrete to break out there under a downpipe.' They gave me a hammer and chisel and I was belting away until six o'clock in the evening when someone said 'Come on, we're going home.' I was at it for about three weeks. Then I was introduced to the concrete mixer – 'twas promotion.

Unlike many of the Irish potato pickers, Frank didn't live in accommodation provided by the farmer. Instead he and his team rented a house in Peterborough. They were collected and left back each day by a farmhand. He had, however, heard of the 'kips': 'I never slept in them but I heard a lot of tales about them from men that actually lived in them. They'd [farmers] run out the cows and whitewash the barn and put the Irish workers in.'

Finding accommodation independently of the farmers was Frank's choice, but it, too, left a lot to be desired, as he admits:

We used to stay in the city. It was maybe twenty miles from the farm. There must be about twenty of us in this house. It was dog rough. But it was no worse than what we left. You paid so much a week and done your own shackling [cooking]. At night time you'd go into your room and you'd put the chair up against the door and the few bob you had under the pillow and make the best of it.

While the wages in England were good, when the cost of living and socialising were factored in to the outgoings, there was little enough left to send home, as he soon realised:

> Knowing the situation at home – when I started on the buildings in '62, £13 10*s* a week was top money and there was many a family man wasn't making that much money and you gave a fiver to the landlady, you sent a fiver home and you did what you could with what you had [left]. You wouldn't go too far on that. You had to save a few quid and you had to live. I loved dancing and if there was a dance coming up – well, yes, I would go.

When Frank went to England initially, he worked at the farmers for the first month or two, picking potatoes. Then, through his father, he got employment in the building trade in the vicinity of Peterborough to take him up to Christmas:

> I could have continued on the whole time in England doing carpentry, if I wanted to, but the wintertime and coming near Christmas – I think you got homesick – you wanted home and there was nothing much doing for the winter in England. We'd try to get as near as possible to Christmas on the buildings and then we'd head home.

As conditions improved in Ireland into the 1970s, he got more work at home and spent less time in England until after twelve years of temporary periods in England he got a full-time job in his home locality where he was able to use his self-acquired knowledge of electrical engineering in a productive manner:

> I was lucky. I was working for Cyril Gibbons of Kilkelly at the time and there was a fairly serious thunderstorm at work. It blew a panel apart. They'd have to wait maybe a month for the new panel and he said to me 'Frank is there any way you could patch it up until we could get a new panel?' It was kinda the break for me. The big panels were expensive and high voltage but were only a bigger version of the radio panels. I worked it out anyways with some of the staff that was there and I got the plant working in about two days. I seen then that I could build a panel.

As new plant came in, Frank began to build the panels and worked in the company for the next eighteen years until it finally closed down: 'I worked as a fitter-electrician for Gibbons', and when the job closed I moved into Harrington's [Harrington Concrete & Quarries]. I went on industrial wiring full time and we used to build the panels and some of them were costing sixty [€60,000] and ninety grand [€90,000].'

Frank and his wife Mary have three adult sons. Noel is employed in Ireland and lives next door to them in Killaturley, while, Eoghan and Shane are global migrants like many young Irish workers of the present time. As in his working life, Frank's innovative spirit hasn't waned and he now finds time to develop new interests and pursuits. Photography is now his passion and in the short span of a couple of years he has travelled 3–4,000 miles around the west coast of Ireland, including the Wild Atlantic Way, capturing on camera the diversity of the ever-changing landscape along this untamed region.

THERESA CONNOR

'I went there in late 1965 and I stayed there until 1968. I had the most wonderful three years of my life.'

The provision of post-primary education in the 1950s and 1960s through the aegis of newly built vocational schools gave young male emigrants from east Mayo an educational foundation they could build on, either at home or abroad. As noted already, convent schools provided secondary education from a much earlier period for girls from this region. However, Theresa Connor, who came from Ballintadder, only a few miles from Ballaghaderreen, chose to receive her post-primary education in the vocational school there, where she felt her aptitudes had a better chance of being fulfilled:

> I went to the technical [vocational] school in Ballaghaderreen where I did my Group [Certificate] and secretarial course. I did commercial subjects and that entitled me to enter for civil service-type exams. This was the first time that the civil service was opening up for people like myself. I was still in school actually when I did the exam, and I got it.

As a member of a family of ten children, Theresa was well acquainted with the narrative of emigration. Both of her parents had been emigrants. Her father spent twenty-five years as a migratory labourer in England and her mother worked in the US for six years before returning home to marry. A number of Theresa's own siblings had already emigrated before she left home. Two of her sisters went to work in the US after training as nurses in England. While her older brothers were engaged in seasonal work in Lincolnshire, Theresa was employed in the civil service in Dublin as a shorthand typist. Because of her youth she found the transition from home to the big city, very difficult: 'Going to Dublin was traumatic – oh absolutely! It was far less traumatic going from Dublin to Paris than it was to go from Ballintadder [near Charlestown] to Dublin! I adjusted immediately in Paris.'

Why did she take a job in Dublin when most of her sisters were working abroad? 'Because it was the first place I was offered a job at that stage. I was the eighth of ten offspring and though we were a little better off at that time [1960] it was still very important I get a job.'

Theresa was hardworking and ambitious and pursued courses that enabled her to upskill and challenge for positions in several prestigious organisations. 'I did the high-school diploma when I was in New York and then I did the diploma in business studies back in Dublin and I also did computer-diploma courses.'

After four years working in Dublin, Theresa decided to move on:

> I didn't have to go abroad luckily enough. When I finished school, which would have been the early Sixties, there were opportunities to work here so I didn't have to go abroad. I just wanted to travel. First I went to work in the OECD [Organisation for Economic Co-operation and Development] in Paris. I worked there for three years. I went there in late 1965 and I stayed there until 1968. I had the most wonderful three years of my life. That's where my sister, Margaret, worked all her life [in the OECD in Paris]. Of course, I had so many sisters in the States that I decided I'd go to there for a while. So then Josephine [sister] decided she'd leave London and come to the States with me. So I worked with the UN [United Nations] in New York for a year which again was a brilliant experience.

The 1960s was an era of economic and industrial expansion in Ireland. This was due in no small measure to the First Programme for Economic Expansion, brought in under Seán Lemass, Taoiseach of the day, and credited to the renowned T.K. Whitaker. This, coupled with the introduction of free second-level education in the mid-1960s, created new opportunities and expectations not available to an earlier generation.

Although Theresa Connor's entry into second-level schooling was ahead of the free-education scheme, she was nevertheless able to avail of the educational opportunities offered at the local vocational school. While progression from these vocational-type courses was limited at that time, she wasn't discouraged from pursuing further studies and attaining higher qualifications. Through hard work and determination she launched herself on a very interesting career that enabled her to attain positions in global organisations, both at home and abroad.

After a year in the US, Theresa returned to Ireland with her sister, Josephine. However, Josephine went back to the US and married Larry Farrell, her Roscommon boyfriend there: 'I came back and I did temporary work for a while and then I joined the IDA [Industrial Development Authority]. I joined them in 1971 and I retired from there as project executive at the end of 2001.' Theresa remained in Dublin on her retirement and is a regular visitor to her home place in Ballintadder, where her brother Eddie still lives.

JOHN BRENNAN

'Everyone's daddy is going to England – why don't you go to England?'

The migrant narrative from the 1970s and going into the 1980s differs considerably from that of twenty or thirty years earlier. Free secondary education in Ireland was well bedded-in by the mid-Seventies and employment opportunities were increasing, which led to a reduction in the numbers migrating or emigrating. John Brennan from Kilbride, Swinford had obtained his Leaving Certificate and subsequently qualified as a carpenter during this relatively prosperous time. His father, a self-taught tradesman, found enough work locally to rear a family of five without leaving the area, in stark contrast with many of his neighbours, who spent part of each year in England as seasonal workers.

After John completed his Leaving Certificate, he worked at home for some time with his father. He didn't emigrate like many of his peers, as he recounts:

> Probably because my father was a journeyman tradesman and he asked me 'Would I stay for a while?,' and the while lengthened and became the rest of my life. Having said that, I moved away from Swinford and round the country. I worked on the gas pipe-line in Cork. Oh, yeah, I worked away. Every year I used to try and get a bit of work away and then come back and work with him [father] for the winter. In the Eighties there wasn't a great amount of work locally but I managed to get employment on the Dublin–Cork gas pipeline in 1982. I started in Dublin and worked my way to Cork – all the way – for over a year. There were Swinford fellows I knew involved in the pipe-line business and that's how I got in on it.

The building of the giant Alcan aluminium plant brought John to work in Limerick for a period. He had contacts there, too, as he recalls:

> There was a Killasser man there. He was after coming back from overseas working with Wimpey and he got a position as boss man down there in Alcan. He got a scatter of different fellows started down there. 'Twas a big job – very big. There were three and a half thousand working there. John Henry from Barnacogue worked there. I knew him well.

As industrialisation forged ahead in the Eighties, John was fortunate enough to find long-term employment in his home area. He got work on the building of Áras Attracta (Residential Home) in Swinford in 1983 and at Sligo Airport in 1989 'and in between I did a couple of bits with my father at home'.

Before settling down to life in his own locality, he decided to seek work on the Continent: 'In the late Eighties and early Nineties there wasn't a great amount of work in Ireland and in 1991 I went to Dublin for an interview for work in Holland. I got the job and I spent a year working there as a carpenter before coming back to Ireland.'

While John and his siblings are all living in Ireland, the migration story of the extended family is much more complex. Most of his aunts and uncles felt it necessary to seek employment outside Ireland. Five of his aunts went to Chicago in the 1920s and spent all their working lives there. Another aunt, who emigrated to America in 1935, returned home permanently in 1988 after fifty-three years in the US. An uncle of his went to Wales in the mid-1930s, married a local girl and settled there. Another uncle migrated in 1935 and spent about sixteen years at seasonal work and nineteen years in construction work, before returning finally to Ireland to retire in 1983. Out of a total of ten aunts and uncles, only two did not emigrate.

The Swinford area was a hotbed of emigration and migration when John was growing up in the 1950s and it was fairly obvious that his home was different from that of many of his neighbours. While his father came home every night, many of the other fathers in the neighbourhood spent some, if not most, of every year in England. When the season's work was finished in England, the migrants began to return, bringing gifts and presents to their offspring, and John and his sister Una felt that they were missing out because their father didn't migrate. At school they were being constantly reminded by other children that 'My daddy is coming home and I'll be getting money', and John recounts one incident which evidenced how children perceived the migrant fathers: 'Una [sister] said to my father when she came home one day [from school] – she said "Everyone's daddy is going to England – why don't you go to England?"' Emigration, it would seem, was so ingrained in the psyche of the people that a husband and father being able to provide for his family by earning a living at home was seen as something out of the ordinary.

Conclusion

The personal stories of some of the e/migrants who left east Mayo in the 1940s, '50s and '60s describing their experiences of life in Ireland before they left and afterwards in their adopted country are shared with us in Part II of this book. Having a network of friends, relatives and neighbours was of major importance in sourcing employment and accommodation and in the subsequent integration of individual e/migrants into their new communities. Nevertheless, employment wasn't guaranteed and wages could vary from job to job. The work the e/migrants engaged in could be arduous, especially for those involved in farm work. Accommodation in the cities for both men and women was often basic, and on farms could, in most cases, be best described as primitive.

Secondary education wasn't accessible to the vast majority of e/migrants from east Mayo during the 1940s and 1950s, thus hindering their upward mobility. Nevertheless, many overcame this barrier and availed of further and higher education courses in their adopted homelands. This enabled them to better their employment prospects, and, indeed, for some it enabled them to progress to positions of authority in their workplaces.

The transient nature of their work on the buildings and their tendency to change jobs frequently – and sometimes illogically – had a negative impact on the promotion prospects of male workers in the construction industry. Female workers led a more sedentary life and this made it easier for them to utilise the education system in Britain to achieve professional status in their chosen careers.

Remittances were a feature of e/migrant life and the tradition of sending money home still lived on into the 1950s and '60s. Living and working abroad gave the e/migrants a perspective on the sacrifices made by their parents – rearing large families on tiny holdings of land – and their appreciation of this comes through in their narratives.

Lack of employment opportunities in the area was the main reason given by most interviewees for 'taking the boat'. Although a small minority of people left east Mayo from a sense of adventure, others just wanted to be united with their friends and relations abroad and a small number left because they resented the repressive lifestyle in Ireland in the mid-twentieth century. The majority admitted, however, that they would have stayed in Ireland if they had constant employment and a standard of living commensurate with what they found abroad. However, as conditions improved and employment increased in Ireland in the 1970s, small farmers were able to supplement the return from the land by working part-time in factories and public works in their own localities. Factories such as Basta in Tubbercurry gave much-needed male employment, while Baxter in Swinford catered mainly for female workers. Concurrent with these developments was the filling of the education lacuna through the provision of new educational facilities and access to them through free post-primary education and free school transport.

The availability of educational opportunities for the younger generation brought a glimmer of hope for the first time in almost two centuries to the people of east Mayo, enabling them to look forward with some optimism to a brighter future for both themselves and their children as we approached the third millennium.

List of Interviewees

Interviewee	Date of taped interview
Mick Foley, Corthoon	9 August 2001
Mary (Foley) Devlin, Corthoon	10 August 2001
Jim Foley, Corthoon	3 August 2002
Stephen Farrell*	2 September 2002
Joe Morrisroe, Barnacogue	2 September 2002
Mary (Waters) Gannon, Montiagh	3 September 2002
John Walsh, Coolrawer	3 September 2002
Tommy Campbell, Cloonaghboy	4 September 2002
Margaret (Mulligan) McIntyre, Madogue	11 September 2002
Eileen (O'Rourke) Killilea, Sonnagh	11 September 2002
John Morley, Corthoon	12 September 2002
Henry Peyton, Madogue	13 September 2002
Jimmy McIntyre, Corthoon	13 September 2002
Martin McCormack, Lisloughna	18 September 2002
Kitty (Breheny) Walsh, Clooncoose	18 September 2002
Tommy McGowan, Lowpark	19 September 2002
Martin Neary, Madogue	20 September 2002
Philip Conway, Lisheenabrone	24 September 2002
Tom Meehan, Brackloonagh	24 September 2002
Maureen (McNeela) Murphy,† Cloonlumney	25 September 2002
Jackie Devine, Tullinahoo	27 September 2002
Paddy Duffy, Madogue	25 October 2002
Brendan Swords, Sandyhill	30 October 2002
Teddy Gallagher, Tavnaglass	7 November 2002
Michael Goldrick, Corthoon	8 November 2002
Bill Madden, Ardara	19 June 2004
Theresa Connor, Ballintadder	4 August 2004
Johnny Conlon, Esker	16 August 2004
Tom Morley, Carrowcanada	9 June 2006
John Mulroy, Lisbrogan	13 June 2006

* Pseudonym

† Interview not taped

Interviewee	Date of taped interview
Jimmy Brennan, Culmore	16 October 2006
John Cafferty, Lurga	17 October 2006
Tommy Grady, Brackloonagh South	19 October 2006
Kevin Walsh, Brackloonagh	19 October 2006
Anthony Dempsey, Graffy	8 March 2007
Paddy Peyton, Tumgesh	10 March 2007
John Brennan, Kilbride	4 September 2007
Tom Goldrick, Corthoon	9 October 2007
Martin McDonagh, Cloonaghboy	4 December 2007
Paddy Foley, Corthoon	3–4 March 2008
Paddy Molloy, Cloonlara	8 August 2008
Ellen (Foley) Reeves, Corthoon	17 July 2009
Frank Gallagher, Killaturley	26 September 2014
May (Henry) Clancy, Barnacogue	26 May 2015

Since the commencement of my research, many of the interviewees have sadly passed away. Among these are Johnny Conlon, Jackie Devine, Philip Conway, Paddy Peyton, Paddy Foley, Jim Foley, Mary (Waters) Gannon, John Cafferty, John Morley, Tom Morley, John Walsh, John Mulroy, Stephen Farrell*, Eileen (O'Rourke) Killilea and Mick Foley. *Ar dheis Dé go raibh siad*.

---

* Pseudonym

Appendices

Notes & References

Bibliography

Index

Appendix I: Enumerators' Figures for Migratory Agricultural Labourers, 1880–1915

Year	Ireland No.	Connaught No.	Connaught Percentage of total for Ireland	Mayo No.	Mayo Percentage of total for Ireland	Swinford PLU No.	Swinford PLU Percentage of total for Ireland
1880	22,900	15,774	68.9%	10,198	44.5%	4,862	21.2%
1881	21,322	16,410	77.0%	10,742	50.4%	5,083	23.8%
1882	16,836	12,507	74.3%	7,918	47.0%	3,523	20.9%
1883	14,780	11,176	75.6%	7,169	48.5%	3,012	20.4%
1884	14,413	10,812	75.0%	7,216	50.1%	3,557	24.7%
1885	13,140	10,128	77.1%	6,586	50.1%	3,061	23.3%
1886	12,375	9,877	80.0%	6,890	55.7%	2,943	23.8%
1887	12,423	10,148	81.7%	7,442	60.0%	3,208	25.8%
1888	11,723	9,941	84.8%	7,087	60.5%	3,122	26.6%
1889	12,028	10,271	85.4%	7,291	60.6%	3,193	26.5%
1890	14,081	12,034	85.5%	8,490	60.3%	3,795	27.0%
1891	13,129	11,069	84.3%	7,271	55.4%	2,982	22.7%
1892	14,783	12,661	85.6%	8,554	57.9%	3,891	26.3%
1893	14,761	12,589	85.3%	8,556	60.0%	3,909	26.5%
1894	15,615	13,474	86.3%	9,508	60.9%	4,258	27.3%
1895	14,119	12,061	85.4%	8,374	59.3%	3,774	26.7%
1896	16,312	13,294	81.5%	8,863	54.3%	4,063	24.9%
1897	16,237	13,224	81.4%	8,701	53.6%	4,079	25.1%
1898	17,902	14,535	81.2%	9,519	53.2%	4,262	23.8%
1899	18,940	15,557	82.3%	10,192	53.9%	4,198	22.2%
1900	19,022	15,878	83.5%	10,331	54.3%	4,144	21.8%
1901*	19,732	15,318	77.6%	10,070	51.1%	4,394	22.3%
1902*	19,176	14,798	77.2%	10,070	52.5%	4,471	23.3%
1903*	17,566	13,530	77.0%	9,264	52.7%	4,073	23.2%
1904*	17,859	13,703	76.7%	9,527	53.3%	4,120	23.1%
1905	14,830	11,349	76.5%	7,619	51.4%	2,744	18.5%
1906	15,286	11,833	77.4%	8,428	55.1%	3,196	20.9%
1907	15,021	11,432	76.1%	7,935	52.8%	3,014	20.1%

Year	Ireland	Connaught		Mayo		Swinford PLU	
	No.	No.	Percentage of total for Ireland	No.	Percentage of total for Ireland	No.	Percentage of total for Ireland
1908	12,200	9,938	81.5%	6,947	56.9%	2,875	23.6%
1909	10,938	9,180	83.9%	6,951	63.5%	2,727	24.9%
1910	10,225	8,325	81.4%	6,221	60.8%	2,619	25.6%
1911	8,878	6,867	77.1%	5,442	58.9%	2,463	27.7%
1912	9,217	6,867	74.5%	5,442	59.0%	2,389	25.9%
1913	8.687	6.547	75.4%	5.060	58.2%	2.451	28.2%
1914	7,341	5,438	74.1%	4,282	58.3%	1,794	25.8%
1915	7,354	5,258	71.5%	4,274	58.1%	1,794	24.4%

* The enumerators' figures for the years 1901–04 include labourers other than 'agricultural', and also female migratory labourers.

Source: Agricultural Statistics, Ireland, 1880–1915. Reports and Tables Relating to Migratory Agricultural Labourers.

Appendix II: Destinations and Numbers of Migratory Agricultural Labourers from Three Selected Areas, 1880–1914

Year	From	No.	To England	To Scotland	Elsewhere in Ireland
1880	Ireland	22,900	16,981	3,771	2,148
	Mayo	10,198	10,019	146	33
	Swinford PLU	4,862	4,857	3	2
1881	Ireland	21,322	17,153	2,725	1444
	Mayo	10,742	10,514	189	39
	Swinford PLU	5,083	5,077	3	3
1882	Ireland	16,836	13,222	2,455	1,159
	Mayo	7,918	7,808	85	25
	Swinford PLU	3,523	3,515	7	1
1883	Ireland	14,780	11,483	2,438	859
	Mayo	7,169	6,913	230	26
	Swinford PLU	3,012	3,003	3	6
1884	Ireland	14,413	11,123	2,262	1,028
	Mayo	7,216	7,103	98	15
	Swinford PLU	3,557	3,553	2	2
1885	Ireland	13,140	10,278	2,018	844
	Mayo	6,586	6,463	108	15
	Swinford PLU	3,061	3,055	6	–
1886	Ireland	12,375	9,983	1,732	660
	Mayo	6,890	6,786	100	4
	Swinford PLU	2,943	2,943	–	–
1887	Ireland	12,423	10,171	1,539	713
	Mayo	7,442	7,291	149	2
	Swinford PLU	3,208	3,201	6	1
1888	Ireland	11,723	9,950	1,216	557
	Mayo	7,087	6,958	121	8
	Swinford PLU	3,122	3,122	–	-
1889	Ireland	12,028	10,268	1,231	529
	Mayo	7,291	7,208	80	3
	Swinford PLU	3,193	3,184	6	3

Source: Agricultural Statistics, Ireland, 1880–1914. Reports and Tables Relating to Migratory Agricultural Labourers.

Appendix III: Migratory Agricultural Labourers, 1905–14

Number of migratory agricultural labourers from three selected areas who were either sons or daughters of farmers and worked on their parents' farms when at home; together with the total number of migratory agricultural labourers from those regions for the years 1905–14 inclusive.

Year	Ireland			Connaught			Mayo		
	Sons	Daughters	Total	Sons	Daughters	Total	Sons	Daughters	Total
1905	8,733	562	14,830	7,022	175	11,349	4,631	164	7,619
1906	8,241	717	15,286	6,319	267	11,833	4,282	259	8,428
1907	8,571	737	15,021	6,801	338	11,432	4,872	327	7,935
1908	6,715	300	12,200	5,933	272	9,938	4,198	271	6,947
1909	6,094	549	10,938	5,228	366	9,180	3,897	366	6,951
1910	5,630	327	10,225	5,120	208	8,325	3,758	206	6,221
1911	5,366	368	8,878	4,548	188	6,848	3,317	188	5,233
1912	5,476	426	9,217	4,022	203	6,867	3,015	198	5,442
1913	5,260	280	8,687	3,913	99	6,547	2,831	94	5,060
1914	4,847	208	7,341	3,638	60	5,438	2,756	60	4,282

Source: Agricultural Statistics, Ireland, 1905–14. Reports and Tables Relating to Migratory Agricultural Labourers.

Appendix IV: Migratory Agricultural Labourers, 1880–1915

Returns of migratory agricultural labourers as furnished by police enumerators for the years 1880–1915 inclusive

Adjusted figures for migratory agricultural labourers as suggested in the 1915 report, p. 3

Year	Total
1880	22,900
1881	21,322
1882	16,836
1883	14,780
1884	14,413
1885	13,140
1886	12,375
1887	12,423
1888	11,723
1889	12,028
1890	14,081
1891	13,129
1892	14,783
1893	14,761
1894	15,615
1895	14,119
1896	16,312
1897	16,237
1898	17,902
1899	18,910
1900	19,022
1901	16,865
1902	16,220
1903	14,798
1904	15,319
1905	14,830
1906	15,286
1907	15,021
1908	12,200

Year	Total
—	—
—	—
—	—
—	—
—	—
—	—
—	—
—	—
—	—
—	—
—	—
—	—
—	—
—	—
—	—
—	—
1896	27,000
1897	27,000
1898	30,000
1899	31,500
1900	32,000
1901	28,000
1902	27,000
1903	25,000
1904	25,000
1905	25,000
1906	25,000
1907	24,000
1908	22,500

Year	Total	Year	Total
1909	10,938	1909	20,500
1910	10,225	1910	18,500
1911	8,878	1911	15,500
1912	9,217	1912	16,000
1913	8,687	1913	15,000
1914	7,341	1914	13,000
1915	7,354	1915	13,000

*The enumerators' figures for 1901–04 in this instance do not include 'other' labourers (see Report for 1915, p. 4).

Source: Agricultural Statistics, Ireland, 1880–1915. Reports and Tables Relating to Migratory Agricultural Labourers.

Notes & References

Introduction
1. John F. Higgins (ed.), *Mayo Association Year Book 2002* (Castlebar, 2002), p. 215.
2. Census of Ireland 1911 [Cd. 6052] Area, Houses and Population: Also the Ages, Civil or Conjugal Condition, Occupations, Birthplaces, Religion and Education of the People. Province of Connaught. County of Mayo (Dublin, 1912), p. 123.
3. *The Parliamentary Gazetteer of Ireland,* vol. II (London, 1846), p. 362.

Chapter 1
1. Henry Coulter, *Flax Growing and Migration in the Eighteenth Century* (1862), p. 199.
2. James McParlan, *Statistical Survey of the County of Mayo, With Observations on the Means of Improvement Drawn Up in the Year 1801 for the Consideration and Under the Direction of the Dublin Society* (Dublin, 1802), p. 110.
3. Frank McManus, 'The Expulsions from Ulster of 1795–97', in *Fermanagh and 1798,* Séamus McAnnaidh (ed.), pp. 44–65.
4. Patrick Tohall, 'The Diamond Fight of 1795 and the resultant expulsions', in Fr Tomás Ó Fiaich (ed.), *Seanchas Ardmhacha*, vol. 3, no. 1, 1958, pp. 17–50. Patrick Hogan, 'The migration of Ulster Catholics to Connaught, 1795–06', in Patrick J. Campbell (ed.), *Seanchas Ardmhacha* vol. 9, no. 2, 1979, pp. 286–301.
5. Liam Swords, *A Hidden Church: The Diocese of Achonry, 1689–1818* (Dublin, 1998), pp. 93–5.
6. James Neligan, 'Parish of Kilmactige, diocese of achonry and county of Sligo', in William Shaw Mason, *A Statistical Account or Parochial Survey of Ireland*, vol. 2 (Dublin, 1816), pp. 349–98.
7. Ibid.
8. Thomas Campbell Foster, *Letters on the Condition of the People of Ireland* (London, 1846), p. 729.
9. E.R.R. Green, 'Agriculture', in R. Dudley Edwards and T. Desmond Williams (eds), *The Great Famine Studies in Irish History, 1845–52* (Dublin, 1956), pp. 89–122.
10. PP [C. 2534] The Agricultural Statistics of Ireland for the Year 1879 (Dublin, 1880), p. 58.
11. John Carr, *The Stranger in Ireland: On a Tour in the Southern and Western Parts of that Country in the Year 1805* (New York, 1806), p. 97.
12. James Neligan, 'Parish of Kilmactige, diocese of Achonry and county of Sligo', in William Shaw Mason, *A Statistical Account or Parochial Survey of Ireland*, vol. 2 (Dublin, 1816), pp. 349–98.
13. PP 1835 (369) First Report from His Majesty's Commissioners for Inquiring into the Conditions of the Poorer Classes in Ireland, with Appendix (A.) and Supplement, p. 370.
14. Ibid. p. 386.
15. Donald E. Jordan Jnr, *Land and Popular Politics in Ireland: County Mayo from the Plantation to the Land War* (Cambridge, 1994), p. 128.
16. Robert E. Kennedy Jnr, *The Irish: Emigration, Marriage, and Fertility* (London, 1973), p. 144.
17. Cormac Ó Gráda, *The Great Irish Famine* (London, 1989), p. 30.
18. PP 1845 [605] [606] Report from Her Majesty's Commissioners of Inquiry into the State

of the Law and Practice in Respect to the Occupation of Land in Ireland (hereinafter known as the Devon Commission) (Dublin, 1845), p. 12.
19   PP 1835 (369) Poor Inquiry (Ireland), Appendix (H.) Part I (London, 1836), p. 12.
20   Kevin Kenny, *The American Irish: A History* (Harlow, Essex, 2000), p. 48.
21   David Fitzpatrick, 'Emigration: 1801–1921', in Michael Glazier (ed.), *The Encyclopaedia of the Irish in America* (Notre Dame, IN, 1999), pp. 254–62.
22   Kevin Kenny, *The American Irish: A History* (Harlow, Essex, 2000), pp. 45–6.
23   Commission on Emigration and Other Population Problems, 1948–54, *Reports* (Dublin, 1954), p. 314.
24   David Fitzpatrick, 'Irish Emigration, 1801–1921', in Peter Roebuck and David Dickson (eds), *Studies in Irish Economic and Social History* (Dundalk, 1984), pp. 1–50.
25   Commission on Emigration, 1954, pp. 314–15.
26   Kerby A. Miller, *Emigrants and Exiles* (Oxford, 1985), p. 360.
27   W.E. Vaughan and A.J. Fitzpatrick (eds), *Irish Historical Statistics: Population, 1821–1971* (Dublin, 1978), p. 337.
28   PP 1833 (612) Report from the Select Committee on Agriculture; with the Minutes of Evidence Taken Before Them, and an Appendix and Index, p. 369.
29   'Emigration from Ireland', *Telegraph or Connaught Ranger*, 31 August 1831, p. 4.
30   PP 1835 (369) Poor Inquiry (Ireland). Appendix (F.) and Supplement (London, 1836), p. 27.
31   PP 1833 (612) Report from the Select Committee on Agriculture, p. 328.
32   Ibid. pp. 329, 335.
33   PP 1835 (369) Poor Inquiry (Ireland). Appendix (F.) and Supplement, p. 19.
34   Ibid. p. 23.
35   Donald E. Jordan Jnr, *Land and Popular Politics in Ireland* (Cambridge, 1994), pp. 70, 71.
36   John Barrow, *A Tour Round Ireland* (London, 1836), pp. 161, 162.
37   PP 1835 (369) Poor Inquiry (Ireland). Appendix (E.) and Supplement, p. 21.
38   Ibid. p. 22.
39   Ibid. p. 23.
40   James Johnson, *A Tour in Ireland: With Meditations and Reflections* (London, 1844), p. 212.
41   Thomas Campbell Foster, *Letters on the Condition of the People of Ireland* (London, 1846), p. 734.
42   PP 1843 (504) Report of the Commissioners Appointed to Take the Census of Ireland, for the Year 1841 (Dublin, 1843), pp. 396, 398.
43   Bernard O'Hara, *The Archaeological Heritage of Killasser, Co Mayo* (Galway, 1991), p. 199.
44   Donald E. Jordan Jnr, *Land and Popular Politics in Ireland* (Cambridge, 1994), p. 57.
45   P.P.1845 [616] [657] The Devon Commission, pt. II (Dublin, 1845), p. 392.
46   Ibid. p. 394.
47   Ibid. p. 437.
48   PP 1835 (369) Poor Inquiry (Ireland) First Report, Appendix (A.), p. 369.
49   PP 1845 [605] [606] Report from Her Majesty's Commissioners of Inquiry into the State of the Law and Practice in Respect to the Occupation of Land in Ireland (Dublin, 1845), p. 201.
50   PP 1845 [616] [657] Devon Commission, pt. II (Dublin, 1845), p. 389.
51   Ibid.
52   'Distress in Ireland', *Morning Chronicle* (London), 11 June 1822.
53   Patrick Fitzgerald, '"The Great Hunger?" Irish Famine: changing patterns of crisis', in E. Margaret Crawford (ed.), *The Hungry Stream: Essays on Emigration and Famine* (Belfast, 1997), pp. 101–22.

54 'Famine in Mayo', *Telegraph or Connaught Ranger*, 13 July 1831, p. 3.
55 Ibid. See also edition 16 March 1831, p. 1.
56 Cormac Ó Gráda, *Ireland: A New Economic History, 1780–1939* (Oxford, 1994), p. 74.
57 PP 1902 [Cd. 1375] Agricultural Statistics, Ireland, 1902. Report and Tables Relating to Irish Migratory Agricultural and Other Labourers, for 1902 (Dublin, 1902), p. 7.
58 PP 1843 [504] Report of the Commissioners Appointed to Take the Census of Ireland for the Year 1841 (Dublin, 1843), p. xxvi.
59 Arthur Redford, *Labour Migration in England, 1800–1850* [1926], ed. William Henry Chaloner (Manchester, 1976), pp. 144–9.
60 PP 1816 (396) Report from the Select Committee on the State of Mendicity in the Metropolis, p. 7.
61 PP 1843 [504] Report of the Commissioners Appointed to Take the Census of Ireland for the Year 1841 (Dublin, 1843), p. xxvi.
62 PP 1819 (314) First Report from the Select Committee on the State of Disease, and Condition of the Labouring Poor, in Ireland, p. 78.
63 John Archer Jackson, *The Irish in Britain* (London, 1963), p. 7.
64 James E. Handley, *The Navvy in Scotland* (Cork, 1970), pp. 18–19.
65 Cormac Ó Gráda, 'Seasonal migration and post-Famine adjustment in the west of Ireland', *Studia Hibernica*, no. 13, 1973, pp. 48–76.
66 PP 1835 (369) Poor Inquiry, Supplement to Appendix (A.) Answers to Questions Circulated by the Commissioners Relative to the Relief of the Destitute Classes in Ireland, p. 20.
67 Ibid. p. 24.
68 Ibid. p. 24.
69 Ibid. p. 26.
70 Ibid. p. 26.
71 Ibid. p. 32.
72 Ibid. p. 152.
73 Ibid. p. 310.
74 Ibid. p. 382.
75 PP 1835 (369), Poor Inquiry, First Report with Appendix (A.) and Supplement, p. 372.
76 Henry D. Inglis, *A Journey Throughout Ireland, During the Spring, Summer, and Autumn of 1834* (London, 1835), pp. 107–8.
77 PP 1835 (369) Poor Inquiry, Appendix (G.) (London, 1835), p. v.
78 T.W. Freeman, 'Land and people, *c*. 1841', in W.E. Vaughan (ed.), *A New History of Ireland, Vol. V, Ireland Under the Union, 1801–70* (Oxford, 1989), pp. 242–71.
79 PP 1828 (513) Report from the Select Committee on the Laws Relating to Irish and Scottish Vagrants, p. 10.
80 Ibid. pp. 7–8.
81 PP 1826–27 (550) Third Report from the Select Committee on Emigration from the United Kingdom: 1827, p. 334.
82 PP 1845 [616] [657] The Devon Commission, pt. II, p. 383.
83 PP 1830 (589) II. First Report of Evidence from the Select Committee on the State of the Poor in Ireland. Minutes of Evidence: 24 March–14 May, p. 33.
84 PP 1835 (369) Poor Inquiry, Appendix (G.), p. xliv.
85 Patrick Fitzgerald and Brian Lambkin, *Migration in Irish History, 1607–2007* (Basingstoke, 2008), p. 27.
86 PP 1836 [43] Third Report of the Commissioners for Inquiring into the Condition of the Poorer Classes in Ireland (London, 1836), p. 3.
87 PP 1845 [605] [606] Devon Commission, p. 51.

88 Donald E. Jordan Jnr, *Land and Popular Politics in Ireland* (Cambridge, 1994), p. 120.
89 Cormac Ó Gráda, *Black '47 and Beyond: The Great Irish Famine in History, Economy, and Memory* (Princeton, 1999), p. 5.
90 PP 1843 [504] Report of the Commissioners Appointed to Take the Census of Ireland, for the Year 1841, County Mayo, p. 400.
91 James Johnson, *A Tour in Ireland: With Meditations and Reflections* (London, 1844), p. 85.
92 PP 1843 [504] Report of the Report of the Commissioners Appointed to Take the Census of Ireland, for the Year 1841, County Mayo, p. xxvii.

Chapter 2

1 J.J. Lee, *The Modernisation of Irish Society, 1848–1918* (Dublin, 1989), p. 2.
2 PP 1852–53 [1542] Census of Ireland for the Year 1851, pt. I, County of Mayo (Dublin, 1852), pp. 147–50.
3 Ibid. p. 142.
4 Ibid. p. 136.
5 Ibid. p. 149.
6 Ibid. p. 140.
7 Ibid.
8 Ibid.
9 'Ballaghaderreen', *Tyrawley Herald*, 4 February 1847.
10 Swinford Historical Society, *An Gorta Mór: Famine in the Swinford Union* (Swinford, 1996), pp. 75–6, 80.
11 IUP series of British Parliamentary Papers: Correspondence Relating to the Measures Adopted for the Relief of Distress in Ireland, Board of Works Series [Second Part] with Index and Commissariat Series [Second Part] With Index, 1847, Famine, Ireland, no. 7 (Shannon, 1971), pp. 10–11.
12 IUP series of British Parliamentary Papers: Relating to Proceedings for the Relief of Distress and the State of the Unions and Workhouses in Ireland [Fourth and Fifth Series]. 1847–48. Famine, Ireland, 2 (Shannon, 1971), p. 60.
13 PP 1847–48 [919] [955] [999] Papers Relating to Proceedings for the Relief of the Distress and State of Unions and Workhouses in Ireland. Seventh series: 1848 (Dublin, 1848), p. 97.
14 IUP series of British Parliamentary Papers: Relating to Proceedings for the Relief of Distress and the State of the Unions and Workhouses in Ireland [Sixth Series]. 1847–48. Famine, Ireland, 3 (Shannon, 1971), p. 477.
15 IUP series of British Parliamentary Papers: Famine, Ireland, 4 (Shannon, Ireland, 1971), p. 13.
16 IUP series of British Parliamentary Papers: Famine, Ireland, 4 (Shannon, Ireland, 1971), p. 86.
17 PP 1881 [C. 2809] Agricultural Statistics, Ireland, 1880. Report and Tables Relating to Migratory Agricultural Labourers (Dublin, 1881), p. 3.
18 Ibid. p. 4.
19 Ibid. p. 7.
20 Henry D. Inglis, *A Journey Throughout Ireland, During the Spring, Summer and Autumn of 1834*, vol. II (London, 1835), pp. 106–7.
21 PP 1845 [616] [657], Devon Commission, pt. II, pp. 382–3.
22 George Nicholls, *Poor Laws: Ireland. Three Reports by George Nicholls, esq., to Her Majesty's Principal Secretary of State for the Home Department, Second Report* (London, 1838), p. 91.
23 IUP series of British Parliamentary Papers: emigration, 4, 1847 (Shannon,1971), p. 270.

24　David Fitzpatrick, '"A peculiar tramping people": the Irish in Britain, 1801–70', in W.E. Vaughan (ed.), *A New History of Ireland, Vol. V, Ireland Under the Union, 1801–70* (Oxford, 1989), pp. 623–60.
25　Ibid.
26　Denis H. Walsh (ed.), *St Mary of the Angels, Batley, 1853–2033* (n.p., 2003), pp. 18, 19.
27　Samuel Jubb, *The History of the Shoddy-trade: Its Rise, Progress, and Present Position* (London, 1860), p. 93.
28　Denis H. Walsh (ed.), *St Mary of the Angels, Batley, 1853–2003* (n.p., 2003), p. 30.
29　Graham Davis, *The Irish in Britain, 1815–1914* (Dublin, 1991), pp. 104–5.
30　Kerby A. Miller, *Emigrants and Exiles* (Oxford, 1985), p. 291.
31　Ibid. p. 347.
32　PP 1912 [Cd. 6052] Census of Ireland for the Year 1911, County of Mayo, p. 173.
33　*Ballina Chronicle*, 7 May 1851.
34　'Emigration from Westport', *Ballina Chronicle*, 30 April 1851.
35　Kerby A. Miller, *Emigrants and Exiles* (Oxford, 1985), p. 357.
36　'The Exodus', *Telegraph or Connaught Ranger*, 6 April 1853.
37　Mary Sullivan, 'The Cavan diaspora', in Brian S. Turner (ed.), *Migration and Myth: Ulster's Revolving Door* (Downpatrick, 2006), pp. 69–80.
38　Ruth-Ann M. Harris and Emer B. O'Keeffe (eds), *The Search for Missing Friends: Irish Immigrant Advertisements Placed in the* Boston Pilot, vol. II, 1851–53 (Boston, 1991) and vol. III, 1854–56 (Boston, 1993).
39　Ibid. vol. II, p. 306.
40　Ibid. p. 461.
41　Ibid. p. 481.
42　Ibid. vol. III, p. 477.
43　Ibid. p. 128.
44　Ibid. p. 212.
45　Ibid. vol. III, p. 136.
46　Ibid. p. 482.
47　Ibid. p. 354.
48　Ibid. p. 377.
49　PP [Cd. 6052] Census of Ireland, 1911, County of Mayo (London, 1912), p. 173.
50　Cormac Ó Gráda, *Ireland: A New Economic History, 1780–1939* (Oxford, 1994), p. 215.
51　Cormac Ó Gráda, 'Seasonal migration and post-Famine adjustment in the west of Ireland', *Studia Hibernica*, no. 13, 1973, pp. 48–76.
52　PP 1870 [C. 31] Reports from Poor Law Inspectors in Ireland as to the Existing Relations Between Landlord and Tenant (Dublin, 1870), p. 45.
53　Ibid. p. 45.
54　John Denvir, *The Irish in Britain From the Earliest Times to the Fall and Death of Parnell* (London, 1892), p. 153.
55　Ibid. p. 154.
56　*Irish Times*, 19 August 1862, p. 2.
57　PP 1866 [3607] Royal Commission on Railways. Evidence and Papers Relating to Railways in Ireland (London, 1866), p. 239.
58　'Overcrowding of Irish steamers', *Irish Times*, 24 July 1877, p. 5.
59　'Fatal railway accident', *Irish Times*, 15 June 1878, p. 5.
60　'Fatal affray among harvestmen – inquest', *Freeman's Journal and Daily Commercial Advertiser*, 12 September 1865.

Chapter 3

1. 'Scarcity of harvest labour', *Irish Times*, 31 August 1859, p. 3.
2. 'The harvest and the labour-market', *The Times*, 26 August 1867, p. 6.
3. *The Times*, 11 June 1862.
4. James Edmund Handley, *The Irish in Modern Scotland* (Oxford, 1947), p. 166.
5. 'Extraordinary exodus of Connaught harvestmen to England', *Irish Times*, 28 June 1879, p. 4.
6. 'Railway and other companies', *The Times*, 6 September 1879, p. 7.
7. Gerard Moran, *Sending Out Ireland's Poor: Assisted Emigration to North America in the Nineteenth Century* (Dublin, 2004), p. 163.
8. Donald E. Jordan Jnr, *Land and Popular Politics in Ireland* (Cambridge, 1994), p. 203.
9. J.J. Lee, *The Modernisation of Irish Society, 1848–1918* (Dublin, 1989), pp. 79, 80.
10. Donald E. Jordan Jnr, *Land and Popular Politics in Ireland* (Cambridge, 1994), p. 204.
11. Gerard Moran, *Sending Out Ireland's Poor: Assisted Emigration to North America in the Nineteenth Century* (Dublin, 2004), p. 164.
12. Gerard P. Moran, 'Famine and the Land War: relief and distress in Mayo, 1879–81, pt. I, *Cathair na Mart* (Journal of the Westport Historical Society), vol. 5, no. 1, 1985 pp. 54–66.
13. J.A. Fox, *Reports of the Condition of the Peasantry of the County of Mayo in 1880* (Dublin, 1881; 3rd edition), p. 11.
14. Ibid. pp. 29, 34–5.
15. Ibid. pp. 16–17.
16. *The Irish Crisis of 1879–80. Proceedings of the Dublin Mansion House Relief Committee, 1880* (Dublin, 1881), p. 136.
17. Ibid. p. 136.
18. Ibid. p. 137.
19. Mansion House Fund, Dublin City Archives, Ch. 1/52/416 (Curry).
20. Mansion House Fund, Dublin City Archives, Ch. 1/52/42 (Carracastle).
21. Mansion House Fund, Dublin City Archives, Ch. 1/52/130 (Charlestown).
22. Ibid.
23. Ibid.
24. Ibid.
25. *Irish Times*, 26 March 1880, p. 2.
26. *Irish Times*, 3 July 1880, p. 5.
27. *Freeman's Journal and Daily Commercial Advertiser*, 23 June 1880.
28. Finlay Dun, *Landlords and Tenants in Ireland* (London, 1881), pp. 204–5.

Chapter 4

1. PP 1877 [C. 1700] Emigration Statistics of Ireland, for the Year 1876 (Dublin, 1877), pp. 4, 5.
2. PP 1881 [C. 2828] Emigration Statistics of Ireland, for the Year 1880 (Dublin, 1881), pp. 3, 12.
3. PP 1912 [Cd. 6052] Census of Ireland for the Year 1911, Co. Mayo (London, 1912), p. 173.
4. Moya O'Connor, 'Of long forgotten far off things …', in Michael Comer, Mairead Golden, Micheál Murphy and Brenda Ormsby (eds), *Swinford Echoes 1997*, vol. II, pp. 77–8.
5. *Connaught Telegraph*, 2 July 1881.
6. *Western People*, 17 August 1889.

7   PP 1828 (513) Report from the Select Committee on the Laws Relating to Irish and Scottish Vagrants, p. 8.
8   PP 1845 [616] [657] Devon Commission, pt. II, p. 213.
9   James Hack Tuke, *A Visit to Connaught in the Autumn of 1847* (London, 1848; 2nd edition), p. 46.
10 Ibid. p. 47.
11 Ibid. p. 49.
12 John Forbes, *Memorandums Made in Ireland in the Autumn* of 1852, vol. I (London, 1853), p. 276.
13 Hans Storhaug, 'European return migration: numbers, reasons and consequences', in Hans Storhaug (ed.), *AEMI Journal*, vol. I, 2003, pp. 69–77.
14 Alan M. Kraut, *The Huddled Masses: The Immigrant in American Society, 1880–1921* (Arlington Heights, IL, 1982), p. 10.
15 PP 1883 (92) Distress (Ireland). Copy of a Report from the Local Government Board for Ireland, Dated 13 March 1883, with Regard to the Distress Existing or Apprehended in Certain Parts of Ireland; and of the Reports from Inspectors of the Local Government Board and Other Papers Enclosed Therewith, p. 5.
16 David Fitzpatrick, 'Emigration, 1801–1921', in Michael Glazier (ed.), *The Encyclopaedia of the Irish in America* (Notre Dame, IN, 1999), pp. 254–62.
17 David Fitzpatrick, 'Emigration, 1871–1921', in W.E. Vaughan (ed.), *A New History of Ireland, Vol. V: Ireland Under the Union, II, 1870–1921* (Oxford, 1989), pp. 606–52.
18 Liam Swords, *A Dominant Church* (Dublin, 2004), p. 218.
19 Willie McNicholas, *Path to the Well: Memories of an Irish Immigrant from Ireland to America* (NY, 2008), p. 5.
20 Gerard Moran, 'Mayo God help us! Emigration from nineteenth-century Mayo', *Cathair na Mart* (Journal of the Westport Historical Society), no. 21, 2001, pp. 119–26.
21 Liam Swords, *A Dominant Church* (Dublin, 2004), p. 221.
22 David Fitzpatrick, 'Emigration, 1871–1921', in W.E. Vaughan (ed.), *A New History of Ireland, Vol. V: Ireland Under the Union, II, 1870–1921* (Oxford, 1989), pp. 606–52.
23 *Western People*, 10 January 1891.
24 David Fitzpatrick, 'Emigration, 1871–1921', in W.E. Vaughan (ed.), *A New History of Ireland, Vol. V: Ireland Under the Union, II, 1870–1921* (Oxford, 1989), pp. 606–52.
25 Tom Holleran, *Rambling Memories: My Memory of the Early Days, 1921–1988* (n.p., 1991), p. 58.
26 Arnold Schrier, *Ireland and the American Emigration* (Minnesota, 1958), pp. 130–1.
27 Aidan Arrowsmith (ed.), *The Complete Works of J.M. Synge: Plays, Prose and Poetry* (Ware, Hertfordshire, 2008), p. 224.
28 PP 1908 [Cd. 4099] Royal Commission on Congestion in Ireland. Second Appendix to the Final Report – Digest of Evidence (Dublin, 1908), p. 522.
29 PP 1908 [Cd. 3748] Royal Commission on Congestion in Ireland. Appendix to the Sixth Report: Minutes of Evidence (taken in County Sligo and County Leitrim 17–27 April, 1907), pp. 12–13.
30 Mark Wyman, *Round-trip to America: The Immigrants Return to Europe, 1880–1930* (New York, 1993), p. 10.
31 Martin O'Malley, [no title] in Patricia Hamill (ed.), *While Mem'ry Brings Us Back Again: A Collection of Memoirs Produced by the Aisling Irish Community Center* (New York, 2006), pp. 157–65.
32 PP 1911 [Cd. 5607] Emigration Statistics of Ireland for the Year 1910 (Dublin, 1911), p. 9.
33 Dudley Baines, *Emigration from Europe, 1815–1930* (London, 1991), p. 42.

34 PP 1907 [Cd. 3481] Agricultural Statistics, Ireland, 1906, Report and Tables Relating to Irish Migratory Agricultural Labourers, for the Year 1906 (Dublin, 1907), p. 16.
35 Diarmaid Ferriter, *The Transformation of Ireland, 1900–2000* (London, 2004), p. 480.
36 *Irish Times*, 15 December 2010, p. 19.

Chapter 5
1 Bernard O'Hara, 'County Mayo', in Bernard O'Hara (ed.), *Mayo: Aspects of its Heritage* (Galway, 1982), pp. 1–9.
2 Ibid.
3 Ibid.
4 Ibid.
5 Ibid.
6 Cormac Ó Gráda, *Ireland: A New Economic History, 1780–1939* (Oxford, 1994), p. 234.
7 PP 1906 [Cd. 3267] Royal Commission on Congestion in Ireland. Appendices to the First Report. Minutes of Evidence (taken in Dublin, 7 September–5 October, 1906) (Dublin, 1906), p. 148.
8 Richard Griffith, *General Valuation of Rateable Property in Ireland*. Counties of Mayo and Roscommon. Valuation of the several tenements in the Union of Swineford – Parish of Kilbeagh (Dublin, 1856), p. 53.
9 Valuation Office, Valuation Lists, no. 16, vol. I, book 7, p. 25; book 6, p. 2; book 5, p. 2.
10 Cormac Ó Gráda, *Ireland: A New Economic History, 1780–1939* (Oxford, 1994), p. 215.
11 David Fitzpatrick, 'Marriage in post-Famine Ireland', in Art Cosgrove (ed.), *Marriage in Ireland* (Dublin, 1985), pp. 116–31.
12 T.P. O'Neill, 'The Food Crisis of the 1890s', in Margaret E. Crawford (ed.), *Famine: The Irish Experience, 900–1900: Subsistence Crises and Famines in Ireland* (Edinburgh, 1989), pp. 176–97.
13 'The distress in Charlestown', *Western People*, 14 February 1891.
14 'Government relief work in Erris', *Western People*, 17 January 1891.
15 PP 1893–94 [C. 6894–xxi] Royal Commission on Labour – The Agricultural Labourer, vol. IV, Ireland, pt. IV. Reports by Mr Arthur Wilson Fox Upon Certain Selected Districts in the Counties of Cork, Mayo, Roscommon and Westmeath with Summary Report Prefixed. Appendix (B.), p. 76.
16 The Congested Districts Board for Ireland, County of Mayo – Union of Swinford. Report of Mr Doran, Inspector, 2nd May, 1892, p. 397.
17 Ibid. p. 399.
18 Ibid. p. 401.
19 Ibid.
20 PP 1906 [Cd. 3267] Royal Commission on Congestion in Ireland. Appendices to the First Report. Minutes of Evidence (taken in Dublin, 7 September–5 October, 1906), p. 130.
21 Ibid. p. 130.
22 Kerby A. Miller, *Emigrants and Exiles* (Oxford, 1985), p. 578.
23 Cormac Ó Gráda, 'Seasonal migration and post-Famine adjustment in the west of Ireland', *Studia Hibernica*, no. 13, 1973, pp. 48–76.
24 Kerby A. Miller, *Emigrants and Exiles* (Oxford, 1985), p. 578.
25 PP 1900 [Cd. 239] Congested Districts Board for Ireland, Ninth Report (Dublin, 1900), p. 18.
26 Ciara Breathnach, *The Congested Districts Board of Ireland, 1891–1923. Poverty and Development in the West of Ireland* (Dublin, 2005), p. 133.
27 Ibid. pp. 134–5.

28 PP 1903 [Cd. 1622] Congested Districts Board for Ireland, Twelfth Report (Dublin, 1903), p. 16.
29 Diarmaid Ferriter, *The Transformation of Ireland, 1900–2000* (London, 2004), pp. 62–3.
30 PP 1900 [Cd. 239] Congested Districts Board for Ireland, Ninth Report (Dublin, 1900), pp. 17–18.
31 PP 1904 [Cd. 2275] Congested Districts Board for Ireland, Thirteenth Report (Dublin, 1904), p. 15.
32 PP 1900 [Cd. 239] Congested Districts Board for Ireland, Ninth Report (Dublin, 1900), p. 23.
33 PP 1908 [Cd. 4099] Royal Commission on Congestion in Ireland. Second Appendix to the Final Report: Digest of Evidence (Dublin, 1908), p. 278.
34 PP 1908 [Cd. 3748] Royal Commission on Congestion in Ireland. Appendix to the Sixth Report: Minutes of Evidence (taken in County Sligo and County Leitrim 17–27 April, 1907), p. 9.

Chapter 6

1 Ciara Breathnach, *The Congested Districts Board of Ireland, 1891–1923* (Dublin, 2005), p. 159.
2 PP 1890–91 [Cd. 6295] Emigration Statistics of Ireland for the Year 1890 (Dublin, 1891), pp. 3, 12.
3 *Western People*, 25 May 1889.
4 Patrick Fitzgerald and, Brian Lambkin, *Migration in Irish History, 1607–2007* (Basingstoke, 2008), p. 8.
5 Dudley Baines, *Emigration from Europe, 1815–1930* (London, 1991), p. 9.
6 Janet A. Nolan, *Ourselves Alone: Women's Emigration from Ireland, 1885–1920* (Kentucky, 1989), p. 2.
7 Breda Gray, *Women and the Irish Diaspora* (London, 2004), p. 175.
8 Maureen Murphy, 'The Fionnuala factor: Irish sibling emigration at the turn of the century', in Anthony Bradley and Maryann Gialanella Valiulis (eds), *Gender and Sexuality in Modern Ireland* (Amherst, MA, 1997), pp. 85–101.
9 J.A. Fox, *Reports on the Condition of the Peasantry of the County of Mayo in 1880* (Dublin, 1881; 3rd edition), p. 36.
10 W.E. Vaughan and A.J. Fitzpatrick (eds), *Irish Historical Statistics: Population, 1821–1971* (Dublin, 1978), p. 338.
11 PP 1909 [Cd. 4919] Agricultural Statistics, Ireland, 1908–9. Reports and Tables Relating to Irish Agricultural Labourers (Dublin, 1909), p. 29.

Chapter 7

1 PP 1881 [C. 2809] Agricultural Statistics, Ireland, 1880. Report and Tables Relating to Migratory Agricultural Labourers (Dublin, 1881), p. 4.
2 PP 1906 [Cd. 2865] Agricultural Statistics, Ireland, 1905. Report and Tables Relating to Migratory Agricultural Labourers for the Year 1905 (Dublin, 1906), p. 6.
3 PP 1881 [C. 2809] Agricultural Statistics, Ireland, 1880. Report and Tables Relating to Migratory Agricultural Labourers (Dublin, 1881), p. 6.
4 Ibid. p. 12.
5 PP 1894 [C. 7533] Agricultural Statistics, Ireland, 1894. Report and Tables Relating to Migratory Agricultural Labourers (Dublin, 1894), p. 4.
6 PP 1881 [C. 2809] Agricultural Statistics, Ireland, 1880. Report and Tables Relating to Migratory Agricultural Labourers (Dublin, 1881), p. 12.

7   Ibid. pp. 7, 9.
8   PP 1900 [Cd. 341] Agricultural Statistics, Ireland, 1900. Report, Maps, Tables and Appendices Relating toMigratory Agricultural Labourers (Dublin, 1900), p. 12.
9   Anne O'Dowd, *Spalpeens and Tattie Hokers: History and Folklore of the Irish Migratory Agricultural Worker in Ireland and Britain* (Dublin, 1991), p. 416.
10 PP 1902 [Cd. 1375] Agricultural Statistics, Ireland, 1902. Report and Tables Relating to Migratory Agricultural and Other Labourers (Dublin, 1902), pp. 21, 25.
11 PP 1907 [Cd. 3481] Agricultural Statistics, Ireland, 1906. Report and Tables Relating to Irish Migratory Agricultural Labourers, for the Year 1906 (Dublin, 1907), p. 8.
12 W.E. Vaughan and A.J. Fitzpatrick (eds), *Irish Historical Statistics: Population, 1821–1971* (Dublin, 1978), p. 338.
13 'A visit to Swinford', *Ballina Journal and Connaught Advertiser*, 18 August 1884, p. 5.
14 PP 1884 (218) Migratory Labourers (Ireland). Copy of Report Made by the Registrar General for Ireland, Showing the Results of Inquiries Made at the Request of the Irish Government by the Local Government Board for England, and the Board of Supervision for the Relief of the Poor in Scotland, as to the Diminution in the Number of Migratory Labourers from Ireland Visiting Certain Districts in Great Britain (London, 1884), pp. 2–3.
15 David Fitzpatrick, '"A peculiar tramping people": the Irish in Britain, 1801–70, in W.E. Vaughan (ed.), *A New History of Ireland, Vol. V: Ireland Under the Union, II, 1870–1921* (Oxford, 1989), pp. 623–60.
16 PP 1826 (404) Report from the Select Committee on Emigration from the United Kingdom (London, 1826), p. 125.
17 PP 1835 (369) Poor Inquiry (Ireland) Appendix (G.) Report on the State of the Irish Poor in Great Britain (London, 1835), p. xxxi.
18 James Hack Tuke, *A Visit to Connaught in the Autumn of 1847* (London, 1848; 2nd edition), p. 45.
19 Ibid. p. 47.
20 PP (IUP series) Report of the Commissioners Appointed to Take the Census of Ireland for the Year 1841 with Appendix and Index. Population, 2 (Shannon, 1968), p. xxvi.
21 Gustave De Beaumont, *Ireland: Social, Political and Religious* [1839] (Cambridge, MA, 2006), p. 193.
22 PP 1909 [Cd. 4919] Agricultural Statistics, Ireland, 1908–09. Report and Tables Relating to Irish Agricultural Labourers (Dublin, 1909), p. 9.
23 PP 1866 [3607] Royal Commission on Railways. Evidence and Papers Relating to Railways in Ireland (London, 1866), p. 239.
24 'Exodus of Western Harvestmen', *Irish Times*, 23 June 1888, p. 5.
25 PP 1881 [C. 2778] [C. 2778–1] [C. 2778–11] Preliminary Report from Her Majesty's Commissioners on Agriculture (London, 1881), pp. 258–9.
26 PP 1900 [Cd. 341] Agricultural Statistics, Ireland, 1900. Report, Maps, Tables and Appendices Relating toMigratory Agricultural Labourers (Dublin, 1900), p. 58.
27 PP 1902[Cd. 850] Agricultural Statistics, Ireland, 1901. Report and Tables Relating to Irish Migratory Agricultural and Other Labourers (Dublin, 1901), p. 8.
28 PP 1907 (Cd. 3481) Agricultural Statistics, Ireland, 1906. Report and Tables Relating to Irish Migratory Agricultural Labourers, for the Year 1906 (Dublin, 1907), p. 13.
29 Ibid. p. 14.
30 PP 1909 [Cd. 341] Agricultural Statistics, Ireland, 1908–09. Report and Tables Relating to Irish Agricultural Labourers (Dublin, 1909), pp. 7–12.
31 James Edmund Handley, *The Irish in Scotland, 1798–1845* (Cork, 1943), p. 39.
32 MH 32/115, National Archives, Kew, London.

33 Seamus Dunleavy and Shirley Thompson, *Finally Meeting Princess Maud* (Studley, Warwickshire, 2006), p. 56.
34 Anne O'Dowd, *Spalpeens and Tattie Hokers: History and Folklore of the Irish Migratory Agricultural Worker in Ireland and Britain* (Dublin, 1991), p. 236.
35 PP 1908 [Cd. 4123] Agricultural Statistics, Ireland, 1907–8. Report and Tables Relating to Irish Agricultural Labourers (Dublin, 1908), pp. 10, 16.
36 PP 1894 [C. 7533] Agricultural Statistics, Ireland, 1894. Report and Tables Relating to Migratory Agricultural Labourers (Dublin, 1894), p. 4.
37 Ibid. p. 7.
38 PP 1890–91 [C. 6519] Agricultural Statistics, Ireland, 1891. Report and Tables Relating to Migratory Agricultural Labourers (Dublin, 1891), p. 7.
39 PP 1906 [Cd. 2865] Agricultural Statistics, Ireland, 1905. Report and Tables Relating to Irish Migratory Agricultural Labourers, for the Year 1905 (Dublin, 1906), p. 10.
40 George Nicholls, *Poor Laws: Ireland. Three Reports by George Nicholls, esq., to Her Majesty's Principal Secretary of State for the Home Department, Second Report* (London, 1838), p. 91.
41 PP 1845 [616] [657] Report from Her Majesty's Commissioners of Inquiry into the State of the Law and Practice in Respect to the Occupation of Land in Ireland, pt. II (Dublin, 1845), p. 437.
42 PP 1896 (321) Report from the Select Committee on Distress from Want of Employment; Together with the Proceedings of the Committee, Minutes of Evidence and Appendix, p. 83.
43 Ibid. pp. 86–7.
44 PP 1900 [Cd. 341] Agricultural Statistics, Ireland, 1900. Report, Maps, Tables and Appendices Relating toMigratory Agricultural Labourers (Dublin, 1900), p. 13.
45 PP 1908 [Cd. 4099] Royal Commission on Congestion in Ireland. Second Appendix to the Final Report. Digest of Evidence (Dublin, 1908), p. 521.
46 PP 1905 [Cd. 2757] Congested Districts Board for Ireland: Fourteenth Report of the Congested Districts Board for Ireland for the Year Ending 31st March, 1905, p. 16.
47 Ibid.
48 Commission on Emigration and Other Population Problems, 1948–54, *Reports* (Dublin, 1954), p. 94.
49 PP 1912–13 [Cd. 6198] Agricultural Statistics, Ireland, 1911. Report and Tables Relating to Irish Agricultural Labourers (London, 1912), p. 21.
50 PP 1907 (Cd. 3481] Agricultural Statistics, Ireland, 1906. Report and Tables Relating to Irish Migratory Agricultural Labourers, for the Year 1906 (Dublin, 1907), pp. 9, 25.
51 PP 1909 [Cd. 4919] Agricultural Statistics, Ireland, 1908–9. Report and Tables Relating to Irish Agricultural Labourers (Dublin, 1909), p. 29.
52 PP 1914–16 [Cd. 8036] Agricultural Statistics, Ireland, 1914. Report and Tables Relating to Irish Agricultural Labourers (London, 1915), p. 19.
53 PP 1908 [Cd. 4099] Royal Commission on Congestion in Ireland. Second Appendix to the Final Report. Digest of Evidence (Dublin, 1908), p. 528.
54 Ibid. p. 528.
55 PP 1907 (Cd. 3481] Agricultural Statistics, Ireland, 1906. Report and Tables Relating to Irish Migratory Agricultural Labourers, for the Year 1906 (Dublin 1907), pp. 38, 39.
56 Aidan Arrowsmith (ed.), *The Complete Works of J.M. Synge: Plays, Prose and Poetry* (Ware, Hertfordshire, 2008), pp. 224, 225.
57 PP 1893–94 [C. 6894–xxi] Royal Commission on Labour. The Agricultural Labourer, vol. IV, Ireland, pt. IV. Reports by Mr Arthur Wilson Fox (Asst. Commissioner) Upon Certain Selected Districts in the Counties of Cork, Mayo, Roscommon and Westmeath; With Summary Report Prefixed, p. 80.

58 Micheál MacGowan, *The Hard Road to Klondike* [1962] (Cork, 2003), p. 50.
59 Personal comment from Mary (Foley) Devlin, granddaughter.
60 John Neary, *Memories of the Long Distance Kiddies* (n.p., 1994), p. 40.
61 PP 1881 [C. 2809] Agricultural Statistics, Ireland, 1880. Report and Tables Relating to Migratory Agricultural Labourers (Dublin, 1881), p. 5.
62 PP 1902 [Cd. 1375] Agricultural Statistics, Ireland, 1902. Report and Tables Relating to Irish Migratory Agricultural and Other Labourers (Dublin, 1902), p. 9.
63 PP 1906 [Cd. 2865] Agricultural Statistics, Ireland, 1905. Report and Tables Relating to Irish Migratory Labourers, for the Year 1905 (Dublin, 1906), p. 11.
64 PP 1893 [C. 7188] Agricultural Statistics, Ireland, 1893. Report and Tables Relating to Migratory Agricultural Labourers (Dublin, 1893), p. 5.
65 PP 1906 [Cd. 2865] Agricultural Statistics, Ireland, 1905. Report and Tables Relating to Irish Migratory Agricultural Labourers, for the Year 1905 (Dublin, 1906), p. 16.
66 PP 1906 [Cd. 2865] Agricultural Statistics, Ireland, 1905. Report and Tables Relating to Irish Migratory Agricultural Labourers, for the Year 1905 (Dublin, 1906), p. 14.
67 PP 1880 [C. 2534] The Agricultural Statistics of Ireland, for the Year 1879 (Dublin 1880), p. 77.
68 PP 1906 [Cd. 2865] Agricultural Statistics, Ireland, 1905. Report and Tables Relating to Irish Migratory Agricultural Labourers, for the Year 1905 (Dublin, 1906), p. 19.
69 PP 1908 [Cd. 4123] Agricultural Statistics, Ireland, 1907–8. Report and Tables Relating to Irish Agricultural Labourers (Dublin, 1908), pp. 10–11.
70 Ibid. p. 11.
71 Ibid. pp. 10–11.
72 Ibid. p. 11.
73 Ibid. p. 12.
74 Ibid. p. 13.
75 John Denvir, *The Irish in Britain from the Earliest Times to the Fall and Death of Parnell* (London, 1892), p. 412.
76 PP 1881 [2951] Royal Commission on Agriculture. Preliminary Report of the Assistant Commissioners for Ireland, p. 3.
77 PP 1902 [Cd. 850] Agricultural Statistics, Ireland, 1901. Report and Tables Relating to Irish Migratory Agricultural and Other Labourers (Dublin, 1901), p. 44.
78 Ibid.
79 Ibid.
80 Ibid.
81 'A visit to Swinford', *Ballina Journal and Connaught Advertiser*, 18 August 1884, p. 5.
82 PP 1893 [C. 6894] Royal Commission on Labour. The Agricultural Labourer, Ireland. A. Summary Report by Mr Arthur Wilson Fox (Assistant Commissioner), p. 11.
83 PP 1906 [Cd. 2865] Agricultural Statistics, Ireland, 1905. Report and Tables Relating to Irish Migratory Agricultural Labourers, for the Year 1905 (Dublin, 1906), p. 15.
84 *Mayo Examiner*, 27 January 1883.
85 PP 1914–16 [Cd. 8036] Agricultural Statistics, Ireland, 1914. Report and Tables Relating to Irish Agricultural Labourers (Dublin, 1915), p. 6.
86 Aidan Arrowsmith (ed.), *The Complete Works of J.M. Synge: Plays, Prose and Poetry* (Ware, Hertfordshire, 2008), p. 224.
87 Finlay Dun, *Landlords and Tenants in Ireland* (London, 1881), p. 205.
88 Micheál MacGowan, *The Hard Road to Klondike* [1962] (Cork, 2003), p. 42.
89 PP 1900 [Cd. 341] Agricultural Statistics, Ireland, 1900. Report, Maps, Tables, and Appendices Relating toMigratory Agricultural Labourers (Dublin, 1900), p. 22.
90 PP 1902 [Cd. 1375] Agricultural Statistics, Ireland, 1902. Report and Tables Relating to Irish Migratory Agricultural and Other Labourers (Dublin, 1902), p. 16.

91 PP 1916 [Cd. 8386] Agricultural Statistics, Ireland, 1915. Report and Tables Relating to Irish Agricultural Labourers (Dublin, 1916), p. 4.
92 PP 1914–16 [Cd. 8036] Agricultural Statistics, Ireland, 1914. Report and Tables Relating to Irish Agricultural Labourers (Dublin, 1915), p. 3.
93 James Edmund Handley, *The Irish in Modern Scotland* (Cork, 1947), pp. 171–2.
94 *Irish Times*, 1 July 1916, p. 3.
95 'Trouble in the Fens', *The Times*, 9 August 1916, p. 3.
96 Ibid. p. 3.
97 'Nationalists and conscription', *Irish Times*, 1 September 1916, p. 4.
98 'Harvesters coming back from Great Britain', *Irish Times*, 15 August 1916, p. 7.

Chapter 8

1 Martin McDonagh, tape, 4 December 2007.
2 John Mulroy, tape, 13 June 2006.
3 John Archer Jackson, *The Irish in Britain* (London, 1963), p. 99.
4 John Walsh, tape, 3 September 2002.
5 John Mulroy, tape, 13 June 2006.
6 PP 1867–68 [4068] [4068–1] Commission on the Employment of Children, Young Persons, and Women in Agriculture (1867), Appendix Part II to First Report: Evidence from the Assistant Commissioners (London, 1868), p. 290.
7 Ibid. p. 315.
8 PP 1896 (321) *Report from the Select Committee on Distress from Want of Employment; Together with the Proceedings of the Committee, Minutes of Evidence, Appendix and Index* (London, 1896), p. 84.
9 PP 1893–94 [C. 6894–xxi] Royal Commission on Labour, The Agricultural Labourer, Vol. IV: Ireland, Part IV: Reports by Mr Arthur Wilson Fox (Assistant Commissioner) Upon Certain Selected Districts in the Counties of Cork, Mayo, Roscommon and Westmeath; With Summary Report Prefixed, pp. 14–15.
10 James Edmund Handley, *The Irish in Modern Scotland* (Cork, 1947), p. 185.
11 Irish Folklore Commission UCD, Ms 2072, Cúige Chonnacht, Co. Mháigh Eo, pp. 68–103: Edward O'Malley, Owenwee, Westport.

Chapter 9

1 Patrick J. Duffy, 'Migration management in Ireland', in Patrick J. Duffy (ed.), *To and From Ireland: Planned Migration Schemes, c. 1600–2000* (Dublin, 2004), pp. 1–15.
2 Peter Campbell, 'The big move of 1941', *Western People*, 23 September 1998.
3 Ibid.
4 Orla Hearns, 'Kildare settlers return to Swinford', *Western People*, 14 March 2006, p. 8.
5 Martin Whelan, William Nolan and Patrick J. Duffy, 'State-sponsored migrations to the east midlands in the twentieth century', in Patrick J. Duffy (ed.), *To and From Ireland: Planned Migration Schemes, c. 1600–2000* (Dublin, 2004), pp. 175–96.
6 Terence Dooley, '*The Land for the People*': The Land Question in Independent Ireland (Dublin, 2004), p. 144.
7 Martin McDonagh, tape, 4 December 2007.
8 Terence Dooley, '*The Land for the People*': The Land Question in Independent Ireland (Dublin, 2004), p. 144.
9 Martin McDonagh, tape, 4 December 2007.
10 Ibid.

11   Terence Dooley, *'The Land for the People': The Land Question in Independent Ireland* (Dublin, 2004), p. 153.

Chapter 10
1   PP 1877 [C. 1700] Emigration Statistics of Ireland for the Year 1875 (Dublin, 1877), p. 12.
2   PP 1901 [Cd. 531] Emigration Statistics of Ireland for the Year 1900 (Dublin, 1901), p. 12.
3   Commission on Emigration and Other Population Problems, 1948–54, *Reports* (Dublin, 1954), pp. 30, 31.
4   PP 1881 [2934] Return of Agricultural Holdings in Ireland, Compiled by the Local Government Board in Ireland from Returns Furnished by the Clerks of the Poor Law Unions in Ireland in January, 1881 (Dublin, 1881), p. 10.
5   PP 1908 [Cd. 4099] Royal Commission on Congestion in Ireland Second Appendix to the Final Report. Digest of Evidence vol. IX, p. 521.
6   Kevin Kenny, *The American Irish: A History* (Harlow, Essex, 2000), p. 152.
7   PP 1893–94 [C. 6894–xxi] Royal Commission on Labour. The Agricultural Labourer. vol. IV. Ireland, pt. IV: Reports by Mr Arthur Wilson Fox (Assistant Commissioner) Upon Certain Selected Districts in the Counties of Cork, Mayo, Roscommon and Westmeath; With Summary Report Prefixed (London, 1893), p. 81.
8   PP 1908 [Cd. 3748] Royal Commission on Congestion in Ireland. Appendix to the Sixth Report. Minutes of Evidence (taken in County Sligo and County Leitrim, 17–27 April, 1907) and Documents Relating Thereto, p. 7.
9   John Neary, *Memories of the Long Distance Kiddies* (n.p., 1994), pp. 41–5.
10 Kevin Kenny, *The American Irish: A History* (Harlow, Essex, 2000), pp. 181, 182.
11 W.E. Vaughan and A.J. Fitzpatrick (eds), *Irish Historical Statistics: Population, 1821–1971* (Dublin, 1978), p. 339.
12 John Archer Jackson, *The Irish in Britain* (London, 1963), p. 13.
13 Commission on Emigration and Other Population Problems, 1948–54, *Reports* (Dublin, 1954), pp. 316–17.
14 Enda Delaney, *Demography, State and Society: Irish Migration to Britain, 1921–71* (Liverpool, 2000), p. 45.
15 Commission on Emigration and Other Population Problems, 1948–54, *Reports* (Dublin, 1954), p. 317.
16 Ibid. p. 25.
17 'Mayo night in Philadelphia', *Western People*, 2 January 1932.
18 'Unemployed British Repatriated from US', *Belfast Weekly Telegraph*, 3 October 1931.

Chapter 11
1   David Johnson, *The Interwar Economy in Ireland* (Dundalk, 1989), p. 43.
2   Jack Foley, 'A powerless story not told: a study of migration from the east Mayo/south Sligo region in the period 1800–2004, with special emphasis on generational migration from the area in the twentieth century', unpublished MSSc. dissertation QUB, 2004, p. 65.
3   Enda Delaney, *Irish Emigration Since 1921* (Dundalk, 2002), p. 14.
4   John Healy, *No One Shouted Stop!*, first published as *The Death of an Irish Town* (Achill, 1988), p. 38.
5   Ibid. pp. 39, 40.

6   Patrick Fleming, 'Recollections', in Fr Leo Henry (ed.), *St. Nathy's College, 1819–2010: Reflections and Memories of Past Pupils* (Ballaghaderreen, Ireland, 2010), pp. 23–4.
7   John Archer Jackson, *The Irish in Britain* (London, 1963), p. 106.
8   Commission on Emigration and Other Population Problems, 1948–54, *Reports* (Dublin, 1954), p. 402.
9   Dermot Keogh, *Twentieth-century Ireland: Nation and State* (Dublin, 1994), p. 273.
10 Jack Foley, 'A powerless story not told: a study of migration from the east Mayo/south Sligo region in the period 1800–2004, with special emphasis on generational migration from the area in the twentieth century', unpublished MSSc. dissertation QUB, 2004, p. 66.
11 Theresa Connor, tape, 4 August 2004.
12 Adrian Redmond and Mary Heanue, 'Aspects of society', in Adrian Redmond (ed.), *That Was Then, This Is Now: Change in Ireland, 1949–1999. A Publication to Mark the Fiftieth Anniversary of the Central Statistics Office* (Dublin, 2000), pp. 45–72.

Chapter 12

1   Commission on Emigration and Other Population Problems, 1948–54, *Reports* (Dublin, 1954), p. 72.
2   Ibid. p. 64.
3   Ibid. p. 92.
4   Enda Delaney, *Irish Emigration Since 1921* (Dundalk, 2002), p. 1.
5   Ibid. p. 7.
6   Mick Foley, Tape, 9 August 2001.
7   Cormac Ó Gráda, *A Rocky Road: The Irish Economy Since the 1920s* (Manchester, 1997), p. 18.
8   Enda Delaney, 'Irish migration to Britain, 1939–45', *Irish Economic and Social History*, vol. 28, 2001, pp. 47–75.
9   Commission on Emigration and Other Population Problems, 1948–54, *Reports* (Dublin, 1954), p. 327.
10 Dermot Keogh, *Twentieth-century Ireland: Nation and State* (Dublin, 1994), p. 164.
11 Teddy Gallagher, tape, 7 November 2002.
12 Linda Dowling Almeida, 'A great time to be in America: the Irish in post-Second World War New York City', in Dermot Keogh, O'Finbarr Shea and Carmel Quinlan (eds), *The Lost Decade: Ireland in the 1950s* (Cork, 2004), pp. 206–20.
13 Ibid.
14 John Cafferty, tape, 17 October 2006.
15 Commission on Emigration and Other Population Problems, 1948–54, *Reports* (Dublin, 1954), p. 230.
16 Terry Connaughton, 'Terry Connaughton, 1952', in Patricia Hamill (ed.), *While Mem'ry Brings Us Back Again: A Collection of Memoirs Produced by the Aisling Irish Community Center* (New York, 2006), pp. 77–85.
17 Linda Dowling Almeida, 'A great time to be in America: the Irish in post-Second World War New York City', in Dermot Keogh, O'Finbarr Shea and Carmel Quinlan (eds), *The Lost Decade: Ireland in the 1950s* (Cork, 2004), pp. 206–20.
18 Ted Nealon, 'Political journalism and the back alley', in Fr Leo Henry (ed.), *St. Nathy's College, 1819–2010: Reflections and Memories of Past Pupils* (Ballaghaderreen, Ireland, 2010), pp. 27–49.
19 Commission on Emigration and Other Population Problems, 1948–54, *Reports* (Dublin, 1954), p. 127.

20 Ibid.
21 Anne Holohan, *Working Lives The Irish in Britain* (Hayes, Middlesex, 1995), pp. 3–4.
22 Adrian Redmond and Mary Heanue, 'Aspects of society', in Adrian Redmond (ed.), *That Was Then, This Is Now: Change in Ireland, 1949–1999. A Publication to Mark the Fiftieth Anniversary of the Central Statistics Office* (Dublin, 2000), pp. 45–72.
23 J.J. Sexton, 'Emigration and immigration in the twentieth century: an overview', in J.R. Hill (ed.), *A New History of Ireland, Vol. VII, Ireland, 1921–84* (Oxford, 2003), pp. 796–825.
24 Seamus Dunleavy and Shirley Thompson, *Finally Meeting Princess Maud* (Studley, Warwickshire, 2006), pp. 53–4.
25 Ibid. p. 105.

Conclusion

1 PP 1835 (369) Poor Inquiry, Supplement to Appendix (A.) Answers to Questions Circulated by the Commissioners Relative to the Relief of the Destitute Classes in Ireland, p. 25.
2 PP 1847 (002) Digest of Evidence Taken Before Her Majesty's Commissioners of Inquiry into the State of the Law and Practice in Respect to the Occupation of Land in Ireland, pt. I (Dublin, 1847), p. 516.
3 PP 1845 [616] [657] The Devon Commission, pt. II (Dublin 1845), p. 379.
4 PP 1881 [C. 2934] Return of Agricultural Holdings in Ireland, Compiled by the Local Government Board in Ireland from Returns Furnished by the Clerks of the Poor Law Unions in Ireland in January, 1881 (Dublin, 1881), p. 10.
5 PP 1902 [Cd. 850] Agricultural Statistics, Ireland, 1901. Report and Tables Relating to Irish Migratory Agricultural and Other Labourers; (Dublin, 1901), pp. 21–5.
6 Anne O'Dowd, *Spalpeens and Tattie Hokers: History and Folklore of the Irish Migratory Agricultural Worker in Ireland and Britain* (Dublin, 1991), pp. 252–3.
7 Cecil Woodham-Smith, *The Great Hunger: Ireland, 1845–1849* (London, 1991), p. 266.
8 Micheál MacGowan, *The Hard Road to Klondike* [1962] (Cork, 2003), pp. 2–3.
9 Horace Plunkett, *Ireland in the New Century* (Dublin, 1983), pp. 54–5.
10 E. Estyn Evans, *Irish Heritage: The Landscape, the People and Their Work* (Dundalk, 1967), p. 51.
11 *Irish Times*, 25, 26, 27 December 2003, p. 14.

Part II: 1940–1970: Migrants' Stories

1 Alistair Thomson, '"My wayward heart": homesickness, longing and the return of British post-war immigrants from Australia', in Marjory Harper (ed.), *Emigrant Homecomings: The Return Movement of Emigrants, 1600–2000* (Manchester, 2005), pp. 105–30.
2 Ibid.
3 Ibid.

Bibliography

Parliamentary Papers (PP)

PP 1816 (396) Report from the Select Committee on the State of Mendicity in the Metropolis (London, 1826)

PP 1819 (314) First Report from the Select Committee on the State of Disease, and Condition of the Labouring Poor, in Ireland (London, 1819)

PP 1826 (404) Report from the Select Committee on Emigration from the United Kingdom (London, 1826)

PP 1826–27 (550) Third Report from the Select Committee on Emigration from the United Kingdom (London, 1827)

PP 1828 (513) Report from the Select Committee on the Laws Relating to Irish and Scottish Vagrants (London, 1828)

PP 1830 (589) II. First Report of Evidence from the Select Committee on the State of the Poor in Ireland. Minutes of Evidence: 24 March–14 May

PP 1833 (612) Report from the Select Committee on Agriculture; with the Minutes of Evidence Taken Before Them, and an Appendix and Index (London, 1833)

PP 1835 (369) First Report from His Majesty's Commissioners for Inquiring into the Conditions of the Poorer Classes in Ireland, With Appendix (A.) and supplement [hereinafter called the Poor Inquiry] (London, 1835)

PP 1835 (369) Poor Inquiry (Ireland) Appendix (G.). Report on the State of the Irish Poor in Great Britain (London, 1835)

PP 1835 (369) Poor Inquiry (Ireland). Appendix (E.) and Supplement (London, 1836)

PP 1835 (369) Poor Inquiry (Ireland). Appendix (F.) and Supplement (London, 1836)

PP 1835 (369) Poor Inquiry (Ireland). Appendix (H.) Part I (London, 1836)

PP 1835 (369) Poor Inquiry (Ireland). First Report, Appendix (A.) (London, 1835)

PP 1835 (369) Poor Inquiry, Supplement to Appendix (A.) Answers to Questions Circulated by the Commissioners Relative to the Relief of the Destitute Classes in Ireland (London, 1835)

PP 1835 (369), Poor Inquiry, First Report with Appendix (A.) and Supplement (London, 1835)

PP 1836 [43] Third Report of the Commissioners for Inquiring into the Condition of the Poorer Classes in Ireland (London, 1836)

PP 1843 (504) Report of the Commissioners Appointed to Take the Census of Ireland, for the Year 1841 (Dublin, 1843)

PP 1845 [605] [606] Report from Her Majesty's Commissioners of Inquiry into the State of the Law and Practice in Respect to the Occupation of Land in Ireland [hereinafter known as the Devon Commission] (Dublin, 1845)

PP 1845 [616] [657] The Devon Commission, Part II (Dublin, 1845)

PP 1847 [002] The Devon Commission, Part I (Dublin, 1847)

PP 1847–48 [919] [955] [999] Papers Relating to Proceedings for the Relief of the Distress and State of Unions and Workhouses in Ireland. Seventh series: 1848 (Dublin, 1848)

PP 1852–53 [1542] Census of Ireland for the Year 1851, part I, County of Mayo (Dublin, 1852)

PP 1866 [3607] Royal Commission on Railways. Evidence and Papers Relating to Railways in Ireland (London, 1866)

PP 1867–68 [4068] [4068–1] Commission on the Employment of Children, Young Persons, and Women in Agriculture (1867). Appendix Part II to First Report. Evidence from the Assistant Commissioners (London, 1868)

PP 1870 [C. 31] Reports from Poor Law Inspectors in Ireland as to the Existing Relations Between Landlord and Tenant (Dublin, 1870)

PP 1871 [C. 1106] Census of Ireland, 1871, part I, vol. IV, no. 3. County of Mayo (Dublin, 1875)
PP 1877 [C. 1700] Emigration Statistics of Ireland, for the Year 1875 (Dublin, 1877)
PP 1877 [C. 1700] Emigration Statistics of Ireland, for the Year 1876 (Dublin, 1877)
PP 1880 [C. 2534] The Agricultural Statistics of Ireland, for the Year 1879 (Dublin 1880)
PP 1881 [C. 2934] Return of Agricultural Holdings in Ireland, Compiled by the Local Government Board in Ireland from Returns Furnished by the Clerks of the Poor Law Unions in Ireland in January, 1881 (Dublin, 1881)
PP 1881 [C. 2951] Royal Commission on Agriculture. Preliminary Report of the Assistant Commissioners for Ireland
PP 1881 [C. 2778] [C. 2778–1] [C. 2778–11] Preliminary Report from Her Majesty's Commissioners on Agriculture (London, 1881)
PP 1881 [C. 2809] Agricultural Statistics, Ireland, 1880. Report and Tables Relating to Migratory Agricultural Labourers (Dublin, 1881)
PP 1881 [C. 2828] Emigration Statistics of Ireland, for the Year 1880 (Dublin, 1881)
PP 1883 (92) Distress (Ireland). Copy of a Report from the Local Government Board for Ireland, Dated 13 March 1883, with Regard to the Distress Existing or Apprehended in Certain Parts of Ireland; and of the Reports from Inspectors of the Local Government Board and Other Papers Enclosed Therewith (London, 1883)
PP 1884 (218) Migratory Labourers (Ireland). Copy of Report Made by the Registrar General for Ireland, Showing the Results of Inquiries Made at the Request of the Irish Government by the Local Government Board for England, and the Board of Supervision for the Relief of the Poor in Scotland, as to the Diminution in the Number of Migratory Labourers from Ireland Visiting Certain Districts in Great Britain (London, 1884)
PP 1890–91 [C. 6295] Emigration Statistics of Ireland, for the Year 1890 (Dublin, 1891)
PP 1890–91 [C. 6519] Agricultural Statistics, Ireland, 1891. Report and Tables Relating to Migratory Agricultural Labourers (Dublin, 1891)
PP 1893 [C. 7188] Agricultural Statistics, Ireland, 1893. Report and Tables Relating to Migratory Agricultural Labourers (Dublin, 1893)
PP 1893 [C. 6894] Royal Commission on Labour. The Agricultural Labourer, Ireland. A. Summary Report by Mr Arthur Wilson Fox (Assistant Commissioner) (London, 1893)
PP 1893–94 [C. 6894–xxi] Royal Commission on Labour. The Agricultural Labourer, Vol. IV, Ireland, Part IV. Reports by Mr Arthur Wilson Fox (Assistant Commissioner) Upon Certain Selected Districts in the Counties of Cork, Mayo, Roscommon and Westmeath; With Summary Report Prefixed (London, 1893)
PP 1894 [C. 7533] Agricultural Statistics, Ireland, 1894. Report and Tables Relating to Migratory Agricultural Labourers (Dublin, 1894)
PP 1896 (321) Report from the Select Committee on distress from want of employment; together with the proceedings of the committee, minutes of evidence, appendix, and index (London, 1896)
PP 1900 [Cd. 239] Congested Districts Board for Ireland, Ninth Report (Dublin, 1900)
PP 1900 [Cd. 341] Agricultural Statistics, Ireland, 1900. Report, Maps, Tables and Appendices Relating to Migratory Agricultural Labourers (Dublin, 1900)
PP 1901 [Cd. 531] Emigration Statistics of Ireland, for the Year 1900 (Dublin, 1901)
PP 1902 [Cd 850] Agricultural Statistics, Ireland, 1901. Report and Tables Relating to Irish Migratory Agricultural and Other Labourers (Dublin, 1901)
PP 1902 [Cd. 1375] Agricultural Statistics, Ireland, 1902. Report and Tables Relating to Irish Migratory Agricultural and Other Labourers (Dublin, 1902)
PP 1903 [Cd. 1622] Congested Districts Board for Ireland, Twelfth Report (Dublin, 1903)
PP 1904 [Cd. 2275] Congested Districts Board for Ireland, Thirteenth Report (Dublin, 1904)

PP 1905 [Cd. 2757] Congested Districts Board for Ireland, Fourteenth Report of the Congested Districts Board for Ireland for the Year Ending 31st March, 1905 (Dublin, 1905)
PP 1906 [Cd. 2865] Agricultural Statistics, Ireland, 1905. Report and Tables Relating to Migratory Agricultural Labourers for the Year 1905 (Dublin, 1906)
PP 1906 [Cd. 3267] Royal Commission on Congestion in Ireland, Appendices to the First Report: Minutes of Evidence (taken in Dublin, 7 September–5 October, 1906) (Dublin, 1906)
PP 1907 (Cd. 3481] Agricultural Statistics, Ireland, 1906. Report and Tables Relating to Irish Migratory Agricultural Labourers, for the Year 1906 (Dublin, 1907)
PP 1908 [Cd. 3748] Royal Commission on Congestion in Ireland. Appendix to the Sixth Report: Minutes of Evidence (taken in County Sligo and County Leitrim, 17th to 27th April, 1907) and Documents Relating Thereto (Dublin, 1906)
PP 1908 [Cd. 4099] Royal Commission on Congestion in Ireland Second Appendix to the Final Report. Digest of Evidence vol. IX (Dublin, 1908)
PP 1908 [Cd. 4123] Agricultural Statistics, Ireland, 1907–8. Report and Tables Relating to Irish Agricultural Labourers (Dublin, 1908)
PP 1909 [Cd. 341] Agricultural Statistics, Ireland, 1908–9. Report and Tables Relating to Irish Agricultural Labourers (Dublin, 1909)
PP 1911 [Cd. 5607] Emigration Statistics of Ireland, for the Year 1910 (Dublin, 1911)
PP 1912 [Cd. 6052] Census of Ireland for the Year 1911, County of Mayo (London, 1912)
PP 1912–13 [Cd. 6198] Agricultural Statistics, Ireland, 1911. Report and Tables Relating to Irish Agricultural Labourers (London, 1912)
PP 1913 [Cd. 6928] Agricultural Statistics, Ireland, 1912. Report and Tables Relating to Irish Agricultural Labourers (Dublin, 1913)
PP 1914–16 [Cd. 8036] Agricultural Statistics, Ireland, 1914. Report and Tables Relating to Irish Agricultural Labourers (London, 1915)
PP 1916 [Cd. 8386] Agricultural Statistics, Ireland, 1915. Report and Tables Relating to Irish Agricultural Labourers (Dublin, 1916)

Irish University Press Series of British Parliamentary Papers
Report of the Commissioners Appointed to Take the Census of Ireland for the Year 1841 with Appendix and Index. Population, 2 (Shannon, 1968)
Correspondence Relating to the Measures Adopted for the Relief of Distress in Ireland, Board of Works Series [Second Part] with Index and Commissariat Series [Second Part] with Index, 1847, Famine, Ireland, 7 (Shannon, 1971)
Emigration, Ireland, 4, 1847 (Shannon, 1971)
Famine, Ireland, 4 (Shannon, 1971)
Relating to Proceedings for the Relief of Distress and the State of the Unions and Workhouses in Ireland [Fourth and Fifth Series]. 1847–48. Famine, Ireland, 2 (Shannon, 1971)
Relating to Proceedings for the Relief of Distress and the State of the Unions and Workhouses in Ireland [Sixth Series]. 1847–48. Famine, Ireland, 3 (Shannon, 1971)

Census of Ireland
Census of Ireland 1911 [Cd. 6052] Area, Houses and Population: also the Ages, Civil or Conjugal Condition, Occupations, Birthplaces, Religion and Education of the People. Province of Connaught. County of Mayo (Dublin, 1912)

Congested Districts Board for Ireland
County of Mayo – Union of Swinford. Report of Mr Doran, Inspector, 2 May 1892

Department of Irish Folklore, UCD
Ms 2072, Cúige Chonnacht, Co. Mháigh Eo: Edward O'Malley, Owenwee, Westport

Dublin City Archives
Mansion House Fund, Ch. 1/52/42 (Carracastle)
Mansion House Fund, Ch. 1/52/130 (Charlestown)
Mansion House Fund, Ch. 1/52/416 (Curry)

National Archives, Kew, London
MH 32/115

Valuation Office
Valuation Lists, no. 16, vol. I, vol. II, vol. III

Newspapers
Ballina Chronicle
'Emigration from Westport', 30 April 1851
'Emigration', 7 May 1851

Ballina Journal and Connaught Advertiser
'A visit to Swinford', 18 August 1884

Belfast Weekly Telegraph
'Unemployed British repatriated from US', 3 October 1931

Connaught Telegraph
3 April 1880
15 May 1880
9 October 1880
2 July 1881

Freeman's Journal and Daily Commercial Advertiser
'Irish harvestmen maltreated in Liverpool', 25 July 1849
'The crops', 13 September 1851
'Distress in the west', 14 March 1862
'Fatal affray among harvestmen – inquest', 12 September 1865
'Diocese of Achonry', 26 October 1877
'Outbreak of famine fever', 23 June 1880
'The famine fever in the west', 7 July 1880

Hull Packet and East Riding Times
'The crisis in Ireland', 4 November 1881

Irish Times
'The exodus', 29 March 1859
'Scarcity of harvest labour', 31 August 1859
'The new race of Irish reapers', 19 August 1862
'Police intelligence', 7 September 1865
'Important: to railway companies', 6 March 1867
27 March 1873
'Late train', 25 June 1873
'Overcrowding of Irish steamers', 24 July 1877
'Fatal railway accident', 15 June 1878
'Overcrowding on Irish steamer', 6 July 1878
'Extraordinary exodus of Connaught harvestmen to England', 28 June 1879
'County Mayo', 23 September 1879
'Meeting at Gurteen', 8 November 1879
'The condition of the west', 2 December 1879
30 January 1880
18 February 1880
'Migratory Irish labour', 21 February 1880
'Contributions', 23 March 1880
'The distress in Ireland', 26 March 1880
'Mansion House Relief Committee', 20 April 1880
'The condition of Mayo', 3 July 1880
'Mansion House Committee', 5 July 1880
'The condition of Mayo', 10 July 1880
'Harvestmen in difficulties', 22 June 1881
'Irish labour emigration', 8 January 1883
'Congestion in the west', 20 October 1883
'Connaught harvestmen for England', 28 June 1884
'State of Swinford Union', 26 April 1886
'Irish harvestmen for England', 3 July 1886
'Rent payment in the West', 5 March 1887
'Exodus of western harvestmen', 23 June 1888
'Distress in Swinford district', 27 August 1890
'Irish farm labourers in England, 11 August 1894
22 September 1897
'Exodus of harvestmen', 25 June 1898
'Exodus of harvestmen', 18 June 1913
'Harvestmen', 16 August 1915
'Harvestmen for Great Britain', 27 March 1916
'Special steamer for harvestmen', 24 June 1916
'Harvesters coming back from Great Britain', 15 August 1916
'Nationalists and conscription', 1 September 1916
'Home is still where the Irish heart is', 25, 26, 27 December 2003
'Foreign nationals send home €274m', 15 December 2010

Leeds Mercury
'An English farmer in Ireland', 21 June 1887

Mayo Constitution
'Correspondence – Swinford', 3 March 1868

Mayo Examiner
'Swinford Union, emigration', 27 January 1883

Morning Chronicle **(London)**
'Distress in Ireland', 11 June 1822

Northern Star and Leeds General Advertiser
17 July 1841

Telegraph or Connaught Ranger
'Westport sufferers', 16 March 1831
'Famine in Mayo', 13 July 1831
'Emigration from Ireland', 31 August 1831
'Irish emigration to the United States', 23 February 1848
'Distress in Mayo', 3 January 1849
'The exodus', 6 April 1853

The Times
11 June 1862
'The harvest in Yorkshire', 11 September 1862
'The harvest and the labour-market', 26 August 1867
'Railway and other companies', 6 September 1879
'Railway and other companies', 8 March 1880
'Affrays between harvestmen', 21 July 1886
'Irish migratory agricultural labourers', 25 September 1886
'Trouble in the Fens', 9 August 1916

Tyrawley Herald
'Ballaghaderreen', 4 February 1847

Western People
'Allan Line', 25 May 1889
17 August 1889
'Evictions on Lord Dillon's estate', 21 September 1889
10 January 1891
'Government relief work in Erris', 17 January 1891
'The distress in Charlestown', 14 February 1891
'Mayo night in Philadelphia', 2 January 1932
24 August 1940
Campbell, Peter. 'The big move of 1941', 23 September 1998
Hearns, Orla. 'Kildare settlers return to Swinford', 14 March 2006

Journals and Periodicals

Delaney, Enda. 'Irish Migration to Britain, 1939–1945', *Irish Economic and Social History*, vol. 28, 2001
Hogan, Patrick. 'The migration of Ulster Catholics to Connaught, 1795–96', in Patrick J. Campbell (ed.), *Seanchas Ardmhacha* Vol 9, no. 2, 1979
Moran, Gerard P. 'Famine and the Land War: relief and distress in Mayo, 1879–1881', part I, *Cathair na Mart* (Journal of the Westport Historical Society), vol. 5, no. 1, 1985
Moran, Gerard. 'Mayo God help us! Emigration from nineteenth-century Mayo', *Cathair na Mart* (Journal of the Westport Historical Society), no. 21, 2001

O'Connor, Moya. 'Of long forgotten far off things …', in Michael Comer, Mairead Golden, Micheál Murphy and Brenda Ormsby (eds), *Swinford Echoes 1997*, vol. II

Ó Gráda, Cormac. 'Seasonal migration and post-Famine adjustment in the west of Ireland', *Studia Hibernica*, no. 13, 1973

Storhaug, Hans. 'European Return migration: numbers, reasons and consequences', in Hans Storhaug (ed.), *AEMI Journal,* vol. I, 2003

Journal of the Royal Society of Antiquaries of Ireland, vol. 27, 1897

Journal of the Royal Society of Antiquaries of Ireland, vol. 32, 1902

Tohall, Patrick. 'The diamond fight of 1795 and the resultant expulsions', in, Fr Tomás Ó Fiaich (ed.), *Seanchas Ardmhacha*, vol. 3, no. 1, 1958

Books

Akenson, Donald Harman. *The Irish Diaspora: A Primer* (Belfast, 1996)

Almeida, Linda Dowling. 'A great time to be in America: the Irish in post-Second World War New York City', in Dermot Keogh, O'Finbarr Shea and Carmel Quinlan (eds), *The Lost Decade: Ireland in the 1950s* (Cork, 2004)

Arrowsmith, Aidan (ed.), *The Complete Works of J.M. Synge: Plays, Prose and Poetry* (Ware, Hertfordshire, 2008)

Baines, Dudley. *Emigration from Europe, 1815–1930* (London, 1991)

Barrow, John. *A Tour Round Ireland* (London, 1836)

Breathnach, Ciara. *The Congested Districts Board of Ireland, 1891–1923. Poverty and Development in the West of Ireland* (Dublin, 2005)

Carr, John. *The Stranger in Ireland: on a Tour in the Southern and Western Parts of that Country in the Year 1805* (New York, 1806)

Comer, Michael and Micheál Murphy. *The Burma Road: Claremorris to Collooney Railway* (Swinford, 1996)

Commission on Emigration and Other Population Problems, 1948–1954. *Reports* (Dublin, 1954)

Connaughton, Terry. 'Terry Connaughton, 1952', in Patricia Hamill (ed.), *While Mem'ry Brings Us Back Again*: *A Collection of Memoirs Produced by the Aisling Irish Community Center* (New York, 2006)

Cowley, Ultan. *The Men who Built Britain: A History of the Irish Navvy* (Dublin, 2001)

Crawford, Margaret E. (ed.). *The Hungry Stream: Essays on Emigration and Famine* (Belfast, 1997)

Davis, Graham. *The Irish in Britain, 1815–1914* (Dublin, 1991)

De Beaumont, Gustave. *Ireland: Social, Political and Religious* [1839] (Cambridge, MA, 2006)

Delaney, Enda. *Demography, State and Society: Irish Migration to Britain, 1921–71* (Liverpool, 2000)

Delaney, Enda. *Irish Emigration Since 1921* (Dundalk, Ireland, 2002)

Denvir, John. *The Irish in Britain from the Earliest Times to the Fall and Death of Parnell* (London, 1892)

Devlin Trew, Johanne. *Leaving the North: Migration and Memory, Northern Ireland, 1921–2011* (Liverpool, 2013)

Dooley, Terence. '*The Land for the People': The Land Question in Independent Ireland* (Dublin, 2004)

Duffy, Patrick J. 'Migration management in Ireland', in Patrick J. Duffy (ed.), *To and From Ireland: Planned Migration Schemes, c. 1600–2000* (Dublin, 2004)

Dun, Finlay. *Landlords and Tenants in Ireland* (London, 1881)

Dunleavy, Seamus. and Shirley Thompson, *Finally Meeting Princess Maud* (Studley, Warwickshire, 2006)

Dunne, Catherine. *An Unconsidered People: The Irish in London* (Dublin, 2003)

Evans, E. Estyn. *The personality of Ireland Habitat, Heritage and History* [1973] (Dublin, 1992)

Ferriter, Diarmaid. *The Transformation of Ireland, 1900–2000* (London, 2004)
Fitzgerald, Patrick and Brian Lambkin, *Migration in Irish History, 1607–2007* (Basingstoke, 2008)
Fitzpatrick, David. '"A peculiar tramping people": the Irish in Britain, 1801–70', in W.E. Vaughan (ed.), *A New History of Ireland, Vol. V: Ireland Under the Union, 1801–70* (Oxford, 1989)
Fitzpatrick, David. 'Emigration, 1801–1921', in Michael Glazier (ed.), *The Encyclopaedia of the Irish in America* (Notre Dame, IN, 1999)
Fitzpatrick, David. 'Emigration, 1871–1921', in W.E. Vaughan (ed.), *A New History of Ireland, Vol. V: Ireland Under the Union, II, 1870–1921* (Oxford, 1989)
Fitzpatrick, David. 'Irish emigration, 1801–1921', in Peter Roebuck and David Dickson (eds), *Studies in Irish Economic and Social History* (Dundalk, 1984)
Fitzpatrick, David. 'Marriage in post-Famine Ireland', in Art Cosgrove (ed.), *Marriage in Ireland* (Dublin, 1985)
Foley, Jack. 'A Powerless story not told: a study of migration from the east Mayo/south Sligo region in the period 1800–2004, with special emphasis on generational migration from the area in the twentieth century', unpublished MSSc. dissertation QUB, 2004
Forbes, John. *Memorandums Made in Ireland in the Autumn of 1852*, vol. I (London, 1853)
Foster, Thomas Campbell. *Letters on the Condition of the People of Ireland* (London, 1846)
Fox, J.A. *Reports of the Condition of the Peasantry of the County of Mayo in 1880* (Dublin, 1881)
Freeman, T.W. 'Land and people, *c.* 1841', in W.E. Vaughan (ed.), *A New History of Ireland, Vol. V: Ireland Under the Union, II, 1870–1921* (Oxford, 1989)
Gallagher, Tom. *Tara's Halls* (North Charleston, SC, 2015)
Gray, Breda. *Women and the Irish Diaspora* (London, 2004)
Green, E.R.R., 'Agriculture', in R. Dudley Edwards and T. Desmond Williams (eds), *The Great Famine Studies in Irish History, 1845–52* (Dublin, 1956)
Griffith, Richard. *General Valuation of Rateable Property in Ireland*. Counties of Mayo and Roscommon. Valuation of the Several Tenements in the Union of Swineford – Parish of Kilbeagh (Dublin, 1856)
Handley, James E. *The Navvy in Scotland* (Cork, 1970)
Handley, James Edmund. *The Irish in Modern Scotland* (Cork, 1947)
Handley, James Edmund. *The Irish in Scotland, 1798–1845* (Cork, 1943)
Harper, Marjory (ed.). *Emigrant Homecomings: The Return Movement of Emigrants, 1600–2000* (Manchester, 2005)
Harris, Ruth-Ann M. and Emer B. O'Keeffe (eds), *The Search for Missing Friends: Irish Immigrant Advertisements Placed in the* Boston Pilot, vol. II, 1851–53 (Boston, MA, 1991) and vol. III, 1854–56 (Boston, MA, 1993)
Healy, John. *Nineteen Acres* (Galway, 1978)
Healy, John. *No One Shouted Stop!*, first published as *The Death of an Irish Town* (Achill, 1988)
Henry, Cathal. *The Charlestown Chronicles* (Dublin, 2009)
Henry, Fr Leo (ed.). *St. Nathy's College, 1810–2010: Reflections and Memories of Past Pupils* (Ballaghaderreen, 2010)
Hill, Myrtle. *Women in Ireland: A Century of Change* (Belfast, 2003)
Holleran, Tom. *Rambling Memories, My Memory of the Early Days, 1921–1988* (n.p., 1991)
Holohan, Anne. *Working Lives: The Irish in Britain* (Hayes, Middlesex, 1995)
Inglis, Henry D. *A Journey Throughout Ireland, During the Spring, Summer and Autumn of 1834*, vols. I and II (London, 1835)
Jackson, John Archer. *The Irish in Britain* (London, 1963)
Johnson, David. *The Interwar Economy in Ireland* (Dundalk, 1989)
Johnson, James. *A Tour in Ireland: With Meditations and Reflections* (London, 1844)
Jordan Jnr, Donald E. *Land and Popular Politics in Ireland. County Mayo from the Plantation to the Land War* (Cambridge, 1994)

Jubb, Samuel. *The History of the Shoddy-trade: Its Rise, Progress, and Present Position* (London, 1860)
Kearney, Richard (ed.). *Migrations: The Irish at Home & Abroad* (Dublin, 1990)
Kelly, Liam. *Kiltubrid, Co. Leitrim. Snapshots of a Rural Parish in the 1890s* (Dublin, 2005)
Kennedy Jnr, Robert E. *The Irish: Emigration, Marriage, and Fertility* (London, 1973)
Kenny, Kevin. *The American Irish: A History* (Harlow, Essex, 2000)
Keogh, Dermot. *Twentieth-century Ireland: Nation and State* (Dublin, 1994)
Keogh, Dermot, O'Finbarr Shea and Carmel Quinlan (eds). *Ireland in the 1950s: The Lost Decade* (Cork, 2004)
Kilbeagh Parish/CBDHS Publication. *A Moment in Time: Celebrating the 150th Anniversary of St. James's Church, Charlestown* (Kilbeagh, 2009)
Kraut, Alan M. *The Huddled Masses: The Immigrant in American Society, 1880–1921* (Arlington Heights, Il, 1982)
Lee, J.J. *Ireland, 1912–1985: Politics and Society* (Cambridge, 1989)
Lee, Joseph. *The Modernisation of Irish Society, 1848–1918* (Dublin, 1989)
Lewis, Samuel. *A Topographical Dictionary of Ireland* (London, 1837)
MacGowan, Micheál. *The Hard Road to Klondike* [1962] (Cork, 2003)
McManus, Frank. 'The Expulsions from Ulster of 1795–97', in Séamus McAnnaidh (ed.), *Fermanagh and 1798* (Dooneen, 2000)
McNicholas, Willie. *Path to the Well: Memories of an Irish Immigrant from Ireland to America* (NY, 2008)
McParlan, James. *Statistical Survey of the County of Mayo With Observations on the Means of Improvement Drawn Up in the Year 1801 for the Consideration and Under the Direction of the Dublin Society* (Dublin, 1802)
McRaild, Donald M. *Irish Migrants in Modern Britain, 1750–1922* (London, 1999)
McRaild, Donald M. (ed.). *The Great Famine and Beyond: Irish Migrants in Britain in the Nineteenth and Twentieth Centuries* (Dublin, 2000)
Micks, William L. *An Account of the Constitution, Administration and Dissolution of the Congested Districts Board for Ireland from 1891 to 1923* (Dublin, 1925)
Miller, Kerby A. *Emigrants and Exiles* (Oxford, 1985)
Mitchell, Brian. *A New Genealogical Atlas of Ireland* (Baltimore, 2002)
Moran, Gerard. *Sending out Ireland's poor. Assisted Emigration to North America in the Nineteenth Century* (Dublin, 2004)
Murphy, Maureen. 'The Fionnuala factor: Irish sibling emigration at the turn of the century', in Anthony Bradley and Maryann Gialanella Valiulis (eds), *Gender and Sexuality in Modern Ireland* (Amherst, MA, 1997)
Nealon, Ted. 'Political Journalism and the Back Alley', in Fr Leo Henry (ed.), *St. Nathy's College, 1810–2010: Reflections and Memories of Past Pupils* (Ballaghaderreen, 2010)
Neary, John. *Memories of the Long Distance Kiddies* (n.p., 1994)
Neligan, James. 'Parish of Kilmactige, Diocese of Achonry and County of Sligo', in Mason, William Shaw, *A Statistical Account or Parochial Survey of Ireland*, vol. 2 (Dublin, 1816)
Nicholls, George. *Poor Laws: Ireland. Three Reports by George Nicholls, esq., to Her Majesty's Principal Secretary of State for the Home Department, Second Report* (London, 1838)
Nolan, Janet A. *Ourselves Alone: Women's Emigration from Ireland, 1885–1920* (Kentucky, 1989)
O'Dowd, Anne. *Spalpeens and Tattie Hokers: History and Folklore of the Irish Migratory Agricultural Worker in Ireland and Britain* (Dublin, 1991)
Ó Gráda, Cormac. *A Rocky Road: The Irish Economy Since the 1920s* (Manchester, 1997)
Ó Gráda, Cormac. *Black '47 and Beyond: The Great Irish Famine in History, Economy, and Memory* (Princeton, 1999)
Ó Gráda, Cormac. *Ireland: A New Economic History, 1780–1939* (Oxford, 1994)

Ó Gráda, Cormac. *The Great Irish Famine* (London, 1989)
O'Hara, Bernard. 'County Mayo', in Bernard O'Hara (ed.), *Mayo: Aspects of its Heritage* (Galway, 1982)
O'Hara, Bernard. *The Archaeological Heritage of Killasser, Co Mayo* (Galway, 1991)
O'Malley, Martin. [no title] in Patricia Hamill (ed.), *While Mem'ry Brings Us Back Again: A Collection of Memoirs Produced by the Aisling Irish Community Center* (New York, 2006)
O'Neill, T.P. 'The Food Crisis of the 1890s', in Margaret E. Crawford (ed.), *Famine: The Irish Experience, 900–1900: Subsistence Crises and Famines in Ireland* (Edinburgh, 1989)
Plunkett, Horace. *Ireland in the New Century* (Dublin, 1983)
Redford, Arthur. *Labour Migration in England, 1800–1850* [1926], ed. William Henry Chaloner (Manchester, 1976)
Redmond, Adrian and Mary Heanue, 'Aspects of Society', in Adrian Redmond (ed.), *That Was Then, This Is Now: Change in Ireland, 1949–1999. A Publication to Mark the Fiftieth Anniversary of the Central Statistics Office* (Dublin, 2000)
Schrier, Arnold. *Ireland and the American Emigration* (Minnesota, 1958)
Sexton, J.J. 'Emigration and Immigration in the twentieth century: an overview', in, J.R. Hill (ed.), *A New History of Ireland, Vol. VII, Ireland, 1921–84* (Oxford, 2003)
Sullivan, Mary. 'The Cavan diaspora', in Brian S. Turner (ed.), *Migration and Myth: Ulster's Revolving Door* (Downpatrick, 2006)
Swinford Historical Society, *An Gorta Mór: Famine in the Swinford Union* (Swinford, 1996)
Swords, Liam. *A Dominant Church* (Dublin, 2004)
Swords, Liam. *A Hidden Church: The Diocese of Achonry, 1689–1818* (Dublin, 1998)
Swords, Liam. *In their Own Words. The Famine in North Connacht, 1845–1849* (Dublin, 1999)
The Irish Crisis of 1879–80. Proceedings of the Dublin Mansion House Relief Committee, 1880 (Dublin, 1881)
The Parliamentary Gazetteer of Ireland, vol. II (London, 1846)
Tuke, James Hack. *A Visit to Connaught in the Autumn of 1847* (London, 1848, 2nd edition)
Turner, Brian S. (ed.). *Migration and Myth: Ulster's Revolving Door* (Downpatrick, 2006)
Vaughan, W.E. and A.J. Fitzpatrick (eds). *Irish Historical Statistics: Population, 1821–1971* (Dublin, 1978)
Walsh, Denis H. (ed.). *St Mary of the Angels, Batley, 1853–2003* (n.p., 2003)
Walter, Bronwen with Breda Gray, Linda Dowling Almeida and Sarah Morgan, *A Study of the Existing Sources of Information and Analysis About Irish Emigrants and Irish Communities Abroad* (Dublin, 2002)
Whelan, Martin, William Nolan and Patrick J. Duffy. 'State-sponsored migrations to the east midlands in the twentieth century', in Patrick J. Duffy (ed.), *To and From Ireland: Planned Migration Schemes,* c. *1600–2000* (Dublin, 2004)
Woodham-Smith, Cecil. *The Great Hunger: Ireland, 1845–1849* (London, 1991)
Wyman, Mark. *Round-trip to America: The Immigrants Return to Europe, 1880–1930* (New York, 1993)
Young, Arthur. *A Tour in Ireland: With General Observations on the Present State of the Kingdom: Made in the Years 1776, 1777 and 1778 and Brought Down to 1779, Vol. I* (London, 1780)

Index

Achill Island 80, 86, 89, 106
Aclare, Co. Sligo 127
Adelaide, Australia 244
Aghamore 24
Alcan Aluminium, Aughinish, Co. Limerick 195, 282
Allan Line (shipping company) 46
Allscott, Shropshire 267
Altamont, Lord 6
American Civil War 10, 31
American Express Company 222
Annagh 55
Áras Attracta, Swinford 283
Armagh, Co. 6, 8–9
Armstrong, John 47
Attymass 1, 55
Australia, emigration to 2, 32, 112, 122, 175, 242, 244
  Assisted Passage Scheme (Australia) 242
Austria, emigration to 71

Bailieborough, Co. Cavan 18
Balla 30
Ballaghaderreen, Co. Roscommon 2, 11, 49, 64–5, 89, 117, 202–3, 274, 280
Ballina 6, 34, 192, 264
Ballinafad College, Belcarra 248
Ballinrobe 18, 34
Ballintadder 41, 96, 119, 125, 280–1
Ballyglass East 26
Ballyglass West 26
Ballyhaunis 30, 36, 38, 40, 60, 64–5, 87, 89, 108, 241
Ballyhine 24
Ballymote [*sic* Ballymoat], Co. Sligo 9
Ballyvary 50
Baltimore & Ohio Railroad 32
Bardney, Lincolnshire 255
Barnacogue 192, 199, 282
Barrow, John 11
Basta (manufacturer), Tubbercurry, Co. Sligo 285
Batley, Yorkshire 30
Baxter Healthcare, Swinford 285
Beaumont, Gustave De 74

Bedfordshire 179
Belcarra 248
Belfast 55, 115, 187
Belgium, emigration from 70
Bellaghy 41, 44–5
Bellanaboy 258
Belmullet 50, 198, 240, 258
Belmullet Poor Law Union 50
Berkshire 226
Birmingham 73, 128, 157, 180, 190, 219
Blackburn 194
Board of Supervision for the Relief of the Poor in Scotland 72
Bohola 1, 24, 55, 118, 136, 178, 212
Bord na Móna 172, 200, 203
Boston, Lincolnshire 176, 179, 187, 189
Boston, Massachusetts 33, 46, 115
Bowling Green, New York 222
Boyle, Andrew 57
Brackloonagh 218, 257
Bradford, Vermont 33
Bradford, Yorkshire 30
Bradwell, Essex 198
Breheny, Ambrose 224
Breheny, Bill 221–2, 224–5
Breheny, Collette 224–5
Breheny, Dolores 224
Breheny, Jimmy (Clooncoose) 221–2, 224–5
Breheny, Jim (New York) 222
Breheny, Madeleine 224
Breheny, Mary 222
Breheny, Maureen 222–4
Breheny, Pádraig 224
Breheny, Patty 224
Breheny, Seán 221–2, 224
Breheny, Teresa 224
Breheny, Vera 224
Brennan, Jimmy 252–4, 256
Brennan, John 282–3
Brennan, Mary 254
Brennan, Michael 252 3
Brennan, Una 283
Brett, Edward 43
Brett, Mary 57
Brett, Michael 57

Brett, Widow (Corthoon) 43
Brigg, Lincolnshire 141, 196
Brooklyn, New York 222–3
  St Francis of Assisi Church 223
Brown and Polson, company, Manchester 193
Browne estate, Cuiltrasna 62
Browne JP, Henry 18
Burgh, Rev. Thomas J. 18
Burke, Bridget 33
Burns family, Charlestown 190
Burns, Jimmy 237
Burns, Mick 176, 237
Burrishoole 18
Bury St Edmunds, Suffolk 200, 262, 264–5

Cafferty, John 125–6
Cahill, Maura 117, 167
Cain jnr, John 33
Cain snr, John 33
Cain, Sabina 33
Cairo, Illinois 32
Cambridge 143
Cambridgeshire 89, 92
Camden, London 137–8, 157, 163, 240
Campbell (Midfield; grandfather of Shane Horgan) 109
Campbell, Ned 143–4
Campbell, Tommy 144, 234–5
Canada, emigration to 2, 112, 122, 158, 195, 253
Cannon brothers (died 1878, Co. Mayo) 36
Canterbury 190
Cardiff 174
Carlisle 154–5, 190
Carndonagh, Co. Donegal 80
Carn [sic Carne] 41, 43
Carracastle 42, 96, 119, 125, 146, 239
Carracastle Relief Committee (Co. Sligo) 42
Carracastle [sic Carrycastle] 40
Carragown 14, 83
Carr, John 8
Carrol, T. 43
Carrowcanada 181, 184, 186
Carrowreagh 151
Cashel, Co. Mayo 40
Cassidy, Thomas 33
Castlebar 29, 36, 88
Castlebarnagh (sic Castlebarnaugh, Castle Barnaugh) 32–3

Castlemore 12, 18
Castlerea, Co. Roscommon 130
Castlerea Poor Law Union, Co. Roscommon 71
Catskills, New York 222
Cavan, Co. 18
Charlestown, Co. Mayo 30, 39, 42–5, 51, 58, 64–5, 78, 84, 88, 117–18, 123, 126, 128, 132, 151–2, 159–60, 162, 164, 167, 172, 176, 187, 190, 203, 207, 212, 218, 221, 225–6, 228, 236, 244, 246, 255, 257, 260, 269–70, 280
  Parsons', factory 207
  St Antoine's Secondary School 117–18, 167
Charlestown Relief Committee 43
Charlestown, Massachusetts 33
Cheshire 216
Chester, Pennsylvania 33
Chicago, Illinois 33, 227, 269, 283
China, emigration to 273
Chiswick, London 179, 235
Chorley, Lancashire 155, 184
Cincinnati, Ohio 32–3
Clancy, John 194–5
Clancy (née Henry), May 192–5
Clare, Co. 107, 155, 181
Claremorris 36, 40, 58–9, 87–8, 144
Claremorris Poor Law Union 80
Clarke, Pat 178
Clayworth, Nottinghamshire 113
Clifden, Co. Galway 241
Cloonaghboy 234
Cloonainra 200, 203
Clooncoose [sic Clooncous] 132, 221, 224
Cloonlara 262
Cloonmore 160
Cloontia 203
Cloontubrid 202, 266
Coleman, Rev. John 14–15
Colleran, Jim 123, 144, 176, 178
Collereen, Luke 15
Collooney 58–9, 88
Commission on Agriculture, 1881 75
Commission on Emigration, 1954 111, 115, 118, 126
Congested Districts Board (CDB) 3, 54–5, 59–62, 71, 84, 111

Conlon, Johnny 146–50
Conlon, Tom 146–7
Connemara, Co. Galway 266
Connor, Bernadette 119
Connor, Eddie 281
Connor, Josephine 281
Connor, Margaret 281
Connor, Theresa 119, 280–1
Conway family, Kinaffe 266
Conway, Peggy 158
Conway, Philip 154–9
'Cookie', Mr (building foreman) 242–3
Coolrawer, Co. Sligo 172
Coolrecuill, Co. Sligo 127
Corbridge-on-Tyne, Northumberland 76
Cork, Co. 46, 178, 191, 241, 259, 269, 282
Corley, Pat 57
Cornwall 218
Corthoon [sic Cartron] 43, 51, 56–7, 159–60, 167, 176, 187, 205, 209, 214, 226, 236, 244
Corthoon National School 117
Costello (barony) 2, 6
Costello, Mr (Edmondstown) 26
Cotton, William 130
County Dublin Vocational Education Committee 117
Coventry 155
Creighton, Rev. Robert 10
Croydon 143
Cuiltrasna 62
Cuiltybo 212
Culmore 40, 45, 254, 256
Curry [sic Currey], Co. Sligo 15, 42, 63, 117
Czech Republic, emigration to 273

Davey, Bridget 30
Davey, Thomas 42
Deal, Kent 190
Deane, A.S. 44
Dean, Edward 14, 83
Deehan, Mary 227
Deeny, James 162
Deeping St Nicholas, Lincolnshire 99, 239
Denvir, John 35, 93
Department of Local Government and Public Health 162
Derby 177, 179, 240
Derbyshire 78

Derenzy JP, Thomas 18
Derrykinlough 203
Derry/Londonderry, Co. 18, 88
Devine, Catherine 141
Devine, Dominic 143
Devine, Jackie 141–5
Devine, Mary 145
Devine, Michael 141
Devine, 'old priest' 144
Devine, Paddy 144
Devine, Pat 143
Devlin (née Foley), Mary 167–71
Devlin, Patsy 170–1
Devlin, Stephen 170–1
Devlin, Tom 170
Devlin, Una 170–1
Devon Commission, 1845 2, 9, 14–15, 17, 20, 22, 29, 48, 83, 129
Digital Equipment Corporation 251
Dillingham Commission, 1911, US 52
Dillon estate, Loughlynn 19, 26, 45, 47, 61–2, 84–5
Dillon, Lord Charles Henry (14th Viscount) 2, 19–20, 26, 47
Diss, Norfolk 161
Doherty, Angela 152
Doherty, Ellen 33
Doherty, John (Lurga; resident in Cairo, Illinois) 32–3
Doherty, John (secretary Charlestown Relief Committee) 43
Doherty [sic Dougherty], Martin 33
Doherty, Michael (Lurga; resident in Gardner, Massachusetts) 32–3
Doherty, Michael J. (secretary Charlestown Relief Committee) 43
Doherty, Thomas (Lurga) 32
Doherty, Tommy (Charlestown) 152, 201
Doherty (travel agent, Charlestown) 64
Donegal, Co. 60, 80, 88–9, 95, 131, 178, 264
Doocastle 118
Doonty 24–5
Doran, Harry 59–60
Dover 212
Drogheda 74
Dromada-Duke 50
Drumshinnagh 231
Dublin, city/county 18, 29, 31, 36, 74,

87–8, 100, 125–6, 144, 172, 191, 193, 201, 218, 250, 255, 262, 280, 282
  County Dublin Vocational Education Committee 117
  Iveagh hostel 201, 255, 262, 267
  Iveagh Public Baths 162
  North Wall 38, 75, 100
  South Wall 100
Dudley Commission, 1907 50
Duffy family, Charlestown 190
Duffy family, Killeen 214
Duffy, Jack 215, 217
Duffy, John 214, 246
Duffy, Martin 151–2, 215
Duffy, Paddy (Madogue) 214–16, 229
Duffy, Patrick (Pat; Corthoon) 43, 57
Duffy's, Miss, commercial school 192
Duggan, Fr (St Wilfrid's, Manchester) 193
Dundalk 9
Dun, Finlay 45, 95
Dún Laoghaire, Co. Dublin 272. *See also* Kingstown, Co. Dublin
Dunleavy, Jack 144
Dunleavy, Seamus 78, 128
Dunne, Lucy 97
Dunne, Molly 97
Durcan [*sic* Duncan], Rev. B. 12, 18, 20, 29, 42
Durham 89, 92, 144, 156, 194–5
Durkan, Bill 136
Durkan, Hugh 82
Durkan, Jimmy 82
Durkan, Patt Nedd 43
Durkin, Ann 147
Durkin, Bridget 33
Durkin, Padhraic 266
Durkin, Pat (Ned) 57
Durkin, Pat (Pat) 57
Durkin, Patrick 177
Durkin, Thomas 57
Dwyer, Kathleen 257
Dyar, Patrick 63
Dyas, John 21

Eagre, building contractor 241
Ealing, London 170
East Lothian 77
Edgware, London 119

Edmondstown 26
Edmonton, London 167
Ellesmore Port, Cheshire 216
Elsham Top Farm, nr. Brigg, Lincolnshire 196
Ennis, Co. Clare 155, 158
Erris 8, 59, 80, 86, 89, 237
Esker 146
Essex 179, 198, 228

Famine 1–3, 6–11, 13–18, 21–4, 26, 28–32, 34–5, 47–8, 54–5, 82, 110–11, 122, 124, 129–31
Fareham, Hampshire 178
Farrell, Larry 281
Farrell, Stephen (pseudonym) 159–63
Faversham 190
Fay, Tommy 197
Feeney, Paddy (agent) 141, 160, 162, 180, 184
Fens, England 93, 99, 239
Ferns, Co. Wexford 18
Fews, Co. Armagh 9
Fianna Fáil 108
First World War 4, 99, 102, 114, 133, 198
Firth of Clyde, Scotland 17
FitzGerald, Garret 133
Fitzpatrick, David 10, 30
Fitzsimmons, Rev. (Pottsville, Pennsylvania) 33
Flannery, John 64
Fleming, Patrick 117
Florida 225
Foley, Andy 43
Foley, Bridie 207–8
Foley, Catherine 179
Foley, John 43
Foley, Kathleen 179
Foley, Mary 240
Foley, Mick 176–9, 205
Foley, Paddy 177, 189, 205, 207, 236–44
Foley, Pake 235
Foley, Sheila 242
Foley, Tom 144, 167, 169, 239
Folkestone 212
Foly jnr, Andrew 56
Foly snr, Andrew 56–7
Foly, John 57
Foly, Thomas 56

Forbes, John 48
Fórsa Cosanta Áitiúil (FCA) 266
Fort Dix, New Jersey 221
Forwood, George 21
Foster, Vere 49
Foster Wheeler, building contractor 240
Fox, A.W. 94, 105
Fox, Bernard 51
Fox, J.A. 39–41, 65
Foxford 6, 30, 40, 64–5, 71, 87–8, 212, 264
France, emigration to 70–1, 280–1
Frehily, Martin 57

Gallagher, Eddy 176
Gallagher, Eoghan 279
Gallagher, Frank 272–9
Gallagher jnr, Michael 273–4, 276
Gallagher snr, Michael 273–4
Gallagher, Joe 273
Gallagher, John 273
Gallagher, Mary 279
Gallagher, Noel 279
Gallagher, Paddy Bawn 202
Gallagher, Patsy (contractor) 151
Gallagher, Shane 279
Gallagher, Teddy 211–13
Gallagher, Tom Strick 202
Gallen (barony) 15
Galway, Co. 32, 35, 39, 49–50, 58, 89, 107, 165, 239, 241, 249, 251
Gannon (née Waters), Mary 164–7
Gannon, Patrick 166
Gannon, Peggy 165
Gardner, Massachusetts 32–3
Garvey, Ben 258, 260
Garvey family, Charlestown 190
Garvey (née Foley), Mary 119
Gateshead 154, 156
Gaughan, John 237
Gaughan, Mick 237
Gaughan, Tony 237
Geesala 237
Germany, emigration to 71
Gibbons, Cyril (Gibbons & Company) 278
Gillingham 190
Gilman, Charley 150
Gleeson's, building contractor 195
Glendining, Alex 10
Glenmullynaha East 26

Glenmullynaha West 26
Glenties, Co. Donegal 80
Gloucester 179, 232, 260
  Pride of Erin GAA club 232
Gloucestershire 250
Goldrick, Bridie 227
Goldrick jnr, Michael 226–7
Goldrick snr, Michael 227
Goldrick, Tom 226, 228–30
Gowdall [*sic* Goudle], Yorkshire 113
Gowel 30
Grady, Mrs (Ballaghaderreen, St Helens) 202
Grant, Capt. (Irish Guards) 169
Grant Lyon, building contractor 241
Gravesend 178–9, 241, 258, 260
Great Depression 4, 67, 101–2, 114–15, 122, 144, 147, 151, 154–5, 183, 257
Great Exhibition, London, 1851 37
Greenwood (née Foley), Bridgie 96
Griffith Valuation, 1856 132
Grimsby 177, 179, 188, 240
Groarke family, Cloontubrid 266
Groarke, Jack 201
Groarke, Jimmy 200
Groarke, Martin 273–4, 276
Groarke, Michael 200
Groarke, Mike 214
Groarke, Paddy 266
Gumley, Rev. John 18

Habsall, Lancashire 106
Hagfield 30
Halligan, John 216
Handley, James E. 17
Hanley, Capt. 28
Hanley, Staffordshire 240
Harrington Concrete & Quarries 278
Harwell, Oxfordshire 238
Harwich 177, 179
Haviland, Rev. A 33
Hawes, Yorkshire 184, 197, 238
Hazleton, Pennsylvania 32–3
Healy, John 117, 223
Henry, Andy 194–5
Henry, Jim 195
Henry, Joe 202
Henry, John 195, 282
Henry, Mark C. 51, 84, 112
Henry, Michael 194

Henry, Pat 194
Henry, Rev. J. 18
Henry, Seán 178
Henry, Tom 194
Hertfordshire 179
Heveran, Martin 18
High Marnham, Nottinghamshire 260
Holderness, Yorkshire 73
Holland, emigration to 283
Holleran, Tom 50
Holmes (landlord, magistrate) 26
Holton Beckering, Lincolnshire 104
Holyhead 75, 99, 138, 154, 161, 262, 270, 272
Horgan, Shane 109
Horkan, John 262
Humber Bridge 195
Hunt, Bartholomew 36
Hunt, Martin 36
Huntingdon, Cambridgeshire 202

Industrial Development Authority 281
Inglis, Henry D. 19, 29
Insurance Company of North America, Philadelphia 248
Inverness 163
Irish Guards 169
Irish National Land League 43
Ironbridge Power Station, Buildwas, Shropshire 267
Isle of Grain, Kent 231, 258
Italy, emigration from 49, 65, 70
Iveagh Hostel, Dublin 201, 255, 262, 267
Iveagh Public Baths, Dublin 162

Jackson, Butty 239
Jackson's farm, Gowdall, Yorkshire 113
Japan, emigration to 273
Jeremiah Thompson (vessel) 33
Johnson, James 12, 22

Keane, Johnny 155, 158
Keane, Mick 155, 158
Keebles, Capt. 36
Kells, County Meath 21
Kennedy, building contractor 118
Kenny, Dr (Mansion House Committee Medical Commission) 41
Kent 179, 241

Kerry, Co. 107, 142, 181, 191, 258, 263–4, 266
Ketton, Rutland 179
Kilbeagh [*sic* Kilbegha, Killebogh] 1, 13, 32–3, 41, 43, 51, 54–6
Kilbride 181, 282
Kilbride, Peter 30
Kilbride, Thomas 30
Kilcock, Co. Kildare 17, 107
Kilcoleman 12, 18
Kilconduff (*sic* Kilicunduff, Killinkillduff) 15, 24, 32, 54–5
Kilcullen, Co. Kildare 107
Kildare, Co. 107–9, 231, 233, 238
Kilgarriff (*sic* Kilgariff) 41, 160
Kilgeever [*sic* Kilgever] 9
Kilkelly 64, 212, 278
Killala 18
Killala, Bishop of 18
Killasser 11–13, 24–5, 50, 55, 107, 109, 129, 147, 213, 282
Killaturley 272, 274, 279
Killedan [*sic* Killeaden] 20, 24, 29, 55, 129
Killeen 214–15
Killilea, Frank 271
Killilea (née O'Rourke), Eileen 269–71
Killmactigue [*sic* Kilmactige], Co. Sligo 7–8, 26, 63
Kilmaclash (now Kilmaclasser) 11
Kilmaclasser (formerly Kilmaclash) 11
Kilmore-Erris 8
Kilmovee 1, 12, 24, 39, 55
Kiltimagh 61–2, 65, 71, 88, 117, 129, 136, 212, 241, 264, 269
Kinaffe 266
Kingstown, Co. Dublin 87. See also Dún Laoghaire, Co. Dublin
Kirkintillock, Scotland 106
Knock 40, 50
Knockfadda 24–5
Korean War 241

Labour News 260
Lacken 52
Laing, John, building contractor 161
Lamb, George 32
Lanarkshire 77
Lancashire 77, 80, 89, 92, 106, 155, 197–8, 219, 253

Land Commission 62, 107–8, 181, 231–2
Larcom, Thomas A. 30
Lavin, Mary 32
Lavin, Patrick 32–3
Lecky, W.H. 16
Leeds 30, 113, 211–12
Lee, Mr (Co. Sligo) 203
Leetch, Thomas 64
Leicester 238
Leitrim, Co. 28, 35, 75, 89, 261
Lemass, Seán 281
Leonard, James Leo 43
Letterkenny, Co. Donegal 88
Leyburn, Yorkshire 184
Limerick, Co. 31, 177, 195, 282
Lincolnshire 35, 89, 92–3, 99, 104, 141, 143, 172–3, 176, 179, 182, 184, 188–9, 196, 223, 229, 236, 240, 253, 255, 272, 274, 280
Lindsay, Thomas 11
Lisbrogan 102, 151
Lisheenabrone 154, 156–7
Lislackagh 151
Lisloughna 200
Liverpool 21, 31, 33, 35–6, 75, 87, 115, 241
Liverpool, New York and Philadelphia Steamship Company 46
Local Government Board 72
Loftus, Fr (P.P. Charlestown) 45
Loftus, Tom 151
London 20, 47, 102, 115–17, 119, 126, 137–9, 143, 152, 161–3, 167, 169, 171, 174, 177, 179, 190, 203, 207–8, 211–12, 214, 218–19, 228–9, 231, 239–40, 245–6, 250, 253, 260, 264, 281
London and North-Western Company 99
Longford, Co. 50, 241
Loughgall, Co. Armagh 6
Loughlynn 19
Lurga 32–3, 41
Luton 137, 171, 178–9, 229
Luzerne, Pennsylvania 32–3
Lynskey's pit (Culmore) 252
Lyons, J., & Co. 208
Lyons, Rev. John Patrick 8

MacGowan, Micheál 88, 95, 131
Madden, Eugene 274, 276
Madogue 214, 245, 248
Magherafelt [*sic* Magherfelt], Co. Derry 18
Malton, Yorkshire 37
Manchester 31, 157, 190–1, 193, 231, 241–2, 270–1
  Brown and Polson, company 193
  St Wilfrid's Catholic church 193
Manchester Ship Canal Company 194
Manly (vessel) 10
Mansion House Committee for Relief of Distress in Ireland 39, 41–4
  Medical Commission 39
Marlborough, Duchess of 39
Marren, Winnie 269
Maryland, US 33
Maye, Butty 144
Maynooth, Co. Kildare 108, 232
Mayo County Council 181, 187, 192, 199, 205, 214, 226, 231, 234, 247, 252, 255, 262
Mayo Men's Association, New York 50
Mayo Men's Ball, Philadelphia 115
Mayo Vocational Education Committee 257
McAlpine's, building contractor 116–17, 141–2, 144, 155, 198–9, 229, 253
McCann, Pake 198
McCormack, Kathleen 204
McCormack, Martin 200–4
McDermott, Pat 234
McDonagh, Hugh 36
McDonagh, Martin 101, 108–9, 231–3
McDonagh, Thomas 56–7
McDonnagh, James 57
McDonnell, Tom 273
McDonough, William 33
McEntire, Andrew 56–7
McEntire, Catherine 56
McEntire, James 56–7
McEntire, John 57
McEntire, Thomas 56
McGoldrick, Tom 261
McGowan, Mary 256
McGowan, Tommy 255–6
McGuinn's pit (Carn) 226
McIntyre, Bridie 191
McIntyre family, Corthoon 214, 216
McIntyre, Jack 229
McIntyre, Jimmy 187–91
McIntyre, Mary Theresa 187

McIntyre (née Mulligan), Margaret 248–9
McIntyre, Paddy 249
McIntyre, Tom 176, 187, 215
McNeela, Pat 146
McNicholas, building contractor 118
McNicholas, Seán 50
McNicholas, Willie 50
McNulty, Rev. John 11
McParlan, James 6
Meath, Co. 18–19, 21, 60, 107–9, 238, 253
Medway (vessel) 10
Meehan, Bríd 218
Meehan, John 218
Meehan, Mary 218
Meehan, Paddy (Australia) 243
Meehan, Paddy (Brackloonagh) 218
Meehan, Paraic 201
Meehan, Tom 218–20
Meelick [*sic* Meeleck] 1, 15, 24, 33, 55, 151, 266
Meenan, James 118
Mellet, P.J. 46
Mellett, M.J. 64
Mellon Migration Centre, Omagh, Co. Tyrone 139
Merseyside 146
Mexborough, Yorkshire 252–3
Middlesbrough 156, 186, 234
Midfield 107, 109, 143, 156, 198, 211–12
Midland Great Western Railway (MGWR) 36, 38, 74, 88, 90, 98
Midlothian 77
Milford Haven, Dyfed 228
Military Service Act 99
Miller, Kerby 10
Millers' (company) 178
Millet, Michael 14
Milton Keynes 229
Moffitt, Nan 162
Moffitt, Val 255
Molloy, Eddie 264
Molloy, John 264
Molloy, Paddy 262
Monaghan, Co. 178
Montiagh, Co. Sligo 164
Moore, Joe 177
Moore, Páidín 177
Moran, building contractor 144
Moran, Patrick 33

Moriarty, Michael 263
Morley, Edward 43
Morley, Patt Thomas 43
Morley, Thomas (Corthoon?) 43
Morley, Tom (Carrowcanada) 184–6
Morrely, Edward 57
Morrely, James 56
Morrely, John 56–7
Morrely, Mary 57
Morrely, Thomas 56–7
Morrisroe, Joe 196–9
Morrisroe, Martin 198
Morrisroe, Mary Frances 196, 199
Morris, Tim 136
Moylough, Co. Meath 108
Moy, River 203
Muckish Gap, Co. Donegal 88
Mulligan, Kathleen 248–9
Mulligan, Mary 248–9
Mulroy, John 102–3, 151–3
Murphy Cabling Company 137–9, 229
Murphy (engineer, Collooney–Claremorris railway) 58
Murphy, Micheál 24

National Radio School, Reading 276
National Services Act 102
Naul, Co. Dublin 19
Nealon, Ted 127
Neary jnr, Martin 266–8
Neary snr, Martin 268
Neary, John 88, 113–14
Neary, Michael 112–13
Neeling (aka Jordan), Martin 33
Neeling, Mary 33
Neill, Henry 64
Neligan, Rev. James 7–8
Newark, Nottinghamshire 254
Newbury, Berkshire 226
Newcastle-on-Tyne 76
New Jersey 221, 249
Newport (Co. Mayo) 50, 109, 231–2
Newport Poor Law Union 50
New York 31–3, 45–6, 50, 115, 127, 222, 225, 281
  United Nations 281
Nicholls, George 29, 82
Norfolk (UK) 161
Northampton 260

North Lindsay Technical College, Scunthorpe 216
Northumberland 89
Norway, emigration from 49, 65
Nottingham 177, 179, 260
Nottinghamshire 113

Oakham, Rutland 146, 149
O'Brien, Cath 33
O'Brien's pit (Bushfield) 255
O'Donnells (master & matron, Swinford workhouse) 27
O'Donoghue, Canon Peter 42
O'Dowd, Anne 78
Offaly, Co. 178
Ó Gráda, Cormac 9, 35
O'Grady, Richard 26
O'Hara, Jim 143
O'Hara, Rev. Denis 49, 61
O'Hara, Tom 143, 232
O'Malley, Donogh 120
O'Malley, Edward 106
Organisation for Economic Co-operation and Development 281
O'Rourke, Bill 269
O'Rourke (née Marren), Winnie 269
O'Shea, Maurice 142
Oughavale 10
Owenwee 106
Oxford 238

Paris 280–1
Parsons', factory, Charlestown 207
Parsons, Ted 239–40
Peterborough 102, 143, 179, 201–2, 214, 229, 273, 275, 277–8
Peyton, Frank 246
Peyton, Henry 245–7
Peyton, Mary 183, 245
Peyton, Paddy 180–3
Peyton, Pauline 245
Philadelphia, Pennsylvania 46, 115, 248
  Insurance Company of North America 248
Plunkett, Horace 131
Plymouth (UK) 115, 190
Poor Inquiry, 1835 2, 8–9, 11–12, 14, 17–19, 21–2, 73, 129
Portsmouth 189–90
Port Talbot 174
Pottsville, Pennsylvania 33
Powell, John Allen 20
Prague, Czech Republic 273
Pride of Erin GAA club, Gloucester 232
Princess Maud (vessel) 272
P&S Pipe Laying, Adelaide, Australia 244

Quebec, Montreal 10, 31–2
Queen Mary (vessel) 221
Queenstown (renamed Cobh) 46, 65
Quinn, Páid 151
Quinnsworth 251

Railway Inquiry, 1835 17
Ratoath, Co. Meath 19
Reading 184, 276
  National Radio School 276
Redford, Arthur 16
Reeves, Bill 209–10
Reeves (née Foley), Ellen 205, 207–10
Regan, Tommy 145
Reilly, Jack 240
Risdale, Jack 236
Roche Brothers, building contractor, Australia 242
Roches Stores 251
Rode, Mark 136
Roe, Peter 36
Roscommon, Co. 17, 20, 28, 35, 49, 65, 71, 89, 126, 266, 281
Rose, Ted 236–7
Rowley, Pat 148, 150
Royal Commission on Agriculture, 1881 93
Royal Commission on Congestion in Ireland, 1908 84, 87, 112
Royal Commission on Labour, 1893 105
Rural Electrification Scheme 257
Rushe, Michael 196
Rutland 179

Sandyhill 250
Schools' Manuscript Collection 126
Schrier, Arnold 51
Scunthorpe 172–3, 184, 187, 189–90, 216, 231, 240
  North Lindsay Technical College 216
Sebright, Sir John 73
Second World War 1, 4, 102, 115–16, 126, 161, 166, 187, 242, 248, 273

Selby, Yorkshire 114
Select Committee on Distress from Want of Employment, 1896 104
Select Committee on Emigration, 1826 73
Select Committee on Irish Vagrancy, 1828 19
Shannon, River, works, 1840s 130
Shepherd's Bush, London 126
Sherrard, W. 15
Shropshire 267
Sigerson, Dr (Mansion House Committee Medical Commission) 41
Skipton, Yorkshire 238
Sligo Airport 283
Sligo, Co. 6–10, 15, 28, 30, 36, 42, 44, 47, 63, 71, 89, 91, 100, 112, 117, 127, 164, 172, 178, 191, 203, 227, 250
Sligo Steamship Company 36
Smith, Tom 145
Snaith, Yorkshire 113
Sonnagh 269, 271
South Africa, emigration to 2
Southampton 177–9, 189–90, 212, 221, 240
South Ayrshire 76
Spalding, Lincolnshire 99, 223, 239
Spotswood JP, Andrew 18
Staffordshire 92, 240
Stamford, Lincolnshire 35, 146, 150, 177, 179
St Antoine's Secondary School, Charlestown 117–18, 167
Staunton, A.J. 83, 104
Stenson, Mikey (Ted) 178
Stevenage, Hertfordshire 178–9
St Helens, Merseyside 146–7, 202
Stirlingshire 105
St Nathy's College, Ballaghaderreen, Co. Roscommon 116–17
Stoke-on-Trent 155
Strickland, Charles 26
Strickland, Jerrard Edward 19–20
Sweden, emigration from 112
Sweeney, Paddy 252
Swinford *passim*
Swinford Poor Law Union (PLU) 8, 26, 28–9, 38–9, 50, 54–6, 70–1, 79–80, 83–4, 87, 89, 98, 104, 111–12, 130
Swinford Union Poor Law Commissioners 27

Swinford workhouse 45
Swords, Brendan 250
Swords, Margaret 251
Swords, Tom 250
Synge, J.M. 87

Tarpey family, Clooncoose 221
Tate (engineer, Collooney–Claremorris railway) 58
Tavnaglass 211
Tavneena 197
Taylor, James 31
Taylor Woodrow, building contractor 219
Tipperary, Co. 259
Toomore 18, 26
Tottenham, London 179
Tourlestrane, Co. Sligo 227
Towey, Maurice 142
Transit (vessel) 32
Tubbercurry, Co. Sligo 45, 47, 63, 71, 112, 117, 164, 285
Tuke, James Hack 48–50, 73–4
Tullachan Bawn 237
Tullinahoo 33, 141
Tully, Mr (Co. Longford) 241
Tumgesh 180–1

UK, emigration to *passim*
United Nations, New York 281
United States, emigration to *passim*
Upper Lurga 41
Utica, New York 33

Vocational Education Act, 1930 116

Wakerley, Northamptonshire 146, 149
Waldron, Dominick 14
Waldron, M.M. 64
Walker, G., and Slater, building contractor 161
Wall's (company) 171
Wall Street Crash, 1929 101, 122, 126, 133, 141
Walsh, James Bernie 202
Walsh, Joe 239–40
Walsh, John 103, 172–5
Walsh, Kevin 257–61
Walsh, Marty 238
Walsh, Maureen 213, 261

Walsh (née Breheny), Kitty 221–5
Walsh, Patrick 249
Walsh, Seán 225
Walsh, Theresa 174
Wanderer (vessel) 32
Warrington 155
Warwickshire 76, 92
Waters, Pat 166
Welton, Lincolnshire 104
Western Health Board 247
Westinghouse Electric Corporation, New York 222
West Kensington, London 170
Westport 6, 10–11, 29, 36, 71, 106, 109, 112
Westport workhouse 48

Whitaker, T.K. 281
　First Programme for Economic Expansion 281
Wimpey's, building contractor 144, 154–5, 161, 189, 238, 240, 282
Windscale Power Station 195
Wisconsin 33
Wolverhampton 219
Woods (townland) 107
Woolworth's (retailer) 270
Wyndham Land Act, 1903 62, 111

York 30, 50
Yorkshire 30, 37, 59, 89, 92, 144, 147, 184, 198, 252